THE CIVIL WAR IN MISSISSIPPI

Heritage of Mississippi Series / Volume V

The CIVIL WAR ── IN ── MISSISSIPPI

MAJOR CAMPAIGNS AND BATTLES

Michael B. Ballard

University Press of Mississippi
for the Mississippi Historical Society and the
Mississippi Department of Archives and History
Jackson

Publication of this book was made possible through
a grant from the Phil Hardin Foundation.

www.upress.state.ms.us

Maps by Bill Pitts

The University Press of Mississippi is a member
of the Association of American University Presses.

First printing 2011

∞

Library of Congress Cataloging-in-Publication Data

Ballard, Michael B.
The Civil War in Mississippi : major campaigns and battles /
Michael B. Ballard.
p. cm. — (Heritage of Mississippi series ; v. 5)
Includes bibliographical references and index.
ISBN 978-1-60473-842-1 (cloth : alk. paper) —
ISBN 978-1-60473-843-8 (ebook)
1. Mississippi—History—Civil War, 1861–1865—Campaigns.
2. United States—History—Civil War, 1861– 1865—Campaigns.
I. Title.
E470.7.B35 2011
976.2'05—dc22   2010024273

British Library Cataloging-in-Publication Data available

TO

MARSHALL SCOTT LEGAN

AND

FRANK ALLEN DENNIS

"What were the people of this beautiful country thinking of to go to war?"

—GENERAL ULYSSES S. GRANT,
speaking of central Mississippi, quoted in Mrs. Dunbar Rowland,
History of Hinds County, 1821–1922 (Jackson, Miss., 1922), 34.

CONTENTS

LIST OF MAPS
- xi -

FOREWORD
- xiii -

PROLOGUE
War Comes to Mississippi
- 3 -

1. CORINTH
The Siege That Was Not
- 13 -

2. VICKSBURG
First Attack
- 35 -

3. IUKA
The Clash and the Quiet
- 55 -

4. CORINTH
Another Van Dorn Debacle
- 77 -

5. VICKSBURG
More Union Failures
- 105 -

6. VICKSBURG
Final Battles and Siege
- 139 -

7. MERIDIAN CAMPAIGN
An Evolution and a Portent
- 172 -

8. BRICE'S CROSSROADS
Confederates Win and Lose
- 195 -

9. TUPELO (HARRISBURG)
Forrest versus Lee
- 220 -

10. MORE RAIDS
Smith and Grierson
- 244 -

EPILOGUE
- 271 -

APPENDIX
The Forgotten
- 273 -

NOTES
- 277 -

SUGGESTED READINGS
- 295 -

INDEX
- 297 -

MAPS

Mississippi at the time of the Civil War
- 2 -

Shiloh to Corinth, April–May 1862
- 24 -

First Attack on Vicksburg, Summer 1862
- 47 -

Battle of Iuka, September 19, 1862
- 67 -

Battle of Corinth, October 3–4, 1862
- 84 -

Grant's Thrust into North Mississippi & Van Dorn's Raid,
November–December 1862
- 112 -

Battle of Chickasaw Bayou, December 29, 1862–January 1, 1863
- 120 -

Yazoo Pass and Fort Pemberton Campaign
- 136 -

Porter's Steele's Bayou Campaign
- 136 -

Grant's Path across Mississippi, March 31–July 4, 1863
- 145 -

Grierson's 1863 Raid
- 148 -

Battle of Port Gibson, May 1, 1863
- 150 -

Battle of Raymond, May 12, 1863
- 155 -

Battle of Jackson, May 14, 1863
- 157 -

Battle of Champion Hill, May 16, 1863
- 161 -

Battle of Big Black River, May 17, 1863
- 163 -

Siege of Vicksburg, May 23–July 4, 1863
- 166 -

Sherman's Routes to Meridian, February 1864
- 177 - & - 183 -

Brice's Crossroads, June 10, 1864
- 205 -

Battle of Tupelo, July 14–15, 1864
- 231 -

A. J. Smith v. Forrest, August 1864
- 249 -

Route of Grierson's 1864 Winter Raid
- 263 -

FOREWORD

$\mathcal{D}$espite the fact that several excellent monographs have been written on the major Civil War campaigns and battles in Mississippi, no study has brought the significant conflicts together in one volume. The purpose of this book is to introduce readers to the stories of those campaigns and battles, the focus being on the struggles that had an important impact on the Civil War in Mississippi. My intent is to demonstrate how these conflicts grew out of strategic planning by both Union and Confederate War departments, planning that included the entirety of the western theater of the war as well as occasional connections to the war in the eastern theater.

My methodology has been to explain the evolution of military actions, how campaigns developed and were carried out, and what factors influenced strategy and tactics. I also look at the ramifications of the outcomes of the military struggles, especially on Mississippi, and the significance of the roles of commanders on both sides. I have tried to avoid minutiae; for those who want to find more thorough examinations of particular conflicts, a recommended reading list has been added to the end of this volume. My narrative is intentionally sweeping and generalized in order to provide a broad view of the state through four years of war.

A companion volume to this study by Timothy B. Smith focuses on the home front in Civil War Mississippi. Together, these two volumes should provide a complete overview of the war in Mississippi, of the experiences of soldiers and civilians alike. These studies are scholarly in nature and content, but they are intended for general audiences, which is the purpose of the Heritage of Mississippi Series.

I trust, too, that these volumes will expand the range of studies in Mississippi and in the western theater of the war as a whole. More and more historians have arrived at the realization that the eastern theater was a stalemate for most of the war, and that the truly decisive struggles occurred in the West.

The war in Mississippi had two decisive regions engulfed by the opposing armies. The foremost was the Vicksburg campaign, which lasted over a year. The other significant area was northeast Mississippi, where control of railroads that connected at Corinth affected strategic operations for most of the war. That region also produced conflicts that were direct results of Union operations in Georgia. William T. Sherman's Georgia campaigning was first tested in his Meridian campaign in early 1864 in Mississippi.

My study is based on primary and secondary sources. I have given those who experienced the war opportunities to speak through their letters, diaries, and the official records of the armies and navies. I have also relied on published studies by other historians so that readers may experience the threads of analysis that have evolved regarding the war in Mississippi. Naturally, none of us agree on every aspect of the war, but those disagreements are what make the study of the conflict enjoyable and enlightening.

I want to thank the Mississippi Historical Society Board of Editors for the opportunity to participate in the Heritage of Mississippi Series. Chrissy Wilson and Elbert Hilliard have contributed greatly with their editorial and other suggestions from having read the manuscript several times. Also I am much indebted to Terry Winschel, Vicksburg National Park Historian; William Shea, professor of history at the University of Arkansas–Monticello; and to anonymous readers who provided excellent analyses and suggestions.

John Marszalek, my mentor and friend for some thirty-six years now, provided his usual sound advice. His support and counsel were, as always, much appreciated and timely.

I have worked with the University Press of Mississippi many times throughout my career, and they are a team that makes the publishing experience an enjoyable one. I especially thank Craig Gill for all his advice, his assistance, and his admirable and remarkable patience. He symbolizes the profound professionalism of the Press. That professionalism includes choosing a talented and a thorough copyeditor, Robert Burchfield. His efforts will not be obvious, but they are reflected very positively throughout this book. His contributions are much appreciated.

As always, my wife, Jan, deserves special plaudits for putting up with yet another Civil War book that leaves our computer room at home cluttered with books and loose papers scattered all over the place. She is never sure how I keep anything organized, and neither am I. I know her encouragement helps, and her occasional questions about how the book is going get me back on the road from which I am so often sidetracked. Everything I publish results as much from her efforts as my own. Without her, you would not be reading this, for this book would still be unfinished.

THE CIVIL WAR IN MISSISSIPPI

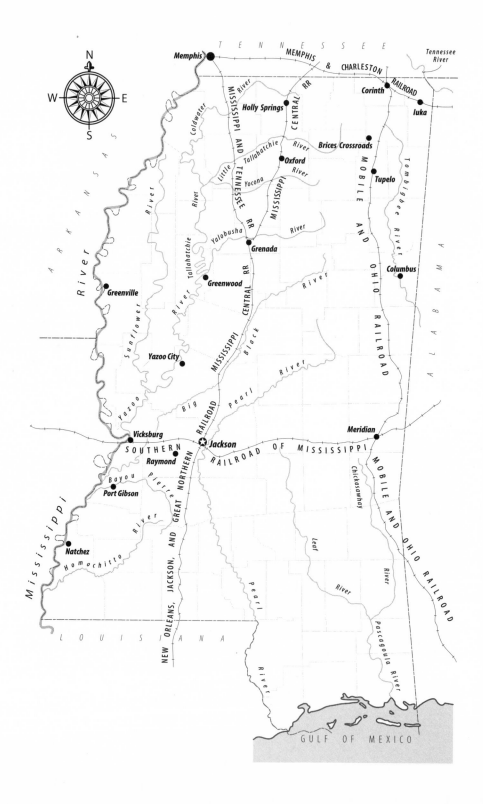

N
W   E
S

T E N N E S S E E

Memphis

MEMPHIS & CHARLESTON RAILROAD

Corinth

Iuka

Tennessee River

MISSISSIPPI AND TENNESSEE RR

Coldwater River

CENTRAL RR

Holly Springs

Brices Crossroads

Little Tallahatchie River

Oxford

Tupelo

Yocona River

MISSISSIPPI

MOBILE AND OHIO RAILROAD

Tombigbee River

A R K A N S A S

River

Tallahatchie River

Yalobusha River

Grenada

Mississippi River

Columbus

A L A B A M A

Greenville

Greenwood

MISSISSIPPI CENTRAL RR

River

Sunflower River

Black River

Yazoo City

Big Pearl River

Yazoo River

Vicksburg

SOUTHERN

Bayou Pierre River

Raymond

RAILROAD

Jackson

RAILROAD OF MISSISSIPPI

Meridian

Chickasawhay River

MOBILE AND OHIO RAILROAD

Port Gibson

NEW ORLEANS, JACKSON, AND GREAT NORTHERN

Mississippi River

Natchez

Homochitto River

Leaf River

Pearl River

Pascagoula River

L O U I S I A N A

GULF OF MEXICO

PROLOGUE

War Comes to Mississippi

The possibility of civil war did not frighten Mississippi fire-eaters, so-called because of their fiery defense of slavery and secession as constitutional rights. John Quitman, a Mexican War hero and prominent state politician, had been one of the major leaders, but he died in 1858, leaving individuals like John J. Pettus, elected governor the next year, to carry on. South Carolina's secession fueled the fires of separation in Mississippi, and though no polls were taken, it seemed the fire-eaters dominated the state, though some of them had reservations about taking Mississippi out of the Union. Many other citizens did not favor secession at all, especially those who relied on the Mississippi River for commerce and those who had no economic interests in slavery. The group called Immediate Secessionists dominated the secession convention elections of December 20, 1860, authorized by the legislature. It seemed likely that another large group, the Cooperationists, not as conservative as their name made them seem, could be swayed to join in the secession movement. As the historian Emory Thomas has noted, the term "Cooperationist" was "ambiguous" in that it implied varying degrees of attitudes. Some in this group "believed in Southern unity"; some did not think drastic measures should be taken until other possibilities could be explored. Still others used the term to screen their pro-Unionist feelings. But in the end, most all of these took the secession route when there seemed to be no other options. The choice to secede was not a wise one, but given the location of the state and the large numbers of slaves within the state, the majority of state leaders apparently did not consider any other option.

Thoughts of a likely war and young men dying on battlefields did not have a sobering effect in the beginning, for the atmosphere in the capital city of Jackson and other locales at the time of the convention was similar to "a holiday mood." A parade and a cheering crowd indicated the dominant feelings, and the shouts of joy grew even louder when news came that the convention had voted 84-15 for secession on January 9, 1861.

The historian John K. Bettersworth described the convention and Jackson: "The drama of revolution proceeded to act itself out in exciting fashion as the ladies of Jackson brought in the Bonnie Blue Flag, and that night at the theater Henry McCarthy purportedly sang for the first time the song that made that flag famous throughout the Confederacy." As cannons boomed and bells tolled, telegraph wires sent the news to Washington, D.C., where the state's congressional delegation, including Senator Jefferson Davis, who had opposed secession, resigned their seats and came home. So Mississippi became the second state to secede, after South Carolina, and the first wave of withdrawals from the Union also included Florida, Alabama, Georgia, Louisiana, and Texas, in that order.[1]

Governor Pettus immediately demonstrated his impetuosity when he sent cannons to Vicksburg to guard the river. The war had not started, and there was no sign of U.S. Navy vessels, but Pettus apparently did not want to take chances. Seven Mississippi companies of volunteer soldiers left to reinforce Fort Pickens, Florida, and a group of militia went south "to raise the Mississippi flag over Ship Island," which lay a few miles out in the Gulf of Mexico from the Mississippi coastline. The convention passed legislation to form a division of volunteer infantry for a year's service and at the same time set up a military board headed by Pettus and a militia officer.

A military tax helped pay the bills for these actions. Another proposed source of revenue proved controversial; J. Z. George, a prominent politician, argued that since slavery had brought on this potential war, then the usual tax of seventy-five cents per slave for all slaves under the age of sixty ought to be increased to a dollar and a quarter. Another delegate went even further, suggesting an increase to two dollars. Slave owners quickly moved to stifle such tax increases "equal to twenty cents on every one hundred dollars in value thereof, the value to be ascertained in the same manner that the value of land is now ascertained." Thus they opened the door for "undervaluation" and avoided paying higher amounts for purchasing slaves. When it came to money, Southern patriotism had its limits.[2]

Despite lack of sufficient funding, Pettus moved ahead in a very reckless fashion. Along with cannons, he sent militia to Vicksburg, and the Mississippians actually fired on a harmless vessel carrying on its normal river business. Fortunately for Pettus, no one was hurt, and when another boat, supposedly loaded with Yankee troops, showed up carrying nothing but passengers and cargo, most of the state's defenders went home. Pettus had embarrassed himself with the use of cannons, and then he showed his lack of acumen with smaller weapons when he bought shotguns that were little more than piles of junk. Obviously Pettus's judgment—whether deploying weapons or purchasing them—left something to be desired. He tried to recover his dwindling reputation with a typical political move. He changed the subject by announcing that he remained committed to an open river.

This was one of several efforts that Pettus and the conventioneers used to soothe the feelings of states in the Northwest, the area now called the Midwest, including such states as Wisconsin, Iowa, Illinois, and Minnesota. The Southerners (Confederate was not yet a commonly used term since a formal central government had not been established), in a strictly political tactic, rejected the idea of opposition to reconstruction of the Union. In effect, they stated that if things went their way, they would lead their states back into, or reconstruct, the Union as it had been. They agreed to affiliate with states not having slavery, and they voted that they had no agenda to reopen the slave trade. Further, they guaranteed the open river that Pettus proposed.[3]

Fire-eaters like Pettus continued to be vocal in many parts of the state, but some attitudes changed in Vicksburg due to worries over probable enemy advances down the Mississippi. Then came exciting news that local favorite son Jefferson Davis had been chosen president of the provisional government of the Confederacy. It was an honor that the moderate Davis did not particularly relish, but his politician's ego kept him from turning it down. When he came to Vicksburg from his home south of the city to catch the train east, he received a hero's welcome. The same plaudits awaited him in Jackson when his train pulled into the station. Back in Vicksburg, a prostitute tried to organize a ball to continue the celebration, but outraged citizens tore her dwelling down. God would not ordain a cause associated with such women. Clearly, the pressures of potential war produced odd situations and reactions.[4]

News of the beginning of war at Fort Sumter fueled the fire-eater cause, and when Abraham Lincoln called for volunteers to put down the rebellion in the South, many people who had wavered came down on the side of the Confederacy. Yet in Vicksburg, citizens continued to hope that secession would not necessarily mean war, though deep down they had to know better. Lincoln's call to squash the rebellion was not exactly a call for a peace conference. But life in Vicksburg continued as if nothing notable had happened. Not until volunteers began loading on trains heading east did a sense of having young men leave the area hit home. Many Vicksburgians realized, too, that threats to the city would not necessarily all come from the north, but also from the south, where Union warships in the Gulf of Mexico could ascend the Mississippi. However much people might have acted nonchalantly, tension grew beneath the surface of calm.[5]

In certain areas, young men did not hesitate to rush to join the Confederate cause and hopefully get into the war everyone expected to start, and end, soon. In their youthful exuberance, they had no appreciation of the horrors and deprivations that awaited them. Mississippi adjutant general W. L. Sykes had reported to Governor Pettus before war became official at Fort Sumter that, in Mississippi, "companies are organized and have been organizing at the rate of seven or eight per week, numbering from fifty to sixty men. The number of companies organized up to the 16th of January, 1861, dated from January 1, 1860, amounts to 65." He went on to state that the "number of men regularly organized into uniformed companies of volunteers amounts to 2,027, armed. Of the thirty-eight companies unarmed, allowing 50 men for an average of each, we have 1,900 unarmed volunteers, which number added to the number of armed men, gives an aggregate of 3,927 belonging to the volunteer companies." The number of men available for duty, he estimated, was 39,623.

Like other Lower South states, Mississippi continued war preparations well in advance of the firing on Fort Sumter. In mid-January Pettus announced that seven companies of Mississippians had been sent to assist Florida and Alabama troops in taking possession of forts and the navy yard at Pensacola, Florida. This had been done as a cooperative action of the three states since the Confederate government had not yet been formed. At the time, these men served under the governor of Florida, which probably was not legal, but obviously that did not matter. The secession convention, on January 23, 1861, organized state regiments into the Army of Mississippi, commanded by Jefferson Davis, before he received his considerably higher position.[6]

Resistance to secession and war did not totally disappear despite the events that pushed the nation in that direction. In the Tennessee River hills section of the state to the northeast and in the piney woods section in the south-central portion, opposition remained widespread. Many people did not care about fighting over slavery and certainly had no desire to be shot while defending the institution. In Tishomingo County in the far northeast corner, for example, Cooperationists dominated, and two had been sent to the secession convention. They represented prevailing attitudes of that area to settle the secession crisis peaceably, not with guns. In Jones County in south Mississippi, which would earn a reputation as a safe haven for deserters, anti-Confederates, and outlaws, the prosecession convention delegate was burned in effigy. Some Jones Countians later tried to declare themselves the "Free State of Jones," disassociating the county from the Confederacy, but the would-be state never had legal status. Pockets of deserters and resisters sprang up in other parts of the state as well.[7]

In Chickasaw County in the north-central part of the state, a native Mississippian and pro-Unionist named Levi Naron offered Governor Pettus his services to raise troops to put down the traitorous rebels who wanted to break up the Union. Naron knew what kind of response he would get, and, according to him, he did. Though no copy of Pettus's angry retort has been found, apparently the governor threatened to hang such men as Naron. Naron also stirred up similar feelings in his own locale and barely escaped trouble several times, but he remained loyal to the United States and scouted for the Union army in northeast Mississippi and west Tennessee during the coming war. Certainly no one could claim that sentiment in the second state to secede was unanimously Confederate. It never was, though we will never know for sure the depths of feelings, for most people who opposed secession found that the most peaceable and least dangerous way to get by was to keep their mouths shut.[8]

Meanwhile General Charles Clark, destined to be Pettus's successor later in the war, went to Pensacola and mustered out volunteer soldiers who had been sent down by Pettus. These men returned to Mississippi, where most were given official status by induction into the state of Mississippi army. By late March Pettus had accumulated thirty to forty companies of volunteers, though the men had not been sufficiently trained for conflict.

New provisional president Jefferson Davis, ruling from Montgomery, Alabama, unaware of Clark's action, then asked Mississippi to send 1,500 troops to Pensacola. Pettus replied that the Army of Mississippi had not yet been completely organized, and he was not sure just how much good the volunteers would be to the Confederate regular army. Davis assured him that the troops were for the provisional army and would be asked to serve only twelve months.

Pettus sent twenty companies, commanded by Clark, and just a few days before the firing on Fort Sumter began the war, Davis asked for 3,000 men to be held in reserve. Once the war began, Davis asked for 5,000 more, raising the total to 8,000. The numbers kept going up, and by June 30 the Confederate government had raised the call to 30,000 Mississippi troops. These men would be gathered as a reserve corps in Corinth in northeast Mississippi, where an eastbound railroad out of Memphis, Tennessee, could carry them to Virginia. By now Virginia and other Upper South states had seceded, Richmond had been declared the Confederate capital, and there seemed little doubt that Virginia would be a major battlefield.[9]

Financially, the Confederacy was not in good shape; it had little currency worth anything, and few coins at all. Except for citizens donating food, a few weapons, and small amounts of money, the state governments, like Mississippi's, would have been in deep trouble. The railroads chipped in with free transportation for militia. Yet Pettus must have been embarrassed when he had to tell the Confederate government that the state was financially unable to make a loan to the new central government. Meanwhile places like Vicksburg, where city fathers worried more and more about their town's vulnerability, worked to organize volunteer companies to prepare for conflict.

In Jackson, a bitter political fight broke out over whether the Confederate Constitution, drawn up in Montgomery by representatives from most of the initial seceded states, should be submitted to the people of Mississippi for an up-or-down vote. Delegates at the secession convention played all sorts of parliamentary games, some wanting the convention to decide the issue, others wanting the people to have the final word. After much manipulation, those opposed to "popular ratification" managed many delays to block resolutions and won a vote on March 29, 78-7. The people of Mississippi, "whether they desired it or not," became "citizens of the Confederate States."[10]

All the confiscated Federal property in the state had to be secured, and delegates had to be chosen to send to Montgomery, still the capital city before it was decided to move the seat of government to Richmond. As one historian summed things up, "Thus the Republic of Mississippi had ended the eighty days of its existence, days in which it had done scarcely more than await the coming of a new union, days in which the Governor had exercised his new authority." Importantly, there was still no war to fight, but the time of peace soon ended. And Mississippians, like it or not, found themselves sucked into the conflict everyone expected, but the demands of which remained unappreciated.[11]

Mississippians noticed the impact of the mass mobilization of the state's young men into military service. Only in large towns did life seem to go on as usual; otherwise, the countryside seemed empty of people. Some worried that without men to do police work and take care of other societal needs, the state would suffer. The reality of war would come slowly to some of the younger men who stayed behind working as home guards of a sort. One youngster noted they had to train themselves and fend for themselves when they camped out. A mother's authority carried more weight than the military, and when a mother called for her son to come home for a while, he went. Private David Holt of Woodville noted that "sisters and sweethearts" visited the camp regularly, and there were plenty of parties to entertain the brave young troops. The time eventually came, however, when these youngsters, most in their late teens or early twenties, were called to go to Virginia to help win the war against the Yankees. Then came tears and sorrowful farewells; departures gave many their first taste of the reality of war. The boys, however, proud of going off to defend their state and country and with practically no knowledge of what they faced, left home feeling joyful and excited. Their families, however, seemed to sense they might never see their loved ones again.[12]

As for Mississippi and the war, the state had blessings and curses. After Tennessee completed the course of secession in June 1861, the northern border of Mississippi was somewhat buffered by Tennessee, along with other Confederate states—Alabama to the east, Arkansas and Louisiana to the west. Farther north, Kentucky and Missouri for a time seemed destined to come into the fold, but Unionists ultimately kept both states out of the Confederacy, though the Confederate government placed a claim on both states.

Early in the war, if Mississippi were to be invaded by Northern forces, it seemed highly unlikely that it would be by land. Even if that should happen, it would not occur very soon. Nor did it seem likely at the time there would be a coastal invasion of Mississippi. Mississippi's tiny Gulf coastal area contained only a few points that conceivably would be of strategic or economic importance. Furthermore, the state was comfortably distant from Washington, D.C., and the eastern population centers of the United States to attract immediate attention. In fact, both the Lincoln and Davis governments placed their emphasis on the eastern rather than the western theater of the war for the obvious reason that the capitals were not far apart.

The Achilles' heel of Mississippi's defense was the configuration of its river system. Unlike Virginia, where the major battles of the eastern theater would be fought and where the Potomac-Rappahannock-York-James east-west waterways afforded natural lines of defense, Mississippi's rivers were essentially north-south streams, which penetrated the state both on its western border along the Mississippi and within the interior. Union naval advantages foretold problems in defending these avenues of invasion, most especially the Mississippi River. The Mississippi flowed past several of the state's richest and most important cities, especially Vicksburg and Natchez. Farther to the east, the Yazoo River and the rivers that fed it— the Tallahatchie, Yalobusha, and Coldwater—allowed passage deep into the heart of north and central Mississippi. Along the eastern edge of the state flowed the Tombigbee, perilously near such important towns as Aberdeen, Amory, Tupelo, and Columbus.

The state's railroad system was also crucial to its defense. Many of the Confederacy's most vital connecting rail lines lay within Mississippi. At

Corinth in the northeast, about five miles south of the Tennessee border and twenty-five miles west of the Alabama line, the north-south Mobile & Ohio and the east-west Memphis & Charleston railroads intersected. This little town would surely have the attention of Confederate and Union military strategists. In central Mississippi, the Mississippi Central Railroad extended north from Canton into central Mississippi and continued north into Tennessee; to the south, under a different name (the New Orleans, Jackson, and Great Northern), it went from Canton to Jackson to New Orleans. At Grenada, in north-central Mississippi, the Central forked, and one, known as the Mississippi and Tennessee, went northwest to Memphis, while the other main line meandered northeast through Oxford and Holly Springs, to LaGrange, Tennessee, and beyond.

Mississippi's capital city was the railroad hub of the lower central part of the state. The east-west Southern Railroad of Mississippi, connecting Vicksburg with Jackson and Meridian, crossed the north-south New Orleans, Jackson, and Great Northern. At Meridian, about eighty miles east of Jackson, the north-south Mobile & Ohio, which descended from Corinth to Mobile, bisected the Southern Railroad.

During 1861 little military action occurred in Mississippi. Governor Pettus sent cannons to arm the bluffs at Vicksburg, angering antisecessionists. After all, there was no Northern threat there, and civilian and economic traffic still plowed the river. Yet in time it became obvious that Vicksburg, because of its strategic location at a sharp turn in the Mississippi, would be a key place of contention, primarily because Jefferson Davis wanted to protect it and Abraham Lincoln wanted it taken. It was true that the Southern Railroad connected Vicksburg with the East, and it was true that across the river a railroad extended a few miles west into Louisiana. These factors did not necessarily make Vicksburg vital, because as the war progressed, fewer supplies traveled those railroads, and the Confederacy could never dominate the river. Yet its location, where Confederate cannons could threaten Union naval vessels, together with the railroads, made Vicksburg important to Davis and Lincoln.

Governor Pettus's efforts to keep Ship Island failed miserably, and soon the few Rebels there evacuated, leaving the place in Union hands from that point to the end of the war. The Federal navy would use the island as a base and staging area for operations along the Gulf and ascension of the Mississippi.[13]

In late 1861 Pettus, to emphasize his preparation activities, reported to the state legislature that Mississippi had twenty-two regiments and one battalion of infantry, one regiment and fourteen cavalry companies, plus eleven artillery companies, or some 23,000 troops altogether. Independent companies that went directly into Confederate service and were out of state likely added another 1,000 to the total. Other troops, including a few enlisted for the war's duration, as well as some Mississippians sent to Confederate western theater commander Albert Sidney Johnston, commander of the so-called Army of Ten Thousand, raised Mississippi's contribution to 35,000. Within the state, four points had been selected where troops would gather for shipment to varying points in the Confederacy. Corinth was the place for those headed to the eastern theater, especially Virginia. Other points included Iuka, several miles east of Corinth; Enterprise; and Grenada. Over the next four years Mississippi would contribute 96,414 men to the Confederate cause, of which 22,843 became casualties, just under a 25 percent casualty rate. Among those lost were surely some men who might have had leadership abilities to help the state recover from the war. Whether such speculation would have been true will of course never be known.[14]

The war meanwhile heated up in far-off Virginia, where Confederates won the first significant battle of the war at Manassas on July 21, 1861. Later that year they won a victory of sorts at Belmont, Missouri, on November 7, 1861, though the postbattle maneuvering forced the Confederates to abandon thoughts of holding a position so far north. The general leading Union forces at Belmont, Ulysses S. Grant, would be heard from again, especially in Mississippi.

Closer to the Magnolia State, the tenuous Confederate line of defense that stretched from eastern Kentucky to the Mississippi cracked when Federals won a battle at Mill Springs, Kentucky, on January 19, 1862. In February 1862 Fort Henry on the Tennessee River and Fort Donelson on the Cumberland fell to Union forces, forcing Albert Sidney Johnston, the overall Confederate commander in the western theater, to abandon Nashville, the capital city of Tennessee. With his defensive line fractured, Johnston fell back to Corinth, where he began augmenting his army. He hoped to add forces commanded by Mississippian Earl Van Dorn, on their way to Corinth from Arkansas, where Van Dorn had, in effect, lost Missouri in the battle at Pea Ridge in northwest Arkansas, in early March 1862.[15]

On the Union side, Grant moved his army south from Nashville and camped on the Tennessee River bluffs at a place called Pittsburg Landing in Tennessee, a little over twenty miles north of Corinth. Grant, like Johnston, expected reinforcements, in particular Don Carlos Buell's Army of the Ohio coming from eastern Tennessee. Johnston attacked Grant's army, camped along high ground above Pittsburg Landing on April 6. After a fierce two-day battle in which the Confederates won the first day and lost the second—when Buell arrived to help turn the tide and Van Dorn did not show up at all—the Confederates, led by P. G. T. Beauregard after Johnston's mortal wound at Shiloh, retreated into Corinth. Beauregard, heavily outnumbered by the Union army now led by Henry Halleck, waited to see what the Federal army would do next. Beauregard knew it was unlikely he could hold Corinth, but he also knew that the town would be Halleck's likely target since there was a vital railroad crossing there. The Union indeed wanted Corinth to facilitate the movement of supplies. But Halleck moved his large army very slowly toward Corinth from the Shiloh battlefield, allowing the Confederates to build up their defenses. War was on the way to Mississippi, both from the Shiloh battlefield and the lower Mississippi River, where the Union navy had begun moving north. So both Corinth and the Mississippi were targets of Federal operations.[16]

1

CORINTH

The Siege That Was Not

*T*wo armies had slugged it out at Shiloh, and, since Union forces held the field and made a half-hearted pursuit of the Confederates, who retreated on the second day of the battle, April 7, 1862, the Federals had won. The cost had been tremendous on both sides. Union troops killed, wounded, and missing in Ulysses S. Grant's Army of the Tennessee, reinforced by Don Carlos Buell's Army of the Ohio on the 7th, numbered over 13,000. The Confederate army, now led by P. G. T. Beauregard after the death of Albert Sidney Johnston, had lost approximately 10,600 men. Though the Confederates had fewer casualties, their strength had been reduced by around 25 percent, while Grant had lost some 19 percent during the bloodbath. The total casualties meant more than percentages, however, for the battle awakened people north and south to the fact that the Civil War would be long and bloody.

The Union army faced the postbattle tasks of reorganizing scattered units, caring for the wounded, and burying piles of dead, friend and foe. Henry Halleck came to the battlefield to take command of the Union forces and found things in disarray. Halleck did not like Grant's style, including his shabby way of dressing, or the fact Grant had been surprised and whipped rather soundly on the first day of battle. What Halleck saw when he reached the high ground above Pittsburg Landing confirmed what he believed, that Grant was not the hero acclaimed by the press after his capture of Fort Donelson in Tennessee.[1]

Before he arrived, Halleck sent Grant a message ordering him to avoid fighting until more troops could be concentrated. Halleck wanted to give

John Pope time to reach Shiloh with his Army of the Mississippi. Pope, with help from the Union navy, captured the strategically important Island No. 10 on the Mississippi above Memphis on April 7, the second day of the Shiloh fight. Pope did not arrive until April 21. Obviously, Halleck did not intend to pursue the Confederates and attack Corinth with alacrity. Yet Halleck's timidity must be viewed in the context of what was going on in Virginia. There Union general George McClellan had accomplished nothing in his campaign to take Richmond, and President Lincoln decided that he would not worry about McClellan and what was going on in the West. Lincoln sent word to Halleck not to force a fight unless he was certain he could win it. With this message in his hand, Halleck determined he would not move rapidly into the unknown toward Corinth.[2]

Halleck did not know how many men Beauregard had, but, based on scouting reports, he accepted inflated numbers, much like McClellan. That uncertainty made Halleck more tentative, as did the fact that Halleck had never led an army in a major military campaign. Within this milieu, Halleck's slow pace was understandable.

Meanwhile Halleck set in motion arrangements to help victims at Shiloh. Halleck also told Grant the army was in no shape to defend itself. The men had become terribly disorganized, artillery batteries needed to be consolidated, and stragglers needed to be rounded up. In effect, much work had to be done "without delay," Halleck said, for the army to resist renewed Confederate attacks. Had Halleck understood the decimated condition of the Confederates, he would not have worried about being attacked.[3]

Don Carlos Buell, whose army arrived from Nashville to turn the tide on the second day, recorded that the battlefield was indeed a mess. Heavy rains, common in the region anyway, often followed battles, and the downpour turned the place into a sea of mud. Provisions had to be carried over long distances from supply boats in the Tennessee River to campsites. The weather conditions, fatigue, wet food, and surrounding swampy areas worked together to create much sickness, and dysentery "prevailed very generally among the officers and men."[4]

An Iowa soldier wrote in his diary on April 8: "The rain kept falling all night[.] There was a great *panic* this morning caused by men firing off their guns to see if the *loads* would go out[.] There was a rally . . . and we expected another fight[.] It is very chilly and thousands of the wounded lay out on the third night with no care[.] Burrial [sic] squads have been busy all day burryiing [sic] the *dead*[.]"[5]

The "horrid scenes and stenches" would never be forgotten by Union soldiers who endured the postbattle privations and terrible weather. Most of the Union dead had been buried in "shallow graves," and many Confederates had been placed in mass graves, the top layer of dirt not deep enough to suppress the smells of decay.[6]

At Corinth, Beauregard's Confederate army rolled along in the beds of wagons or staggered on foot into the small town like a great plague. Corinth was originally known as Cross City, because the railroads, the west-to-east Memphis & Charleston and north-to-south Mobile & Ohio, intersected there. That intersection made the town important to both armies, for railroads carried supplies and reinforcements. Most Corinthians had already left their homes to get out of harm's way when Johnston began concentrating troops there before Shiloh. Those who had not wished they had.

Confederate wagon trains from Shiloh, bearing broken bodies covered with both wet and dried blood, accompanied by hideous sounds of groaning and shrieking, snaked into Corinth streets, horrifying the few Corinthians who remained in town. Local volunteers and surviving soldiers worked to deal with the multifaceted problem of trying to save masses of men, but their efforts came too late for many, their corpses riding among the living. Estimates of the number of wounded ranged from 5,000 upward, a mixture of Confederates and captured Federals. As Corinth did not have facilities to cope with the onslaught, some men had to remain in wagons or lie on the ground, or on elevated places like porches, awaiting transfer to whatever structures could quickly be adapted to something resembling hospitals. The sparsely settled area contained few doctors or nurses who had not fled, but those who could be rounded up, helped by many well-intentioned volunteers, worked hour after hour doing what they could to alleviate suffering and save lives. Amputations created grotesque piles of arms and legs, which attracted all sorts of insects. Some wounded were given painkillers and left to live or die when doctors concluded nothing could be done medically to save them. Practically every home in the town soon bore bloodstains on floors, walls, and furniture.[7]

Tennessean Sam Watkins recalled, "We became starved skeletons; naked and ragged." Diarrhea became epidemic, and Watkins noted, "Almost the whole army attended the sick call every morning." Soon it became obvious that the wounded must be sent elsewhere to relieve the logjam in Corinth. Many were loaded into train cars running east into Alabama and south into Mississippi. Beauregard and his officers realized that many regiments, shadows of their original strengths, must be consolidated. Meanwhile soldiers able to function took shovels and bayonets and anything else they could dig with and started building a line of massive breastworks and abatis around the northwest, north, and northeast approaches to Corinth several hundred yards north of the center of town. Estimates of the length of the entrenchments went as high as forty miles. Swampy areas, bad water, and insects made the work miserable. The Confederate sick list grew longer daily.[8]

Food became more and more scarce. Biscuits made from flour and cooked over campfires were pitiful excuses for the real things. Pickled beef, barely palatable, had to be gulped down by soldiers who then fought their body's efforts to send it back up and out. Diarrhea spread like a communicable disease. Wells had to be dug to find anything close to good water. Rain helped the water situation. One Confederate soldier said regular water had a "bluish color and greasy taste," something like "castor oil." The water beneath the ground reached by shovels was no better. Some of it resembled "coal tar, dish water and soap suds mixed."[9]

Braxton Bragg wrote pointedly of the pathetic condition of the troops, as a long column of Shiloh survivors continued drifting into the Corinth area. Bragg told Beauregard: "Our condition is horrible. Troops utterly disorganized and demoralized. Road almost impassable. No provisions and no forage; consequently everything is feeble. Straggling parties may get in to-night. Those in rear will suffer much." He begged for fresh troops to relieve the rear units of the army, but the rain and mud did not make sending reinforcements feasible. Bragg admitted relief would be difficult. "It is most lamentable to see the state of affairs, but I am powerless and almost exhausted. Our artillery is being left all along the road by its officers. . . . Relief of some kind is necessary, but how it is to reach us I can hardly suggest, as no human power or animal power could carry empty wagons over this road with such teams as we have."[10]

Bragg indicated clearly that the condition of the troops struggling into Corinth was not much better than that of the wounded. Fortunately for the Confederates, Henry Halleck's waiting gave Beauregard's troops time to recuperate and reinforcements time to arrive. Yet Beauregard realized that his 35,000 men, many of whom were barely able to fight, plus Van Dorn's 15,000 troops still pushing toward Corinth, would leave him far short of the multitude Halleck would bring to Corinth. Beauregard knew that all he could do was continue building up defensive works and deploy his men to stall the Union advance. He knew, too, that if he received no reinforcements in addition to Van Dorn's troops, he would eventually be forced to hand over Corinth to the Yankees.

Beauregard wrote Richmond, "If defeated here we lose the Mississippi Valley and probably our cause, whereas we could even afford to lose for a while Charleston and Savannah for the purpose of defeating Buell's army, which would not only insure us the valley of the Mississippi, but our independence." At that point Beauregard obviously did not know that Halleck was in command and that Buell's force was only one of three Union armies he faced. In fact, Beauregard guessed there were 85,000 Union soldiers, but the enemy army soon to be heading his way numbered well over 100,000 men, probably as many as 120,000. His urgent messages to Van Dorn to move quickly to Corinth from Memphis were more critical than Beauregard imagined.[11]

From east Tennessee, Kirby Smith sent a brigade and two regiments to Corinth from Chattanooga, and Smith assured Richmond that he could spare no more. John Pemberton sent four regiments from South Carolina, two short of the six Beauregard requested. Beauregard wanted all of Smith's forces and for Smith to come to Corinth; Smith was agreeable, but Richmond was not. The troops that came to Corinth were too few to make a difference in the coming showdown with Halleck. The War Department wanted Smith to be active in Tennessee to threaten Union communications. From a distance, Samuel Cooper and Robert E. Lee in Richmond tried to move troops around to the Confederacy's greatest advantage. It was obvious that they, and Jefferson Davis, were not willing to abandon a presence in Tennessee to protect Corinth and the railroads there. Their decision ultimately made the loss of Corinth inevitable.[12]

In setting up his defensive positions around Corinth, Beauregard placed his Third Corps, commanded by Braxton Bragg, in the Farmington area to the east. William J. Hardee had orders to protect the region from Farmington to the Memphis & Charleston Railroad south of Farmington. Hardee's deployments on the Confederate right were designed to protect the railroad and to block any Union attempt to flank the Confederates from the east. Leonidas Polk's First Corps aligned on the left, where Polk's left extended just past the Mobile & Ohio Railroad. Thus the defensive line extended from the Mobile & Ohio north of Corinth in a slight arc to the Memphis & Charleston to the east.

Bragg's Second Corps occupied the center of the line. Earl Van Dorn finally arrived, and his men were held in reserve to support either flank and to assist wherever needed. Beauregard ordered John C. Breckinridge's Reserve Corps to the south of Corinth to protect the Confederate rear and to support Hardee on the right. Beauregard obviously expected the Federals to be more of a threat to his right since the roads from Pittsburg Landing to Corinth would lead the enemy more toward the right and right-center of the Rebel line. Also, the Federals might attempt to cut the Confederate supply line to the east via the Memphis & Charleston, hence Beauregard's determination to have strong support for Hardee. Cavalry would scout the Federal advance and fall back to guard both flanks of the Confederate line as circumstances might dictate.[13]

Beauregard also attempted diversions intended to force Halleck to send reinforcements to middle Tennessee and Kentucky, as any move that could force reduction of Yankee troop strength and slow Halleck's advance or perhaps even postpone his march would be worth trying. Beauregard sent John Hunt Morgan's cavalry into middle Tennessee and Kentucky. Morgan and his troops had success interrupting Union lines of communication. Kirby Smith in Tennessee proposed operations in Kentucky as a diversion to help Beauregard. Beauregard also sent a small cavalry expedition to Paducah, Kentucky, which came to nothing, mainly due, according to Beauregard, to incompetent leadership. A counterproposal to Kirby Smith to use his small force to threaten Nashville, a part of the plan to use his troops to attack enemy communications, failed due to Richmond's inability to send him sufficient reinforcements. Beauregard's diversions failed to force Halleck to deplete his army, for there were enough Union troops scattered throughout the surrounding country to deal with Rebel threats without needing help from Halleck.[14]

Despite the disappointments, Beauregard determined to get his army, numbering some 50,000 men thanks to the addition of Van Dorn's troops, ready to oppose Halleck's advance. If Beauregard had known the truth about Halleck's numbers, he might have reconsidered going to the trouble of deploying his army north and east of Corinth. Jefferson Davis did not want to lose Corinth, but would he want to risk having one of his major armies crushed? Beauregard, however, could not warn Davis about that possibility since Halleck's numbers were unknown. Though he had no idea why Halleck moved slowly, Beauregard was fortunate he faced a tentative opponent. Most historians do not regard Beauregard as a successful general; his main problem was his dislike of Jefferson Davis. He believed he had not been treated very well, despite leading an army to the first major Confederate victory at Manassas in Virginia. Yet he had military talents, and his understanding of army operations was extensive, as his plans at Corinth indicated.

His orders stated that each regiment should camp 400–800 yards to the rear of its place in the line of defense, and each regiment would be responsible for building a good road from camp to the front. The roads were to be built to accommodate the movement of artillery. The defensive front should have 3,520 men stretched out per mile. Each division should have a brigade in reserve 400 yards to the rear. Beauregard also issued specific instructions regarding Van Dorn's troops and the use of heavy and light artillery. Any roads approaching the left and right flanks of the army should be blocked in all swampy places, making them even more difficult to negotiate by enemy troops. He thought this tactic especially important on the left flank, where the obstructions should force the Yankees to move toward the Mobile & Ohio Railroad, where Polk's artillery could effectively shell the enemy. The plans indicated the depth of Beauregard's knowledge.[15]

The continuing unhealthy situation at Corinth and the lack of sufficient supplies threatened to undermine Beauregard's dispositions before Federal forces ever arrived. The deadly situation regarding men's health as described by Bragg did not seem likely to improve. Bad water and summer heat took a heavy toll on the Confederates. Food, what there was of it, continued to be barely edible, and Beauregard complained bitterly to Richmond that Lucius B. Northrup, head of the Confederate commissary, was so incompetent that he might single-handedly starve the army at Corinth. Beauregard finally took matters into his own hands, sending "agents to northern Texas and Arkansas," who arranged the purchase of herds of cattle. The beef alleviated Beauregard's situation, but once Richmond got wind of his success, he received orders to send some of the food to other armies. What the Jefferson Davis government could not give, it did not hesitate to take away. Beauregard had another reason to detest Davis.

As Beauregard pondered his army's situation at Corinth, he decided to look into future options, whether forced to by Halleck or ever-present sickness. He knew the War Department expected him to protect north Mississippi as well as Fort Pillow, a stronghold north of Memphis on the Mississippi River. He considered the possibility of moving west to Grand Junction, Tennessee, which would put him in position to hit the Union right flank and also block the Federal army from moving west into Memphis or getting to Fort Pillow. At the same time, Halleck could send troops north and west around Beauregard's position and take Fort Pillow. The loss of Fort Pillow would possibly open the Mississippi all the way to the Gulf of Mexico, for Beauregard was not sure defensive positions at Vicksburg at the time were strong enough to stand up to the Union navy. In effect, too many factors, including water problems, eliminated the Grand Junction strategy. Beauregard decided to try to hold Corinth and make the best of his bleak situation. He had no faith that Richmond would send him more men.[16]

Confederate scouts toured the country south of Corinth and found that the closest place where good water and food and adequate defensive positions existed was Tupelo, situated on the Mobile & Ohio Railroad some fifty miles south of Corinth. While he examined his situation at Corinth,

Beauregard attempted to get heavy artillery sent to Vicksburg and urged the construction of earthworks there. He later claimed more credit for initiating the defenses at Vicksburg than he deserved, but he understood better than the Confederate War Department the importance of the town's defenses to the prevention of free access up and down the Mississippi by the Union. Yet he would later express his feelings that focusing on Vicksburg or other places was not as important as unchaining Confederate forces from places so they could roam and fight more freely.[17]

While Beauregard worked feverishly to prepare for Halleck's arrival, Halleck prepared to move his force of three armies southwest to Corinth. John Pope's forces composed the left of Halleck's line, Buell's army occupied the center, and Grant's Army of the Tennessee was placed on the right, but without Grant. Halleck assigned George Thomas to command Grant's army, and he assigned Grant to remain at headquarters as second in overall command. This was a slap in the face for Grant, and another indication that Halleck did not trust Grant's leadership abilities on the battlefield.[18]

After the war, Grant observed that he "was little more than an observer." Orders from Halleck's headquarters "were sent directly to the right wing [Grant's army] or reserve, ignoring me, and advances were made from one line of intrenchments to another without notifying me. My position was so embarrassing in fact that I made several applications during the siege to be relieved." Grant indeed came close to resigning, but, fortunately for the Union war effort, his friend William T. Sherman talked him into staying on. Halleck, when confronted by Grant regarding his do-nothing position, responded that he was surprised at Grant's anger. Halleck wrote, "You have precisely the position to which your rank entitles you. Had I given you the right wing or reserve only it would have been a reduction rather than increase of command, and I could not give you both without placing you in the position you now occupy." Halleck denied he had done Grant "any injustice" and claimed that he had defended Grant during recent months from attacks made by others. Halleck lied, for he had indeed been the instigator of some, in fact most, of those complaints.[19]

Preparations went forward for the march to Corinth, but Halleck made clear to all his commanders that he would not move rapidly and take great risks. Halleck had never before led an army into battle, and what he had seen when he arrived at Pittsburg Landing no doubt convinced him that caution was the best strategy. Grant, in Halleck's mind, had not exercised enough caution, and the army had paid a high price. Halleck did not intend to make the mistakes Grant had made; Halleck would not allow the combined armies to be vulnerable to attack.

Halleck believed in massing forces and overpowering the enemy, and he also embraced the strategy of digging in for protection. He had written *Elements of Military and Science* years before the war, detailing his military science views. He had translated a work on Napoleon by Antoine Henri de Jomini, a leading French military theorist. West Point instructor Dennis Hart Mahan's *Advanced-Guard, Out-Post* also influenced Halleck's thinking. With this background affecting his thinking on this, his first and last time to lead a military campaign, Halleck could be expected to move slowly and dig in every evening. If Beauregard attacked, Halleck intended to meet him from a position of strength. Though Halleck at the time was criticized, and has been ever since, for the snail-like pace of his army, when all factors are considered, his thinking is more understandable. Halleck believed that taking a strategic point was more important than destroying Beauregard's army, so if he pressured Beauregard to abandon Corinth without a major battle, so much the better. Halleck's thinking mirrored Lincoln's view that Halleck should not risk a failed campaign.[20]

Halleck chose the obvious approach to Corinth. The Mobile & Ohio Railroad ran slightly west of north from the town, and the Memphis & Charleston stretched southeast of Corinth before turning to a generally eastern course to Iuka and beyond. Halleck stretched his armies to fill the gap between the two railroads. As the Federals neared Corinth, they would become more compact if Halleck kept his soldiers between the railroads, and he intended to maintain that alignment, though, especially on his left, where the aggressive John Pope commanded, troops did at times overlap the Memphis & Charleston. Since Halleck thus plotted the route of his army, the campaign could hardly be called the siege of Corinth, as it was at the time and since, for Beauregard had access to a wide range of territory he could use to retreat if necessary. At no time did Southern forces even come close to being penned in by Halleck's armies.

Within the wide "V" created by the railroads, several roads and trails led to Corinth. Heavy rains held up Halleck's advance by turning main roads into quagmires. The roads were not a great hindrance to infantry, which could avoid them, but they slowed supply wagons and artillery to a crawl. In effect, they disrupted Union efforts to guard and maintain supply and communication lines from Pittsburg Landing to Halleck's army. Buell characterized them as "narrow, unimproved, dirt roads," and in truth they were more wagon and horse trails than roads.[21]

The Union right, Grant's army, led by George Thomas, followed a route defined by a road from Pittsburg Landing southwest to the village of Monterey, where it turned and led directly to Corinth. Buell's army, the center, moved forward, with its guide one of the Hamburg-to-Corinth roads. Hamburg was a Tennessee River town a few miles southeast of Pittsburg Landing, and two main roads stretched from Hamburg to Corinth. Buell took his army on the route "farthest west," which put the Army of the Ohio in the center of Halleck's approach with its left adjacent to the right of John Pope's Army of the Mississippi traveling to Corinth via the other road, called the Old Hamburg and Corinth. Pope's route led to Farmington, a community due east and about three miles from Corinth. Farmington also was a short distance north of the Memphis & Charleston Railroad. Federal control of the railroad would cut Beauregard's eastern supply line and slow any Confederate efforts to get reinforcements to Beauregard.

Pope understood the importance of his position, and he did his best to take advantage of it. Beauregard already understood the necessity of keeping the railroad open, and he did his best to keep Pope at bay. This sector of the campaign proved to be the only one in which significant fighting took place. Halleck warned Pope not to push ahead of Buell and break contact between the center and left. Halleck had no desire to risk flank attacks or Rebel offensives that might succeed due to his forces becoming scattered. He preferred having Pope wait on Buell rather than ordering Buell to speed up. Halleck stayed with his determination to be slow and careful, no matter what opportunities Pope might have.[22]

The Union march dragged on. Begun around May 1, the pace amounted to about 1,200 yards a day. Grant later said he expected a two-day campaign to capture Corinth, but it would take a month to reach and occupy the town. Halleck himself bragged to Secretary of War Edwin Stanton in a May 3 message that his forces would be in Corinth by the evening of the next day. Grant had not foreseen Halleck moving so slowly and entrenching every night. Halleck quickly backed off his bombastic prediction. As days dragged by, he reminded Stanton and Lincoln, lest they grow weary of his slow pace, that the "country is so wooded and marshy that we are obliged to feel our way step by step." Not only that, but "the enemy is strongly intrenched, and his number equal if not superior to ours," making caution all the more necessary. Despite limited resistance by Confederate scouts and pickets, Halleck refused to take any risk and kept his three armies moving methodically and coherently. He believed he could defeat Beauregard, but he predicted it would be a "a terrible battle," something he likely thought worse than Shiloh. Halleck was convinced that Beauregard's reinforcements made the Confederates a much more formidable force than Grant had faced.[23]

The Union move on Corinth settled into Halleck's version of a siege. Soldiers in blue pushed forward slowly morning until evening and then built fortifications of dirt and logs. The tactics resembled a siege, but the temporary earthworks were the extent of any resemblance to actual siege operations. Nevertheless, Halleck's tactics supported his determination to carry on a defensive-offensive strategy, more the former than the latter.

On the Federal right, George Thomas reported on May 4 his wing moved toward the Purdy-Corinth road, protecting flanks with dug trenches. Three days later Thomas ordered his divisions forward again, spreading between the Monterey-Corinth and Purdy-Farmington roads, and once more threw up defensive works. Nothing happened until May 16 when Thomas ordered another forward movement, using connecting roads as a guide, moving between the Monterey and Purdy roads toward Corinth. Thomas noted that each of his flanks repelled enemy attacks—"strong resistance" he called it— and that evening his men dug in once more. His report included a description that characterized the majority of Halleck's campaign: "From this time until our next advance there was considerable skirmishing between our pickets and those of the enemy, our pickets cautiously but steadily advancing from day to day and always holding the ground they had gained."[24]

On May 21 Sherman's division, on Thomas's right flank, made progress, crossing a creek and driving Confederates away from a strong position around a house called Russell's. Sherman's success had a ripple effect, as the rest of the wing moved slowly forward to high ground, experiencing but token opposition from Beauregard's troops. Thomas's men had drawn close enough to Corinth to hear a "great commotion" in the town, and he assumed that Beauregard was preparing to attack the Union right. Beauregard was not; there was a reason Union troops had met little opposition. Two days passed and nothing happened. Rebel deserters reported that an attack was planned but canceled after Beauregard's generals learned that Sherman had taken a position on high ground.

Sherman pushed forward again, after receiving orders on the night of May 27 to move out the next morning and "drive the rebels from [the] house in our front on the Corinth road." The house Halleck referred to was a "double log building, standing on a high ridge on the upper or southern end of the large field," which had been occupied already by pickets. The Confederates had pulled back. As Sherman pushed closer to Corinth, the skirmishing picked up, artillery dueled, and Union forces pushed closer to Rebel lines. Sherman noted later that the Union right pushed so near that "we could hear the sound of his [Rebel] drums and sometimes of voices in command and the railroad cars arriving and departing at Corinth were easily distinguished." The sounds of railroad engines and cars became constant in the town, and Sherman knew something important was going on, though it was difficult to understand what it was.[25]

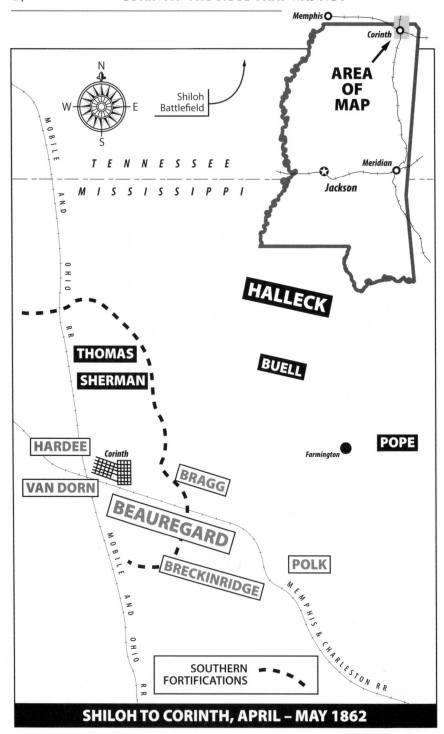

AREA OF MAP

Memphis
Corinth

TENNESSEE
MISSISSIPPI

Shiloh Battlefield

Meridian

Jackson

MOBILE AND OHIO RR

HALLECK

THOMAS
SHERMAN

BUELL

HARDEE
Corinth

POPE

Farmington

VAN DORN

BRAGG

BEAUREGARD

MOBILE AND OHIO RR

BRECKINRIDGE

POLK

MEMPHIS & CHARLESTON RR

SOUTHERN
FORTIFICATIONS

SHILOH TO CORINTH, APRIL – MAY 1862

In the Federal center, Don Carlos Buell's Army of the Ohio began moving toward Corinth on April 29, crossing the Lick Creek bottom after his troops constructed several bridges. He followed the Hamburg-Corinth road, trying to keep alignment with Pope's left wing. Pope eventually branched off onto the old Hamburg-Corinth road toward Farmington. Heavy rain and Confederate resistance slowed Buell's army, and the muddy roads forced Buell to depend on horsemen rather than wagons to provide logistical support from the Tennessee River.

Pope advanced more quickly and aggressively, but Halleck was not pleased. Pope's faster pace often left gaps between his right and Buell's left. Buell complained that he had to shift his lines and move faster to protect Pope's right. On May 17 Pope and Buell personally scouted ground around the Purdy-Farmington road. They led their troops forward to within two miles of outer Confederate works. Meanwhile Buell also had to make sure his right extended to Thomas's left. On May 21 some of Buell's men engaged Confederates around the Serratt house, which sat on a hill. The outnumbered Rebels made a strong stand before retreating, no doubt reinforcing Halleck's determination to be cautious.

Not until a week later did Federal forces occupy Serratt's hill. The position put Buell within less than 1,000 yards from the outer Confederate defense line. Buell ordered his troops to dig in the evening of May 28. The next day Buell told Halleck that an advance should be made in cooperation with Pope, but Halleck, perhaps unnerved by Pope's impetuosity, told Buell that he and Thomas should move forward to test the Rebel strength. Pope should stay where he was, since he had pushed closer to enemy lines than the other two wings. Soon intelligence reports indicated that Beauregard had massed his troops to assault Pope, and Buell must be ready to provide support. Pope had certainly caused the Confederates more trouble than any other part of Halleck's army, but the news about an attack proved to be a red herring.[26]

Pope's aggression made Halleck as nervous as Beauregard. On May 3 Pope attacked a small force of Confederates near Farmington. The heavily outnumbered Confederates retreated back to Farmington. Pope ignored the distance his position put him from Buell's left, and, as Pope pushed to Farmington, Seven Miles Creek separated his right from Buell. Pope smelled a possible breaking of enemy lines, and he forgot about Buell. Beauregard, aware that Pope's advance had isolated his command, decided to attack Pope, "cut him off from his base," and force him to give up any thoughts of constructing defensive works at Farmington.

Beauregard's attack, however, did not materialize as planned. Van Dorn, on the right flank, had orders to move before dawn against Pope's left. But

Van Dorn's inept local guide, combined with problems of getting his whole command to move quickly, doomed the surprise he hoped for. Pope's officers learned of Van Dorn's presence and immediately withdrew to avoid a flank attack. Van Dorn sent his men forward anyway, and part of Braxton Bragg's men, ordered to attack Pope's front while Van Dorn hit the Yankee left, came rushing forward to join the charge. The front and flank tactics that Beauregard envisioned failed, but his troops did kill and wound quite a few of Pope's men, and the Rebels raided abandoned Yankee camps. Beauregard reported 200 men killed and wounded, most of whom fell during Pope's initial attack. Pope made light of the fighting, focusing on the success of his attack, reporting that his men "are all returning" to camp a couple of miles from Farmington. He reported only fourteen casualties, though Beauregard claimed the Federals had "quite a number" of losses.[27]

Pope sent word to Halleck the next morning that his command had advanced and had captured a formidable position east of Farmington. However, he said, his situation had drawbacks, like the nearby creek and a heavy "jungle and swamp" on his left. Rebel reinforcements had come to protect the Memphis & Charleston Railroad south of Pope's position. Pope had confidence he could prevail, though, if "Buell's force will keep pace on our right." By focusing on the positive, Pope avoided criticism for separating his army from Buell's and put the onus on Buell to keep up. At the same time, Buell reported to Halleck that his army continued to deal with bad roads and swampy creek terrain. Buell wanted to be sure Halleck understood his problems, for Buell did feel especially obliged to save Pope. Buell, who was not particularly fond of Halleck or Pope, likely thought he had tried to follow the framework of Halleck's plans, and Pope had not.[28]

Pope sent Halleck more messages, describing a massive buildup of Confederate forces in his front and reporting that scouts indicated the Rebels had decided to pull out of Corinth. Obvious conflicting reports led Pope to ask Halleck's permission for a reconnaissance on May 8 to ascertain if the Confederates were withdrawing. Halleck agreed and asked Pope if he needed help from Buell. Pope replied that he wanted Buell only to protect his right flank to make sure no enemy force got between them. Pope's concern indicated he did not yet believe news of Beauregard's evacuation.[29]

Beauregard already knew he would soon have to abandon Corinth due to the enemy's overwhelming numbers. He determined to keep the Yankees guessing. He ordered his men on the right to prepare to attack and hoped that by striking the Yankees "another blow," he would at least "blind him [Halleck] as to the future movements" being planned.[30]

To give Pope more to think about, Beauregard sent Van Dorn orders to move forward on the evening of May 8. Van Dorn marched his men to a position with his left near a mushy creek bottom, his center on the Danville road, and his right held by Sterling Price's troops. The next morning Van Dorn moved his battle line to his right, "crossing the three roads leading to Farmington from the south," that is, the Danville and two Jacinto roads. Van Dorn then ordered an advance toward Pope's line. The Federals fell back, abandoning Farmington and crossing Seven Mile Creek. Confederates burned the bridge across the creek. Unfortunately for Van Dorn, his plan for Price to attack and get into the rear of Pope's troops to cut off the Union retreat failed due to rugged, overgrown, ravine-riddled terrain. A disappointed Van Dorn regretted that the speed of the Yankee retreat spoiled his plans.

Pope notified Halleck that his army had been attacked by 20,000 Confederates and that his line held for some five hours before retreating to avoid entrapment. Pope thought he was safe, unless the Confederates got between him and Buell. Up until that point, Pope had been nonchalant about the gap. Confederate aggressiveness had gotten his attention. Pope reported his losses as "considerable," though he did not report a number. He thought the Rebels had suffered greatly too, but Van Dorn reported only nine men lost.[31]

Ulysses S. Grant remained a spectator during all the activity in Pope's sector. Pope later recalled that Grant established a camp at the rear of Pope's army and rarely interacted with anyone other than his own staff. He did visit Pope's headquarters occasionally, but, according to Pope, Grant spent most of that time lying on a cot, saying little. Pope wrote, "I never felt more sorry for anyone."[32]

Grant never mentioned visits to Pope's camp in his memoirs, but he did write that sometime in mid-May he suggested to Halleck that Pope's army go by night around the rear of Buell and Thomas and attack at daylight. Perhaps Grant, despite his melancholy, had noticed, and appreciated, Pope's fighting attitude. Grant did not believe that Pope would find much, if any, opposition or difficult terrain on such a march. But Halleck, Grant wrote, dismissed the idea without hesitation, and Grant "felt that possibly I had suggested an unmilitary movement." From Halleck's point of view, uncovering his left would be much too risky. If Beauregard ordered an attack on Buell's left before Pope could get his army in place on the Union right, things could get ugly, for Halleck would find himself fighting on two fronts. He still did not believe he had a great advantage in numbers, and he would not be moved from his original strategic campaign concepts. Halleck, no doubt, also remembered Lincoln's admonition: "Be very sure to sustain no reverse in your Department." His rejection of Grant's plan was a mere reflection of his refusal to take risks.[33]

On Pope's front, Van Dorn's failure to do little more than push Pope back a few hundred yards increased Beauregard's worries over the ever-increasing pressure of Halleck's army. Halleck had taken his time, but now the entire Federal force had gotten close enough to Corinth to convince Beauregard that he could not hold the town for long. Scouting reports indicated the Yankees were increasing their presence and pressing hard on the Confederate left, so it was time for Van Dorn and Bragg to quit operations on the right and spread the army all across the front to face Halleck's approach. Beauregard realized that Halleck's numbers were "too near together for us to be able to strike a great blow."[34]

Beauregard could not bring himself to leave Corinth just yet, however. He knew that, despite the odds, he would be heavily criticized in Richmond if he gave up Corinth, which meant losing the vital railroad crossing. From May 10 to 30, when he finally ordered the evacuation, Beauregard kept his forces in line of battle, and skirmishing between the armies became commonplace. Each passing day made it more obvious that the Confederates could do nothing but try to hold their entrenched positions, and the time they could do so was quickly running out. In late May Beauregard contemplated another assault against Pope, but bad weather and other problems forced cancellation of the operation.[35]

When Beauregard concluded retreat had become essential, following a May 25 conference with his commanders, he began working on the particulars of the evacuation. Beauregard sent out detailed instructions on routes south that the cavalry, Braxton Bragg's troops, and Earl Van Dorn's men should take. Van Dorn had orders to retreat to Baldwyn, located on the Mobile & Ohio to the south between Corinth and Tupelo. Train cars would be used to carry supplies southward. On May 29 the retreat got under way in earnest. Union soldiers and officers could clearly hear trains coming and going, and they had varying opinions about what the Rebels were doing.

In fact, if anything good can be said about having to retreat, Beauregard's version at Corinth could be classified as a model for other generals. While wagon trains moved south, a band walked around town playing retreat, tattoo, and taps, while some drummers beat out reveille. The sounds were intended to confuse the Federals about Beauregard's intent. Was he getting ready to leave or settling in part of the army for the night, and possibly getting others ready to attack? To add to the mixed signals, Beauregard ordered campfires to burn brightly all along his line. One empty train ran back and forth a short distance on the Memphis & Charleston rail line. Each time the train got close to town, Rebels cheered as if welcoming reinforcements. They also cheered when supply trains returned from the south on the Mobile & Ohio to reload. So-called Quaker artillery-poles the length of cannons, some coated with ashes, and scarecrows imitating gunners and pickets, were part of Beauregard's ruse. He also sent a few men to portray deserters who wandered into Union lines talking about a major attack by Beauregard in the morning and saying they wanted no part of it.[36]

All the Confederate activity indeed caused confusion among Halleck and his officers. About 1:20 on the morning of May 30 Pope sent a message telling Halleck that trains were bringing many reinforcements to the Rebels. He told Halleck "the cheering is immense every time they unload in front of me." Pope became convinced that he would be attacked "in heavy force" come daylight. Halleck received word from Buell that the Rebels had in part moved west and would attack the Union right. Halleck sent word to Grant, addressing Grant as "Commanding Army of the Tennessee," an unusual appellation considering Grant's actual position, that the enemy would attack the Union left the morning of May 30, "as troops have been moving in that direction some time."

Suddenly sounds of explosions came from Corinth after some of the Confederate commotion had died down for quite a while. The Rebels blew up anything of military value that could not be evacuated. Sherman wanted an explanation. "The whole is now enveloped in dense smoke, yet the rebels are in my front. Cars ran all night with long trains." Halleck responded to Sherman, "I have no explanation." Halleck mentioned Pope's earlier message and concluded that the current thinking at headquarters was that the Rebels might pull out of Corinth proper and make a stand "in the angle between the two railroads." By 6 a.m. on May 30 Pope decided the explosions indicated a retreat, and at 8:25 he informed Halleck, "The enemy evacuated yesterday and last night," to the south. Pope said his men were pushing into town. Beauregard's retreat strategy had indeed worked to perfection.[37]

Beauregard stopped his army initially at Baldwyn, but he decided the area was not good as a defensive position, so the Confederates moved on to Tupelo, arriving June 9, where Beauregard and his staff found good water and good defensive terrain. On June 12 Beauregard wired Richmond that, despite Halleck's claims of a great victory, the Confederate "retreat was a most brilliant and successful one." In Beauregard's mind, the giving up of a railroad junction was minor compared to the fact that Halleck had found a deserted town and had captured no supplies or armaments, and Beauregard had saved his army from being forced to surrender. Halleck took the opposite view. He had captured Corinth, and that was his great objective.

John Pope stayed on Beauregard's trail for a time, sending back frequent reports to Halleck, at one point asking that both Buell and Thomas send reinforcements. Halleck replied, "The main object now is to get the enemy far enough south to relieve our railroads from danger of an immediate attack. There is no object in bringing on a battle if this object can be obtained without one." In Halleck's mind, as long as Beauregard kept up a retreat, that was all that mattered. Halleck's assignment had been to take Corinth, and he intended not to fight Beauregard unless ordered to do so. Going to battle with Beauregard had never been foremost in his mind, except to bring about the fall of Corinth.[38]

Secretary of War Edwin Stanton congratulated Halleck: "Your brilliant and successful achievement gives great joy over the whole land." Stanton asked for more news, declaring that the president was especially eager to be kept informed. One Halleck report proved to be a thorn in his side. He informed Washington that Pope had reported the capture of 10,000 prisoners and 15,000 guns. Pope heatedly denied that he ever sent any such thing to Halleck. Pope had informed Halleck that there were many enemy stragglers to the south: "Not less than 10,000 men are thus scattered about, who will come in within a day or two." Obviously someone, perhaps a Halleck staff member or one of Pope's, had misstated the facts. The occasion created hard feelings between the two, and in 1865, after the end of the war, Pope contacted Halleck and asked for a copy of the report that he had allegedly sent. Halleck replied that he had been ordered to California, and his papers were all boxed up. Halleck insisted, however, that he "never reported to the Secretary of War dispatches received from you which were not so received." That answer did not satisfy Pope, who immediately sent a long message back to Halleck, continuing to deny he ever sent any such message to Halleck, and he was disappointed that Halleck was not willing to produce a copy that could settle the issue one way or another.

Halleck appeared to let the matter drop after that, and there is no evidence in the official records of the war that Pope sent such a message, only that Halleck received it. The exchange illustrated how often personal conflicts infiltrated command relationships. Halleck also had run-ins with Buell and, of course, Grant during various stages of the campaign. He managed to keep the army moving, and he succeeded, but his inexperience in field command showed, for he never managed to form a team of commanders whom he could trust or who trusted him. Yet Grant and Sherman admired Halleck for most of the war, perhaps because they respected his military acumen, but they could not warm up to him personally.[39]

At the time of the capture of Corinth, Halleck also became a target of disgruntled Northern reporters. By allowing Beauregard to get away, Halleck had, in the words of a Cincinnati reporter, "achieved one of the barren triumphs of the war. In fact, it is tantamount to a defeat." Another reporter wrote of Beauregard's evacuation: "I do not know how the matter strikes abler military men, but I think we have been fooled. The works are far from being invulnerable, and the old joke of quaker guns has been played off on us."[40]

Some Union soldiers agreed that the taking of Corinth had been an empty victory, but, whether they liked him or not, most of Halleck's officers, like Sherman and Grant, agreed that the campaign was very successful. Few lives had been lost, and the railroad crossing had been taken. Corinth, not Beauregard's army, had been Halleck's target, and the town was in Union hands and would remain so until the latter days of the war. Grant, with an obvious ax to grind, wrote later in his memoirs that the capture of Corinth was strategically significant, "but the victory was barren in every other particular." As the war progressed, Grant, like Beauregard, became convinced that enemy armies were much more of a threat than places. But early in the war, that kind of thinking had not yet come into vogue. Abraham Lincoln recognized the flawed logic and did his best to convince his generals in the East to go after Robert E. Lee's army rather than worrying about Richmond. Jefferson Davis took the opposite position, and ultimately his insistence on saving places contributed significantly to Confederate defeat in the western theater.[41]

If Halleck's army was not going to pursue Beauregard, what would it do? There were three large armies massed at Corinth after Pope returned from chasing Beauregard. Stanton mentioned in a message to Halleck that he assumed the offensive would continue on to Vicksburg. Halleck never responded to the comment, and Stanton never mentioned it again, largely because President Lincoln was still dealing with George McClellan in Virginia. McClellan wanted Union forces sent into middle Tennessee in an attempt to force the Confederate government to pull some of its troops out of Virginia.[42]

Initially, Halleck broke up his massive armies, sending them in different directions to fix railroads, dig better earthworks around Corinth, and find supplies. Pope had his Army of the Mississippi, Buell was in charge of the Army of the Ohio, and Grant was put back in command of the Army of the Tennessee. As the summer wore on, Halleck dealt with stomach ailments, Pope was called to Virginia to lead a newly organized Army of Virginia, and Lincoln and Stanton kept insisting on more troops to help McClellan. Halleck grew frustrated with continual demands for troops from practically every direction, but on July 2 he received word from Lincoln to come to Washington for consultation. On July 11 Lincoln published an order making Halleck commander "of the whole land forces of the United States, as General-in-Chief." Halleck left Corinth on July 17, after calling Grant from Memphis to Corinth to take command there.

Halleck had little to say to Grant about what was going on, about what plans might be in place, so Grant wrote later that he was in command of the West Tennessee District, but in reality he became a departmental commander. However, the departmental position did not come to him officially from Washington until October 25. The two generals had had a strained relationship, and an ironic twist awaited them in the future. When Halleck left, Grant had to busy himself trying to keep enough men present to hold on to the Corinth-Memphis corridor. Demands for troops from Arkansas, Tennessee, and Virginia had melted the 100,000 Halleck once had, and Grant wondered if he could scrape together enough of those still around to go on the defensive. In September Grant had only 45,500 left to defend a broad front.[43]

To the south, General Beauregard quickly found out that Jefferson Davis did not have nearly as high an opinion of the Confederate retreat as did his general. Davis took the unusual step of sending Beauregard a list of questions about why Corinth had been given up. Davis sent his aide-de-camp, William Preston Johnston, to deliver the questions, which included a query as to why the army retreated in the first place. Beauregard said he had no choice. Could the damage be undone? Beauregard said future operations depended on what the Yankees did. If Halleck divided his forces, then there would be an opportunity to go on the offensive. If enemy forces did not divide, Beauregard would seek ways to force them to do so.

Davis then asked if the army had made proper use of the terrain, and Beauregard said the defensive positions had been chosen by himself, Sidney Johnston, and Bragg, and they could find no stronger positions. Why was there so much sickness? Bad water and food and no fresh supplies, Beauregard replied. Could not the Union rear have been attacked? Beauregard said that if that were possible, he would have done so. What had been done, Davis asked, to prevent Union descent on the Mississippi after Pope had captured Island No. 10? One must wonder at Davis's state of mind to ask Beauregard such a question. The Confederacy had no navy to speak of, and Beauregard did not command the navy, nor was he in a position to monitor what naval defenses there were on the Mississippi. Davis went on to ask what had been done to defend Memphis, which had fallen. Beauregard said building up Fort Pillow on the river had depleted Confederate forces, and that holding Fort Pillow and Corinth was the only way to protect Memphis. And those efforts failed due to lack of manpower. Finally, Beauregard assured Davis the army had suffered very few losses.[44]

The incident demonstrated just how out of touch Davis was with the situation in the West in general and in his home state in particular. If he had any idea how badly Beauregard was outnumbered, and why an army facing two-to-one odds could not be expected to make a long stand at Corinth, he would have understood Beauregard's decision. Davis did not understand, but he thought he did. He considered himself well-schooled on conditions in the western theater. Therefore he believed Beauregard had lost Corinth due to the general's incompetence. Davis never seriously analyzed his armies' situations in the West. His perceptions were coated in delusions. Just because Beauregard was in command did not mean he could be everywhere at once, and he could not impact operations over a wide area with the limited resources he had available. Davis, like Halleck, had the illusion that every effort must be made to protect places, like towns and railroads. Halleck, with his huge army, could afford that philosophy at the time; Davis could not. Davis refused to accept the idea that the only way Confederate armies in the West could be effective was to go on the offensive at times and places of their choosing.

As for Beauregard, he received signed documents from physicians to prove to Davis that a leave of absence was necessary for "restoration of my health." He wired Richmond on June 15 from Tupelo that he was stepping down for a short time and placing Braxton Bragg in command of the army. Beauregard departed for Mobile, where he intended to spend his sick leave. Davis was not impressed by Beauregard's untimely departure, no matter the reason. Beauregard had lost Corinth, and that obviously made Davis sicker than Beauregard claimed to be. On June 20 Davis sent a wire to Bragg acknowledging news of Beauregard's departure. Bragg no doubt did not expect what the rest of Davis's message said: "You are assigned permanently to the command of the department, as will be more formally notified to you by the Secretary of War. You will correspond directly and receive orders and instructions from the Government in relation to your future operations." Beauregard could take his time recuperating.[45]

Bragg now had to make decisions and recommendations, and he ultimately decided to take most of his army, some 30,000 men, into Tennessee to counter Don Carlos Buell's operations there. Buell had gone into Tennessee after the fall of Corinth, mainly to try to run Confederate general Kirby Smith out of the east Tennessee region. President Lincoln worried about east Tennessee throughout the war due to the presence of many loyal Unionists in the area. He continually urged his western commanders to defend the region against Rebels. Slavery was not an issue there, and many citizens had risked their property and lives by openly supporting the Union. Buell, however, would soon be threatened by more

Confederate forces entering Tennessee, and he never carried out Lincoln's wishes.

Bragg could not have his men sit around Tupelo and allow Federal forces to exercise whatever initiative they chose. He left behind 16,000 men under the command of Sterling Price to watch northeast Mississippi and made plans to move into Tennessee to coordinate operations with Smith against Buell. At Vicksburg, Earl Van Dorn had approximately the same number of troops and could perhaps work with Price if necessary. Bragg envisioned Van Dorn and Price invading western Tennessee, while he and Smith cut Buell's supply line that stretched from Chattanooga to Nashville. All these movements centered around operations in Tennessee set up the next battles in Mississippi.[46]

2

VICKSBURG

First Attack

$\mathcal{D}$uring the Civil War, Vicksburg, Mississippi, sat, as now, on high bluffs between Memphis and New Orleans, overlooking the Mississippi River. In the early spring of 1862 the Union navy on the lower Mississippi seemed formidable. After victory in New Orleans, the Federal boats had ascended the river and taken Baton Rouge, Louisiana, and Natchez, Mississippi, without a fight. Neither of those towns had been prepared for defense, however, especially from attacks from an enemy navy. So the Union navy's fighting abilities, despite victory at New Orleans, had not been tested over an extended period of time. Yet the string of successes, despite their nature, convinced Union naval officers, especially the leader of the expedition, David Farragut, that Vicksburg, too, would fall quickly.

In time the naval commanders on the Mississippi and Union strategists in Washington learned they had been far too optimistic. The mighty river does not now flow through the same channel past Vicksburg as it did during the Civil War. There was a hairpin turn there, which challenged the power of vessels going upstream against the current and skilled pilots going downstream with the current. One can stand on those bluffs today and easily imagine the river as it was then and why military minds, both Union and Confederate, considered Vicksburg the key to controlling the river and its supply lanes that connected the trans-Mississippi with the rest of the Confederacy.

Abraham Lincoln, not a professional military man but endowed with much common sense, looked at a map of the region early in the war and saw clearly that Vicksburg was "the key" to the area. Lincoln knew about the twists and turns of the Mississippi at Vicksburg, and he knew the slopes of the bluffs would no doubt be fortified with Confederate cannons, making Union vessels easy targets as they tried to negotiate the turns. As long as Rebel cannons sat among the heights and crevasses, Union naval forces could obviously not claim control of the entire length of the river. The string of Union naval victories did not convince him that Vicksburg defenders would be easily forced to surrender.

While Lincoln considered the fall of Vicksburg essential, Jefferson Davis thought holding it was vital to Confederate fortunes in the West. Union victory would assure that no supplies shipped by boat could be carried up to the Southern Railroad of Mississippi, which terminated at Vicksburg from its route across central Mississippi and carried east. Some of these supplies reached Vicksburg via a railroad that ran from several miles into Louisiana across the river from Vicksburg.

To the south, the Red River, flowing northwest to southeast from Louisiana, emptied into the Mississippi. Confederate supplies came via the Red River from Texas and northwest Louisiana, and many of these goods were carried upriver to Vicksburg. Union control of the Mississippi would make the Red River logistically irrelevant to the Confederacy east of the river. Thanks to the Southern Railroad, Vicksburg had the potential of being a supply hub, though historians of the Vicksburg campaign do not agree that the amount of supplies sent east from the city reached the high volumes feared by Lincoln and hoped for by Jefferson Davis.

Some supplies were held up on the Louisiana side of the river for soldiers there, other supplies were held in Vicksburg for troops defending the town, and still others were carried across the river at varying points along the eastern bank of the Mississippi. So the question arises: was Vicksburg as vital as Jefferson Davis and Abraham Lincoln seemed to think, or was its significance more symbolic than real? Did Davis and Lincoln make it more important than it was? Such questions may be debated, but as long as both sides thought the town was important, it was, and much blood would be expended before it eventually was surrendered.

While Union strategists realized that progress ascending and descending the river above and below Vicksburg had to be accomplished before any attack could be made on the city itself, the town remained on their minds early in the war. During the dawning of 1862, with the completion of several ironclad boats upriver, Union naval strategists decided it was time for action on the Mississippi. They envisioned the river as an avenue of invasion, both from the Gulf of Mexico on the south end and from Missouri to the north. As in Halleck's vision, the Federal navy would approach Vicksburg from two directions, challenging the Confederacy's ability to defend it.

To the south, Flag Officer David Farragut of the Union navy, a Tennessee native, led a successful assault on New Orleans, which fell in late April after relatively weak Confederate resistance. Baton Rouge and Natchez soon surrendered with no resistance at all. Farragut's ascent up the Mississippi had been remarkably easy, so he could be excused if he felt confident about taking Vicksburg. Why should it be any different than Baton Rouge and Natchez? Farragut, who much preferred the open sea to rivers, longed to get back to the Gulf of Mexico. He sent a detachment upstream from Natchez to take Vicksburg quickly. Once Vicksburg fell, Farragut could cut the Red River supply route, turn around, and hastily go south to his beloved ocean waters.

Union navy captain Samuel Phillips Lee led the way north from Natchez in the early summer of 1862. Since unwelcome instructions from Secretary of the Navy Gideon Welles had arrived ordering Farragut to take Vicksburg, Farragut urged Lee to be quick about it. With the end of his part of the river campaign in sight, Farragut wanted no delays. He gave Lee, who departed on May 18, five vessels, including Lee's own *Oneida*. Other vessels included the *Pinola*, *Kennebec*, *Sciota*, and *Winona*.

The Union excursion up the Mississippi had resulted in hundreds of fires on both the Louisiana and Mississippi sides of the river. Confederate military officials had ordered plantation owners and farmers to burn cotton and sugar to keep the crops out of enemy hands. These agriculturists were none too happy to destroy their income. And all the while they fought high river levels to keep their farmland dry. These were angry people, staring with hatred in their eyes at the Yankee invaders.

The Federal sailors no doubt stared back with looks of amusement, for they felt unstoppable, but their thus far easy journey was about to hit a snag. Farragut's hope for a quick end to his river campaign ended at Vicksburg. Lee became quickly frustrated after sending a message to Confederate outposts demanding, upon the authority of Flag Officer Farragut and Major General Benjamin Butler, controversial Massachusetts politician and now the military commander of New Orleans, that Vicksburg surrender. Lee promised the protection of "private property and personal rights."

James Autry, having been appointed military governor and post commander of Vicksburg by Mississippi governor Pettus, refused, noting that "Mississippians don't know, and refuse to learn, how to surrender to an enemy." He invited Farragut and Butler to offer surrender instructions, if they dared. General Martin Luther Smith, a New Yorker with a Georgia wife, commanded Confederate forces in the city and also rejected Lee's message, with the comment that he had been ordered to hold the city and he intended to do so. The mayor of Vicksburg sent a message rejecting any notion of surrender. Rebuffed by these responses, Lee ordered his squadron back downriver to await further instructions from Farragut.[1]

General Smith welcomed the reprieve. Since taking command in Vicksburg on May 12, he had been working his men and slave laborers to build up the city's defenses. The only troops he had on hand were the Eighth Louisiana Battalion and the Twenty-seventh Louisiana regiment. By May 18 six artillery batteries had been readied for action. Still, the beleaguered general did not feel comfortable. He assumed that with such a small force, he would be outgunned no matter what the enemy tried. He recommended that Vicksburg residents leave town to avoid the dangers of an expected Union naval bombardment. A majority took his advice; many of those who did not would regret their decision once artillery shells started screaming from the river into the streets.[2]

Another message from Lee, this one on May 21, echoed Smith's call for civilian evacuation, and Lee urged that the city be cleared of nonmilitary personnel within twenty-four hours. David Farragut had finally arrived, and Lee's words were surely intended to impress his boss. Lee tried a little psychology on the mayor and other city officials: "I had hoped that the same spirit which [induced] the military authorities to retire from the city of New Orleans, rather than wantonly sacrifice lives and property of its inhabitants, would have been followed here." The mayor, knowing that many had already retreated east of town, assured Lee that his warning would be circulated.

The large numbers of residents who left town relieved Smith's concerns. The Vicksburgians took whatever they could and camped in woods, fields, barns, carriage houses, and other places that seemed far enough from the range of Yankee guns. If they could find nothing with a roof on it, they covered themselves with sheets, quilts, and blankets and hoped it would not rain. These refugees surely had their lives disrupted, but at least they would be safe from gunboat missiles that soon would fall on Vicksburg.

In his message, Lee further warned city officials he had the option to open fire whenever he deemed it necessary. He seemed to want Confederate officials to know he was not trying to give them an opportunity to avoid having his guns shell their town. Whatever his intent, Lee did nothing for several more days. His delays and Farragut's apparent inclination to let him get away with it did not please official Washington. If Lee expected Farragut to be furious at the impudent Rebels, he was wrong. Farragut seemed surprisingly content to keep his guns silent. Abraham Lincoln and his advisers wanted the Mississippi cleared past Memphis at least (they hoped the boats coming down from the north would take care of the rest of the river, as they indeed did) so the navy could offer additional logistical support to Halleck's army as it moved toward Corinth. Halleck knew of navy successes on the river, but he never appreciated Farragut's difficult situation at Vicksburg trying to deal with hardheaded Rebels.[3]

Farragut considered other plans by the time he learned of the War Department's dissatisfaction with his inaction. The flag officer looked over Vicksburg's defenses, observed the spring floodwaters, and talked with General Thomas Williams, who commanded army detachments carried upriver by river transports to assist Farragut's attempt to capture Vicksburg. Williams, a career officer from New York, assured Farragut that his troops were insufficient to storm the bluffs. At the time, no one thought about flanking the town to the south, as Ulysses S. Grant eventually would do, and even if such a thought had crossed his mind, Williams did not have the manpower to make such a move with any hope of success.

Farragut, tired of waiting and becoming more disgusted at the recalcitrance of enemy officials and commanders in Vicksburg, wanted to launch an all-out bombardment anyway, just to teach these people a lesson. His naval commanders convinced him that nothing worthwhile would be accomplished, and some vessels might be lost or damaged trying to cope with unpredictable river currents and the Confederate artillery. This town would not be a pushover. The steep bluffs frowned down on Federal sailors as if daring the navy to try to force the city's surrender.

Farragut yielded to his officers' common sense, and he may well have been delighted with their opposition. Maybe he could simply leave Vicksburg and go back to the Gulf. Without sufficient army support, he knew he could do little more with his naval guns than make noise. He sat down and penned a litany of complaints to Butler. He pointed out that the Confederates had positioned their guns on the riverbanks in such a manner that attempts to shell them from the river would bring negligible results. He also exaggerated the number of enemy soldiers in town and argued that even should the navy and Williams's men take the place, they did not have sufficient numbers to hold it. Farragut had not worried about such things until now, but the determination of Vicksburg defenders and the visibility of their big guns depleted his confidence. And then there was the inland river with its high water and shifting, swirling currents that he hated to navigate.

Farragut decided to leave a detachment of his squadron south of Vicksburg to blockade the river and harass the city with occasional shells. Williams took his men to the mouth of the Red River to increase the firepower of the blockade against Confederate supply boats, while Farragut returned to the Gulf to direct operations along the coastline. In a letter to Secretary of the Navy Gideon Welles, Farragut reiterated much of what he had told Butler, and he mourned that while on the upper reaches of the Mississippi, he was "at least 300 miles farther" than he had been from the sea since his childhood. Clearly, the old salt had had enough of river campaigning.[4]

Before departing, Farragut appointed James Palmer to command the fleet stationed at Vicksburg. Palmer's *Iroquois*, along with the *Katahdin*, had been added to the naval force brought north by Lee. Palmer was senior to Lee, and this, ostensibly, was Farragut's rationale for the change. In truth, Farragut had not been thrilled with Lee's earlier inaction, though he had done nothing about it. Perhaps Farragut simply did not like Lee. Whatever the cause, the move infuriated Lee, who eventually requested and received reassignment elsewhere.[5]

While Palmer prepared vessels for the blockade, other action erupted downriver toward Baton Rouge. Guerrilla activity along the river increased markedly, making Union sailors and soldiers very nervous. The presence of guerrillas along the banks of the river opened what amounted to a second front and no doubt contributed to Farragut's, Williams's, and other commanders' reluctance to concentrate for an assault on Vicksburg. Their timidity gave Martin Smith more time to solidify Vicksburg defenses.[6]

Additional Confederate troops poured into Vicksburg, including the Twentieth and Twenty-eighth Louisiana, a few companies of the Sixth and Twenty-eighth Mississippi, and one battery from the First Mississippi Light Artillery. Some of these men were ill, many were inexperienced, and too many were "indifferently armed." Eventually the Fourth and Fifth Louisiana regiments arrived. The improvement in numbers did not necessarily guarantee quality, and Smith worried about the reaction of these new, raw men to enemy naval guns. He later stated that, given the inexperience among his soldiers, his incomplete batteries—which included cannons not mounted for service—and no qualified officers to train recruits, he knew that an aggressive assault by the enemy might be difficult to repulse. Farragut, however, had given Smith the most precious thing he needed—time.[7]

The Confederates worked to set up seven artillery batteries, two above Vicksburg to guard against Union vessels coming from the north and five facing the threat posed by Farragut's fleet. The batteries Smith concentrated on Farragut's flotilla totaled twelve cannons of various sizes and one ten-inch mortar. The smaller cluster of guns to the north totaled five heavy guns, including a rifled eighteen-pounder that became a legend at Vicksburg. The gun was dubbed "Whistling Dick" due to the sound the shells made when fired. In addition, General Smith had two forty-two-pounder guns, but these had been sent to the naval yard at Yazoo City to protect a construction project—the Confederate ironclad *Arkansas*. Smith did not have the firepower he wanted or needed, but he had enough to be noisy, keeping enemy sailors on the alert.[8]

The summer of 1862 would be memorable to a population that had never endured a barrage of shot and shell from heavy military artillery. On May 26 Federal iron missiles fell periodically among the town's streets and hills. Sporadic shelling had been going on for some time, but the 26th marked the beginning of the systematic harassment Farragut wanted. To preserve ammunition, Smith ordered gunners not to fire long range and only occasionally from medium range. He realized that enemy shells did very little damage to Confederate works, so why tire his men and waste shells by shooting back? The general understood, too, that by having his men maintain a low profile, he could keep the enemy "ignorant of our real strength as well as the effect of their own shot."[9]

Palmer's men kept up the shelling with varying intensity through the remainder of May and into the second week of June. By then Halleck had taken Corinth and had adopted the view that the navy could clear the river of any Confederate threats. He had no intention of sending troops from Corinth to Vicksburg. Halleck believed his men had more important duties to perform. Halleck's attitude caused Palmer to worry about his flotilla becoming isolated. He had heard nothing from Farragut since the latter left Vicksburg for Baton Rouge. Palmer needed to discuss several concerns with his commander. He feared that the Confederates might be constructing batteries below Vicksburg to cut off Union supplies coming up from New Orleans. Expected coal shipments to Vicksburg from Natchez had not arrived. Palmer sent the *Winona* to Natchez on a scouting mission, where the crew learned that Farragut had ordered coal stockpiled at Natchez back to Baton Rouge. Farragut's action was a clear indication that he had lost interest in Vicksburg. Reports downriver also indicated that Confederates were indeed erecting river batteries at the river town of Grand Gulf between Natchez and Vicksburg.

Palmer took a detachment downstream to check personally on the Grand Gulf situation. General Williams, who earlier returned his troops to Baton Rouge, had been angered by Confederates firing at his men from Grand Gulf. He led a detachment ashore to chase off Rebel guerrillas, but he did not burn the town, and grateful citizens supplied the Yankees with food. Then the guerrillas returned.

When Palmer arrived at Grand Gulf, he ordered the *Wissahickon* and *Itasca* to shell both the town and Confederate artillery positions, but Rebel gunners held their own. The firm enemy resistance convinced Palmer to order the rest of the Vicksburg fleet down to eradicate the Rebels. On June 10–11 massed Union naval guns pounded Grand Gulf, and sailors went ashore and set eight fires in a failed effort to burn down the town. The assault intimidated the Confederates, who quietly melted into the surrounding countryside. They would be back, however, and Grand Gulf continued to be a thorn in the side of Union naval operations.[10]

The Federal fleet went to Natchez, where Palmer sent word to Farragut that news from the Vicksburg front was not good. The Rebels were supposedly building an ironclad somewhere up the Yazoo River, which emptied into the Mississippi north of Vicksburg. Also, intelligence reports indicated that Confederates had evacuated Fort Pillow on the Mississippi above Memphis. Enemy troops deserting Fort Pillow were headed for Vicksburg. Further, Palmer's detachment had suffered from much illness. After sending the message, Palmer led his entourage back toward Vicksburg, accompanied by the *Tennessee*, which carried much-needed coal.

Union sailors saw several Grand Gulf fires still burning, and gunners lobbed a few rounds into the area. Confederate troops, however, showed no inclination to be goaded into another fight. The boats moved on while Palmer kept an eye to the south, hoping that Farragut had received the message and would be coming up with reinforcements. Farragut did get the news, and he would return, no doubt very disappointed.[11]

Palmer's report had greatly alarmed Farragut, dissipating his cavalier attitude toward Vicksburg. He sent a letter to Secretary Welles filled with exaggerated warnings about the Rebels fortifying all the bluffs between Baton Rouge and Vicksburg. Obviously, he wrote, the enemy was concentrating all its strength for a showdown at Vicksburg. Farragut, his fighting spirit somewhat renewed by events, promised Welles he would personally direct operations against Vicksburg, and army forces would come up from Baton Rouge to help. General Williams concurred with Farragut that the Rebels would make a stronger stand, and, indicating he had been pondering the situation, Williams stated his belief that army infantry and artillery would be needed to attack the rear of the town in conjunction with the naval assault from the river. He still had too few men, but Williams's judgment proved to be accurate. Halleck's refusal to send troops meant it would be months before Union strategy proved Williams's observation to be correct. By that time, Williams would be dead.[12]

While Union planning proceeded, Confederates supposedly putting together a concentrated effort to defend Vicksburg were actually in disarray. The news about the evacuation of Fort Pillow caught General Smith by surprise, and he was angry he had not been informed sooner. After all, the collapse of Confederate positions north of Vicksburg affected the overall strategic situation on the Mississippi, as had the loss of New Orleans. Smith complained to his boss, General Mansfield Lovell, a Marylander blamed perhaps unjustly for the loss of New Orleans. Lovell then commanded the Department of Southern Mississippi and East Louisiana, which included Vicksburg, and he had set up headquarters in Jackson. Lovell agreed with Smith that this kind of information should have been forwarded quickly, and he complained to his superior, P. G. T. Beauregard.

Beauregard was already in a bad mood, especially finding himself grilled by President Davis after evacuating Corinth. Beauregard wrote an angry reply to Lovell, in which he pointed out that the Confederate retreat in north Mississippi had dominated his time. He might as well criticize Lovell for not letting him know in advance of the latter's evacuation of New Orleans. Beauregard made it clear that he expected Lovell to take care of his own problems rather than complaining. Further, Beauregard considered the loss of Vicksburg inevitable, and he seemed to be ready to give up the entire lower Mississippi valley. This attitude no doubt contributed to his illness and his being replaced by Bragg.[13]

Lovell learned that Jefferson Davis did not share Beauregard's pessimism. Davis wired Smith on June 14 asking for a progress report on the construction of the *Arkansas* and the condition of Vicksburg defenses. He offered governmental aid and made the obvious comment that Confederate losses above and below Vicksburg increased the significance of the town. Davis's chief military adviser, Robert E. Lee, wired Lovell on June 16 and likewise stressed that the Vicksburg area was too important "to be thought of being abandoned." Lee promised additional weapons and encouraged Lovell to recruit additional troops. He made clear none of Beauregard's army would be available. Lee assured Lovell that the government had confidence in him, further proof that, from Richmond, the view westward was very foggy.

Events took the burden off Lovell. On June 20 Earl Van Dorn was named departmental commander. Van Dorn, the dashing Mississippian who had mismanaged his army and suffered defeat at Pea Ridge in northwest Arkansas, received his orders from Braxton Bragg, who had just taken over for Beauregard. Thus the command situation directly affecting Vicksburg operations during this period of an enemy naval threat from the Mississippi was hardly stable. Yet the absence of Union infantry and artillery at Vicksburg certainly gave Van Dorn an advantage.[14]

Bragg and Van Dorn moved quickly to support Smith. On June 23 John C. Breckinridge's division of 4,000 men entrained at Grenada, bound for the hill city. Breckinridge, a Kentuckian and former vice president of the United States, had developed a good fighting force. Another 2,000 troops would be on their way as soon as they gathered supplies in the Grenada area. Daniel Ruggles, commander of these troops, received orders to depart for Tangipahoa, Louisiana, and take command there. Ruggles had a reputation for being a troublemaker, and his departure was part of the Lovell-Beauregard housecleaning. With reinforcements en route, Van Dorn hurried from his Jackson headquarters to Vicksburg.[15]

Ever confident in his own ability, Van Dorn sent Jefferson Davis a message assuring the Confederate president Vicksburg would be held unless overwhelmed by a "superior force. Foot by foot the city will be sacrificed." Van Dorn also asked Davis to place the *Arkansas* under his command when the ironclad was ready for combat. This seemingly innocent request, to which Davis agreed, would have disastrous consequences for the Confederacy later that summer.[16]

Meanwhile Van Dorn toured Vicksburg and approved the city's defenses. Smith had done a good job of setting up artillery, and more arrived almost daily from Mobile, Richmond, Columbus (Mississippi), and other points around the Confederacy. The entrenchments were not as good as they might have been, for slave labor had been used, and the slaves, tiring of the constant digging, frequently escaped and went back to their masters. The owners often did not return them, because they needed their slaves in their fields. Confederate patriotism often took a backseat to planters' economic interests.

Breckinridge's men soon arrived and filed into earthworks. Smith's men manned the batteries, and Breckinridge sent detachments to reinforce outposts along the river and the army's flanks above and below town. Light artillery covered approaches to the main defensive line, and cavalry roamed north along the Yazoo and south in the Warrenton area.[17]

Confederate soldiers forced themselves to remain in the trenches while Federal shells flew into Vicksburg. A Mississippian observed, "One feels utterly defenseless unless there is a chance to strike back, which in this case, is out of the question." When not on duty, men lay under the shade of trees, and at night watched naval shells streaking through the sky. They also coped with stagnant water, which caused much illness. Sometimes soldiers poured water through pieces of cloth, in vain efforts to remove scum and other impurities. Men continued to sicken and die. Mosquitoes also made life miserable, as did red bugs (chiggers). Food that consisted mostly of sugar and rice was better than nothing, but not much. Water and food problems, camping near the city cemetery while in harm's way, and inflated prices in Vicksburg stores made many men wish they were any-where else.[18]

Despite the misery, Confederates had remained on the alert. The effec-tiveness of Smith's and Breckinridge's dispositions had yet to be tested. They seemed judicious and certainly superior to conditions at Vicksburg when Smith's small force had been the town's only resistance. Now Confederate defenders numbered about 7,000, more than enough to offset Thomas Wil-liams's brigade of five regiments and two light artillery batteries, assuming the Yankees might be foolish enough to attack the bluffs. Additional heavy artillery helped counter Union naval firepower.

Farragut now had some twenty-six vessels on hand, and the imminent arrival of Charles Davis and his fleet, victors at Memphis on June 6, would increase that number to over forty. The ever-optimistic Van Dorn felt good about his chances, especially if the *Arkansas* could be finished in time to neutralize or, better yet, chase away the Yankee navy.[19]

While the Confederates improved their defensive situation, David Far-ragut, pressured by Washington and frustrated that his string of successes had suddenly stopped at Vicksburg, renewed his campaign to take the city. On June 13 he started sending vessels from Baton Rouge to Natchez. The sloop of war *Richmond* carried Williams's small army, while the *Brooklyn* scouted the riverbanks looking for Rebel artillery. Farragut ordered his commanders to be sure they had sufficient supplies for the trip back up-river. Aboard his flagship *Hartford*, Farragut reviewed reports of guerrilla activity along the Mississippi and found to his satisfaction that all enemy operations in the Grand Gulf area apparently had ceased. One sailor noted that the people of Grand Gulf, providers of food or not, were the "most treacherous and rabid secessionists" he had ever seen, and he was delighted that most of the town had ceased to exist, after being set on fire and repeat-edly shelled.

Pennsylvanian David Porter, destined to play a key role in the coming months of the Vicksburg campaign, joined Farragut for the trip upriver. Porter's father, after whom he had been named, had been Farragut's men-tor; in fact, the younger Porter and Farragut were foster brothers. Porter had remained behind in New Orleans, where he became disenchanted with Benjamin Butler's bureaucracy. Butler promised to provide towing help for Porter to get his mortar flotilla upstream to help at Vicksburg. Porter had a sharp tongue and told Farragut that Butler had deliberately deceived him, and that it was aggravating to have to fight traitors on two fronts. Farragut reacted by complaining about Butler in a message to Secretary of the Navy Gideon Welles.

Despite the many problems he faced getting Porter's and other vessels upstream, Farragut persevered. He arrived at Vicksburg aboard the *Hartford* on June 25 and immediately ordered preparations for an attack. Porter would initiate things with a bombardment by his mortar boats the next morning. The rest of the Union vessels would advance past Vicksburg in staggered formation, so each boat would have an open line of fire. Farragut's lengthy orders took time to distribute, and the attack he envisioned did not occur until June 28. Porter began shelling the city on June 26, and Confederate gunners replied, but neither side suffered notable damage. Intermittent fire continued through June 27, rising and falling in intensity. Finally Farragut decided that his men and boats were ready to make the main attack.

Farragut continued hoping that Charles Davis's fleet would show up as expected, but Davis apparently was in no hurry: there was no sign of a flotilla. Davis, a native of Massachusetts, a flag officer, and a longtime navy veteran, was in fact still in Memphis, preparing for the trip to Vicksburg. He did send an advance detachment of five vessels commanded by Alfred W. Ellet, a Pennsylvanian whose brother Charles had invented the steam-powered rams used to great effect at Memphis. Ellet arrived on June 25 and anchored above the Confederate right flank at the head of the peninsula. He led a small detachment through swampy terrain, avoided Rebel pickets, and contacted Farragut.

Farragut decided that the assault would go forward without Ellet's help, since he did not think Ellet had sufficient strength to do any damage to Confederate positions upriver. A frustrated Ellet fired off a message to Davis, encouraging the latter to hurry. Perhaps Ellet alone could not do much damage, but he knew Davis's entire fleet would have considerable impact. Despite Ellet's pleadings, Davis, refusing to be rushed, did not arrive in time to join in Farragut's assault.

Ultimately, Davis's absence did not matter. Farragut's attack produced much noise, but only proved what was becoming more and more obvious: the navy alone could not capture Vicksburg. Union naval artillery caused panic in the city, a naval officer noted, where residents had been lulled into feeling safe, as "shot and shell went hissing through trees and walls, scattering fragments far and wide in their terrific flight; men, women, and children, rushed into the streets, and, amid the crash of falling houses, commenced their hasty flight to the country for safety." Some Confederate soldiers thought the city, with its inflated prices, was getting what it deserved. Confederate gunners returned fire, damaging several Yankee vessels. Federal wounded, some with severed or nearly severed limbs,

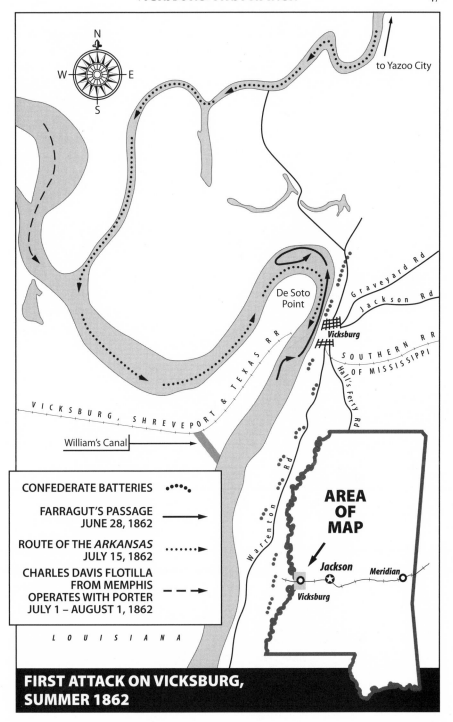

N
W E
S

to Yazoo City

De Soto
Point

Graveyard Rd
Jackson Rd

Vicksburg

SOUTHERN RR
OF MISSISSIPPI

Hall's Ferry Rd

VICKSBURG, SHREVEPORT & TEXAS RR

William's Canal

Warrenton Rd

CONFEDERATE BATTERIES

FARRAGUT'S PASSAGE
JUNE 28, 1862

ROUTE OF THE *ARKANSAS*
JULY 15, 1862

CHARLES DAVIS FLOTILLA
FROM MEMPHIS
OPERATES WITH PORTER
JULY 1 – AUGUST 1, 1862

AREA
OF
MAP

Jackson   Meridian

Vicksburg

LOUISIANA

**FIRST ATTACK ON VICKSBURG,
SUMMER 1862**

littered some decks, as sailors who had endured the heat and insects faced much more dangerous Rebel shot and shell. One Confederate shell crashed through the boiler of the *Clifton*, scalding six sailors to death and causing horrible wounds for many others.[20]

Martin Luther Smith proudly watched his artillery neutralize Farragut's fleet, and concluded that Vicksburg could safely withstand any attack directly from the river. In his postaction report, Smith, like Federal officers, concluded that "the ultimate [enemy] success hinged upon a movement by land." Union infantry approaching the city from the south, north, or east might well present problems. Union ships and infantry trying to take Vicksburg from the river would continue to fail. Farragut informed Henry Halleck that success at Vicksburg required army assistance and in much greater numbers than Thomas Williams's small force. But Halleck had focused on Corinth and had captured the town, and he would send his land forces to Arkansas and Tennessee, wherever they might be needed, before sending men to Vicksburg. He had not responded to Edwin Stanton's mention of Vicksburg, and he obviously had no interest in focusing on helping the navy capture the town. He showed no indication of changing his mind.[21]

Farragut became more frustrated when he learned that Alfred Ellet had decided on his own to take one of his rams, the *Monarch*, on a foray up the Yazoo River north of Vicksburg. Ellet ventured up to the confluence of the Sunflower River and the Yazoo; there he spotted several Confederate boats that had been set on fire and set adrift to discourage Union ascendancy up the Yazoo. Ellet also saw Rebel guns on bluffs at a community called Liverpool and thought he spotted the *Arkansas*, the long-rumored Confederate ironclad, which had made a trial run from Yazoo City as far as Liverpool. Whether Ellet actually saw the ironclad is debatable, but whatever he did see convinced him to turn and go back to the Mississippi. So ended the late June Union offensive, and the Federal navy remained practically dormant for the next several weeks.[22]

Ellet's experience worsened David Farragut's disposition. In the wake of the June 28 failure, he feuded with one of his officers and continually complained to Halleck and Welles that the navy had done all it could do. He could keep sending his boats back and forth, mostly unscathed, in front of the Confederate fortifications at Vicksburg, but nothing would be accomplished. Without joint navy-army operations, the Rebel bastion would never surrender. By the second week in July Farragut asked Welles to allow the fleet to return to the Gulf. Davis's squadron could stay on the Mississippi to block river traffic from Vicksburg north. Farragut thought he could make a much better contribution to the Union cause operating along the Gulf coast.[23]

Farragut sent his message and, while waiting for an answer, met on July 14 with Ellett, Williams, and Davis. Ellett wanted to go back up the Yazoo, in part to get back at Confederates who fired at his boat from the banks and also to clear the stream of Confederate vessels. After an evening of discussion aboard Farragut's *Hartford*, the four agreed that Davis should send three of his boats on a scouting trip up the Yazoo the next morning.[24]

In the early hours of July 15 the *O. A. Tyler*, the *Carondelet*, and the *Queen of the West* entered the Yazoo "to procure correct information concerning the obstructions and defenses of the river." Suddenly the Confederate ironclad previously spotted by Ellet appeared on the horizon. The *Arkansas* had been finished and tested, and was steaming down the Yazoo on its maiden voyage.

On the *Arkansas'* deck stood Captain Isaac Brown, who had personally resurrected the ironclad project when it seemed doomed due to bureaucratic ineptness and inefficient contractors. His persistence had paid off, and he no doubt felt great satisfaction as the formidable *Arkansas* moved toward the Mississippi and war. The *Arkansas* was 165 feet long, carried a crew of 200, had ten guns, and was plated with railroad iron four and a half inches thick. Earl Van Dorn exercised his command authority over the *Arkansas* by constantly urging Brown to hurry to Vicksburg and challenge the Union naval presence there. Brown understood, but he would not move until he was sure his prized vessel was ready. To Van Dorn's relief, Brown had the *Arkansas* on its way the night of July 14. In the early dawn the next morning, Brown spotted the enemy ships.

As the *Arkansas* moved ever closer, the *Tyler* and the *Queen of the West* turned back toward the Mississippi, but the commander of the *Carondelet* decided to fight. The *Arkansas* and *Carondelet* pounded each other at close range until the *Carondelet's* steering mechanism jammed, causing the boat to drift ashore. The *Arkansas* suffered damage, too, most notably the wrecking of its pilothouse, but Brown ordered the ironclad on down the Yazoo, leaving the *Carondelet* crew to tend to their battered boat and sixteen wounded. The *Tyler* turned momentarily to assist, but upon seeing the *Carondelet's* fate, fled again. Brown followed, and the *Arkansas* steamed into the Mississippi into the midst of Davis's and Farragut's fleet.

The Confederate ironclad ran the gauntlet, the *Arkansas* and its crew enduring the pounding of heavy shells coming from all directions, and yet somehow making it through to the Vicksburg port. The heat of battle and machines was tremendous, and many men seeking relief stripped to their underwear. One of Brown's subordinates, John Wilson, reported that he was "cut in the arm and leg by fragments of wood and iron. The heat on the gun deck from rapid firing, and the concussion from shot and shell alike was [sic] terrific." By the time the battered vessel anchored, it presented scenes of carnage that many would never forget. One witness reported that "blood and brains bespattered everything, whilst arms, legs, and several headless trunks were strewn about." Cheering crowds celebrating the *Arkansas'* arrival quickly quieted and retreated when they saw the grisly sights on deck.[25]

A furious Farragut thought his fleet had been unnecessarily caught napping and thus had suffered considerable damage from Brown's guns. He sent Davis a blunt message: "we must go down and destroy" the enemy ironclad. "It will be warm work," he admitted, "but we must do it." Accordingly, Union vessels able to function carried out a late-evening assault on the *Arkansas* and inflicted additional damage, but Rebel guns on board the ironclad and along the river slopes kept Farragut's boats at bay. Williams's infantry joined in the fray, sharp-shooting at enemy sailors from the distant Louisiana side of the river.

Though the night assault fizzled, Farragut remained determined to destroy the *Arkansas*. On July 16 he urged Davis to join in a combined assault. After all, Davis had ironclads, too, and surely would be expected by Washington to dispatch the Rebel version. Farragut said he would do his part and urged that the attack be carried out on June 17. Davis did not receive Farragut's message until that morning and quickly wrote back disagreeing with Farragut's plan. An all-out attack, without consideration of the possible consequences, would hardly justify the probable disadvantages of losing ground that had been gained by Union forces on the Mississippi. Davis had obviously been impressed by the *Arkansas*. He wrote Farragut that the navy controlled the Mississippi except for the small stretch in front of Vicksburg and that surely the government would eventually send a sufficient army to help take the town. Meanwhile the *Arkansas*, as long as it stayed where it was, would not be a problem. Davis did not rule out an attack, but he did not want to wreck his flotilla in the process. Farragut disagreed, pointing out that the *Arkansas* could move out at any time and do damage upstream or down. Farragut especially worried over what the ironclad might do to his supply line stretching tenuously back to New Orleans.[26]

Davis demurred and decided to send the *Essex*, his largest and most powerful ironclad, to attack the Confederate ironclad and to satisfy Farragut. Commanded by William D. Porter, this impressive vessel moved downstream from Davis's position above Vicksburg and attacked the

Arkansas on July 22. Porter ordered his crew to ram the Rebel ironclad, and the *Essex* struck a glancing blow and then grounded for about ten minutes. The *Arkansas'* guns, plus Confederate sharpshooters and heavy artillery on the bluffs, battered Porter's boat. Once the *Essex* got free of the bank, it continued to pour shot and shell into the *Arkansas*, but when Porter realized that no help was forthcoming, he disengaged. Ellet took the *Queen of the West* down later, but likewise withdrew when other Federal commanders failed to assist. Both Farragut and Davis later condemned Porter for the latter's complaint that promised help did not show up. Obviously, everyone did not have the same understanding of the operation. Internal bickering reflected the problem of two commanders with divergent views trying to work together. Farragut feared the *Arkansas*, and Davis did not think it worth attacking.[27]

Farragut, too, suddenly lost interest in the *Arkansas* after Secretary Welles sent word he could return to the Gulf. Farragut notified Davis of his imminent departure and warned his colleague there would not be enough ships below Vicksburg to contain the *Arkansas* if the ironclad went in that direction. Farragut bluntly told Davis not to expect any help from New Orleans. He would assist where he could, but he did not intend to send boats to patrol the Mississippi north of New Orleans. In effect, Farragut was turning his back on Vicksburg.[28]

Davis responded by requesting General Williams to stop the transfer of his troops south. Williams said that disease had reduced his effective force to about 800 men, too few to be of any use in the Vicksburg area. Davis's calls for help from other parts of the region went unheeded, so he finally sent the *Essex* and the *Sumter* downstream to Baton Rouge to block the Rebel ironclad if necessary. These two boats were still south of the Vicksburg guns after the failed attempts to destroy the *Arkansas*. Davis hoped the combined firepower of his two vessels would keep the *Arkansas* bottled up between the Louisiana capital and Vicksburg.[29]

On August 1 Davis decided to follow Farragut's example and leave the Vicksburg area. He ordered his fleet upstream to Helena, Arkansas, and wired Secretary Welles regarding his decision. He had done so, he said, because he could not communicate with naval forces below Vicksburg; he believed his supply line back to Helena was shaky due to guerrilla activity; reports indicated that the Rebels might be concentrating their forces in Arkansas, threatening his Helena base; and sickness had increased markedly among his men. The continual "breathless . . . red-hot, gasping days" had taken a toll. Considering all these circumstances, Davis thought his continued presence at Vicksburg was pointless. At Helena, he could effectively keep the river clear of Rebels between his base and Vicksburg, and he would be in a good position to cooperate with armies in Arkansas and north Mississippi. Welles was not happy about Davis's decision; the navy secretary was already furious that the *Arkansas* had not been destroyed. Yet he too finally understood that without an army presence, Vicksburg could not be taken.[30]

Confederates in Vicksburg celebrated when news reached town that the last of the Union fleet had withdrawn. Residents moved back into their abandoned homes, though a timid few held back, fearing the Yankees would return. Those who came back were surprised that the city had suffered relatively little damage from the lengthy bombardment. Authorities in Richmond sent warm congratulations to Van Dorn and his army and to Brown and his crew. The Confederate Congress passed a resolution commending the *Arkansas*' exploits, and Van Dorn praised Brown's accomplishments. As one historian has noted, "With one ironclad, a handful of guns, and 7,000 troops, the Confederates had regained control of 250 miles of the Mississippi." This assessment is an exaggeration, for the Union navy still ruled the river, except in front of Vicksburg.

The South nevertheless had reason to be optimistic, especially after the loss at Shiloh and Beauregard's abandonment of Corinth. Unfortunately, a bad choice by Van Dorn soon cast a cloud over Southern elation. That decision grew out of another questionable decision by Van Dorn to send Breckinridge with a force from Vicksburg to attack Baton Rouge. If the Confederates could retake the Louisiana capital city, then the Red River would be open to commercial traffic once more and an important supply artery restored. Van Dorn further wanted to recapture New Orleans, thereby extending Confederate control of the Mississippi from Vicksburg to the Gulf. Such grandiose ideas came easily to Van Dorn, but he consistently had trouble implementing them. With the approval of President Davis, Van Dorn pushed ahead and developed plans for the campaign against Baton Rouge.[31]

In late July he wrote orders instructing Breckinridge to take his troops by rail and by foot from Vicksburg to Baton Rouge. Breckinridge had some 4,000 men on paper, but his men had become worn down and sickly in the hot Vicksburg summer, and the trip south had a further deteriorating effect. By the time the weary Rebels reached the vicinity of Baton Rouge, Breckinridge had only about 2,600 fit to attack. Inside the city, Thomas Williams had 5,000 men, though his numbers fit for duty were, like Breckinridge's, much lower.

Williams's men, stationed on the Louisiana side of the Mississippi in swampy terrain, had suffered more from exposure to unhealthy elements than had their Confederate counterparts. Breckinridge did not know the condition of the Yankees in Baton Rouge, but his own depleted force convinced him he needed help. So he asked Van Dorn to send the *Arkansas*. He hoped the ironclad could drive away Union naval vessels at Baton Rouge and lob shells among Williams's infantry and artillery. Otherwise, Breckinridge's men would be dodging naval shells as well as infantry and light artillery missiles.

Van Dorn immediately ordered the *Arkansas* to assist Breckinridge. His hasty decision did not take into account that the battered ironclad was not ready for more action. The engine was not functioning properly, and repairs to torn iron plating on the hull had not been completed. Compounding the situation, Commander Brown had become ill and had gone home to Grenada, Mississippi, to recuperate. Brown's second in command, Henry Stevens, hesitated to obey Van Dorn, due to Brown's absence and because he knew the boat was not fit for combat. Van Dorn appealed to Brown's superior, Flag Officer William Lynch, who ordered Stevens to obey.

Lynch, in Jackson at the time, had no way of knowing the *Arkansas*' condition, and he did not see fit to check with Brown. Lynch accepted without question Van Dorn's assurances that the ironclad was ready to go. Stevens sent word to Brown about the situation, but Brown arrived in Vicksburg too late to stop the *Arkansas*' last voyage. The boat broke down repeatedly, and finally, on August 6, a few miles above Baton Rouge, the ill-fated vessel stalled, and its crew blew it up to prevent its capture by the Union navy. Becoming impatient, Breckinridge had attacked on August 5 and had been repulsed, primarily due to the firepower of the enemy navy. Thomas Williams died during the fighting, and afterward Breckinridge claimed an important consolation prize when a portion of his command occupied Port Hudson, a key strategic port on the Mississippi above Baton Rouge. Port Hudson provided Confederate forces with a strong outpost on Vicksburg's southern flank.[32]

The loss of the *Arkansas* cost the Confederacy dearly. The Union navy could now move along the Mississippi practically unfettered, for there were few Confederate vessels afloat to harass the Federal navy and none as threatening as the ironclad. When the *Arkansas* went down, all Confederate hope of extending Rebel control of the Mississippi beyond Port Hudson disappeared. Still, though the river was mostly in Union hands, the bastions at Port Hudson, batteries being set up at Grand Gulf, and of course the forces at Vicksburg meant that Union vessels navigating the river could not do so without risking damage and casualties from Confederate guns. On the other hand, the *Arkansas*' demise forced Confederate commanders to reassess strategy to protect Vicksburg and the Red River supply artery. Having shore batteries but no navy obviously limited Confederate options.

Contrary to Confederate optimism, events during the hot summer months along the river in front of Vicksburg did not prove that the fortress was impregnable. Union officials had simply miscalculated. Successes above and below Vicksburg had given them a false sense of security. Once Union commanders understood that an army would be an essential component to forcing the city's surrender, it was only a matter of time until they attempted joint operations to produce that result. Van Dorn's troops and the *Arkansas* had given the Confederacy hope, and Confederate troops would maintain their hold on Vicksburg for most of another year. But Van Dorn had to forget about taking Baton Rouge and New Orleans. Port Hudson was a consolation prize, but it was an important Southern bastion for the successful defense of Vicksburg. Without an ironclad, holding the town would be tenuous. Indeed, the forced destruction of the *Arkansas* portended a waning of the Confederate cause in Mississippi.

Farragut's decision to leave Vicksburg ironically was a factor in Henry Halleck's decision to break up his massive army at Corinth. Without the logistical support of Farragut's and Davis's combined fleets, Halleck proceeded with his plans to send detachments not only to Arkansas and Tennessee but also to Alabama. Other military and political factors affected Halleck's thinking, but certainly the lack of success at Vicksburg, along with the escape of Beauregard's (Bragg's) army, impacted the course of the war in the West, especially in Mississippi.

Western theater strategists on both sides gave Vicksburg a respite. Ulysses S. Grant, who eventually became mired in the second and third efforts to take Vicksburg, had other priorities. Grant, Van Dorn, and Sterling Price had to cope with constant calls for reinforcements from an evolving Don Carlos Buell versus Braxton Bragg campaign in Tennessee. The ongoing Tennessee campaign was rooted in Buell being sent to Chattanooga, another city of significant railroad junctions. To complete the strategic situation in Tennessee, Bragg decided to go into Tennessee to challenge Buell and to try to go all the way to Kentucky to entice men there to enlist in the Confederate army. Bragg had no way of knowing at the time that the propaganda about thousands of Kentuckians being eager to fight for the Confederacy was largely untrue. The Bragg-Buell campaign led to two battles in northeast Mississippi, the first resulting from both Grant's and Price's efforts to keep each other from sending reinforcements to Buell and Bragg. That situation set up a showdown in the northeast Mississippi town of Iuka.[33]

IUKA

The Clash and the Quiet

$\mathscr{B}$raxton Bragg made recommendations to Richmond, and he had asked that most of his army, some 30,000 men, go to Tennessee to counter Don Carlos Buell's operations there. Buell had marched his men to Tennessee after the fall of Corinth, mainly to try to take east Tennessee away from Confederate general Kirby Smith, though establishing control of Chattanooga would also be significant. Receiving permission to carry out his plan, Bragg left behind 16,000 troops under the command of Sterling Price to watch northeast Mississippi. At Vicksburg, Earl Van Dorn had approximately the same number and could cooperate with Price if necessary. Bragg envisioned Van Dorn and Price joining forces to invade western Tennessee, while Bragg wanted to join forces with Smith and cut Buell's supply line that stretched to Nashville. All these movements led to combat in northeast Mississippi.[1]

Buell's men had been at work on the Memphis & Charleston Railroad after the fall of Corinth, repairing rails and bridges, trying to make the line serviceable all the way to Stevenson, Alabama, where it met the Louisville and Nashville line that ran north through Nashville and into Kentucky, making the Louisville and Nashville an important supply line for Federal forces.

Union troops commanded by Ormsby Mitchel, stationed at Nashville, had come south to work on the Memphis & Charleston from Huntsville, Alabama, and they had repaired much of the line westward from the Chattanooga area to Tuscumbia. Union forces would eventually be in position to take Chattanooga and perhaps turn south toward Atlanta. Smith must be taken care of first to satisfy Lincoln. If Buell joined with Mitchel, their combined forces would be between Beauregard's (now Bragg's) Rebels, who had evacuated Corinth, and Smith, making it difficult for the Confederates to consolidate the two armies.

Meanwhile Bragg moved east, traveling south of the Memphis & Charleston, while Buell moved east along the railroad itself. Bragg's presence made Union plans more problematical, but not as much as Union strategy based on isolating Smith. Railroads in north Alabama and in Tennessee all had breaks and bridge damage caused by military operations, each side trying to cause logistical problems for the other. None of those situations affected Smith, who could be supplied from Virginia by the East Tennessee and Virginia Railroad, which also connected Knoxville with Chattanooga. The section of the line between Chattanooga and Knoxville required repair work, which meant Buell would be slowed if he tried to follow that route to Knoxville to confront Smith. Rebel cavalry raids continually added to Union problems.

Bragg, with Richmond's approval, decided to take his forces south by rail to Mobile and then northeast to Atlanta and on to Chattanooga. This movement, though roundabout, took him beyond Buell, who was concentrating west of Chattanooga. The maneuver allowed Bragg to get into middle Tennessee, where he and Smith could cooperate in a plan to invade Kentucky and cut off Buell's supply base on the Ohio River. A key to the Confederate strategy was the belief that many Kentuckians wanted to fight for the Confederacy and that a Confederate army entering the state would bring thousands of new recruits. The theory proved false, for by the fall of 1862 most Kentuckians who wanted to fight for the Confederacy already were. Nevertheless, the politically tainted notion dominated Confederate strategic thinking. Another problem lay in Bragg's immediate future. Kirby Smith had no intention of cooperating; he did not want to serve under Bragg, and he wanted whatever glory there was to be gained in Kentucky to go to him. Bragg, of course, did not know what obstacles awaited him.

Confederate strategists believed Bragg's offensive should produce other possibilities to be dictated by events. Perhaps Buell would hurry north to chase Bragg and Smith away, thus bringing on a major engagement. A Confederate victory could certainly turn the tide in the western theater. Bragg's campaign led to constant calls for reinforcements from Price in Mississippi and, for Buell, from Grant.

Another Confederate force became part of the situation. Earl Van Dorn had failed to take Baton Rouge, so he prepared to move a large portion of his Vicksburg force by rail to Jackson and then north on the Mississippi

Central Railroad to Holly Springs. Van Dorn's failure to recapture Baton Rouge led him north to cooperate with Price. The two would drive their troops through Grant's lines and go north into west Tennessee, thus protecting Bragg's left flank and possibly joining him in the Kentucky campaign. Events, however, did not wait for Van Dorn to put together his campaign.

William Rosecrans had his detachment from Grant's army scattered across northeast Mississippi east of Corinth. Buell's call for reinforcements caused Rosecrans to prepare part of his troops to cross the Tennessee River and join Buell. A Union supply base was at Eastport, on the Tennessee, north of Iuka. But when Grant received reports of Van Dorn coming north and news about Price shifting his army as if to come north toward Corinth, he decided that the two Rebel generals were about to join forces and attack Corinth. So Grant got in touch with Rosecrans, whose troops were still in Iuka, to concentrate with other forces Grant had begun pulling close to Corinth to meet the Confederate threat.

On the Confederate side, John Breckinridge had been ordered to take his division to Tennessee to join Bragg. That left Van Dorn an opening to go into west Tennessee with or without Price, though certainly he preferred having Price join him. But Bragg wanted Price to stay east of Corinth to block reinforcements from reaching Buell by rail. Price occupied Iuka not long after Rosecrans had departed. Price thought he was a good position to turn back Yankee reinforcements. Van Dorn and Price stayed in contact and decided at one point to do as Grant expected—that is, combine forces and attack Corinth. Jefferson Davis worried about the seeming lack of coordination in north Mississippi. As usual, Van Dorn had his own grandiose ideas, while Price tried to do what Bragg wanted. However, Bragg, far away from the area now, was not well acquainted with the situation, and threw up his hands in frustration and left the two generals to work things out on their own.

It seemed for a time that was impossible. Van Dorn sent word to Price on September 8 that if Rosecrans had gone to Tennessee, which he had not, then Price should join Van Dorn and clear west Tennessee, and then go on to Kentucky and the Ohio River. That way they could help Bragg whenever the opportunity arose. On the other hand, if Rosecrans had not left Mississippi, Van Dorn would march to join Price, and they would attack Rosecrans. But Price responded that Bragg had ordered him to move toward Nashville. Price assured Van Dorn that he wanted to do as the latter suggested, but he must obey Bragg's order.

Price must have been reminded of a visit with President Davis in Richmond a few months earlier in June. Price wanted to command an invasion of Missouri, and he wanted to take his Missouri troops with him. His troops never should have been sent east of the Mississippi, he argued. Davis did not like Price's presumptuous attitude, and he made it clear that Price's troops were more needed in Mississippi than in Missouri. Price claimed that an invasion of Missouri would force Henry Halleck to break off his Mississippi invasion. Davis did not agree, and after he and Price exchanged insults, Price said he would resign and go to Missouri anyway. Davis said he would accept the resignation happily.

After a few hours of considering political repercussions, Davis changed his mind, turned down the resignation, and said that as soon as things settled down a bit in Tennessee and Mississippi, Price could take his men and go to Arkansas and prowl the trans-Mississippi. Price would eventually see that the promise was, at least in part, hollow. His troops were among the Confederacy's best, so ultimately Price would leave, but his men would not. To Price's credit, he remained faithful to the Confederate cause in spite of Davis's treatment and in spite of Van Dorn's weak leadership.[2]

Van Dorn turned the decision over to Secretary of War George Randolph. Van Dorn, hearing that Union forces were evacuating Memphis, was more eager than ever to drive into west Tennessee. However, the certainty that Rosecrans had not gone anywhere, except back to Corinth, changed the strategic landscape. Rosecrans's army must be defeated, whether at Corinth or anywhere else he might go. Van Dorn on September 17 wrote a panicky note to Price saying they should meet west of Corinth, to keep enemy forces in Bolivar, Tennessee, from reinforcing Rosecrans. Van Dorn clung to the belief that the best way to help Bragg was to invade west Tennessee, but uncertainties continued. Richmond authorities reminded Van Dorn that he was senior in command, and that he and Price had been expected to cooperate after Breckinridge left to join Bragg. It seemed no one could make a firm decision about what to do. Bragg wanted Price to shadow Rosecrans, and Van Dorn wanted to invade Tennessee and, if Rosecrans's plans could be determined, then attack him. Bragg remained in the dark, for he had thought Rosecrans had arrived in Nashville on September 12.

During this period, Grant had to deal with constant calls from Washington to send reinforcements to Buell, and he finally sent word to the War Department that there was no doubt the Confederates planned to attack Corinth. He could not afford to send any more men to Tennessee. Also Grant knew that Van Dorn had come north to the Holly Springs area. Grant moved quickly by organizing, with Rosecrans's input, a two-pronged assault on Price, whose forces were still in Iuka. If they moved quickly, Grant believed his army could capture Price before Van Dorn reached him. Then

Grant's forces could turn west and attack Van Dorn. Grant believed decisive action would prevent Price and Van Dorn from reinforcing Bragg.[3]

Price meanwhile informed Van Dorn that he did not want to stay in Iuka.
Either he and Van Dorn must unite and strike Rosecrans, or, Price said, he
would go to Kentucky to join Bragg. On September 17 Price received a
September 12 telegram from Bragg urging Price to come to Nashville. Bragg
continued to believe, erroneously, that Rosecrans was in Nashville. Bragg's
words weighed on Price, who thought he had to do something, with or
without Van Dorn.

Early on September 19 Price informed Van Dorn that he would move to
unite their forces, as Van Dorn had requested two days earlier. Van Dorn
had not given up on invading west Tennessee to pressure Buell and assist
Bragg. Price's scouts intervened with reports that the enemy planned to attack Iuka. He urged Van Dorn to make a demonstration toward the town of
Rienzi, south of Corinth, to divert Grant's attention from Iuka, so he could
march and join Van Dorn. In a second message the same day, Price said he
would be attacked. News arrived that Union general E. O. C. Ord was leading Grant's left wing down the railroad from Corinth to Iuka. This made
Van Dorn's demonstration at Rienzi all the more necessary. Then Price read
another report that more Yankees were moving from the southwest toward
Iuka. Whether or not Price understood this was Rosecrans's wing, he did
know he was in trouble. After all the uncertainty about what to do, Grant
had made the Confederates' decision for them. Price must fight at Iuka or
find a way to avoid being trapped.[4]

Grant pushed the Iuka campaign at a more rapid pace than he would
have preferred. He did not want to lose three divisions to Buell, which was
what Halleck wanted to happen. Grant had earlier set himself up for Halleck's request when he told Halleck that Corinth was secure. When Grant
backpedaled and complained about giving up men, Halleck told him to
abandon Corinth if necessary. Halleck's position was strange since he had
once considered his occupation of Corinth of great significance. Clearly official Washington deemed Buell's operations in middle Tennessee more important. By informing Halleck that an opportunity had arisen to whip both
Price and Van Dorn separately, Grant made a strong case that he could not
deplete his numbers and carry out his mission to keep Confederates from
going to Bragg.

Grant went ahead with his plans, strongly influenced by Rosecrans, who
claimed to be very familiar with the Iuka area due to his previous occupation of the town and surrounding area. Rosecrans suggested that one wing
of the army, under Ord, move east via the Memphis & Charleston Railroad

to attack Iuka from the northwest. Rosecrans, meanwhile, with some 9,000 men, would go south to Jacinto, turn east on the Jacinto road, and at a place called Barnett's Crossroads turn northeast to Iuka. He would divide his army there, sending most of his men north on the Fulton road, while the rest stayed on the Jacinto road. His troops could block both possible routes to prevent Price's escape, and then merge near Iuka where the roads came close together. With Ord on the northwest side of town and Bear Creek (which had no bridges thanks to cavalry on both sides) on the east and the Tennessee River to the northeast negating other possible retreat routes, Price would indeed, theoretically anyway, be forced to fight his way out of Iuka by breaking through Rosecrans's troops. Grant agreed, writing later that Rosecrans's familiarity with Iuka led him to trust his subordinate's suggested plan.[5]

The plan had flaws that Rosecrans or Grant ultimately could not overcome, for the campaign that unfolded fell victim to many problems, including fatal problems with communications, most attributable to rugged, swampy, and hilly terrain that had not been well scouted by Union cavalry, and to Grant's unwieldy leadership. Grant had little knowledge of the area's geography and placed his trust in Rosecrans. Rosecrans claimed to know the area, but time proved his overconfidence. Grant later learned that scouts could have warned him that there were potential problems caused by lack of good roads and rugged terrain.[6]

By wanting to move with speed not only to keep from sending troops to Buell but to also defeat Price quickly in order to turn and fight Van Dorn, Grant went ahead with the campaign. He was sure that he could take Price out of the strategic picture, if not by totally defeating him on the battlefield, then by trapping him geographically.[7]

While Rosecrans got under way, Ord, with 6,000 troops, prepared to travel by rail east from Corinth to Burnsville, detrain, and be poised to attack Price from the northwest. In his after-action report, Grant claimed Ord had 6,000 men, but in his memoir he wrote 8,000. Perhaps the latter figure included detachments left to guard Burnsville and other areas. Grant made his headquarters at Burnsville, thinking he could keep in touch with both wings by courier. If things went well, Price would be trapped between the two Union forces and crushed on the battlefield. Price only had some 14,000 men, so he would be slightly outnumbered. But the timing had to be perfect, and it was not. Rosecrans was to move his troops to a point just south of Iuka by the night of September 18. Ord would attack the next day, and then Rosecrans would move forward and hit Price from the rear.[8]

Splitting an army anytime can be hazardous, especially if one wing is moving in darkness. Despite Grant's assumption that Rosecrans's comment about knowing the area was true, it seemed obvious that Rosecrans was not very familiar with the route he took. He knew where roads were, but not well enough to be negotiating them at night, especially if anything went wrong, and it did. Also communications between the two wings would rest solely on the shoulders of couriers carrying messages back and forth, mainly from Burnsville to Jacinto. From Jacinto, the riders would have to ride to Rosecrans's army. Thus, once Rosecrans started moving east, the time necessary for sending and receiving correspondence increased. The messengers could have traveled on a straight line between Burnsville and Rosecrans and connected more rapidly, but to do so they would have had to traverse tricky terrain that was swampy in spots and thick with trees. They could easily get lost, compounding the communications problem.

Union officers tried to find guides familiar with the Rienzi-to-Iuka corridor and the countryside between Ord and Rosecrans, but few locals were willing, and some proved, intentionally or not, to be untrustworthy. In effect, the campaign as laid out was a gamble. Ord would have no trouble making the initial attack, but it seemed unlikely that Rosecrans could carry out his part of the timetable. If he did not, then Grant would have to make adjustments, and given his post-Shiloh state of mind, it remained to be seen if he could handle a crisis. He still had little confidence, and he still feared losing battles and his job. He certainly knew that if attacking Iuka did not make it possible to save Corinth, he would likely lose his command, and his army career might end.[9]

Trouble started early. On the afternoon of September 18 Rosecrans experienced all sorts of delays. David Stanley's division did not arrive to join the rest of Rosecrans's force until after dark, because a guide misled the column. Charles Hamilton's division was ready with nowhere to go. Rosecrans kept Grant informed, and he wrote optimistically that he hoped to be in position by the evening of September 18. When Ord began the attack at 4:30 the next morning, Rosecrans, massed on the Fulton road, would go north as planned and smash Price from behind.[10]

Meanwhile Ord's wing left the train and Burnsville, Grant's headquarters, and marched to within six miles of Iuka to wait for orders to attack. They ran into a few Rebel skirmishers and brushed them aside. Grant later called it a "sharp engagement," but there is little evidence that it amounted to much. Ord would be in place, on time, and ready to assault Price on schedule.[11]

Rosecrans would not make it, for he could not make up lost time quickly enough to be where he was supposed to be. His problems began with difficulties in concentrating his force in rain and darkness and peaked when a guide erroneously led Stanley's division northeast into the right rear of Ord's army. Stanley's errant march cost Rosecrans four to five hours. Stanley had to countermarch in the dark. Rosecrans informed Grant that his forces were temporarily divided, but he hoped to move out at 4:30 a.m. on September 19, continuing his advance at the same time Ord's wing would be awaiting orders to attack. Rosecrans estimated he could be in place south of Iuka before one or two o'clock the afternoon of the same day. Rosecrans moved before 4:30 a.m., and by midnight his divisions reached Barnett's Crossroads, where Rosecrans intended to turn north by northeast toward Iuka.

Grant, disappointed and seemingly unnerved when he learned that Rosecrans was running behind schedule, told Ord not to attack until Rosecrans got into position, "or he should hear firing to the south of Iuka." Grant insisted later that he sent the change in plans to Rosecrans, but the message is not in the official records of the war, and Rosecrans never received it. In his memoirs, Grant does not mention informing Rosecrans of the change in tactics. Grant, strangely enough, wired Henry Halleck that Rosecrans was moving up from the south, while Ord attacked Price. He gave no hint that anything was wrong. It is not surprising that Grant would put the best face on the situation to Halleck, but why send the message at all? Grant implied that he did not consider Rosecrans's problems to be disruptive. The wire also indicated that Grant still intended for Ord to commence the battle.

Grant, however, had already told Ord not to move until he heard sounds of battle from Rosecrans's attack. Ord was not to do anything until he knew that Rosecrans was fighting Price. Why Grant did not have scouts monitoring Rosecrans's progress and reporting back to Grant is a mystery. By leaving it to Ord to wait for infantry and artillery fire, Grant ruined his chances of catching Price in a trap. Grant did not know, of course, about the acoustical problems that would doom his operation, but he did pass control of what happened to Ord rather than personally coordinating his two wings. The confusion did not stop there. Grant said he sent Ord the same message in the early morning hours of September 19, but Ord said he did not receive it until about 10 a.m. that day. Ord surely must have wondered why he had not received orders to charge as planned. Grant simply told Ord to be cautious and not to attack unless it could be ascertained that Price was retreating from Iuka. Not until 4 p.m. on September 19, not after midnight as Grant later claimed, did Ord receive orders to move closer to Iuka, but still four miles out, and wait for battle noise. About that time, Ord was told that smoke could be seen from the direction of Iuka. But everyone assumed that this resulted from Price's men burning supplies and whatever else they needed but could not carry as they moved south from Iuka.

On the 19th Grant received a September 17 message from Halleck, who worried about Price: "Do everything in your power to prevent Price from crossing the Tennessee River. A junction of Price and Bragg in Tennessee or Kentucky would be most disastrous. They should be fought while separate." Grant replied that Corinth was secure, and Ord and Rosecrans were closing in on Price at Iuka. Unless an unexpected attack on Corinth by other Confederates forced him to return Rosecrans and Ord to Corinth, he did not think it possible for Price to get into Tennessee. While giving himself an out in case something went wrong, Grant declared, "I will do all in my power to prevent such a catastrophe." He again did not mention his problems at Iuka.[12]

Rosecrans informed Grant at 6 a.m. on September 19 that the army was eighteen miles from Iuka and in fine spirits due to news from the eastern front. He said he expected to be in position south of Iuka by 2 p.m. A Federal agent—code-named Chickasaw, real name Levi Naron, a pro-Union native Mississippian—recalled that one of his scouts, L. Bennett, arrived about 4 a.m. with a message from Grant. The order, Naron said, told Rosecrans to move at once and attack from the south by 4 p.m. A letter with the message gave Rosecrans news that George McClellan had won a great victory in Maryland at Antietam, which was not true, but to the soldiers it was good news. Grant asked Rosecrans to have the information read at the head of his command, which he did. The message Grant sent is not in the official records.[13]

Rosecrans responded, "If Price is there he will have become well engaged by the time we come up," and Rosecrans predicted that his firepower would force Price to surrender. Again, there is no known response from Grant. But Rosecrans's words indicated that he had no idea that Ord had been told to delay his assault on Iuka. Rosecrans further stated that he would send Hamilton up the road from Fulton to Iuka and Stanley up the Jacinto road. Clearly, Rosecrans at this point fully intended to block Price from escaping to the south.[14]

If Grant received Rosecrans's message and did not respond, his silence is puzzling. Surely he could tell that Rosecrans gave no indication he knew of the change in plans. The fact that Rosecrans's message is in the official records would indicate that Grant received it, though if he did, there is no way to know when he read it. The predictable communications problems had indeed come into play, but some of the particulars of the breakdown in communications are elusive.

In any event, Rosecrans soon realized that the terrain dictated a change in his plans of a two-front approach to Iuka. The Fulton-Iuka road and the road into Iuka from Jacinto did run on a parallel course, but several miles apart, much more than he expected, so his divided army would be widely separated. The thickly brushed, swampy land between the two roads made mutual support impossible, even if a connecting road had been along the route. Such a road did not exist until the roads almost merged very close to Iuka. Rosecrans had no choice but to stay on the Jacinto road with Hamilton in the lead, followed by Stanley. The situation proved that Rosecrans had little knowledge of the Iuka region. It is unthinkable that he based his campaign strategy on roads that neither he nor his scouts had checked. When he later saw the terrain, Grant agreed that Rosecrans had made the right choice. Rosecrans does not mention his error in judgment in the official records.[15]

Rosecrans's error could be salvaged, however, if he managed to get his army close enough to Iuka to take advantage of the near merger of the two roads. South of Iuka the Bay Springs road connected the Fulton and Jacinto roads, giving Rosecrans the opportunity to send Hamilton's division over to the Fulton road. Then his two divisions could approach Iuka and Price as he had envisioned. Yet his chance to salvage his part of the campaign was a two-edged sword. If Price blocked the way before Rosecrans reached the Bay Springs road, then the Fulton road would be open if Price needed it to escape the Union trap. Rosecrans did nothing to block it, likely because he figured that with Price being attacked from the front and rear, his army could spread out as it went north, thereby denying Price access to the road.

As Rosecrans continued moving along, around noon he encountered two of Grant's staff, apparently scouting on their own or looking for Rosecrans. Rosecrans mentioned their presence in a 12:40 p.m. note to Grant written from Barnett's. He also reported skirmishing and Hamilton advancing. Grant claimed he did not receive the message until after the battle. The Grant staffers, Lyle Dickey (a cavalry commander apparently temporarily attached to Grant's staff) and Clark B. Lagow, told Rosecrans there had been no skirmishing on Ord's front since 3 p.m. Grant never mentioned personally sending the two men, though he must have, since he did acknowledge their encounter with Rosecrans. Apparently, so it would seem, he did not order them to seek Rosecrans, for they had no messages from Grant.

Their presence is interesting, since they seemed to have materialized for no obvious reason. As time went on, however, it became clear they wanted to be sure Rosecrans understood what was going on and what Grant expected of him. Yet they carried no written messages, and perhaps their presence was Grant's response to Rosecrans's earlier message. Since they came from Grant, he likely told them that he had informed Rosecrans of the changed plans for attack. If they knew about the change, they never made it clear to Rosecrans.[16]

Their interaction with Rosecrans was obtuse. They asked him if he thought the Rebels were concentrated at Iuka. Rosecrans said he believed so, though he must have been a bit puzzled answering a question to which these two should know the answer. Rosecrans commented that his men only had about six miles to go, and they had expected to hear Ord's guns by now. The scouts indicated that perhaps Ord had waited for Rosecrans to begin the fight. Rosecrans quickly responded that that could not be, for the plan called for Ord to attack first to draw Price's attention, while Rosecrans struck the Confederate rear. Lagow told Rosecrans that he must attack immediately to keep the Rebels from getting away. Rosecrans said he understood his role, but by attacking first he would have Price moving toward his line of communications, and he had to make sure those lines were secure so he could communicate to Grant and Ord. The two staffers continued riding with Rosecrans, and soon up ahead they heard the sound of fighting along Hamilton's front. Grant's aides rode away at 4:30, presumably to report Rosecrans's arrival, but Grant said later they got lost and did not make it back to his headquarters until the next morning.

The two never said Grant had changed plans, but they certainly gave transparent hints, dancing around the situation rather than speaking frankly to Rosecrans. Rosecrans cannot be blamed if he believed he had not been warned, but the conversation should have caused Rosecrans to ask pointedly if the plans had been changed. And the two Grant staffers should have asked Rosecrans if he was not aware that the original plans had been changed. It is incredible that, assuming the conversation occurred as reported, none of them seemed to grasp there was something terribly wrong with what Grant expected of Rosecrans.

There was no direct, simple order, the kind for which Grant would become known. Grant seemed to have reached a point where he had no concern about Rosecrans. He may have had his mind on Corinth, for he still worried that Van Dorn might attack there before Rosecrans and Ord could make the return trip. False reports also indicated that John Breckinridge, at that time on his way to Bragg, might join forces with Van Dorn.

Grant seemed to be in a daze during the whole Iuka campaign. As the historian Peter Cozzens observed, "Grant distanced himself from the operation against Price early. By headquartering at Burnsville, he seemed to not want to be heavily involved with the attempt to beat Price." Grant's reaction to Rosecrans's part of the operation is difficult to understand. He was upset about Rosecrans falling behind schedule, but he seemed reluctant to make adjustments once his timetable had to be changed. He made little effort, it seems, to stay in touch with Rosecrans; Ord and Rosecrans should have been fully informed once Grant changed his original plan. Neither was. Grant seemed satisfied to wait on news from Rosecrans rather than actively seeking his whereabouts. Why he bothered sending the Antietam news to Rosecrans is also curious. Grant also told Ord to send the Antietam story to Sterling Price, who sent back a sharp rebuff. He did not believe the news, but even if it were true, he and his men would keep fighting. Ord grew frustrated because he feared Price might react by leaving Iuka. Ord understood that Grant's decision to wait on Rosecrans gave Price a chance to withdraw unscathed. Ord thought he should attack at once rather than wait. He was not impressed with Grant's decision to depend solely upon Rosecrans to strike the first blow in order to whip Price.[17]

As for Rosecrans, he was about to find he was too late to take advantage of the Bay Springs connecting road. The crossroads was open, but just beyond he found his way blocked by a portion of Price's army, eventually a whole Rebel division, about two miles from Iuka. Obviously Rosecrans could not divide his army, sending Hamilton across to the Fulton road, with the Confederates so close. Price's men would not just watch Rosecrans redeploy. Rosecrans was therefore forced to fight before he intended, and he heard nothing to indicate Ord's wing had attacked. He must have felt confused, isolated, and betrayed. Rosecrans later wrote he was "profoundly disappointed," and he would be far less diplomatic in comments to Ord. His predicament resulted from the lack of communication with Grant's headquarters, and the strange assumption by Grant's two staff members that Rosecrans knew about a change in plans, which he obviously did not. Rosecrans had been left to his own devices, and there was no excuse for Grant to have allowed such a situation to develop.[18]

Charles Hamilton's division, being in the lead, bore the brunt of the fighting south of Iuka. Stanley, being behind Hamilton, could not, due to terrain restrictions, do much to help without creating a logjam, which would give the Confederates targets they could not miss. The battle took place along two ridges with a ravine in between. The heavy growth of trees on each side left "no room for development," as Rosecrans later wrote. Tactics took

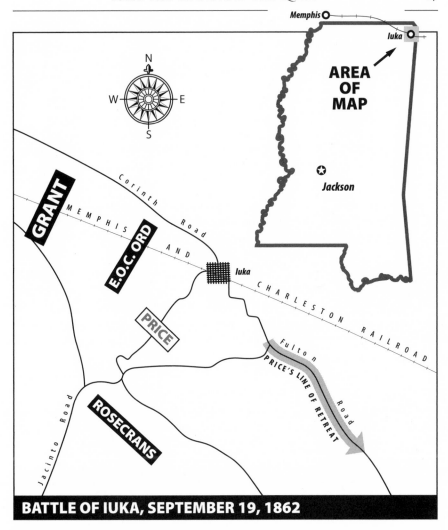

BATTLE OF IUKA, SEPTEMBER 19, 1862

a backseat to a necessary slugfest. Price's Confederates, due to lively skirmishing that had begun with Hamilton's advance five miles from Iuka, had been alerted, but also surprised to run into Rosecrans's advance, and Price had to rush part of Henry Little's division forward to block Hamilton.[19]

Hamilton's advance became seriously engaged 300 yards north of the crossroads around 4:30 p.m., and Ord had been told to move against Price from northwest of the town at that time. However, he had also been told to move only when he heard sounds of battle on Rosecrans's front. Ord heard nothing and did nothing, factors that led to the great controversy coming out of the Iuka battle.

The troops at the head of Hamilton's column found before them the crest of the hill covered by trees. The hill sloped downward both right and left. The underbrush and timber got so dense that Hamilton's men had to take a position across the Jacinto road, and the regiments out front had to make a flank march that exposed them to Confederate fire. Moving through a storm of Confederate rifle and artillery fire, the Fifth Iowa took their position in woods on the right of the road, near the protective artillery fire of the Eleventh Ohio battery. The Twenty-sixth Missouri deployed on the Iowans' right and the Forty-eighth Indiana on the left. When the battle began in earnest, Hamilton had only three regiments on his front line.

The Confederates had to deploy on the fly. Ord's presence had so occupied Price that he had not considered a rear attack. So his troops had been caught off guard, if only momentarily, by Rosecrans. Price's scouts had not gone far down the Jacinto road earlier and therefore had not sounded any alarm. Price did not learn until around 2:30 p.m. that a large enemy force was moving toward him from the south. He rushed Louis Hebért's and John Martin's brigades of Henry Little's division to meet the emergency, though turning the men away from Ord's threat and marching them south took time. But they made it just in time to prevent Rosecrans from deploying on the two incoming roads. A Michigan officer noted, "the enemy's long roll was beat and they formed line of battle. Soon the armies became engaged and a terrible conflict ensued." An Ohioan concurred that before the Federal lines could be formed, "the rebels open[ed] fire along the entire front of the Union line, having approached them entirely unseen, owing to the dense underbrush and broken character of the ground, and at the same time attempting to turn the Union position by an attack on their flanks."

As fighting continued to heat up along the battle front, it became apparent that the Rebels had to descend into the ravine at the foot of the hill and go up the bank on the other side to carry out an effective attack on the Yankees. Otherwise a stalemate would result, and with Ord within striking distance, Price had to settle with Rosecrans as quickly as possible. Hamilton knew his main job was to keep the Rebels at bay by pinning them in the ravine. Hebért's brigade proved formidable. All the while Rosecrans and his generals must have listened for sounds of fighting on Ord's front, but they heard nothing. As time passed it became apparent that Rosecrans would not get help from Ord, so he reacted accordingly. He gave up his plan of putting a division on the Fulton road and pushing into Iuka. The enemy he faced kept getting reinforcements, obvious evidence that Price was not fighting Ord. Whatever the reason, and he had no way of knowing what that could be, Rosecrans had no doubts that Ord had not attacked. Rosecrans would not find out why until the next day.

As the battle developed, units from Hamilton's division deployed piece-meal along the Federal battle line. Soon the Iowans, Ohioans, Missourians, and Indianans were joined by the Fourth Minnesota to the left of the Indianans, and the Sixteenth Iowa and Twenty-sixth Missouri took their position behind the Fifth Iowa, the Indianans, and the Ohio battery. Eventually the Tenth Iowa came up on the extreme left, supported by the Twelfth Wisconsin Battery. Other regiments eventually joined in the fight, but the seven infantry regiments and two batteries made up the main Union battle line.[20]

Price's troops initially included the First Texas Legion, the Fourteenth and Seventeenth Arkansas, the Third Louisiana, and the Fortieth Mississippi, all in Hebért's brigade. When Martin's troops arrived they split to help cover the Rebel flanks, the Thirty-seventh and Thirty-eighth Mississippi to the right, and the Thirty-sixth Mississippi and Thirty-seventh Alabama to the left. Two batteries from Missouri divided their guns to cover each Rebel flank and in the middle. Price left Dabney Maury's division near Iuka to keep an eye on Ord.

These were the basic opposing lines for most of the fighting, although with other units arriving at staggered intervals, the fighting continually grew louder and fiercer. Yet Ord continued to hear nothing. With each side bringing some 4,000 men into a small battlefield area, close fighting and many casualties resulted. Hebért's and Martin's troops led the first charge of the Confederate efforts and with remarkable success, considering they had to negotiate the ravine to clash with Hamilton's line. Union units fought well, except for the green Indianans, who broke and ran a couple of times. The Sixteenth Iowa also retreated after taking heavy casualties, and neither of the two regiments participated any further in the fighting.

When the battlefield became covered in smoke, both sides had trouble with visibility, and on more than one occasion Federals and Confederates fell victim to friendly fire. As a member of the Third Louisiana noted, "So close were the lines to each other at the termination of the battle, that the opposing forces unknowingly walked into each other's lines and were forc-ibly seized and taken prisoner." When darkness came, conditions worsened, but brutal fighting did not diminish. A Confederate who was not in the fight observed later that the Third Louisiana was "cut all to pieces." But he also said, with a hint of admiration, that the Federals fought desperately.[21]

Union efforts to save one of their batteries typified the struggles that day. The battery had been disabled, all its men dead or wounded, and the horses lay dead. Stanley ordered a charge to drive the Rebels away, but Confederate sharpshooters rose up and fired into the Union flank. Stanley ordered a retreat, the Confederates charged, and they were driven back by the Yankees who had re-formed their line. And so it went, and as the darkness increased, more men fell dead from friendly fire.

The entire battlefield became a scene of memorable carnage, though neither side would know the extent of the macabre situation until morning light. A Confederate Missourian recalled for years thereafter "groans and cries of the wounded for help and water," and the "floundering of crippled horses in harness." He confirmed there were breezes, for the "night wind rose and fell, swelling with louder, wilder note. . . . It seemed an invocation from the ghosts of the dead, and a requiem to the departed spirits of the dying."

Confederate casualty numbers are suspect, but Price reported 86 killed and 408 wounded, for a total of 494. He also wrote that about 500 sick and wounded were eventually left behind in Iuka. More reliable accounts indicate Price's losses as 260 or more killed, 1,100 wounded and missing. Other figures are a little lower, but there seems no doubt that Price lost more than he reported. Official reports on Hebért's brigade stated 63 killed, 305 wounded, and 40 missing. Considering that this brigade was in the heat of battle from its inception, those numbers seem quite understated. One Union soldier wrote about walking across the battlefield the day after the fight, and he and his comrades found 160 Rebels "in a heap and covered with a tarpaulin." Obviously Price's men did not have time to bury all their dead.[22]

The Union figures told the story of what happened to Rosecrans's troops. David Stanley's division, behind Hamilton's, suffered 8 killed, 81 wounded, and 4 captured, most in Joseph Mower's brigade sent to the front to help Hamilton. Hamilton reported 141 killed, 613 wounded, and 36 captured, for a total of 790. Hamilton's men fought mostly on the defensive, a charge late in the battle being the only major exception, explaining their low number of casualties, considering the hard fighting. The regiments that initially went into battle lost 127 killed and 434 wounded, obviously the bulk of Union casualties. The Fifth Iowa, the first regiment to advance into battle formation, had more losses than any other Union unit, 37 killed and 179 wounded.[23]

Official regimental reports detailed the severity of the fighting. A Union Missouri colonel wrote, "From the opening to the end of the engagement my command was constantly under a galling and destructive fire, and my loss in killed and wounded was severe." An Iowa officer noted that during the fighting, "the left wing of my regiment was suffering terribly from a cross-fire coming from the left of the battery, nearly every officer of the three left companies being either killed or wounded." A Mississippi colonel reported that he was ordered to move on the far right of the Confederate line. They ran and climbed a fence, and he noted his men "received a heavy cross-fire upon our right and in front. Under this sudden and unexpected heavy fire by a force evidently more than three to one, with all advantages as to position, and finding my command confronting this greatly superior force alone . . . I ordered my men to fall back in rear of the fence." Price wrote that when the fighting began, it "was waged with a severity which I have never seen surpassed." General Hamilton agreed, stating, "I never saw a hotter or more destructive engagement."[24]

The cruelest loss for Price was his friend and division commander, Henry Little. Little had ridden forward during the fury of the fighting with Price and Price's staff. Price ordered Little to bring up his remaining two brigades; at that moment a minié ball hit Little in the head, and he toppled from his horse, instantly killed. Price was emotionally distraught for some time. That night Little was buried by "torchlight" in Iuka.[25]

The Confederates buried what dead they could, but certainly not all. Some of the bodies were too close to enemy lines. Moving around could be dangerous. General Hamilton wrote, "The smoke of battle added to the coming night, and it was soon too dark to distinguish the gray from the blue uniform."

Thus the fighting finally stopped around 8 p.m., though scattered shooting continued for a while longer. From the initial contact at some point around 4:30 p.m., the struggle had continued mostly unabated until darkness forced an end to the carnage. Who had won? Neither side, though Rosecrans and Grant would claim victory. It was true that the Confederates had initially driven the Federals back a few hundred yards, but mostly the lines of battle swayed forward and backward, and with the battlefield hemmed in as it was by terrain, neither side could do much more than fight hard, and both did. Certainly Grant could have won a great victory if he and Ord and Ord's wing had not sat out the battle.

It is as difficult today as then to fully account for the claim of both generals that they did not hear the struggle going on just a few miles away. Other Union troops deployed at much farther distances, guarding the railroad or performing other duties, claimed to have heard the sounds of battle. One soldier wrote that he and his comrades did not hear heavy fire until the next morning, and Grant and Ord both claimed the wind blocked the noise of Rosecrans's fight, though men in the battle said they did not notice any wind or breezes of any magnitude. Those who insisted that they did not hear, including Grant and Ord, must be believed, for it would be incredible to conclude that, if they had known Rosecrans was in a major fight, they would have done nothing. Certainly Rosecrans always wondered if he had been left to fend for himself, and if so, why? Rosecrans later asked Ord why he had remained in place, and why he had had to fight the battle alone. Ord supposedly said nothing; he simply handed a copy of Grant's revised orders. Ord was likely embarrassed when he learned that Rosecrans had not been informed. Ord explained that he had not heard sounds of fighting. Rosecrans became very angry, and as time passed his ill feelings for Grant and Grant's inaction grew and never went away.

Rosecrans never believed the story that Ord and his army had not heard anything. Whatever had prevented Ord and Grant from hearing the roar of battle—whether an acoustical aberration, the hills around the battlefield, heavy air, or north-to-south wind—Rosecrans would not be convinced by any argument. And even with all those possibilities, it is still difficult to understand why the sounds of such a raging battle could not be heard just a few miles away. Assuming the truth of it, then the question lingers as to why no scouts from Ord's front, checking southern approaches to Iuka, did not hear the fight and report the news to Ord and Grant. All that mattered was Grant's and Ord's insistence they personally had not heard anything. Rosecrans's army, whatever the reasons, fought the battle at Iuka by itself.[26]

As for Sterling Price, Ord's inaction gave him time to consider his next move. Price wanted to continue the battle the next day. He pulled Maury's division south of town to reinforce his battle lines. In doing so, he left only cavalry to observe Ord. In retrospect, Price had made a silly move. No matter the reason for Ord's inertness, chances were slim that his soldiers would continue to remain in place. Price could not excuse that kind of gamble. He went to a private home to rest and left orders not to be disturbed. But around midnight Hebért, Maury, and cavalry officer Wirt Adams came to talk with Price. They told Price's adjutant that it would be a disaster to resume fighting Rosecrans come morning. The army must retreat from Iuka or risk getting pinned between the two Union wings. About that time messages from Earl Van Dorn arrived.

As dawn approached, the delegation was permitted to wake Price, and he thought they had come to tell him it was time to resume the fight. When they expressed their opinions that retreat was urgent, he tried to change their minds. Price seemed so enthralled with his army's successes, as he saw them, against Rosecrans, that he had all but put Ord out of his mind. The officers insisted, and he eventually accepted their arguments. He did refuse to leave behind the wagon train filled with Union supplies captured since the army had first arrived in Iuka, supplies left behind by Rosecrans when he returned to Corinth. In his official report, Price downplayed his resistance to leaving, saying that having learned of how many Yankees were in the area, and fearing for the safety of his wagon train, he did as originally planned and went to join Van Dorn.

Things moved quickly, and by the time the sun came up on September 20 the Confederate army, with its supply wagons, had left town and was moving down the Fulton road, the road Rosecrans had not been able to block. Price himself helped hurry the wagons along, threatening to hang any driver who lagged behind. Rosecrans, Ord, and Grant were in for a big surprise when daylight spread across Iuka.[27]

Did Price's march south create enough noise to be heard by Rosecrans and his troops? Indeed, Rosecrans admitted he heard the wagons of an army in motion, so no doubt many of his men did also. Rosecrans, still isolated, had no idea what might be going on. Were the Confederates changing position to renew their attacks, or were they indeed retreating? And if they were retreating, why had Ord not attacked? Rosecrans could be excused if he suspected Ord and Grant had gone back to Corinth.

Since Rosecrans had no answers, he instructed his officers to wake their men sometime between 3:30 and 4 a.m. and have them ready to fight as soon as light spread over the battlefield before them. He intended for Hamilton to shift eastward to hit the Confederate left. Before dawn Rosecrans had concluded that the noise heard during the night was Price's wagon train moving out of harm's way. He also falsely believed Confederate troops had massed to renew the battle.

In his report, he stated rather dramatically: "Day dawned. No firing on the front. Our skirmishers, advancing cautiously, found the enemy had retired from his position." Rosecrans threw out skirmishers, and Stanley led his fresh division toward Iuka. Stanley saw some scattered enemy stragglers and had his artillery lob a few shells toward the town. At that point Rosecrans knew that it was not only Price's wagon train but his entire army that had departed during the night down the Fulton road. Part of Stanley's force occupied Iuka, while the rest marched south on the Fulton road in pursuit. Stanley's cavalry rode from the Jacinto to the Fulton road via the connecting Bay Springs road. Hamilton issued orders for his men to about-face and go back down the Jacinto road to Barnett's to watch for an opportunity to strike Price's right flank.

At 8:45 a.m. Rosecrans sent Grant a message, addressing Grant as being in Booneville rather than Burnsville, a mistake that perhaps indicated

Rosecrans's frustrated state of mind. He briefly summarized the previous evening's fighting, estimated his losses at 400 men, and mentioned the noise heard during the night. He said he now believed Price was retreating down the Fulton road. If that proved to be true, he would pursue and try to push Price east into the lowlands of Bear Creek. An hour later Rosecrans sent a second message to Grant reporting what had happened, his pursuit strategy, and estimates of Confederate dead and wounded. He concluded with "Why did you not attack this morning?" He also asked for reinforcements at Barnett's. The message wound up in Ord's hands, who responded to Grant that he had heard no battle noise the previous evening; hence he had not attacked. He did hear guns that morning, Stanley's few artillery rounds no doubt, and moved his wing forward to three and a half miles from Iuka "as per order till I could hear from General Rosecrans." Rosecrans meanwhile sent word to Grant detailing the deployment of his army in pursuit.

Grant advised Ord at 8:35 a.m. on September 20 that he had just received a message written by Rosecrans the previous evening at 10:30 p.m. announcing the battle that had been going on. Rosecrans had told Grant that Ord must attack that morning "and *in force*." Grant immediately notified Ord that he must get his troops into Iuka and "attack as soon as possible" to create a diversion. When Grant and Ord heard Stanley's artillery, Ord "pushed on with all possible dispatch without waiting orders." Grant eventually went to Iuka and found Price gone and heard about the Rebel departure, perhaps from Rosecrans's messages or from Ord. Grant made a point to note in his after-action report: "This was the first I knew of the Fulton road being left open to the enemy for their escape. With it occupied no route would have been left them except east, with the difficult bottom of Bear Creek to cross, or northeast, with the Tennessee River in their front, or to conquer their way out."[28]

After Rosecrans sent his troops in pursuit of Price, he met with Grant, who had ridden in with Ord's wing. Grant told Rosecrans to continue the pursuit of Price as long as the pursuit produced "benefit to us or injury to them." The two then rode together down the Fulton road. As they rode, Grant, seeing the lay of the land, understood why Rosecrans had not divided his army, which would have been required to cover the Fulton road. Grant thus agreed with Rosecrans's decision. Meanwhile the chase continued until Union forces were worn down, and Rosecrans, with Grant's permission, ordered his men back to Iuka. The Federals had withstood an ambush by a detachment of Confederates along the way, which did not amount to much but undoubtedly made Stanley and Hamilton more cautious, thus slowing their columns.

Though Grant expressed an understanding of how Price had managed to get away, as time passed he tended to blame Rosecrans for Price's uncontested retreat, and the more Rosecrans learned about Grant's change in orders, which he had not known about, the more furious he became. After the war, Grant manipulated the facts in his memoirs to show that he had done everything right, and Rosecrans made mistakes. Grant wrote that the unblocked Fulton road was "neglect" on Rosecrans's part, contradicting his postbattle comments. William Lamers discusses all the points at issue between Grant and Rosecrans, and he convincingly demonstrates that Grant ultimately treated Rosecrans unfairly. The botched campaign had been partly caused by Rosecrans not knowing the countryside as well as he claimed, but Grant's change in orders had been fatal.

In the final analysis, Price's escape must be laid at the feet of Grant. The Fulton road would not have been open if Grant had allowed Ord to seize the initiative and attack Price. If that had happened, Rosecrans could have deployed from the Jacinto road across to the Fulton, as he intended, and moved in behind Price. Unforeseen circumstances had delayed Rosecrans from expanding his front, but having to fight Price alone did not mean he could have succeeded in blocking the Fulton road even if one wing of his army had been on it. Ord's absence from the battle doomed Rosecrans's adjusted route. An Ord attack could certainly have allowed Rosecrans to shift troops onto the Fulton road. But since Ord and Grant assumed Rosecrans was approaching on both roads, by not attacking, as ordered by Grant, Ord assured that Rosecrans could not use his troops to block both roads. While it is true Ord did not know Rosecrans's situation, an Ord attack would have solved the Union dilemma anyway. When one side of Grant's trap never sprang, mainly due to Grant being an observer rather than a fighter, Price not only had a chance to fight, and he fought well, but also the opportunity to escape.

Grant afterward trumpeted that if Price had intended to go to Kentucky, he was "defeated in that," and if he intended to stay in Iuka until Van Dorn came to join him, he was "defeated in that." "Our only defeat was in not capturing the entire army or in destroying it as I had hoped to." He had also been defeated in that. Grant had eased Halleck's fears of a Price advance into Tennessee, but he had not ensured that Price would not do so in the future. In the bigger western theater picture, Price's presence in Tennessee at the time of the fight at Iuka would have been of little help to Bragg, who was already in Kentucky, trying desperately to coordinate operations with Kirby Smith and to decide where Don Carlos Buell was and what to do about it. Bragg and Smith had been unable to coordinate or cooperate with much success, and they would not be in Kentucky much longer. Whatever happened in northeast Mississippi now would have no impact on Bragg or Buell in Kentucky.[29]

So the northeast Mississippi situation had evolved into a contest between armies that had tried to assist their respective sides in Tennessee and Kentucky. Now neither was being ordered to send reinforcements, but only to keep each other bottled up. Soon eyes on Kentucky would shift to north Mississippi, for what happened between Rosecrans, Grant, Price, and Van Dorn would decide if, and how soon, the Union could once again turn toward the Mississippi River and Vicksburg. Before that happened, there would be a bloody encounter between Rosecrans, Price, and Van Dorn.

4

CORINTH

Another Van Dorn Debacle

$\mathscr{O}$n March 7–8, 1862, Earl Van Dorn lost a battle at Pea Ridge (also called Elkhorn Tavern), in northwest Arkansas. Logistical problems and poor tactics had doomed Van Dorn's army there, which included Sterling Price's troops. Van Dorn's biographer wrote of the Pea Ridge outcome that the general "chose to believe in the axiom that battles and campaigns are not won by idly standing by." But Van Dorn had trouble realizing that the armies that fight those battles and conduct those campaigns must be trained, fed, and fit to fight. Van Dorn also believed in surprising the enemy. He had failed to do so at Pea Ridge; time would tell if he could do it at Corinth.[1]

Despite the mess at Pea Ridge, Price was willing to go into battle with Van Dorn again because he believed it was the best chance the Confederacy had to do anything positive in northeast Mississippi. Price's adjutant, Thomas Snead, remembered Arkansas all too well, and in a lengthy letter to Price said he would resign before he would be a part of anything involving Van Dorn. Price soothed Snead's anger by pointing out that duty came before personal feelings. Price had no enthusiasm about Van Dorn, and he knew that Van Dorn, senior in rank, would be in charge of whatever their combined forces did. Price set aside his doubts and hoped his army would do likewise. He knew that many, perhaps most, of his men shared Snead's attitude.[2]

While Price's army recuperated from Iuka in the Tupelo-Baldwyn area, he began corresponding with Van Dorn to choose where the junction of their armies should be. Price reviewed all the reports he had regarding enemy activity and suggested Ripley in northwest Mississippi as the best place. Van Dorn agreed. While Van Dorn and Price planned their campaign, Braxton Bragg sent word from Bardstown, Kentucky, to Van Dorn on September 28, 1862, saying that he had forced the Federals to retreat toward the Ohio River. Bragg still wanted Van Dorn and Price to push into Tennessee and Kentucky and join him. Van Dorn did not receive the telegram until November 2. By that time, situations in north Mississippi and Kentucky had changed drastically.[3]

Price's march to Ripley was not a pleasant one and seemed to forecast the coming campaign. One of his Missouri soldiers wrote that darkness and a driving rain made the trip from Baldwyn miserable. The heavy rain turned roads into mud, which got worse as the army marched. He recalled, "some of the boys often lost their footholds and tumbled broadside into" the quagmire.[4]

The army reached Ripley on the 28th, and Van Dorn quickly organized his forces, designating them as the "Confederate Army of West Tennessee." He called Price's troops "Price's Corps, or Army of the West," which included Louis Hebért's and Dabney Maury's divisions. His "District of the Mississippi" troops from Vicksburg would be commanded by General Mansfield Lovell, who still had the stigma of losing New Orleans hanging over him. Van Dorn estimated his total troop strength, when concentrated, at 22,000 men.[5]

Van Dorn had advanced into west Tennessee while Price was in Iuka. The idea was to draw attention away from Price so that he might cross the Tennessee River to support Bragg. Van Dorn had gone almost to Bolivar, where he sparred with Federal troops and caused one Union division under Ord, Leonard Ross's, to reinforce the Union position at Bolivar. (In his postbattle report, Van Dorn mistakenly writes that he forced Ross to return to Corinth.)[6]

On September 28 Van Dorn shared with his generals his determination not to go back into west Tennessee but to attack Corinth. He believed that if his army moved with alacrity, he could create a diversion at Pocahontas, where his men would fake the building of a river bridge and then turn east and hit Corinth from the northwest. He would send cavalry to destroy the track somewhere along the Mobile & Ohio Railroad north of Corinth, thus impeding Federal reinforcements trying to reach Corinth from that direction.

In his postcampaign report, Van Dorn elaborated on his reasons for targeting Corinth. He believed that taking Memphis would be a forlorn hope. Bolivar was fortified, and the Hatchie River provided a further obstacle, so it could not be captured quickly, and Federal reinforcements could be sent quickly from Jackson, Tennessee, located to the northeast of Memphis but not very far away. Also he could not adequately protect his flanks and rear if he ignored Memphis and Corinth and marched north toward Bolivar. Therefore Van Dorn decided that to accomplish anything in west Tennessee, he must take Corinth and hopefully push Rosecrans back to the Tennessee River. He believed that with Corinth in his hands, Federal troops would have to abandon Bolivar and Jackson, and by then exchanged prisoners from Fort Donelson, rearmed, would have arrived, and he could gain control of west and middle Tennessee and be in an excellent position to help Bragg. If all went well, Memphis would be irrelevant, for a while anyway. The Federals could not afford to abandon the river city to send additional troops with those from Jackson and Bolivar after Van Dorn.

Van Dorn claimed he knew Rosecrans was growing stronger, and that the Federals continued to build and improve defensive works, but there is no mention in his report of where and how those works were being built. He commented on Rosecrans's situation to support his decision to attack quickly. He knew he had about as many men as Rosecrans, and, he wrote, "I had a reasonable hope of success." Van Dorn did not know how strong the inner defensive works at Corinth were, so even if he broke through Beauregard's outer line of defenses, built to hold off Halleck, he would have much more formidable positions to breach. Corinth had become much more defensible since Van Dorn had seen the area.[7]

Once Van Dorn made up his mind about anything, a vote by his generals was hardly necessary. For the record, Dabney Maury supported the plan. Lovell suggested another move on Bolivar, this time a full-fledged attack, but he agreed that the Van Dorn plan might work. Sterling Price made clear that he did not agree with anything about Van Dorn's proposal. He wanted to wait until the paroled prisoners could join the army. Without them, Price could not see anything positive about attacking Corinth. Even victory would be hollow, for Van Dorn would not have enough strength to hold it, and if, as Van Dorn envisioned, the army used Corinth as a point of departure to move north into west Tennessee and Kentucky, perhaps joining Bragg, the Confederate flanks would still be exposed to Federal attacks on their left from Bolivar and in the rear and left from Memphis. Taking Corinth would not make all those troops suddenly disappear.

Price's arguments were cogent, but Van Dorn paid them no mind. Van Dorn had many negative qualities as a commander, and inflexibility was one of them. He did notice that Price seemed almost depressed and said so. Price said he had only stated his beliefs, but Van Dorn should not worry that Price's men would give all they had at Corinth. Van Dorn must have felt affirmed, for if there was one general there whom he truly respected, it was Price. It is questionable whether he knew how little Price respected him, but it is unlikely that had he known, he would have listened. In any event the die was cast. The army would march the morning of September 29.

Van Dorn ordered three days of rations cooked and a wagon train loaded with bacon, flour, and salt. How much thought Van Dorn gave to the effects of weather on the march is not clear. It would be a hot march, unlike the freezing weather in Arkansas. Van Dorn seemed either to lose sight of or not consider such things. He rarely displayed concern for his men. When the army marched out of camp, Price's army, especially Hebért's division, had experienced battle at Iuka only ten days earlier and had been on the move much of the time since then. Their respite had been relatively brief. Now they were on the road again, battling heat and soon the enemy.

Three days' rations would not be enough to sustain Van Dorn's army. And what of water? Union and Confederate soldiers knew Corinth had a notorious reputation for bad water, but there is no indication that the Confederate wagon train carried barrels of the precious liquid. Van Dorn did not know that on September 30, as the Corinth campaign continued, John C. Pemberton had been named to replace him, enabling Van Dorn to invade west Tennessee. Richmond authorities obviously were still more concerned with assisting Braxton Bragg than the situation in northeast Mississippi. Also, some Mississippi political leaders had complained to President Jefferson Davis that they had no faith in Van Dorn. Corinth would underscore the validity of their concern.[8]

On September 24 Ulysses S. Grant, lulled into a false sense of security by Price's and Van Dorn's lack of activity, decided it was quiet enough to take a trip up the Mississippi to St. Louis. He wired Halleck that, given Van Dorn's failure to do much damage at Bolivar, he thought it safe to make the trip so that he could confer with Samuel Curtis, commanding the Department of the Missouri, about sending detachments to the Yazoo River in central Mississippi. Supposedly the Rebels were working on more ironclads, and, if true (it was not), then something should be done to stop it. Memories of the *Arkansas* lingered. Grant also said his recent health had not been good, and though he felt better, he thought the trip would help. He had moved his headquarters to Jackson, Tennessee, perhaps to get away from unhealthy Corinth. During the Iuka campaign, Grant had expressed great concern about Van Dorn attacking Corinth, but now he was ready to leave the area and go to St. Louis. He appeared to still be under the cloud of the post-Shiloh period when he was chastised by Halleck. Grant could be excused for wanting a respite, but he picked a strange time to take it.

He received no objection from Halleck and prepared to leave, but before doing so he issued an order regarding the organization of the District of West Tennessee. Sherman would be at Memphis in command of the First Division, which included an area east to Bolivar and south of the Hatchie River that ran from Tennessee into Mississippi. Ord headed the Second Division, including all territory north of Bolivar to the Kentucky line, and Rosecrans would command the Third Division, which mainly included Corinth and vicinity. Isaac F. Quinby was named to head the Fourth Division, which would be responsible for a wide area from Cairo, Illinois, to the Fort Donelson region. The positioning of the troops demonstrated Grant's determination to hold what had been gained since the fall of Forts Henry and Donelson.

Grant then departed, leaving behind memories of the march from Shiloh to Corinth and the problems of the Iuka campaign. No doubt he had also been worn down by the pressure of Washington constantly badgering him to send men to Buell, while he tried to keep both Price and Van Dorn at bay in northeast Mississippi and to keep them from sending troops to Bragg. He had been stressed, and whatever health problems he had may have been the result. If he had any notions of going on a major offensive, he thought he could not do so. Iuka had been trying enough. He surely believed that just being with his wife, Julia, would calm him, and he doubtless needed and relished her reassurance. She had always been positive and supportive. In her memoirs, Julia does not mention her husband's visit to St. Louis, leaving one to wonder if she thought it best not to discuss his absence where a battle was brewing in his department.[9]

By the time Grant returned, Union scouts reported that Van Dorn and Price had joined forces. Yet Grant misread the situation. He thought Van Dorn had targeted an area above Memphis. If true, Grant told Halleck, troops from Helena, Arkansas, would be needed. Grant insisted, "Threatened at all other points, I cannot send out forces to drive him away." Other reports indicated combined Confederate forces would move north into Tennessee from the Ripley area. On October 1 Grant notified Halleck, "For several days there has been a movement of the rebels south of my front." He admitted that he could not tell if the enemy was going to attack Bolivar or Corinth, but he had determined that it must be Corinth and that the town would be attacked from the west or southwest. He concluded, "My position is precarious, but hope to get out of it all right."

A day later news came that Van Dorn and Price had moved north to Pocahontas. Grant grew more concerned. From Pocahontas, the Confederates could move on to Bolivar or turn east toward Corinth. Rosecrans had no doubts Corinth was the Rebel target, and he began pulling in troops from surrounding areas to reinforce the town's defenses. He knew by then that John Breckinridge's division had been sent to Bragg, but he had false reports of numerous reinforcements coming to Van Dorn, boosting the Confederate numbers to 40,000 men.

Rosecrans probably did not accept the inflated figure, for he did not panic. He would soon have some 23,000 men on hand, about the same as Van Dorn, but Rosecrans had the advantage of strong outer and inner earthworks. Van Dorn knew nothing of inner works circling the town limits and anchored by well-constructed battery fortifications armed with large-caliber rifled guns. Van Dorn was blindly leading his men into what would be a meat grinder even if his men broke through the outer Federal line.

He would find out within a few hours after he completed his Pocahontas feint and led his army across the Hatchie and Tuscumbia rivers northwest of Corinth. Before crossing the bridge across the Hatchie, named Davis' Bridge after a local man, Van Dorn met with his generals in the Davis home at Metamora on the west side of the Hatchie. Van Dorn drew a map of the area, based in part on his memory and in part at the direction of a local guide, perhaps Davis. General John Bowen of Lovell's division thought the map was worthless, and Sterling Price later commented that he had given Van Dorn an excellent map, but for reasons unknown, Van Dorn had not used it. Van Dorn's arrogance was such that he thought he needed no map. He likely felt certain that his knowledge of the country made a map unnecessary.[10]

The Confederate attack on Rosecrans's outposts did not take the Yankees by surprise, as Van Dorn later claimed. Rosecrans, having determined Van Dorn was coming, had been hampered in making his defensive dispositions, ironically by the lack of a good map. But he had spread a brigade out beyond his outer defenses to watch for an enemy approach. On October 1 Colonel John Oliver of the Fifteenth Michigan, commanding the Second Brigade of Thomas McKean's division, led his men toward Chewalla, northwest of Corinth on the Memphis & Charleston Railroad just across the state line in Tennessee. Rosecrans believed that the Chewalla road would be Van Dorn's most likely route. Oliver could quickly determine if the main Rebel force approached from that direction. For most of October 1 and early on the following day Oliver adjusted his lines according to scouting reports, so his men stayed on the move. He shifted his front toward Bolivar to the north and toward Kossuth, Mississippi, to the southwest. On October 2 skirmishing, some of it heavy, broke out along the brigade's shifting front. Oliver pulled back to make sure he could cover both the Chewalla road and "an old road from Kossuth" that forked into the Chewalla road. The main road from Kossuth to Corinth was a few miles south and entered Corinth from the southwest.

Rosecrans grew concerned. The skirmishing over a wide area left him hoping Van Dorn might come directly at him from the northwest, over well-fortified ground between and just to the left of the Memphis & Charleston and across the built-up Beauregard fortifications to the Mobile & Ohio. Such an advance into the "V" formed by the railroad tracks as they approached Corinth would give Rosecrans's troops the advantage of concentrating fire and interior line flexibility to shift troops. The closer the Rebels moved toward the bottom of the "V," the more lethal the fire from Rosecrans's forts. But if Van Dorn's army came directly down the Mobile & Ohio, Rosecrans would have to shift a large portion of his troops from behind their fortifications to meet the Confederate attack.

Rosecrans feared such a move because he did not think Van Dorn would be reckless enough to come straight at the arcs of Union fortifications. Confederate general John Bowen, who, after the battle, preferred charges against Van Dorn for mishandling the campaign, said Van Dorn told him, before the Corinth attack, that he hoped to maneuver the Federals out of Corinth, Jackson, Bolivar, and Memphis, and that Van Dorn's intention at that time was that he would not directly attack enemy defensive works. Later, Bowen claimed, when he asked Van Dorn about attacking Bolivar, Van Dorn "replied to me that he would not sacrifice his men against the fortifi- cations." Bowen's thinking, then, as the army marched toward Corinth, was the same as Rosecrans's. It would soon become clear that when it came to sacrificing men, Van Dorn would do so without hesitation. His lust for vic- tory and glory outweighed his humanity.

The action on October 2, 1862, convinced Rosecrans that most of the Rebel army, perhaps all of it, was indeed approaching between the two rail- roads. Rosecrans must have believed his chances to repel Van Dorn were excellent. Even if the Rebels broke through the outer defensive line, the inner forts and entrenchments should be almost impenetrable. He sent orders to troop commanders to concentrate to receive the expected at- tack. On October 3 Rosecrans deployed his army along the outer defensive works. Thomas Davies's division occupied the ground to the northwest

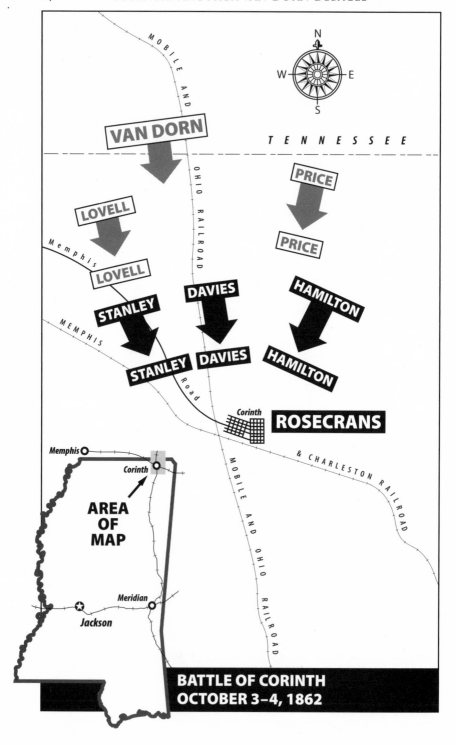

BATTLE OF CORINTH
OCTOBER 3–4, 1862

between the two railroads, Thomas McKean's was on Davies's left, and Charles Hamilton's veterans of Iuka spread out over the northeast angle between the railroads. David Stanley's division would be held in reserve.

As Van Dorn's army approached on the 3rd, Mansfield Lovell's division, composed of John Villepigue's, John Bowen's, and Albert Rust's brigades, was on the right, south of the Memphis & Charleston Railroad. Dabney Maury's division was on the right of Price's corps and on the left Louis Hebért's. As the Confederates reached the outer Yankee works, both of Price's divisions were between the railroads.

The armies began fighting on October 3 with heavy skirmishing early in the morning, and by 9 a.m. the Confederates pushed aggressively toward Rosecrans's outer defenses. Van Dorn's attack on the 3rd surprisingly brought him closer to victory than Rosecrans expected. The more progress his troops made, the closer they came to the inner line of strong points that Van Dorn did not know existed. Battery Lathrop was several hundred yards southwest of the railroad depot near where the Mobile & Ohio and the Memphis & Charleston crossed. West of Lathrop was Battery Tanrath, and north of Tanrath was Battery Phillips. About 400 yards to the northeast was Battery Williams, set up on a rise on the south side of the Memphis & Charleston. North across the track and over 600 yards west of the city stood Battery Robinett, which proved to be one of the decisive points on the second day's fighting.

As the battle progressed on the 3rd, for several hours it seemed Van Dorn and his army would get their initial view of the forts by simply strolling through them after taking Corinth. John Oliver placed his brigade on a prominent hill along the outer defenses, and by 9 a.m. Dabney Maury's right flank slammed into Oliver's position, and Oliver found himself in danger of being flanked and captured. John McArthur's brigade moved up on Oliver's left, the terrain leaving him unaware for a time that Maury's troops were endangering Oliver's position. It became clear once McArthur reached the hotly contested hill that more reinforcements would be needed. Rosecrans sent word to Thomas Davies on the Federal right to send help to McKean's front on the left. Meanwhile Davies arrived with his division at the junction of the Chewalla and Columbus roads, the latter leading north, the former to the northwest. He realized that Oliver and McArthur were in a tight spot. Davies decided that by moving north on the Columbus road, he could outflank Maury's troops, and, with Rosecrans's permission, Davies pushed forward.

Soon a panicky message came from Oliver that he must have immediate help, and Davies sent two regiments and two pieces of artillery. Davies also heard from Rosecrans that he must keep the attacking Rebels from getting through the outer works. Rosecrans preferred beating Van Dorn before the Rebels broke through the old Beauregard works, for he did not want to be forced to depend totally on the strong inner lines and forts. If the Confederates had too much momentum, anything could happen. Davies posted two brigades across the Columbus road, while trying to cover the space between his left and his other brigade assisting Oliver on his extreme left. Realizing that his division was stretched much too far, with large gaps not only along his line but also within McKean's troop alignment, he sent word to Rosecrans that reinforcements were essential. Shortly, Charles Hamilton's division moved up on Davies's right, allowing the Union line to close up. By focusing too much on defending the outer works, the long arc at the top of the "V," Rosecrans had stretched his line very thin.

Sterling Price aligned his troops with Dabney Maury's division on his right, extending to the Memphis & Charleston Railroad. Louis Hebért's division was on the left, and both divisions attacked Oliver and Davies. Price watched proudly as his men moved forward through abatis, piles of timber, and entrenched Union troops. He wrote later: "My troops charged the enemy's position with the most determined courage, exposed to a murderous fire of musketry and artillery. Without faltering they pressed forward over every obstacle, and with shouts and cheers carried in less than twenty minutes the entire line of works, the enemy having fled." McKean's and Davies's thinly spread line had indeed been punished by Price's concentrated attack. The assaults pushed Union forces to the rear of the outer entrenchments for about 1,000 yards. While this action went on, the highlight of the day's fighting for the Confederates took place on Maury's right, when Lovell's division slammed into Rosecrans's left, held by McKean's troops, who had already been fighting off Maury's attack.

Lovell's three brigades—Rust on the right, Bowen in the center, and Villepigue on the left—reached John Moore's brigade of Maury's division at the Memphis & Charleston. McArthur could see the danger, but he did not deploy his reinforcements well, and in any case he did not have enough troops to stop Lovell. The Confederates had the advantage of being shielded by heavy undergrowth, so when they broke into the open, the waiting Federals were not prepared to receive the attack. Lovell summed up the fight very simply: "The conflict was short and bloody." But it was not that easy. Rust's brigade took heavy casualties, especially from canister, but his men refused to quit, and they eventually prevailed against an Illinois regiment and a section of the First Missouri Light Artillery. The Confederates captured the "Lady Richardson," a prized twenty-pounder rifled Parrot gun of Henry Richardson's artillery.

Bowen's and Villepigue's troops charged across the railroad onto the Chewalla road, chasing and capturing Yankees for several hundred yards. The hill that Oliver had occupied fell into Confederate hands. Then, for reasons never fully understood, but indicative of his performance for the rest of the day and the next day, Lovell lost all interest in continuing his offensive. It was true that both Bowen's and Villepigue's troops were scattered, but they could have easily regrouped, especially with the enemy in retreat. Bowen's First Missouri, one of the western Confederacy's best combat units, became separated from the rest of the brigade, and were recalled along with the rest of Lovell's division. The Missourians joined with other Confederate units in the fighting. Bowen did not care, for he knew his men would rather fight than observe. He made no effort to call them in. Lovell may have tied his hands, but Bowen knew that by ignoring these troops' absence, at least part of his brigade would continue contributing to the Confederate effort.

Peter Cozzens, historian of the Corinth battle, surmises that Lovell thought he had lost enough men and simply did not want to continue, and Lovell did practically freeze for the rest of the battle. Lovell had not shown combat capability until the one charge, and after the one success he never would again. According to one account, when Lovell and his staff came to see Bowen, one of the staff, not Lovell himself, asked Bowen about making an attack. Bowen said he was willing to attack and die if an attack was ordered. No more was said, Lovell and his men walked away, and Bowen knew there would be no assault. After contributing greatly to Van Dorn's failure to capture Corinth, Lovell would quietly exit the army. Later in the war he served as a volunteer aide to Joseph E. Johnston, but Johnston failed in efforts to get a division command for Lovell.[11]

While Lovell forced his division to sit and watch, John Moore led his brigade, plus two regiments of Arkansans from W. L. Cabell's brigade, to the sounds of guns along the Memphis & Charleston Railroad. Moore ordered a charge against re-formed regiments from McKean's division, commanded by John McArthur. McKean, not a young man, seemed to suffer more than most from stress and heat, and he allowed McArthur to command the division. John Oliver re-formed his battered troops to assist in this Federal stand taken after McKean's troops fell back toward Corinth. McArthur's left began near Battery F, where Minnesota and Ohio artillery filled a gap, and from there his men formed an arc that stretched northeast across the Memphis & Charleston and from there faced north, directly in front of Moore's brigade. The shock of Moore's attack drove back McArthur's troops, but then McArthur counterattacked. Moore's men retreated, regrouped, and advanced again. Moore brought up two Arkansas regiments held in reserve, which extended his battle line beyond McArthur's on the Union right. Then Bowen's First Missouri, roaming and fighting, showed up on McArthur's left rear.

One of Bowen's veterans wrote of a long sheet of flame pouring from enemy rifle pits, and the usual iron and lead filled the air all around them. The Federal firepower had a devastating effect; many gaps opened in the Confederate lines, were filled quickly, and opened again. It seemed "every instant death smote."

Moore attacked again, the Federals once more fell back, and McArthur sent word to McKean that he desperately needed reinforcements. McKean responded stupidly by ordering John Oliver's troops forward. Worn down by heat and earlier fighting, Oliver's troops shifted from behind McArthur's battle line to a support position, but they ran into McArthur's retreating brigade. Union regiments became mixed and confused. Oliver's troops fired into the Seventeenth Wisconsin, which broke into a run toward Corinth. McArthur considered reorganizing some of his exhausted men to make a stand, but he knew they could not. Moore gave the Federals a respite when he stopped to re-form his line.[12]

Marcellus Crocker's brigade of McKean's division, held too long in reserve, finally received orders to advance, and the men deployed facing Moore, while McArthur's battered men retreated. Crocker placed his left near Battery F, one of the inner defensive anchors (in his postbattle report, Crocker mistakenly calls the battery "E," an indication of the confusion that day). To close a gap in the Union line, his right had to reach the left of Davies's division. Crocker then learned McKean had ordered part of his brigade back, in the direction of Corinth, to the inner works. Crocker sent two regiments to form his front line and two others in the rear of the line. The Confederates had aligned on the northeast of the Memphis & Charleston, and Crocker's troops were on the southwest side. Moore attacked again, and Crocker's Iowans on the front line fought well, causing Moore to stop and rest his troops while he reported to Maury and asked for orders. Crocker now learned that once all batteries passed through to Corinth, he should concentrate his four regiments into a single line to provide concentrated firepower. Sporadic firing continued until Crocker pulled his troops into the inner defenses as dark approached.

On McKean's right, Thomas Davies and his division had an active day that ended in a rather bizarre fashion. He provided McKean with reinforcements, and his line was very secure. With pressure coming from Price's left, Davies realized he needed reinforcements to avoid being outflanked on his right. He asked Rosecrans for more men while he waited, and then sent the last of his reserve units to keep his left from being overwhelmed. Richard Oglesby's brigade, Davies's division, covered a so-called bridle path that Rosecrans feared the Rebels would use as an access path to advance. Oglesby and Pleasant Hackleman, a fellow brigadier general, had orders to pull back to where the Columbus and Chewalla roads forked, the Columbus from that point leading north by northwest and the Chewalla veering off directly west.

Martin Green, commanding a brigade in Louis Hebért's division, charged McKean's position and eventually wrecked Oglesby's men, and Oglesby fell mortally wounded. The fighting went back and forth, for Green's men had to cross an open field, at times subject to heavy Union fire, then he had to pull them back. Green continually sent his men back and forth until they compelled the Yankees to retreat. While Oglesby's troops fought to hold Davies's line, Hackleman's brigade, on the right of the Columbus road and to the east of Oglesby's brigade, was, as Davies later wrote, "not engaged." Hackleman for the moment was Rosecrans's Lovell. On both sides, tactical support was at best inconsistent and at worst totally absent.

Davies ordered both brigades to retreat down the Columbus road, while his remaining brigade, led by Silas Baldwin, covered the retreat, but the messenger did not get through, so Baldwin's troops continued fighting Moore. Davies made his last stand for the day at a battlefield landmark simply called the "white house." McArthur pulled troops back to help cover Davies's left flank, where severe fighting continued until late evening. During the fight against Green, Hackleman was shot dead, so Davies lost two brigade commanders due to Green's attack. The contest between Green and Davies dragged on for some time; at one point Davies received a circular from Rosecrans's headquarters that ordered commanders not to fall back to the "extreme position" unless they were driven to it. The language was unnecessarily vague, and Davies and other commanders interpreted it to mean the inner works protected by the strategically located big batteries. Davies learned that David Stanley's division, held in reserve, had never been ordered anywhere because one of Rosecrans's aides could not find him. Finally Stanley was located, and he ordered his troops forward to assist Davies, but the fighting ended for the day before Stanley could get into position.

Before Stanley advanced and while his struggle continued with Green, Davies heard that Charles Hamilton was moving toward the Mobile & Ohio in an attempt to get into Price's left rear. Hamilton had spent the day guarding northeastern approaches to Corinth, and his front had been quiet. Hamilton shifted his front and saw the opportunity to hit the Confederate rear and relieve pressure on Davies. Had Rosecrans been more aware of the battlefield situation, he could have ordered Hamilton much earlier to strike Price's flank and rear and perhaps have sent Van Dorn in retreat in one day. Certainly Lovell would have been no threat. Price would have been forced to change fronts, leaving his right flank vulnerable to Davies.

As Hamilton's army finally moved, one of his brigade commanders, Napoleon Buford, took off to the northwest in pursuit of Confederate skirmishers, wasting much valuable time. Hamilton refused to continue until Buford returned from his, under the circumstances, ridiculous foray. But Hamilton's tactical move never came to fruition because, for reasons understood perhaps only by himself, Hamilton got into an argument with Rosecrans about an order he received from one of the commanding general's aides. The message directed Hamilton to form on Davies's left, using the point where the two lines met as a pivot, and then to swing his troops to hit the Rebel rear. Clearly, the wording of the message was a simple mistake; it should have instructed Hamilton to use Davies's right as a pivot and swing around to the northwest and west to strike Green's rear. Hamilton made a big deal of it, however, sending a message back to Rosecrans saying he did not understand the order. Was he supposed to march behind Davies's battle line to get on Davies's left, or in front of him, where the Rebels would undoubtedly have seen his troops and opened fire? Night ended the fighting before Hamilton could do anything.

Hamilton's motive perhaps has roots in some of his earlier comments. According to one source, Hamilton said he had no confidence that Corinth could be held. He believed the Confederates had terrain advantages and could not be driven from their positions. He expected Rosecrans to order a retreat the night of October 3 to try to cross the Tennessee and find Buell. Hamilton expected he would be left behind to fight a rearguard action. In later years Hamilton blamed Buford's wild-goose chase for his failure to act as ordered. If Hamilton indeed thought the army would evacuate Corinth, the wrongly worded message from Rosecrans's headquarters must have seemed a godsend. With Buford's help, Hamilton managed to avoid fighting, and, in his own mind, he and his men could escape Corinth with relatively few casualties. Whatever the case, the next day, October 4, Hamilton would find himself and his men holding the Union right flank, and he could not avoid going into battle.[13]

By the end of October 3 Davies had at last become disengaged, and Union forces pulled back into the inner lines of defense and realigned and concentrated for renewed Confederate attacks the next morning. Davies later wrote, "I regret exceedingly that I had not the advice and suggestions of our commanding general on this day, but with the exception of the order heretofore referred to . . . , I do not remember to have received any." Levi Naron, aka Chickasaw, recalled leading Mower's brigade to Davies's relief and then reporting back to Rosecrans that Mower was "in position." This seemed a typical example of how Rosecrans operated. His use of Naron and Naron's scouts to deliver messages to his officers demonstrated that he reacted to events as they unfolded. He was not proactive, staying on top of developments to guide his generals' movements and tactics.

In fact, there is no indication that Rosecrans ever became aggressive in directing the battle. His report of the first day's fight showed clearly he let his commanders coordinate the fighting. He sent reinforcements when he could, but he seemed never to understand the evolution of the battle. If he ever got close enough to the combat to watch, his report does not say so. Such expressions as "word came" and "orders were accordingly given" mark the tone of Rosecrans's participation. The only time he seemed to get personally involved with the battlefield operations was the Hamilton situation, in which Rosecrans's authority as commander of the army did not impress one of his division commanders. Of course, Hamilton's division had borne the brunt of the Iuka battle, so perhaps Hamilton held a grudge against Rosecrans about that mismanaged campaign.[14]

As Rosecrans sat down that evening to plan the disposition of his troops for the next day, he did so with the impression that he was outnumbered "probably two to one." Earlier he had not believed the inflated numbers reported about Van Dorn's strength, but the ferocity of Price's attacks may have convinced him he was facing more men than he expected. He did decide to rely on his inner defenses and forts to stave off the Rebel attack the next day. He decided that protection of the left flank of the army would rest with his main battery forts, for Phillips, Williams, and Robinett, supported by McKean's and Stanley's divisions, had a good field of fire to cut down charging Confederates. His center, which included Stanley's right and Davies's left, would be supported by several field batteries, and the big guns in Williams and Robinett could shell Rebels attacking the center. Davies's division stretched from the right center of Rosecrans's line to the right to

Purdy road and followed that road north to support Battery Powell. Field batteries would also provide Powell with flank support. Purdy road was east of the Mobile & Ohio and led northeast out of Corinth.

From the point where Davies's line ended, the left of Hamilton's division touched it, and from that point Hamilton's ran east at a ninety degree angle from Davies's. In this position, Hamilton's men could protect the Union left, swing north to northwest to strike the Rebel rear, or change fronts and move into Corinth to provide support where needed. Rosecrans had a conference with his division leaders so all would understand the deployment plan. Rosecrans had been in touch with Grant, who remained at his Jackson headquarters and ordered reinforcements to Corinth to help Rosecrans. The additional men would not provide support during the October 4 fighting.[15]

Earl Van Dorn kept his army in basically the same position they had been in most of the day. Lovell remained on the right, while Price's divisions, Maury in the center and Hebért on the left, made up the rest of the line. Van Dorn was disappointed that his army had not finished the job on the 3rd, and he believed that one more hour of daylight would have made total victory possible. He still had no appreciation of the strength of Rosecrans's inner line, nor did he understand that by forcing a tight concentration of enemy troops, their position would make possible more intense firepower. Also, Union commanders could freely take advantage of interior lines, shifting men wherever needed, usually out of the vision of attacking Rebels. Van Dorn perhaps hoped that the cool evening, in marked contrast to the heat of the day, would reinvigorate those who survived. The thought of a night attack crossed Van Dorn's mind, and such an attack was supported by two of Lovell's brigadiers, Rust and Bowen, who earnestly wanted to make up for doing so little during the day. But Van Dorn decided it would be illogical to attack enemy lines that could not be seen clearly, and even he could see the troops needed more rest. Anyway, many of the men felt good. They had pushed the Yankees back and could now see Corinth. If they had a good day tomorrow, they would be inside the town.

Van Dorn's plan for renewing the fight on the 4th included having three batteries deploy on a ridge west of Corinth and open fire at 4 a.m. After their signal, Hebért would swing his brigade toward Corinth by sending forward his left flank, arched to attack the Union far right. These troops would be William Cabell's brigade, transferred to the left from Maury's division. Hebért would proceed with an en masse attack south down the Purdy road. At the sound of Hebért's assault, Lovell would advance with two brigades, holding one in reserve, from the area between the Smith Bridge road on his right and the Memphis & Charleston Railroad on his left. Once Hebért's attack was heard, Lovell would "move rapidly to the assault and force his right inward across the low grounds southwest of town." Maury, meanwhile, would strike directly from the center position into Corinth. The timing of the attacks hinged on Hebért's dawn strike.[16]

Van Dorn's cannons fired on time, not only alerting his army to prepare for attack but also getting the attention of Rosecrans's forces. Dawn came and with it a great silence. Van Dorn wrote, "there was no attack on the left. A staff officer was sent to Hebért to inquire the cause. That officer could not be found. Another messenger was sent and a third; and about 7 o'clock General Hebért came to my quarters and reported sick." Why Hebért took so long to report his illness to Van Dorn has never been explained. Surely Hebért had aides who could have passed along the information much sooner. Whatever his reasons, Hebért had disrupted the timing of the attacks and given the enemy plenty of time to prepare for the fight. Martin Green, appointed by Price to take command, said Hebért told him about dawn that he could not take the field. It is obvious from Green's battle report that he was not aware that he should step in and immediately launch an assault. He did order an attack, but it was not aggressive at first, not surprising for a general suddenly thrown into such a situation. As Price noted, Green moved forward as soon as he could make the necessary disposition of troops, something that Hebért should have done during the night. If he was too sick to do that, news of his illness should have been known well before dawn. A Missouri soldier recalled that Green "was hopelessly bewildered, as well as ignorant of what ought to be done."[17]

On the Confederate right, Lovell had moved forward at daylight, Villepigue and Bowen out front and Rust in reserve. Within a short time, Rust moved up to take the center position. Lovell's full division then advanced to "within a few hundred yards of two strong works of nine guns each protected by heavy infantry forces." The "strong works" were Batteries Phillips and Robinett, which could hit Lovell's men on their right and left flanks and sweep his center. Between the two batteries were four infantry regiments and several others within supporting distance. While Lovell looked at the enemy strength in front of him, he received an order from Van Dorn to detach a brigade to Price to strengthen his center. He intended to send Villepigue, but he dragged his feet most of the day until the fighting ended and he received orders to withdraw.

Except for a brief attack on Villepigue's left and Bowen's personal decision to move forward to test the enemy's firepower, which Bowen quickly realized he could not challenge alone, Lovell's contribution to the second day's battle came to nothing. He did not try to move to his right, which he could have done without putting his division out in the open. If he had done so, he would have least carried with him the attention of a part of Rosecrans's left flank, perhaps easing the pressure on Price's right flank. Possibly it is too strong to call Lovell a coward, but he acted like one, and from the tone of their reports, Rust and Villepigue were glad of it. Only Bowen showed any initiative. Thus one of Van Dorn's divisions, as during most of the previous day, did little more than observe while Price's two divisions were fighting and dying in repeated attacks.[18]

While the Confederates tried to regain some sort of coordination, the ground shook beneath them from the roar of the big guns in the Union fortresses. A Texan said, "bombs burst before, behind & over us." Of course, minié balls and canister filled the air, but the Rebels kept advancing until it became obvious that, with no reinforcements, their efforts were bound to fail. This same problem plagued Rebel attacks all day and forced a retreat. Price's men knew and were angered that Lovell's division "scarcely fired a gun during the whole fight." The silence was Lovell's fault, not his men's. The gallant charges and ultimate failures left men feeling a "hopelessness sinking of the heart." One soldier said he had never felt that way before and hoped he never would again.

On the left, lack of organization and coordination, due largely to Hebért's absence, quickly got the Confederates in trouble. The two brigades on the far left were supposed to swing out as the top of an arch-shaped tactic and hit Hamilton's left and Davies's right. But both brigades lagged behind Elijah Gates's, William Cabell's, and W. H. Moore's brigades, which, to be fair, had a shorter distance to go, being closer to the pivot point. But with the two outer brigades lagging, the left flanks of other brigades became vulnerable. In his postaction report, Green does not mention the problems caused by his slow brigades, but he was impressed by Gates and Cabell. Moore did well, too, but he was shot dead while his men charged all the way into the streets of Corinth. Though Green finally got the two outer brigades to swing their left flanks forward, providing some protection for the Rebel left, Hamilton's division stretched beyond Green's left, and Hamilton surged to his left to meet the enemy charge.[19]

The key fortification on the Union right was Battery Powell, flanked by numerous field batteries. William Cabell moved forward to support Gates, whose men took and occupied Powell, quite a feat under the circumstances. Yet Gates was under increasing pressure from Union forces rushing to the area to throw back the Confederates. Cabell's men made a gallant charge, but they could not beat back the Yankees. The tight Union formation worked well, for just as Confederates fought their way through one line, other Federal brigades moved up to block them. If Cabell had been able to attack earlier, he might have fared better. But he had been sent to Hebért from Maury, who turned him over to Green, and Green told him to continue taking orders from Maury.

Green's sudden responsibility to command combined with the fog of battle to muddle his judgment. He quickly changed his mind, but the command situation kept Cabell from coordinating with Gates, and the two brigades might have shattered Davies's exhausted division. Davies had warned Rosecrans the previous evening that his men, due to the loss of officers and men in the ranks, were in no condition to do much the next day. Rosecrans told Davies that he would be put in a reserve position. Green's and Maury's assaults, however, forced Davies's men to fight, and many broke and ran, just as Davies had feared. The retreat of Davies's troops left several small batteries temporarily vulnerable, but four Union regiments rushed up to fill the void, and a Wisconsin battery fired into the Confederates, trying to take advantage of the gap created by Davies's retreat. Union forces charged and chased away the Confederates who had pushed through the center of Rosecrans's line.

The action that took place where Davies's men had been deployed before their retreat typified the day's fighting, which became a general melee, as battle lines became segmented, surging back and forth. An Illinoisan watched in amazement as Union guns mowed down the charging Confederates and the infantry fired volley after volley, "but all in vain, on they came and scaled our guns," forcing some Federals to pull back into town. One Confederate summed up the turmoil as a "perfect tornado of grape and canister," and "a rattle of musketry and minie balls." Amazingly, some of Green's men reached the streets of Corinth, but the Yankees counterattacked, regaining Battery Powell. Price praised his troops for getting into Corinth and their effectiveness in house-to-house fighting. He also noted that enemy "batteries were in mask, supported by heavy reserves, behind which the retreating enemy took shelter, and which opened upon our troops a most destructive fire at short range."

Union artillerists manning the big guns of Battery Williams, located southeast of Battery Robinett and bolstering the center of Stanley's line, had a clear line of fire at the right flank of the charging Confederates. Price's men fought on, but shortages of ammunition, fatigue, and devastating fire from the big Union guns took a heavy toll. Union troops from Stanley's and Hamilton's divisions took up the slack left by Davies's hectic retreat. Green's troops got so scattered that those who triumphantly entered the town had no reinforcements. They made it to the Tishomingo Hotel, when, as a Texan so aptly put it, "the gas ran out of the Confederate attack." So while Price's troops achieved a measure of glory by taking Powell and forcing their way into Corinth, in the end they simply could not hold what they had won. The uncoordinated attacks in Green's drive forward against the Federal right depleted whatever chances of success they might have enjoyed. The fighting had been vicious, and official and personal battle reports of the blue and gray survivors on the Federal right and Confederate left indicated mutual respect for each other's fighting abilities.[20]

The last notable fighting of October 4 took place on the Confederate right, where John Moore's brigade assaulted Battery Robinett. The struggle around Robinett came to symbolize the Corinth battle in years to come. The fighting proved to be as vicious as in any battle of the war and, except in numbers engaged, compares well with the fighting at Spotsylvania Courthouse in Virginia in 1864 when Robert E. Lee's army held off Grant's attack at the mule shoe.

While Lovell's division continued to watch, Moore's brigade fearlessly attacked Battery Robinett, but not as early as planned, again due to delays caused by Hebért. About 10 a.m. Moore heard the heavy fighting on the Confederate center and left and ordered his men forward. William Cabell's and C. W. Phifer's brigades provided flank support. After advancing some 100 yards, Moore's men came under heavy fire after being seen by Rosecrans's troops on his left. Moore wrote: "the enemy seemed to discover our designs and at once opened on us, and kept up the severest fire I ever imagined possible to concentrate on one point in front of a fortification [Robinett], yet we suffered but little, being protected by timber until we reached the fallen timber and open space which extended about 100 yards in front of their works. On reaching this point we charged and carried the enemy's works the whole extent of our line." From there some of Moore's men made it to Corinth, and even fought their way into Robinett, but like other Rebel successes, the place could not be held, because the Federals again shifted troops, whereas Moore had no more to shift.

John Fuller, commanding the First Brigade of Stanley's division, deployed his men to meet the assault against Robinett, which came from the northwest. Had Lovell provided any support for Moore's right, the fighting might have become more interesting, but there is no way to know if the results would have been different. Lovell's decision to freeze made sure the question would never be answered. Fuller realized that both Phifer's and Moore's men were coming at him, and he shifted troops to cover his flanks. Fuller admitted in his report that several of his regiments took a beating in the initial attack. Battery Williams, not far south of Robinett, pitched in during the fighting, forcing some Federal infantry to lie down to avoid getting hit by friendly artillery from behind. This proved to be a common tactic for Union infantry who found themselves in front of their artillery.

The Federals recovered, and the Confederate attack lost momentum, but the fight was not over. Around 1 p.m. Fuller saw the Rebels coming again, this time extending their line farther west (where Lovell again could have helped), so that Robinett would be hit from the north, northwest, and west. Wager Swayne, commanding the Forty-third Ohio and positioned on the left and rear of Robinett, saw the Rebels "had gained the parapet and opened fire on our rear from the opposite [right] side of the earthwork on our right [Robinett]." Swayne shifted his regiment to the left and pulled his right back, so his men could fire directly at the Confederates. Confusion reigned in Federal ranks around Robinett until Stanley led the organization of the defensive lines, and the Rebels were finally beaten back.

Swayne's account is, as are many reports, vastly oversimplified, but likely is based only on what he saw. The truth was that the fighting at Robinett was fierce, often hand to hand. Soldiers on both sides, so caught up in the battle, did not care if they lived or died. Henry Robinett, after whom the battery was named, was killed. Federals inside the fort tossed shells with short fuses among the Rebels, who sometimes grabbed them and threw them back. The fighting in and around Robinett could be summed up as bloody bedlam.

William P. Rogers of the Second Texas gained particular notoriety after he was killed on the slopes of Robinett. Soldiers on both sides praised his bravery, perhaps as symbolic of the reckless courage showed by men on both sides. He rode up to the fort on his horse, which, given the roar of gunfire, was not exactly a smart thing to do. He stayed in the saddle as long as he could, leading his men. Apparently he saw that his soldiers must surrender to stop the slaughter and tried to find a white flag. He at last held the flag aloft, but in the smoke and hysteria of battle, Colonel John Sprague of the Sixty-third Ohio did not see the flag, and he ordered some of his men to cut down the Rebel on horseback. Rogers had at least seven wounds in his body when he was found after the Confederates retreated. He is buried on the site of Battery Robinett.

Rosecrans commented later that the fighting that resulted in the deaths of Rogers and so many others convinced him "it was about as good fighting on the part of the Confederates as I ever saw. The columns were plowed through and through by our shot, but they steadily closed up and moved forward until they were forced back." He also encountered a wounded

Arkansas lieutenant who broadened Rosecrans's regional culture. The Arkansan said, "you licked us good, *but we gave you the best we had in the ranch.*"[21]

After the Confederate retreat all along the line, Van Dorn ordered Lovell to cover the rear while the army gathered at Chewalla to camp for the evening. Some officers wondered why the army should not go farther in case Rosecrans decided on an immediate pursuit. Van Dorn seemed not to care what Rosecrans did. He sent cavalry to the south along the Mobile & Ohio Railroad to the hamlet of Rienzi. There the army would assemble and attack Corinth from the south. Price was astonished when Van Dorn told him about this plan. After Van Dorn had retired for the night, Price, Maury, and other officers went to Van Dorn's tent and awakened him. They argued strongly that the army was in no condition to continue fighting the next day. They believed the men should be led farther west, to Ripley, where they could rest and dig in, in case Rosecrans came after them.

Van Dorn relented and sent orders to commanders to ready their men to retrace the army's approach to Corinth, which, if things went well, would get them back to Ripley safely. Maury told Van Dorn that evening that Van Dorn was the only officer he ever saw who loved danger just for the sake of danger, and when he was in that zone, he simply ignored relevant factors. Van Dorn did not agree, of course, but he said he would not let his personal feelings bring more misfortune to the army.[22]

Rosecrans was in no hurry to pursue immediately. His own forces had been bloodied and his losses heavy. He did eventually pursue, and Grant had already set in motion troops from Tennessee to try and cut off the Confederates at Davis' Bridge over the Hatchie. The pursuit caused more tension between Rosecrans and Grant, adding to the strained relations left over from Iuka. On the morning of the 5th, Rosecrans sent a message to Van Dorn assuring him that Confederate dead left on the battlefield would be properly buried, "and a soldier's tribute will be paid those who fell fighting bravely, as did many in Maury's division." Rosecrans also issued orders regarding details of his army's pursuit of Van Dorn.

On October 5 Van Dorn's army moved west. He found waiting on the west side of the Hatchie, on the high ground at Metamora, nine Union regiments and four artillery batteries, sent by Grant from Jackson, Tennessee, under the command initially of Stephen Hurlbut, who would be replaced by E. O. C. Ord.

The Confederate advance the morning of the 5th consisted of John C. Moore's brigade. Moore's men marched within two to three miles of Davis' Bridge, and he was given orders "to push forward, cross the bridge, form a line of battle on the right of the road, and then advance, take, and hold the heights of Metamora, which command the crossing at Davis' Bridge." Moore pushed forward as rapidly as possible, but Moore noted, "the men being greatly exhausted and weak for want of food and the previous two days' marching and hard service, when we reached the crossing and formed line we did not have more than 250 or 300 men in ranks." Moore filed the remnant of his command across the bridge and to the right of the road as ordered. At that point Federal cannons opened up from the ridge. One regiment, the Second Texas, Rogers's unit, was cut off by the fire and stayed on the east side of the Hatchie. Moore's men found themselves in a narrow timbered area with open fields to their front and rear. The ground in their front extended all the way to and up the heights held by Ord's men.

Moore knew it would be suicide to march his men forward and attack. He sent for reinforcements and in his message warned Price and Van Dorn that he could not hold his position very long without immediate reinforcements. Moore shifted his troops, trying to avoid Ord's fire as much as possible, but the air became increasingly filled with shot, shells, and bullets, especially against Moore's right flank. He realized that not all of Ord's army was on the ridge. Facing the possibility of capture, Moore ordered his men to fall back across the Hatchie as best they could, since enemy artillery focused on Davis' Bridge. Moore's men naturally got scattered, so those who made it across joined either Cabell's or Phifer's brigade, whichever was handiest.[23]

The Federals Moore encountered were part of General George Veatch's brigade. Veatch had occupied the Metamora high ground and had been ordered by Ord to advance after exchanges of artillery with the Confederates. Veatch put two regiments on the left of the road to the Hatchie and three on the right. Those on the right ran into Moore's fire first. Moore's men fought stubbornly, but then the two regiments on the left hit Moore's right. The fighting continued for a time, but Moore obviously had no chance with his few men, and he had already suffered more losses. He had to retreat, for he stood no chance at all against five enemy regiments.

The Federals captured quite a few of Moore's men who did not make it across the Hatchie. Part of Phifer's brigade, led by Sul Ross, went across the bridge to help but quickly came back after seeing that Moore had retreated. Moore's withdrawal set up the second phase of the fighting. Ord, not satisfied with taking the bridge and cutting off Van Dorn's expected retreat route, ordered his troops to cross the Hatchie, and they ran into heavy fire from Ross's and Cabell's brigades. The Confederates had the advantage of high ground on the east side of the Hatchie, and Ord had made a big mistake by sending his men across the river where the enemy waited on high ground.[24]

William Cabell's depleted brigade was walking across the Tuscumbia River bridge when he heard sounds of artillery coming from Moore's fight at the Hatchie, some five miles away. Maury told Cabell to move as rapidly as possible to assist Moore. All Van Dorn's men suffered from lack of water, making a fast march a challenge. When Cabell arrived, he found Phifer's brigade under Ross and remnants of Moore's brigade fighting on the east side of Davis' Bridge as Ord's army attacked. Cabell aligned his men on Ross's right; a battery Cabell had sent on ahead was already in action. The battle continued until Cabell's ammunition began to run out. He ordered ten rounds given to each infantryman, and his troops kept firing "until the enemy had ceased firing, except their skirmishers and my cartridges had given out." He notified Maury, who ordered Cabell to retire back to a timber line where more ammunition awaited. While his men pulled back, Cabell's horse fell on him, severely injuring his hip and leg.[25]

A Rebel soldier came away from the Hatchie with renewed respect for the enemy. "Their thin ranks sufficiently attest the fact that Union men *will fight*—whatever prejudiced persons—self conceited *Generals* or such old grannies as the wives may say to the contrary." The fighting at Corinth had tested men on both sides, and the two-day clash had produced many more brave men than cowards.

By the time the Hatchie fight withered, another route bypassing Davis' Bridge had been found, the Boneyard road, which branched off to the southeast. Maury pulled back his men, and they followed the rest of Van Dorn's army. John Villepigue's division came up and held the line at the bridge after Maury's troops pulled back. The Union attack began to fizzle. Ord fell wounded, and Hurlbut took command, and he ordered Veatch to send his troops across the Hatchie to shore up the battle line. Veatch admitted that during the fighting on the east side of the Hatchie, the Confederates "kept up a most destructive fire of musketry, grape, and canister, principally directed on the bridge and upon our forces who were crowded in masses on the right." After the Confederates pulled back, Union troops did not follow.[26]

Hurlbut blamed Ord's ignorance of terrain east of the Hatchie for the unfortunate massing of troops that gave Confederates easy targets. Hurlbut pushed across reinforcements, and had the numbers, combined with Maury's withdrawal to gain the high ground. During the action, Veatch fell wounded, though not seriously. Rebel troops kept up token resistance, including artillery duels with the Yankees until around 3:30 p.m. Hurlbut reported afterward, "The total want of sufficient transportation, the loss of battery horses, the shortness of provisions, and the paramount necessity of burying my dead, taking care of my wounded, and securing the prisoners and captured munitions of war prevented my pursuing." He did not add that the Confederates had put up such strong resistance he decided he did not want to fight any longer. More than that, Hurlbut had filled himself with too much whiskey to lead a pursuit.[27]

To the east, John Bowen's brigade, in the rear position of Lovell's division, successfully kept the Yankees at bay. On the east side of the Tuscumbia River, on a hill called "Big Hill" above Young's Bridge, Bowen's men stood aside to allow Van Dorn's wagon train to cross. Union troops, commanded by James McPherson, came up and tried to cut Bowen off to keep the Confederates from escaping via the bridge. A spirited fight broke out. Bowen reported that he personally went to the center of his front and took command of the Fifteenth Mississippi. The fire of that regiment, Bowen penned, "must have proved destructive, as the advance was not only thus checked, but their whole force fled from the field. I then crossed the Tuscumbia at my leisure, tore up and burned the bridge, obstructed the ford near by, and joined the division about 3 miles beyond." Bowen noted his losses were "2 or 3 killed and 8 or 10 wounded." McPherson put a better face on the action, saying his troops took the crest of Big Hill, probably long after Bowen's troops had left. The next day McPherson's troops rebuilt the destroyed bridge and continued following the Confederates until breaking off pursuit and returning to Corinth. McPherson did not report his losses.[28]

Van Dorn's army completed their escape down the Boneyard road, crossing the Hatchie well south of Davis' Bridge at a place called Crum's Mill. The army continued its dreary retreat until Holly Springs, where the exhausted survivors of Corinth drifted in, usually in small groups, and the ragged groups moved on to Ripley. Rosecrans's pursuit had been held up by the rebuilding of Young's Bridge and the clearing of Boneyard road, where trees chopped down by Confederates had to be removed. Rosecrans's troops also had to rebuild Crum's Mill bridge, which had been destroyed. With McPherson in the lead, the Federal pursuit continued.[29]

Grant, who had not been on the scene and therefore had no knowledge of the violent fighting at Corinth, was not pleased that Rosecrans had not vigorously and immediately pursued Van Dorn. Despite the fact that Rosecrans's troops kept after Van Dorn nearly all the way to Ripley, Grant suddenly called off the pursuit. At the time, this very un-Grant-like decision was based on his belief that Van Dorn would have been reinforced before

Rosecrans caught up. This was not the case, as Grant found out very shortly after telling Rosecrans to return to Corinth. Certainly Union forces had an opportunity to overwhelm and capture Van Dorn's entire army. Henry Halleck wondered why Grant had stopped the pursuit, but he did not criticize Grant, for he concluded Grant was on the scene and should know what he was doing.

Rosecrans was extremely angry, and he believed he not only might have wiped out Van Dorn's army but also could have gone south and taken Vicksburg. He was no doubt overly optimistic about the latter, but Rosecrans had trouble forgiving Grant for stopping what might have been a resounding end to the Corinth campaign. Grant obviously had not regained his self-confidence since his post-Shiloh experience. His actions at Iuka had been anything but sterling, and his decision not to be present at Corinth was telling. Now he had called off a promising pursuit of an enemy army. Perhaps he simply did not want to risk Rosecrans's misfortune, which might result from chasing Van Dorn. Grant had won at Iuka, at least technically since Price had abandoned the battlefield, and Rosecrans had won convincingly at Corinth, and with back-to-back victories, why should he risk a black mark in Washington? Grant may have thought that Halleck was just waiting for one wrong move to lash out again. Whatever the case, for the Union army at Corinth, the battle and campaign ended with a whimper. The Rosecrans-Grant hard feelings continued until Rosecrans finally received command of the Army of the Ohio, replacing Don Carlos Buell.[30]

During the fighting at Corinth, Rosecrans lost 355 killed, 1,841 wounded, and 324 wounded or missing, for a total of 2,520 out of approximately 22,000 who were engaged. An additional 570 were killed or wounded in the fighting at the Hatchie. Van Dorn also had approximately 22,000 men, and his casualties included 323 killed, 1,117 wounded, and 1,657 missing. The Confederate figures as given in the official reports are likely too low. One source has Van Dorn losing slightly over 500 killed, over 2,100 wounded, and over 1,600 missing. Casualties at the Hatchie were included in Confederate figures, though exactly what they were is not spelled out in post-battle reports. Losses there may have contributed to Van Dorn's problematic casualty reports. There are a paucity of battle reports by regimental commanders in the Confederate army. One set of striking figures are of the losses of Lovell's division—77 killed, 285 wounded, and 208 missing. Compared to overall Confederate losses, whichever figures one chooses to embrace, Lovell's list demonstrated his small contribution to the fighting at Corinth and thereafter.

Some of the Confederates captured did not seem to mind. They were probably better fed and had water to drink, which they would not have had if they had been with their comrades. They did rail at some of the Yankees, calling them "vandals for invading their country and ravishing their property." They threatened a "no quarter" policy (shooting down enemy soldiers rather than accepting their surrender) from then on, a rather silly statement coming from prisoners. One also said if he had a chance to shoot at a crowd of the enemy, he would only aim at one—Abraham Lincoln.

On a more curious note, "Old Abe," the mascot eagle of the Eighth Wisconsin, survived the fighting, and Douglas the camel, with the Forty-third Mississippi, also came through unscathed. Camels had come into the country during the 1850s when Jefferson Davis was secretary of war. The theory was they would be more reliable than horses for service in the West. The experiment went nowhere, but some of the camels were still around. Douglas would be shot and killed later at the siege of Vicksburg.[31]

For Earl Van Dorn, the loss at Corinth confirmed low opinions of his generalship held by many. He still did not know that John Pemberton had replaced him, and he would not be happy about it. In early November 1862 a court of inquiry met to examine charges against Van Dorn by John Bowen. The gist of Bowen's position was that Van Dorn had not properly reconnoitered the area at Corinth, had not made proper preparations for supplying the army, and had unwisely ordered the attack at Corinth. Much of this was true, but Van Dorn was acquitted, which was the usual result of such proceedings. General officers tended to take care of their own in such cases. So Van Dorn remained in north Mississippi and would eventually have an opportunity to redeem his shattered reputation. It is surprising that Bowen did not include Lovell in his charges.[32]

The Confederate defeat at Corinth opened the way for the first Union campaign against Vicksburg. North Mississippi from Corinth to Memphis was now mostly controlled by Grant's forces, although he complained loudly to Halleck that he did not have enough men to do anything. The Corinth battle, following on the heels of Price's forced retreat from Iuka, signaled the ebbing of Confederate fortunes in the West. Three days after Van Dorn began his retreat from Corinth, Braxton Bragg met Buell near Perryville, Kentucky. Bragg's army fought Buell's to a draw, but Bragg decided he must retreat back into Tennessee. Kentuckians had not rushed to join his army as he had hoped and expected, and he believed that to remain left him too isolated from reinforcements. This was in many ways typical of Bragg, who often seemed to grab defeat from the jaws of victory.[33]

After Corinth and Perryville, there was a lull in major action in the war until November 1862. Ambrose Burnside replaced George McClellan in Virginia, and Grant finally began gathering forces to invade north Mississippi.

5

VICKSBURG

More Union Failures

After Henry Halleck left for Washington, D.C., Union forces cleared out Confederate influence in north Mississippi, and now Grant, his confidence still shaky, had a decision to make. The decision was not what to do; official Washington wanted the surrender of Vicksburg. What Grant had to decide was how to achieve it. Ultimately he took the risky action of moving his army south into Mississippi via the Mississippi Central Railroad.

Like most commanders, Grant claimed he needed more troops before he could proceed to do anything. Halleck, now commanding all Union armies, was in a position to oblige, and he did so to the best of his ability. Men from Cairo, Illinois, and other staging points throughout the Midwest rode riverboats to Tennessee, and soon Grant had a force of nearly 50,000 men strung out on a rough line between Memphis and Iuka. Grant received word that he now headed the Department of the Tennessee, a newly created area by the War Department that included the portions of Tennessee and Kentucky west of the Tennessee River, Cairo, and as much of north Mississippi as he could conquer.[1]

Grant informed Halleck that his plans included a thrust into Mississippi along the convenient Mississippi Central, which ran south from Tennessee all the way to Canton, some twenty-five miles north of the Mississippi state capital at Jackson, and continued on to and through Jackson under a different name (New Orleans, Jackson and Great Northern) all the way to New Orleans. If he could make it to Jackson, Grant reasoned, he could turn west and force Vicksburg's surrender.

What Grant did not know at the time, though he would get wind of it soon enough, was that John A. McClernand, a well-connected Illinois politician who had performed decently enough under Grant as a civilian general at Belmont and Shiloh, was intriguing with the Lincoln administration to put together a separate force for the purpose of coming down the Mississippi and capturing Vicksburg. Once Grant heard about the scheme, he hurried up his own plans in the hope that he could take Vicksburg before McClernand arrived. Official Washington, especially Secretary of War Edwin Stanton, initially bottled up McClernand's plans, which, whether intentional or not, gave Grant more time. By November 3, 1862, Grant's army moved into north Mississippi.[2]

Grant divided his forces into two wings totaling some 37,000 effectives, not including men stationed along the Tennessee-Mississippi state line to watch for Rebel raids. James McPherson, a well-liked Ohioan who had ranked first in his class of 1853 at West Point, commanded the right, and Charles Hamilton, the Iuka/Corinth veteran who had graduated with Grant at West Point, led the left wing. Grant specifically wanted to take Holly Springs and then push as far south as Grenada. If all went well, he would then decide whether to proceed to Jackson. His supply line stretched via the Mississippi Central, plus the Mobile & Ohio Railroad that ran south from Corinth, all the way north to Columbus, Kentucky. That invaluable line would become more tenuous the farther south his troops traveled. This was the gamble Grant had decided to take. He believed, or at least sincerely hoped, the supply line would remain secure from Confederate attacks in his rear.

As partial protection, he ordered William T. Sherman, his good friend commanding at Memphis, to send a force out to cover the army's right and to threaten the Confederate left. Meanwhile plans proceeded to assemble a force at Helena, Arkansas, a river town below Memphis. These troops would cross the river and march inland across the Mississippi Delta and further threaten the Confederate left flank.

Grant had no trouble taking Holly Springs, for the Confederates had evacuated the town and moved south. Union soldiers noticed that, aside from slaves, the town seemed mostly occupied by women, women not at all happy to see the enemy in their midst. The Federals thought Holly Springs to be a "beautiful town," but they would remember how "citizens scowled" at them and warned them that Sterling Price would get them for coming into Mississippi. Grant's men ignored the snubs, but many were struck by the plight of slaves, and the next time Holly Springs citizens saw the

Federals, the shadow of slavery and military reverses would cause Grant's army to lash out bitterly at the town.[3]

While Grant continued his march south, John C. Pemberton, now commanding Confederate forces in Mississippi, worked feverishly to stop him. Pemberton faced problems, not the least of which was his Pennsylvania nativity. Many Southerners did not trust him, and his first departmental command in the South Carolina and Georgia area had demonstrated that he had difficulty dealing with native political leaders. Protests against his leadership in South Carolina reached such a fever pitch that Jefferson Davis removed him from command and sent him west to take over the Vicksburg theater. Pemberton's administrative talents and his well-trained staff combined to do a good job of cleaning up a departmental bureaucracy in disarray, wrought by Earl Van Dorn. Pemberton was not a field general, nor did he want to be, and Grant's invasion presented strategic and tactical challenges the Pennsylvania West Pointer had not encountered.

Since he felt more comfortable behind a desk covered with papers at his Jackson headquarters, Pemberton left daily field command decisions to Earl Van Dorn, who had been removed from overall command of the department before his Corinth disaster. The situation was not comfortable, but Van Dorn and Pemberton handled it well enough. Van Dorn kept Pemberton informed, and the latter made occasional train trips to the front to check on the state of things. Despite his preferences, Pemberton could not escape the responsibility of countering Grant's offensive, though he continued to rely on Van Dorn and on advice from Braxton Bragg, who commanded the Army of Tennessee in Tennessee.[4]

Pemberton had about 21,000 troops to cover a large area. Nine thousand more were en route from Tennessee, but even 30,000 would be too few to defend adequately the wide north Mississippi front. Grant's forces did not greatly outnumber Pemberton's, but Union forces, being on the offensive, could dictate how the campaign proceeded, and Pemberton and Van Dorn had to be ready for all possibilities. This made concentration of Confederate troops impossible. Both flanks of Pemberton's army would be vulnerable if he lingered in any one position too long or if he stretched his line too thin. While Grant had options of calling on additional troops, such as Sherman's in Memphis and others in Helena, Pemberton did not have any reserves. Initially Pemberton had Van Dorn pull the army back from Holly Springs to dig in on the Tallahatchie River's south bank. Anchored by where the Mississippi Central crossed the river, Confederate works spread to the right and left as far as their numbers allowed, and scouts checked for other bridges and fords that might give the Yankees opportunities to flank the Rebel line. The generals hoped the river would be an effective, though obviously not a permanent, barrier against Union progress.

Pemberton wired Richmond for assistance, but the Confederacy simply did not have enough men to reinforce him adequately. He could not order troops in the trans-Mississippi area to come to his rescue, because his authority stopped at the east bank of the Mississippi. His immediate superior, Joseph E. Johnston, likewise had no authority across the river, and the Davis government, for political reasons, stupidly refused to order unequivocal cooperation from trans-Mississippi commanders. The best Pemberton could hope for was that Grant would order assaults against the strong Confederate Tallahatchie position and suffer enough losses to force Grant to go back north. Grant, of course, had no intention of pursuing such a reckless strategy.[5]

On November 27 the Union column at Helena swung into action. Led by Brigadier General Cadwallader C. Washburn, whose brother Elihu was an intimate of Lincoln and Grant, these troops included Washburn's cavalry, supported by Alvin P. Hovey's infantry. This force crossed the Mississippi and tramped across the north Delta region toward Pemberton's exposed left. Pemberton sent Colonel John S. Griffith and his Texas cavalry brigade to block Washburn. Griffith won the duel and prevented Washburn from destroying bridges that would have placed Pemberton's mobility in jeopardy. The Delta invasion, along with concerns about Federal cavalry activity on his right flank in the area of the Mobile & Ohio rail line, nonetheless forced Pemberton to give up the Confederate position on the Tallahatchie. He ordered a withdrawal farther south to his next line of defense behind the Yalobusha River at Grenada. Grant's strategic successes had removed the Tallahatchie barrier without his army there having to make any kind of attack.

Grant's forward units crossed the Tallahatchie at Abbeville just north of Oxford on December 1, skirmishing all the while with Pemberton's rear guard. The Yankee advance and the Rebel cavalry covering the Confederate retreat stayed in close contact for several days. Pemberton sent infantry to help his cavalry hit the Federals hard at Coffeeville on December 5.[6]

The Confederates noticed that people there seemed "depressed and destitute," with a "general air of gloom" all around. Pemberton's retreat obviously had disheartened many civilians. Nevertheless, the repulse gave Pemberton's army some breathing room, and the next day his tired troops busied themselves shoring up entrenchments behind the Yalobusha. William H. Jackson, a Tennessee-born West Pointer nicknamed "Red," whose cavalry had played a key role in keeping Grant's advance at bay, had his men camp several miles north of Grenada to keep an eye on Union movements.[7]

Grant decided to stop for a while so that his army could rest and regroup in the Oxford area. Sherman arrived with three divisions from Memphis, and Grant had to think about what to do next. He had been toying with the idea of sending Sherman back to Memphis to lead an expedition down the Mississippi to Vicksburg. Meanwhile he would remain with his army in north Mississippi. He did not think the Confederates could fight effectively on two fronts, and he also wanted to have his own man, Sherman, leading the river expedition rather than have John McClernand show up and take over. Furthermore, Grant hoped that success by Sherman would ease concerns about the vulnerable supply line to the north.

Grant discussed his thoughts with Sherman in Oxford on December 7 and explained that while the push against Pemberton could continue, the river expedition would set up a second front, forcing Pemberton to make tough decisions. Sherman agreed, and on December 9 he started back to Memphis with one division, leaving the other two with Grant. Sherman added troops to his expeditionary force to make up for the loss of the two divisions. Soldiers from Samuel Curtis's command (Curtis was another West Pointer and New Yorker who commanded the Department of the Missouri, which included Arkansas) provided the necessary manpower. Sherman worked out transportation details with Flag Officer David Porter, who now commanded the lower Mississippi naval fleet.

Grant's army received the same sort of welcome in Oxford as in Corinth. Oxford residents thought the Yankees the most profane bunch they had ever encountered. The Federals had endured long marches and wet, muddy trails and thus were not in the greatest of moods when they arrived. Vandalism abounded, forcing locals to hide food and valuables wherever they could. Kansas soldiers, known for their rough behavior and hated even by other men in Grant's army, were particularly rapacious. Fences disappeared to become firewood for the Yankees, and salt became so scarce people had to boil dirt from smokehouse floors to extract salt.

Some Union soldiers became bored, wrecked stores and homes, dressed in clothes confiscated from Confederates, and surrounded a dwelling where some of their officers were staying. The men rushed in, crying out, "Guerrillas!" and forced the officers to plead for their lives; then the "Confederates" issued paroles. The next day the officers bragged about their heroism in driving off the guerrillas, while the men who had pulled off the prank smirked, winked, and wisely kept their mouths shut.[8]

Though many Federals were abusive and destructive, many of their actions were caused by their experiences with Confederate guerrillas. While Rebel guerrillas were usually not in the regular army, their bullets were just as dangerous, and they often shot at Union soldiers from ambush. Sometimes they captured and executed Yankee soldiers. In some cases guerrillas were captured and given similar treatment. The problem for the majority of civilians was that they were, in the minds of Grant's men, linked to this sort of thing, often being accused of giving succor to guerrillas who infested the area. Thus local people and Federal soldiers had strained relationships on several levels.

Grant managed to salvage some good feelings among Southerners by setting up a kind of welfare program for those who had lost food to both armies and faced starvation. His system included asking loyal Unionists in the area to sell their provisions via military posts to families based on need. Disloyal residents would be taxed to create a fund to provide free food for those who could not purchase goods from the military posts. Thus supplies would be coming from two sources. Inspectors oversaw the program. For many months Grant held out hope that such soft handling of civilians would fuel a desire on their part to come back into the Union voluntarily, thereby shortening the war. Indeed, the Lincoln administration supported such a strategy early in the war.[9]

Meanwhile Confederate scouts reported to Pemberton that Sherman was in Memphis gathering troops for an excursion down the Mississippi. Pemberton knew this meant an attack on Vicksburg. He ordered Martin Luther Smith to inspect the bluffs along the Yazoo River north of the city for possible battery sites. He also told Smith to use slave labor to place obstructions in the Yazoo and to increase security measures in the area, especially at railroad bridges. Pemberton knew that if he had to fight both Grant and Sherman, he would need serviceable rail lines all the way from Grenada to Vicksburg. Having the advantage of interior lines to shift forces meant nothing if trains could not move freely. Pemberton continually pleaded with Richmond for reinforcements, but Jefferson Davis continued to refuse transfer of men from Louisiana and Arkansas without permission of commanders there. Davis knew those generals would not give up their men unless ordered to do so from Richmond, orders which they knew would not come.

Many Confederate leaders, including Davis, apparently did not understand, or take time to ponder the fact, that the war could never be won unless territorial limitations were replaced by total cooperation. Davis knew that there was much anger in Arkansas that Van Dorn's army had been sent

from that state to Mississippi. Therefore he hesitated to force commanders
to send troops to Pemberton. In later months Richmond would plead for
cooperation, but no orders came from the Davis War Department. When
political concerns dominated military thinking, as often happened, Confederate military operations suffered.

While Pemberton worried about his lack of troops, Grant gave the Confederate commander something more to think about. In mid-December
Grant sent cavalry to raid the Mobile & Ohio. The raid threatened Pemberton's exposed right and wreaked havoc on Confederate lines of communication between Mississippi and middle Tennessee. The resulting expedition
was not that spectacular, but Grant's riders did destroy Rebel supplies and
gave the Confederate high command anxious moments. Grant then issued orders to his wing commanders to scout their fronts; the march south
would continue. Grant did not know that two key developments would
greatly threaten his army's security.[10]

The Confederates launched two cavalry raids, one in Grant's rear and the
other that began in his front and continued into his rear. Far behind enemy
lines, Nathan Bedford Forrest led his riders into west Tennessee. Forrest,
a Tennessean and a soldier with a genius for leading small strike forces,
had orders to damage Yankee lines of supply and communication to relieve
the pressure on Pemberton. Forrest and his men crossed the Tennessee
River between December 13 and 15, 1862, and hit the Mobile & Ohio and
the Mississippi Central, at one point riding near the Tennessee-Kentucky
border. The raid resulted in major damage to Union supply and communication lines. After a hard fight at Parker's Crossroads in Tennessee, Forrest
recrossed the Tennessee River on January 1, 1863.

The idea for the other raid came from Lieutenant Colonel John S. Griffith, commander of the Texas cavalry brigade. Griffith had obviously become familiar with the geography of north Mississippi during the campaign, and he understood that a fast-moving cavalry force could get behind
Grant's front and strike the Federal supply and communication lines to
the north of Grant's position. Griffith thought Holly Springs and Memphis
were excellent targets and that Earl Van Dorn would be the perfect choice
to lead the raid. Griffith penned his ideas in a letter to Pemberton, who
liked what he read. He summoned Griffith to discuss the matter further
and notified Van Dorn. Van Dorn no doubt loved the proposed mission,
for it would give him a chance to grab headlines and redeem himself for
Corinth.

Before Pemberton gave the order to set the raid in motion, he had to
check reports of a Union naval threat to the Yazoo City naval yard on the

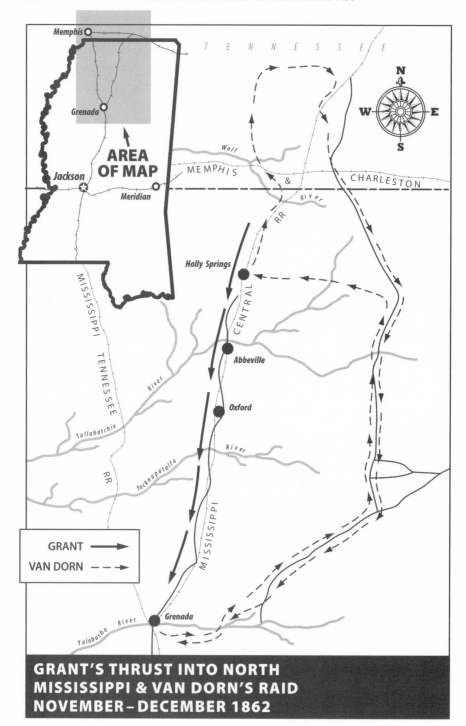

GRANT ——▶
VAN DORN - - -▶

**GRANT'S THRUST INTO NORTH
MISSISSIPPI & VAN DORN'S RAID
NOVEMBER–DECEMBER 1862**

Yazoo River. The report was false, but from his Jackson office he ordered additional heavy guns placed along the Yazoo bluffs. After messages to and from General Smith, Pemberton responded to the need for additional troops in Vicksburg to replace those sent to reinforce defenses on the Yazoo bluffs. Pemberton then started back to Grenada, and along the way he received welcome news that an enemy ironclad, the *Cairo*, had struck a mine and sank on December 12, albeit with no casualties. The boat's escorts fled back to the Mississippi, easing Pemberton's mind about Union pressure on the Yazoo.[11]

After these brief diversions, Pemberton again turned his attention to the Van Dorn raid. He issued orders on December 12, placing all available cavalry under Van Dorn's command. Three days later the horsemen crossed the Yalobusha at Graysport east of Grenada, and on the evening of December 17 Van Dorn led his force of some 2,500 men northeast toward Pontotoc; none of the men, except Van Dorn and his brigade commanders, knew where they were going. The ride proved uneventful until the raiders got to Pontotoc, where they narrowly missed running headlong into Grant's cavalry returning from the Mobile & Ohio sortie. Fearing that they were outnumbered and that the Confederates were after them, the Yankees avoided a major confrontation. Skirmishing occurred, but Van Dorn continued on north, for he did not want to be distracted from his mission and alarm the Yankees. So a fight that neither side wanted did not happen.[12]

Van Dorn kept his column moving until the evening of the 18th, when he ordered a halt on the west bank of the Tallahatchie River at New Albany. He purposefully moved northeast to disguise his intent to attack Holly Springs, which was northwest of his position. The men spent a rainy, cold night and were back in the saddle early the next day. As the riders continued toward Ripley, they came to an old, barely passable road that forked to the left. Scouts told Van Dorn that the road led to Ripley; to give his column cover and rest he led them down the rugged passage. Later, after dusk, Van Dorn, worried about the condition of the road, ordered a countermarch and turned north to the main Ripley–Holly Springs road. Van Dorn did not plan this forth-and-back movement, but if any Union scouts were trying to track the Confederates, they surely must have been confused.

Around 10 p.m. the advance reached an area where yet another road paralleled the main road into Holly Springs. The men undoubtedly knew where they were going by now, and after the long ride they were ready to attack. Van Dorn divided his column, and his men rode silently until within about five miles of the town. Here they rested, confident that their presence was unknown to the enemy in Holly Springs. Van Dorn had sent spies on ahead to check out the Federal presence, and several people who lived along the way had thought the Confederates were Yankees and had warned them of rumors that Rebel cavalry were in the area. While they may have seethed at this blatant lack of loyalty to the Confederacy, Van Dorn's troopers said nothing to dispel the mistaken identity.

Confederate scouting reports indicated that the Yankees in Holly Springs were concentrated in three locations: the courthouse and other buildings in the center of town, near the railroad depot, and on fairgrounds just outside the city. Rather than risk a security breach and the scattering of his men, Van Dorn decided to attack en masse with his entire force. Once the column got into town, the troopers had orders to branch out and hit their assigned areas. The First Mississippi cavalry would hit the fairgrounds; Missouri cavalry would strike the depot; and the Texans would ride into enemy camps on the town square. Any prisoners would be turned over to the Twenty-seventh Texas, while the Sixth Texas and the Seventh Tennessee units were assigned to scout roads leading south and north, respectively.

While Van Dorn plotted his attack, he did not know that a misunderstanding of orders among Union cavalry aided the Confederate cause. Colonel Lyle Dickey, leader of the Union detachment that encountered Van Dorn's column in the Pontotoc area, sent two men on ahead to warn Grant. But the two became confused about the intent of their orders, and Dickey learned when he reached Grant's headquarters at Oxford on December 19 that his two messengers had never arrived. Shortly after Dickey's arrival, Grant received messages from scouts confirming a large enemy presence in his rear. The angry general immediately ordered cavalry to pursue the Rebels.

Grant did not know for certain where the Confederate cavalry was, and his messages expressed no great sense of urgency. He underestimated the size of Van Dorn's forces and how deeply they had penetrated the area behind Union lines. He had no idea that any actions he took could not save the Holly Springs garrison and supply depot from Van Dorn's attack. To compound Grant's frustrations, his cavalry commanders reacted very slowly, and his commander in Holly Springs, Colonel Robert Murphy of the Eighth Wisconsin infantry, reacted hardly at all, other than alerting Illinois cavalry to ride the next day in search of the Rebels. Grant approved Murphy's action, and the latter went to bed the night of the 19th blissfully unaware of the threat hovering outside the city.

At 5 a.m. on December 20 one of Murphy's soldiers took a black man to headquarters at one of Holly Spring's mansions. The man claimed to have seen Confederate cavalry near town. Murphy did not believe the story and in a huff ordered the man taken away. Then, having second thoughts, Murphy wired Grant that there was a report of a large force (5,000) of Rebel cavalry poised to strike Holly Springs. Murphy ordered trains readied for quick trips north and south to bring reinforcements and construction crews in case the Confederates were somewhere close and damaged track. Finally Murphy alerted the Second Illinois to send six companies to watch the railroad depot at dawn. After this flurry of activity, which Murphy likely instigated as a precaution to protect him from Grant's wrath, the sleepy commander, who still did not believe the gossip about the proximity of Rebel cavalry, returned to bed without putting his entire force on alert.

Shortly before sunrise on December 20, Van Dorn's column, four abreast, rode close to Holly Spring's town limits and paused until enemy pickets had been surprised and neutralized. Then the Confederate horsemen broke the morning silence and went thundering into the streets of Holly Springs. Van Dorn sat astride his horse by the road and waved his hat in response to cheers from his men. The combined noise of bugles, men's cheering voices, and horses' hooves fell on sleeping Union soldiers and Confederate civilians like a sudden storm. Men of the 101st Illinois infantry, the first Federal unit hit by the Rebel raiders, panicked, many simply running in the other direction to get away.

An Alabama reporter captured the chaos of these early moments of Van Dorn's attack: "Yankees running, tents burning, torches flaming, Confederates shouting, guns popping, sabers clanking, abolitionists begging for mercy, rebels shouting exultantly, women en dishabille clapping their hands, frantic with joy," all calling on Van Dorn's riders to kill the Yankees. This day would be long remembered by those who experienced it.

Amid the calamity, Union cavalry at the fairgrounds tried to make a stand, but most had to surrender to avoid being shot down. Others flung themselves on their horses and got away, some seventy of them making it to the safety of Union lines in Memphis. Infantry never offered any organized resistance, and individual Federal soldiers who did not successfully run away, or ride away if a stray horse could be found, soon surrendered. By 8 a.m. Van Dorn's men controlled all of Holly Springs and began carrying out their mission of mass destruction of Union supplies.

Van Dorn meanwhile ordered a guard placed at the Walter House, where he thought General Grant's wife, Julia, was staying. She was in Oxford at the time, visiting her husband. Van Dorn's intentions were good; he felt duty-bound to take care of his old friend's spouse. There is no evidence he personally checked to see if she was there. In Oxford, Grant worked to organize some kind of pursuit of the Rebel cavalry. In Holly Springs, Murphy became a prisoner while still wearing his nightclothes, according to Confederate accounts; according to his own report, he was captured while trying to escape from the railroad depot. Either way, Murphy's military career was over; Grant would soon fire him.

Holly Springs' brief liberation from Federal rule became a wild, destructive party, and Confederate conquerors and Union captives joined together to partake of liquor and other supplies strewn about the railroad depot and the downtown streets. Freed slaves and the town's white citizenry also participated in the impromptu party, and Van Dorn's officers had to struggle mightily to regain control of their men. Van Dorn offered paroles to the prisoners of war to avoid the burden of taking them along on the rest of his raid. Van Dorn knew that by now the alarm had been sounded all across north Mississippi, and he and his men could not dally too long or they might be trapped in Holly Springs.

Murphy agreed to the paroles, and the Rebels marched their 1,500 prisoners to the rail station and paroled them. Van Dorn's troops spent the rest of the morning and early afternoon systematically destroying everything beneficial to the Union army, as well as filling their own saddlebags with as much as they could carry. Fires set to destroy ammunition soon spread to various buildings, including the hospital. The Confederates did their best to control the blazes, but the estimated dollar damage ranged from $400,000 to $4,000,000. The bottom line was that Grant, thanks to Van Dorn and Forrest, had lost more than he could quickly replace.

Around 4 p.m. the raiders left Holly Springs and rode northeast. The fact that none of Grant's cavalry had shown up demonstrated the general's problems of getting a pursuit under way. At Davis Mill on December 21, Van Dorn's men attacked a Union garrison at the Wolf River railroad bridge, but the well-positioned Yankees beat the Confederates back. Van Dorn, knowing he did not have time to get bogged down in a fight, called off the attack. The raiders continued on a north/northeasterly course and then turned back south toward Mississippi.

At Middleton, Tennessee, Van Dorn tried again, unsuccessfully, to dislodge a Union garrison. After a brief exchange of fire, he ordered his men to stop firing and to mount up and ride for Ripley. Federal pursuers had finally shown up, and their pressure on Van Dorn's column intensified. Van Dorn left a detachment at Ripley to slow the Yankees and continued southwest, avoiding the road that led back to Holly Springs. The Ripley detachment skirmished briefly with Union cavalry, who were just far enough behind that Van Dorn led his column to the safety of Confederate lines at Grenada on December 28. Confederate casualties during the raid are uncertain, but it is certain that Van Dorn and his men had dealt a severe blow to Grant's north Mississippi campaign at a small price.

The Holly Springs debacle forced Grant to retreat north toward Tennessee. His unhappy troops wrought much destruction in Oxford before leaving, and vengeful Union soldiers ransacked Holly Springs, setting fires and, as one of them noted, changing the town "from one of the prettiest places I ever saw to a heap of ruins." Several Federals were arrested for destructive binges. The aftermath of Van Dorn's raid and Grant's retreat seemed to fuel increased partisan attacks on Grant's army, which in turn lashed back at the perpetrators. It was not a good time for north Mississippi civilians.

Sherman heard news of Van Dorn's success, but he did not give much credence to it because he assumed that, if indeed something had happened, his friend Grant would take care of it. Sherman should have made a greater effort to verify, or debunk, the news before he continued his operation against Vicksburg. He proceeded, however, with his campaign. Sherman would not receive official word of Grant's withdrawal from north Mississippi until after he had suffered a severe repulse himself.

His soldiers left Memphis on December 20, traveling by boat to Helena, Arkansas. There his force increased from 20,000 to 32,000 men, and this formidable army left Helena on December 22. While traveling down the Mississippi, Sherman's troops had to keep their heads down to avoid attacks by Rebel guerrillas from the riverbanks. Sherman retaliated by sending men ashore to burn areas where the shots came from. Civilians, as in Grant's campaign, paid a high price for guerrilla activities. On Christmas Day, Sherman sent a detachment to Milliken's Bend, Louisiana, to burn Rebel supplies and to tear up the Vicksburg, Shreveport, and Texas Railroad, which terminated at the Mississippi's western shore. It would be difficult to get troops in Louisiana to help Pemberton fight off the Union attack. Sherman had no way of knowing that Pemberton had seemingly insurmountable problems getting help from across the river, with or without the railroad. On the morning of December 26 Sherman's forces arrived at both the Johnson and Lake plantations on the Yazoo River north of Vicksburg. That evening a frigid, drenching rain fell.[13]

In Vicksburg, Confederate leaders, who had been kept informed by telegraph operators along the banks of the Mississippi north of the city, rushed to prepare a warm welcome for Sherman's cold army. General Pemberton and his immediate superior, Joseph E. Johnston, a Virginian, West Pointer, and former commander of the army in Virginia until receiving a severe wound, had been working with Richmond to add to the number of troops necessary to defend Vicksburg, but with a two-front campaign in progress, the size of the armies favored the Union. Now with Grant out of the picture, thanks to Van Dorn and Forrest, Pemberton could concentrate on Sherman.

Pemberton was entertaining President Jefferson Davis and General Johnston when he received the news of Sherman's foray down the Mississippi. Davis and Johnston hurried to Jackson, and the president, after stopping on December 26 to make a ninety-minute encouraging oration to the Mississippi legislature in Jackson, proceeded from there back to Richmond. Johnston also addressed the politicians and, according to a reporter from the *Vicksburg Whig*, promised to be "watchful, energetic and indefatigable" in defending Mississippi. His words proved to be meaningless.

Davis's action seemed symbolic. A key western theater confrontation was about to happen, but the president seemed more anxious about the Virginia front. If Pemberton felt snubbed, he did not show it. He immediately ordered troops at the Grenada front to Vicksburg. He and his staff would work tirelessly the next few days to get reinforcements in place to stop Sherman.

In Vicksburg, General Smith had received a telegram on Christmas Eve that a huge Union armada was coming down the Mississippi and turning into the Yazoo. The news interrupted a ball being held at the Balfour mansion in the city, attended by several Confederate officers, including Smith. Initially annoyed at the courier's interruption of the festivities, Smith changed his demeanor quickly when told that eighty-one Federal troop transports were closing in from north of the city. He ended the ball and rushed to his headquarters. On Christmas Day he ordered the Vicksburg defenders to get ready to fight, and he put General Stephen D. Lee in charge of the defenses along the Walnut Hills area that protected the northern approaches to Vicksburg. Sherman knew that Farragut had accomplished nothing along Vicksburg's riverfront, so he determined to attack overland, smash Confederate resistance, and march his army into the streets of the Mississippi River town.[14]

Smith's men had built impressive defensive works along the base of the bluffs in front of the so-called River Road, which ran from the hills along the Vicksburg side of the Yazoo all the way to Yazoo City. Another road followed the bluff line in the same direction. The roads gave Lee opportunities to shift his troops as needed to block Union assaults. The land between the baseline along the bluffs and the Yazoo has best been described as "a triangular belt of lowland, about five miles across at its base; its apex abutted against Snyder's Bluff. Except for cleared fields adjacent to the three plantations located in the area, this bottomland was densely wooded and intersected by a number of bayous and sloughs." In effect, the terrain Sherman's men would have to negotiate to get to the Walnut Hills bluffs provided many challenges.

High water usually flooded most of this triangle. Landmarks included the plantations of W. H. Johnson and Annie E. Lake, where Sherman's troops had first disembarked. The plantations lay west of Chickasaw Bayou, a stream "bisecting the triangular belt of land," which flowed northeast of the bluffs before turning north and emptying into the Yazoo. The bayou's source was McNutt Lake, a large body of water to the southwest of the Confederate Walnut Hills line. The lake provided a natural defensive barrier for Lee's left flank. The third plantation, Benson Blake's, was east and north of Thompson Lake, a considerable body of water that lay east of Chickasaw Bayou and emptied into the Yazoo. Northeast of Thompson Lake, Bliss Creek flowed out from among the bluffs and into the Yazoo a few miles below Snyder's Bluff. The small patch of ground, also somewhat triangular and bordered by the creek, Snyder's Bluff, and the Yazoo, contained two lakes named Cypress and Goose.

Stephen Lee, a South Carolinian and West Pointer who had already served with distinction in Virginia, must have felt great satisfaction when he looked out over this ground. If the Yankees attacked, they would have to deal with all these natural water barriers. Their advance would be slowed, and the Confederates should be able to shift and concentrate and successfully repulse whatever strategy Sherman tried. Normal tactical movements by the Yankees would be difficult at best.

Lee realized that only five avenues of approach were available to the enemy, and he ordered fortifications built up in each area and placed his troops accordingly. Looking at the triangle from southwest to northeast, Lee readied his defensive positions at a racetrack along the road from Johnson's plantation to Vicksburg; at an Indian mound where Chickasaw Bayou was very shallow; northeast of the mound where a road to the Lake plantation crossed Chickasaw Bayou on a corduroy bridge; close to the Blake home where a levee on the east side of Thompson Lake provided egress to the River Road; and at Snyder's Bluff. Snyder's Bluff had been fortified for some time, and the road from Johnson's had been blocked by abatis. Lee ordered defensive infantry trenches dug at the Indian mound and the bridge crossing of the bayou, and he ordered men to chop down trees to block the Thompson Lake levee.

Lee's initial deployments included the Thirty-first Louisiana, divided to cover the Indian mound and the bayou bridge. Companies D and E, First Mississippi Light Artillery, provided cover for the Louisianans and later

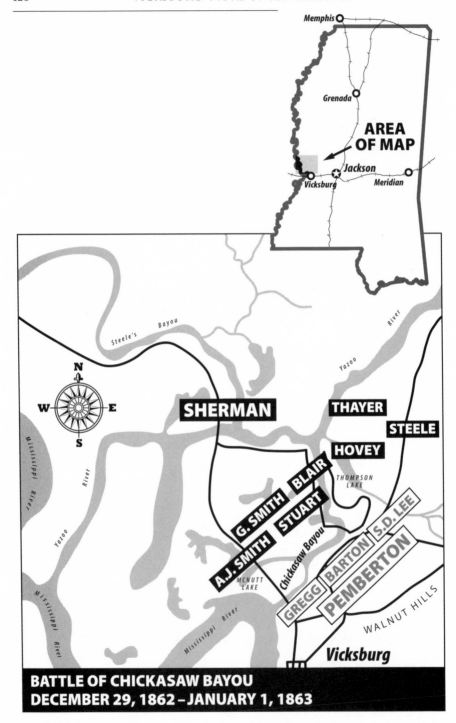

BATTLE OF CHICKASAW BAYOU
DECEMBER 29, 1862 – JANUARY 1, 1863

for the Seventeenth Louisiana and the Forty-sixth Mississippi. Two guns of Company D went with the Seventeenth and Forty-sixth on December 26 to block Sherman's troops taking the road from the Johnson to the Lake plantation.

Pemberton had just arrived at Smith's headquarters when he received news that the Yankees were off their boats and marching. He immediately fired off a message to Grenada that expressed the urgency of speedy transfer of troops to Vicksburg. He told General Dabney Maury to rush his division of 4,000 men to the Vicksburg front. Maury, a Virginian and West Pointer who had performed well at Pea Ridge, could not come all the way by train, for the transfer of General Carter Stevenson's division from Tennessee to Mississippi had tied up the railroad from Jackson to Vicksburg. Maury would have to detrain at Vaughan, north of Canton, and march his men over to the Yazoo, where river transports would carry them to Snyder's Bluff. Pemberton sent messages to his staff and to Johnston, who was still in Jackson, to do everything possible to facilitate the movement of troops from Jackson to Vicksburg.[15]

While the Confederates rushed to meet Sherman's threats, General George Morgan's Union Division assembled December 26 at Johnson's plantation and marched toward Annie Lake's plantation. There is no evidence that any occupants of the homes and plantations dotting the battlefield stayed on their property during military operations. They had likely been warned since they had gone into Vicksburg seeking safety. As if to underscore the danger to civilians, Union gunboats sent shells over the heads of Morgan's infantry, trying to encourage Rebels to fall back, giving Morgan a strong foothold from which to attack.

Stephen Lee and the man he placed in charge of defenses in the Chickasaw Bayou area, Colonel William Withers, rode out the morning of the 26th to inspect defenses when they were met by scouts who reported Morgan's landing. Withers immediately sent forward the Twenty-sixth Louisiana and a portion of the Forty-sixth Mississippi to set up skirmish lines in the woods along the bayou.

Colonel Withers had an ambush in mind; he did not believe he had enough men to stop Morgan, but he could delay him until reinforcements arrived. The ploy failed when an anxious Confederate fired too soon, and Federals in Morgan's advance deployed and moved toward Withers's small force. A gun from Company D, First Mississippi Light Artillery, hit the Union flank with canister charges. The fire gave Withers time to pull back his infantry and re-form, setting up a defensive line on either side of the road that crossed the Lake property. With darkness coming on, and being unsure of the size and nature of the enemy force in his front, the Union commander on the field, Colonel John De Courcy of Morgan's Third Brigade, pulled his troops back to the woods bordering an open field, where his and Morgan's other two brigades camped. During the evening, Frederick Steele's and Morgan Smith's divisions came ashore on the Johnson property and camped east and southwest, respectively, of Morgan's division. Withers meanwhile brought up the Seventeenth Louisiana to relieve the Twenty-sixth and no doubt waited anxiously for news of reinforcements arriving in Vicksburg. The fact that Withers now had three enemy divisions spread across his front demonstrated how desperately Lee needed reinforcements.[16]

Up to this point, Sherman felt satisfied. His men had gotten ashore with relative ease, and now he could plan his attack for the next day. Morgan's division would push forward, cross Chickasaw Bayou, and use the River Road to advance to Walnut Hills. Steele's division would advance and line up on Morgan's right and move toward the hills. Morgan Smith, an experienced prewar officer, would cross Chickasaw Bayou near Steele and set up a roadblock on the River Road. Andrew Jackson Smith received orders to march his First Division from Johnson's south to the racetrack. His men would have the doubly difficult task of breaking through Rebel abatis and drawing fire from Confederate cannons to divert shelling away from the rest of the Union advance. Later Sherman altered the plan slightly; part of Steele's division would take boats upstream to the mouth of Chickasaw Bayou, where they were to chase away Confederates and march down the east levee of the bayou.

On the morning of the 27th Sherman's army moved, but things did not go as well as the commanding general had hoped. Steele's men landed and cut their way through to the bayou levee, but detachments had to work with the navy to drive off Rebel sharpshooters. After this delay, Steele resumed his march, slowed occasionally by Confederate obstructions. Soon he learned that Sherman had sent his troops to the wrong place. The levee his men had worked so hard to clear was in fact the levee bordering Thompson Lake, not Chickasaw Bayou. Nevertheless, Steele pushed his men on, and skirmishing soon broke out between his advance troops and Confederates of the Twenty-sixth Louisiana plus guns of Company A, First Mississippi Light Artillery. As night fell Steele, still uncertain about enemy numbers and his proximity to the rest of the army, camped on the levee.

Distant to Steele's right, Morgan's division marched that morning with De Courcy in the lead. General Frank Blair, a Missourian from a prominent political family and assigned to Steele's division, advanced to cover

Morgan's right as Steele's division had initially been ordered to do. Thus Colonel Withers discovered that the Yankees were coming from two directions, Morgan from the north and Blair from the west. Withers sent the Seventeenth Louisiana and cannons from the First Mississippi Light Artillery to block Morgan. The Forty-sixth Mississippi and more cannons waited for Blair. Knowing that he did not have enough firepower to stop the two columns, Withers pulled his men back.

Meanwhile Morgan Smith's men came up behind Blair, and the two jointly probed Withers's position. Acting on reports of enemy concentration around the Indian mound, located on the other side of Chickasaw Bayou, Union commanders pushed the Fifty-fifth Illinois and Fifty-fourth Ohio regiments forward, while keeping up pressure on Withers. At the Indian mound, Charles Morrison, commanding the Thirty-first Louisiana, had his men dig trenches and construct abatis as the Yankees opened fire. The rest of the day the two sides skirmished. During the evening, gunners of the First Illinois Artillery, assisted by some of the 116th Illinois infantry, set up a battery close to the Confederate position.

De Courcy's advance bogged down due to Twenty-sixth Louisiana flanking fire. More Union troops came up, and by nightfall the Louisianans had to retreat, but they had fulfilled their mission of holding up the enemy advance. The Confederates had accomplished much with very little. One regiment, parts of two others, and one section of artillery, with geographic assistance, had kept Sherman from getting his army across Chickasaw Bayou. During the evening, reinforcements poured into Vicksburg, and Pemberton organized his defense. General John C. Vaughn and his Tennessee brigade took their position on the left, General Seth Barton and his Georgians were in the center, and Stephen Lee commanded a division of Louisianans and Mississippians on the right. Alabama native John Gregg and his brigade of Tennesseans were held in reserve, and Pemberton received word that two brigades from Dabney Maury's division at Grenada were on the way to Vicksburg. By dawn of the next day Pemberton heard more good news; Confederate guns on Drumgould's Bluff had beaten back Union gunboats attempting to knock out the Rebel battery.

On December 28 Union forces tried all day to break through the Confederate defenses along Chickasaw Bayou. Sherman realized that enemy works were more solid than expected; he did not know that Rebel reinforcements continued to arrive by train in Vicksburg and that others were already on battle lines to contest his army's offensive.

General Steele made some progress, but when his second and third brigades, commanded by Generals Charles Hovey and John Thayer, respectively, massed between Blake's Levee and Thompson Lake to charge, Confederate guns of Company A, First Mississippi Light Artillery, plus the firepower of the Forty-sixth Mississippi infantry, inflicted numerous casualties on the tightly packed Union position. Hovey rushed to Steele's headquarters and reported the situation. Steele broke off the attack, and Sherman ordered the men to reboard river transports to bring them back to Johnson's, where they could support Morgan.

Morgan started the day by sending his artillery to pound a passage at the junction of the road from Annie Lake's plantation and the River Road. Strong Confederate positions there had to be knocked out before Morgan's infantry could break through. By 10 a.m. De Courcy thought Confederate fire had been reduced enough for Morgan to assault. The Union advance forced the Twenty-ninth Louisiana to give up its forward line and retreat, ultimately back across Chickasaw Bayou. By then it was 12:30, and Colonel Allen Thomas was satisfied that his heavily outnumbered troops had held up the Yankees for such a long time.

Indianans and Ohioans cautiously crossed the bayou and with strong support advanced. A vicious artillery duel ensued between the First Mississippi Light Artillery and gunners from Michigan and Wisconsin. The Mississippians, outnumbered two to one in firepower, ultimately had to retreat, but De Courcy's caution left the Confederate position in good shape. On the Confederate right of the crossroads area, the Twenty-sixth Louisiana fought well, holding up the Forty-ninth Indiana and 120th Ohio before retiring.

Frank Blair's brigade had an active day, moving first around De Courcy's right and trying to break across the bayou through the Forty-second Georgia defenders. The Georgians did not budge, and later Blair received orders to come to De Courcy's aid, but soon Blair's men received friendly artillery fire. Ordered to retire, Blair later was sent to cross the bayou behind Union lines and support the attack against the Twenty-sixth Louisiana, but the day ended before he could get his troops in position. Blair's experience symbolized the day's frustration for Sherman's troops.

On the Union right, Morgan Smith's division made headway at the Indian mound, but like their comrades elsewhere could not break through. Along the Confederate line, the Fortieth Georgia and the Sixty-second Tennessee arrived to reinforce the Thirty-first Louisiana. The Sixty-second Tennessee shifted to reinforce General Lee's sector, so the Third Tennessee helped hold the line. Guns of the First Illinois Light Artillery pounded the Confederate position most of the day. The Illinoisans drove off two guns of the First Mississippi Light Artillery, but four guns of the Fourteenth

Mississippi Light Artillery arrived and effectively dueled the Yankee artillery. Union attempts to breach the crossing at the Indian mound failed because Rebel rifles consistently cut down Union fatigue parties attempting to remove obstructions. On the far right of the Union position, Kentuckian Stephen Burbridge and his brigade of A. J. Smith's division (finally on the scene after much delay) built rafts to try crossing McNutt Lake to turn the Rebel left, but their efforts failed.

A day of much jockeying and bitter fighting ended with Confederate advance positions keeping Sherman's men from the base of Walnut Hills. Union gunboats played a supporting role, maintaining a threatening presence near Drumgould's Bluff to keep Pemberton from shifting troops from there to the fighting along Chickasaw Bayou. Sherman spent the evening of the 28th deciding what to do next, while Pemberton looked to the disposition of troops, leaving defensive plans to his commanders in the field.[17]

As December 29 dawned, Sherman still hoped for decisive results. He issued orders calling for a breakthrough at the center of the Confederate lines, occupation of Walnut Hills, and then either a direct attack on Vicksburg or a sweep up the Yazoo to knock out Rebel batteries at Drumgould's and Snyder's bluffs. Specifically, Morgan was to push across the bayou near the junction of the River Road and the road to Annie Lake's; Steele's entire division would provide support. On the right, A. J. Smith led his and Morgan Smith's divisions across the bayou at the Indian mound (Morgan Smith had been wounded on the 28th).

George Morgan hoped to catch the enemy by surprise the morning of the 29th. He had scouted his front the night of the 28th and thought of sending a detachment of engineers to bridge Chickasaw Bayou where Confederate presence seemed minimal. Sherman approved, but when morning came Morgan found his engineers lacked the necessary equipment. The bridging could be accomplished, but cutting trees meant that the completion of the task would take a couple of hours. Once trees began to fall, Confederate artillery and infantry took notice. Stephen Lee rushed the Twenty-ninth Louisiana and the Forty-second Georgia to the scene. Lee also sent word for the Fourth Mississippi to reinforce the troops contesting the crossing. Whatever surprise Morgan had hoped for was gone.

Meanwhile Frank Blair received an order from Morgan to push toward Morgan's left. Blair found the Confederates had retreated from their positions of the 28th, but the terrain in front, both naturally and thanks to Rebel obstructions, provided a considerable challenge. Blair did not know that Lee had pulled his troops back in the hope that Yankees would follow. Lee's men waited quietly in ambush, allowing the bluecoats to get close.

Firing between Morgan's and Lee's artilleries increased as the minutes ticked by. The Confederates lost a caisson when shells from the First Wisconsin Light Artillery blew it up. The increased intensity of shelling and rifle fire convinced Morgan that Lee had massed too many men for Morgan to follow through on an earlier boast that his men would soon reach the crest of Walnut Hills. He shared his feelings with Sherman, who by now had lost his patience with the stalemate. Sherman pointed to the hills and made clear to Morgan that he expected them to be taken. Sherman later sent one of his staff members to Morgan with a message: "Tell Morgan to give the signal for the assault; that we will lose 5,000 men before we take Vicksburg, and may as well lose them here as anywhere else." Accordingly, Morgan sent word to De Courcy and to Blair to charge. De Courcy protested but promised to obey.

Morgan quickly planned the assault. Blair, Thayer, and De Courcy would send their brigades forward to make a frontal attack. Morgan's First and Second brigades, commanded respectively by Colonel Lionel Sheldon and Colonel Daniel Lindsey, had to flank Lee's position, getting between Lee and Barton's Georgians, thus blocking Lee's nearest reinforcements. General Pemberton, aware that such an attack might be coming at Lee's front, sent Lee the Seventeenth and Twenty-sixth Louisiana and a cannon from the First Mississippi Light Artillery. Around noon Federal artillery signaled the attack to begin, before Morgan's bridge had been completed. Morgan decided that Sherman's orders did not allow time for the engineers to finish their work.

Blair advanced on the left, and his men moved remarkably across rugged ground, obstructions, and a storm of musketry and artillery fire. They overran Lee's forward positions, and Blair's men encountered the main Confederate line held by three Tennessee regiments, the Third, Thirtieth, and Sixty-second. Over to his right, Blair could see that De Courcy's men were having success against advanced Rebel positions, but the well-entrenched main Confederate line proved too strong. First Blair and then De Courcy admitted defeat. The field became covered with smoke, and the flying lead and cannon shot proved too much for some Union soldiers, who sought shelter rather than attack. As lack of support left the Fourth Iowa isolated, the regiment suffered heavy losses before Thayer pulled them back.

Stephen Lee observed his soldiers' success and decided on a counteroffensive. Many Union soldiers other than the Fourth Iowa had been left behind during the retreat, and Lee sent the Seventeenth and Twenty-sixth Louisiana forward. The Louisianans took some 300 prisoners and captured

around 500 rifles. Eighty Union wounded were taken and sent to Vicksburg hospitals. The repulse of Blair and De Courcy forced Morgan to recall
Lindsey's and Sheldon's brigades. Morgan refused his officers' requests to
resume assaults after the men had time to rest and re-form. He asked Sherman to issue orders for a flag of truce to allow retrieval of the dead and
wounded. Sherman refused at first, changed his mind, and darkness came
on, making it impossible for a white flag of truce to be seen. The Union
truce party had to retreat after being shot at by Lee's men. Thus the fighting
along the River Road ended.

On the Union right, the day began with A. J. Smith ordering Giles Smith
to get his brigade across the bayou and storm the heights near the Indian
mound. To prepare, Giles Smith sent out skirmishers and work parties. A
company from the Sixth Missouri would cross the bayou and assist a work
party to cut a pathway up the opposite bank. When they finished, the rest
of the Sixth, followed by the Eighth Missouri, 116th Illinois, and a company
of the First Illinois Light Artillery, would advance. On Smith's right, Stephen Burbridge's brigade continued to operate around McNutt Lake, trying
to get a bridgehead across the bayou. William Landrum's brigade moved
down the Vicksburg road toward Confederate works at the racetrack.

On the Confederate side, Seth Barton had the Sixty-first Tennessee,
supported by the Sixtieth, in position to meet Landrum. The Thirty-first
Louisiana and Fifty-second Georgia waited opposite Giles Smith while the
Fortieth Georgia watched Burbridge. The Confederates waited and then
heard Morgan's guns to the north signal the enemy attack.

Giles Smith also heard the guns. Smith's advance rushed forward, forded
the bayou, and saw they could not cut a path there as planned. The engineers began mining operations, and Smith sent the advance company, the
Sixth Missouri, to the spot where they crossed the bayou. Here they waited
under the cover of the high bank while the engineers worked.

Meanwhile patrols of Union Missourians tested Confederate works held
by the Thirty-first Louisiana. The Louisianans did not budge, prevailing
against five different Union patrols that tried to break the line. Though the
Confederates held, Rebel commanders remained concerned, and the Fifty-
second Georgia took position on the left of the Louisianans. The action at
the Indian mound grew hotter.

On the Confederate right, part of Thayer's brigade formed in Morgan's
rear. Skirmishers from the Thirtieth Iowa moved forward to where the
Thirteenth U.S. Infantry was exchanging fire with Confederates across the
bayou. Thayer's men supported the Thirteenth until recalled to the Lake

house. Charles Hovey's brigade came up in the late afternoon and moved to where Blair had formed for his earlier attack. Hovey prepared his soldiers for a charge, but Sherman decided to end action for the day in this sector.

Back at the Indian mound, Giles Smith had concluded that he was not going to break through the enemy works, but he had to find a way to extract the Sixth Missouri without the regiment being decimated. Darkness, the Eighth Missouri, the Thirteenth U.S. Infantry, and the Fifty-fourth Ohio provided enough cover for the Missourians to escape. Smith had chosen wisely; by nightfall the Sixtieth Tennessee arrived to further strengthen the Confederate hold on the Indian mound area.

During the evening, Sherman pondered his army's failure and his next move. In response to an inquiry by Joseph Johnston, Pemberton wired Jackson that all available men should be sent at once to Vicksburg, including Carter Stevenson's division, which just arrived by rail from Braxton Bragg's army in Tennessee. Stevenson and advance elements of Edward Tracy's brigade of Alabamians reached Vicksburg in cold, rainy weather. During the night, Sherman ordered retrieval of the pontoons, and Confederate cannoneers, hearing the noise, lobbed shells at the Yankees. The action convinced the Confederate high command that Union attacks would resume the next morning, but their assumption proved inaccurate.

During the day, David Porter's gunboats continued throwing shells into Confederate lines, especially in the Drumgould's Bluff area. Porter's guns made plenty of noise but produced little results. Sherman contacted Porter late in the day and urged that a boat be rushed to Memphis to secure small-arms ammunition. Soon the *Rattler* steamed upriver into the night.[18]

On December 30 Sherman decided to refocus. Instead of continuing the hopeless hammering of Confederate defenses along Chickasaw Bayou, he determined to knock out Rebel positions on the Yazoo bluffs. Success would give him a path to reestablish communications with Grant; obviously Sherman still planned his moves based on the assumption that Grant was nearing Jackson and would soon arrive at Vicksburg. Sherman should have wondered how Grant could be coming from Jackson when Confederate reinforcements had reached Vicksburg by rail from the capital city. Yet Sherman refused to admit defeat. He figured that if he could get past the Confederate right, he could divert Confederate attention from bayou lines and allow Union successes there.

While Sherman wrestled with his options, skirmishing broke out at several points along the bayou, and Pemberton continued to receive reinforcements. Dabney Maury's division arrived late in the afternoon of the 30th. Still, Pemberton did not feel comfortable. For all he knew, Union reinforcements might be headed downriver to join Sherman. Grant's retreat had given Pemberton some flexibility, however, and he felt comfortable enough about the security of the Grenada front to order Louisianan Louis Hébert and his brigade to Snyder's Bluff via the Yazoo River.

Unaware of Pemberton's shuffling of troops, Sherman proceeded to write orders for an assault on Snyder's Bluff. Steele's division and Giles Smith's brigade would transfer upriver on Porter's boats, disembark, and attack. Porter endorsed a proposal by Charles Ellett to attach a large rakelike apparatus to the lead boat to clear any torpedoes in the river, like the one that sank the *Cairo*. Ellett also led an effort to blow up a Confederate raft obstruction near Snyder's Bluff.

The plan might have worked; certainly the Confederates had no idea what the Yankees were up to. However, nature intervened on the side of the Rebels. The night of December 31, a thick fog covered the area, and Porter decided that his boats could not negotiate the Yazoo in such conditions. The attack had to be postponed. Porter told Sherman that landing troops had to be done in the daytime, which would cost the essential element of surprise.

A frustrated General Sherman finally accepted that the campaign was over. Not only had the weather turned against him, frequent sounds of trains pulling into Vicksburg convinced him that more Rebel reinforcements had arrived. Furthermore, if the waters suddenly rose, as could easily happen in winter, his men might be stranded along their bayou lines. The final nail was a December 23 message from Grant that finally reached Sherman's headquarters, detailing Grant's retreat. Sherman understood now, and should have already guessed, how Pemberton had been able to bring in more men. On New Year's Day, 1863, the Union army began withdrawing from the Yazoo.

Stephen Lee, fearful when he first received word of a Federal buildup at Snyder's, breathed a sigh of relief when he saw the enemy leaving. He organized a pursuit force of Tennesseans and Texans, while Colonel Withers led Alabama, Louisiana, and Mississippi troops after the bluecoats. The two columns converged, but they were too late to block the retreat. Skirmishing broke out with Union troops covering the withdrawal, but the Confederates did not have enough firepower to counter Porter's naval artillery. By early afternoon, January 2, Sherman's army was on the way back to Milliken's Bend. He had lost 1,776 killed, wounded, and missing. Pemberton troops had suffered only 187 casualties. Sherman had 208 killed, Pemberton 57. A comparison of wounded was even more striking; Sherman had 1,005 fall, while Pemberton counted only 120.[19]

The grand scheme concocted by Grant and Sherman had failed miserably. Perhaps both deserve criticism for trying to hurry up the campaign in order to have Vicksburg in hand before John McClernand arrived. In doing so, they failed to grasp the risks that lengthy supply lines, geography, and weather conditions could impose on an army. Geography had especially worked against Sherman as he vainly tried to coordinate the movements of his army in the Chickasaw Bayou swamp. Had they continued to hammer away in north Mississippi, Grant and Sherman may well have reached Jackson, turned west, and besieged Vicksburg before the end of December. In trying an end run, Grant rushed things and lost the campaign. He did not despair, however. He still had his eyes on Vicksburg. While Confederates celebrated a hard-earned victory, their merriment would have been tempered had they understood just how tenacious this rumpled general could be.

Grant reminded his subordinates that the capture of Vicksburg remained their goal, and they were not to let up until that goal was accomplished. He emphasized that point to John McClernand, who by now had arrived on the scene. McClernand took command of Sherman's force and led an amphibious campaign up the Arkansas River that resulted in the capture of Arkansas Post and Fort Hindman on January 11, 1863. The Union victory meant that the Confederates had lost a base of operations connecting southern and central Arkansas to the Mississippi. Not impressed, Grant termed McClernand's campaign a "wild-goose chase" and ordered the politician-general to withdraw to the Mississippi for further operations against Vicksburg. He changed his tune when he learned that Sherman had supported McClernand's foray.

Grant received official Washington's blessing to take command of all operations around Vicksburg, and he made sure that McClernand got the message. Grant then turned his attention to what became a series of failed efforts aimed at finding a feasible way to take the city.[20]

Grant tried bypassing the seemingly impregnable defenses north of Vicksburg and the fortified bluffs along the town's riverfront. Sherman had failed against the former, and Farragut and Davis had experienced the strength of the latter. Initially Grant turned his attention to the old canal project begun by Thomas Williams's men during the Farragut campaign. He liked the concept and hoped that success would give the navy an opportunity to help the army gain a foothold south of Vicksburg.

So work began, but high water and engineering problems ensured slow progress. Yet Grant did manage to force a dilution of Pemberton's forces. To ensure that the Federals did not catch him unawares, Pemberton scattered his men "over a 17-mile front, extending from Snyder's Bluff on the Yazoo to Warrenton." Aware of the problems he had handed the enemy, Grant examined more options. By late March he gave up on the canal; the erratic Mississippi provided too many setbacks, and Pemberton's artillery made work on the ditch dangerous.

Other failures compounded Grant's frustration. On the west side of the Mississippi, some seventy-five river miles north of Vicksburg, lay Lake Providence, a crescent-shaped body of water that could link the Mississippi via Louisiana bayous and rivers to the mouth of the Red River, miles south of Vicksburg. If successful, Grant's army and Porter's navy could get safely past Vicksburg and increase options for approaching the hill city out of the range of Pemberton's guns. Grant's engineers cut levees and created immense flooding, thus making it difficult to secure safe channels for the passage of Porter's boats. The project dragged on, and Grant eventually gave up on it in favor of a new strategy to bypass Vicksburg.

In the back of his mind, he considered moving his army down the Louisiana side of the Mississippi and using Porter's boats to ferry his men across to the Mississippi side, well below Vicksburg. And though it took him a while to embrace the idea as workable, the Lake Providence project produced a future benefit for the operation Grant had in mind. Massive flooding provided a water barrier that would protect Union troops marching south along the Mississippi's west bank.[21]

Before any of that happened, Grant tried other ideas. An ambitious Federal project took place well north of Vicksburg. Just south of Helena, Arkansas, on the Mississippi side of the river, flowed a waterway called Yazoo Pass. The pass emptied into the Coldwater, which flowed into the Tallahatchie. The Tallahatchie flowed through the Mississippi Delta region to the town of Greenwood, where it joined with the Yalobusha to create the Yazoo. A successful ascent via this route by Union forces would outflank Pemberton's position on the Snyder's Bluff heights overlooking the Yazoo northeast of Vicksburg.

To access the pass, Union engineers had to blow up a levee that protected area farmland in the north Delta from Mississippi River floods. Once Federal vessels entered the pass, they could maneuver across wide Moon Lake and enter a small channel that led to the Coldwater. Confederate naval commanders understood the potential the pass offered for enemy penetration deep into the Delta, but not until the threat materialized did Rebel fatigue parties rush to fell trees to obstruct the channels.

Grant thought the Yazoo Pass gambit worth the effort, and he told his engineers to investigate. The engineers liked what they saw, and on February

3 loud explosions sent high waters from the Mississippi roaring into the pass. The waters washed out a wide gap, and pro-Union planter and future Mississippi governor James Lusk Alcorn informed Grant's chief engineer that the navy should have few problems getting down to the Yazoo. Grant quickly put together an amphibious force to take advantage of a seemingly golden opportunity.

The water roaring down rivers that led south into the heart of prime Mississippi farmland caused much damage. Slaves had to build levees to keep the water away from animals and farmland vulnerable to erosion, but it was a losing battle. Farmers moved everything of value they could to high ground, while watching their homes flood and many animals drown. By the time the water receded, the landscape was littered with ruined homes, dead animals, and fences scattered everywhere or simply gone, and the Delta black gumbo mud seemed to cover everything. Illness struck many farm families trying to salvage their livelihood.

Union operations continued, and David Dixon Porter sent instructions to one of his commanders, Watson Smith, to command a squadron that included seven vessels: *Rattler, Romeo, Forest Rose, Signal, Cricket, Linden*, and the ironclad *Chillicothe*. Later the ironclad *Baron de Kalb* and the tinclad *Marmora* joined Smith's fleet. The *Cricket* and the *Linden* did not arrive in time for the expedition. Accompanying the naval detachment would be 600 infantry Sherman assigned to the operation. Smith's mission was to get to the Tallahatchie, then to the Yazoo, then to the Big Sunflower. Smith must damage all things beneficial to the Confederacy and get as much information as possible about Rebel ironclads on the Yazoo. The possibility of another *Arkansas* worried Porter.

Natural barriers of large tree limbs hung over waterways, and driftwood, plus obstructions caused by Confederate axes, also worked to hold up the Union flotilla. By February 21 the last obstructions between the Mississippi and the Coldwater had been removed. Grant watched and waited. He turned down a request from McClernand to take 21,000 men and make another incursion into Arkansas. Grant would not be deterred; he needed all the men at his disposal to clear the Mississippi. Grant built up the Yazoo expedition, which now included two divisions. The Union force also included thirty pieces of field artillery and nearly four regiments of cavalry. Other boats, including two rams, *Dick Fulton* and *Lioness*, joined Smith's squadron. Numerous troop transports further clogged the waterways. Grant modified his plan to include an assault on Grenada via the Yalobusha. Afterward, the amphibious force would return to Greenwood and descend the Yazoo.

Delays in getting troops to the pass, keeping channels clear, and engine problems among the vessels held up the long column's entrance into the Coldwater until February 28. The actual ascent down the Coldwater toward the Tallahatchie did not commence until March 3. The head of the column reached the latter on the evening of the 5th. Curious slaves lined the banks, and smoke from burning cotton filled the nostrils of Federal soldiers and seamen. Landing parties managed to retrieve much cotton before planters had time to set their bales ablaze. The bluecoats also scavenged planter property for food, throwing scares into white plantation mistresses. Federal officers issued death threats to those who attacked civilians and their property. The trip downriver proved to be a slow one, due mainly to the cautious naval commander Smith. Not until March 11 would the Union force be positioned to attack Confederates awaiting in a stronghold at Greenwood called Fort Pemberton.

Commander Isaac Brown, of the ill-fated *Arkansas*, had been keeping an eye on Union activity at Yazoo Pass and sent word to Pemberton about the blown levee. Pemberton got the message on February 9 and responded to Brown's request for heavy artillery with the news that no such guns were available. Anyway, Pemberton did not think a Union threat from that area very feasible. He soon changed his mind when messages about enemy activity continued to pour into Jackson. The Yankees were trying to get to the Coldwater, and one look at a map told the rest. Grant was trying to outflank Pemberton's line on the Yazoo. Brown rushed to get two steamboats, *Mary Keene* and *Star of the West*, ready for combat. Pemberton hurried infantry to Yazoo City, where William Loring arrived to take command of Confederate forces gathering at Fort Pemberton.

Pemberton and his staff worked frantically to get additional reinforcements to Greenwood. Two heavy artillery pieces, suddenly available, were sent up the Yazoo from Vicksburg, and Thomas Waul's hard-fighting Texas Legion stood by at Yazoo City. In Jackson, Lloyd Tilghman, an old friend of Pemberton's, reported with his brigade to Loring. News about enemy activity to the north continued coming to Pemberton's headquarters—some positive, some negative—but there could be no doubt that the threat he had earlier shrugged off was very real.

When Loring arrived in Greenwood, he toured a site selected by Brown and others for a defensive position. Preliminary construction work had already begun, and Loring approved. The place lay "two and one-half miles by land and about four by water west of and upstream from Greenwood." Loring had the option of making a stand at Greenwood or Yazoo City; he decided to fight at the former. Even if the Federal fleet should drive him off, Loring could slow down the enemy advance, thus giving Pemberton more time to transfer men and guns to the Yazoo front. Loring placed his big guns on the high south bank of the Tallahatchie; from there the guns could be depressed enough to hit Federal boats. Also, at the fortress site, the Tallahatchie and the Yazoo flowed some 500 yards apart, a distance easily covered by the guns. Waul's Texans came up and occupied trenches dug across the peninsula.

Loring wired Pemberton that construction of rafts to block the river would begin at once. If they were not completed in time, Loring suggested sinking the captured Union vessel *Star of the West* in the Tallahatchie. This was the same boat that had carried out Abraham Lincoln's attempt to resupply Fort Sumter just before the war began. Loring further ordered steamboats protected by cotton bales to do battle with the Union navy if necessary. To stay in better touch with Pemberton, Loring set up a line of couriers to ride between the Mississippi Central, from a point north of Jackson, and Greenwood.

While his men worked and waited, Loring took a patrol up the Tallahatchie to look for enemy signs. Waul, who studied law in Vicksburg before moving on to a political career in Texas, supervised construction of Fort Pemberton and bombarded General Pemberton's headquarters with pleas for more artillery. Loring heard enough reports and rumors on his reconnaissance that, when he returned, he called in all reserves within supporting distance, including detachments from Tilghman's brigade and infantry at Grenada.

Waul and Loring understood the danger of losing Fort Pemberton; if it fell, Union troops and vessels could block the river network north of Vicksburg, which provided much-needed supplies to the city's defenders. Still Pemberton refused Loring's request to continue weakening the Grenada front; Loring should instead call in more of Tilghman's troops from Yazoo City. Pemberton pointedly wired Loring that he thought Loring had as many troops as he could manage in the Greenwood area. The message indicated the continuing hard feelings developing between Loring and Pemberton, and soon Tilghman, influenced by Loring and an incident in which Pemberton unjustly accused Tilghman of disobeying orders, joined the anti-Pemberton clique. Pemberton had admitted his error in the Tilghman case, but Tilghman never forgot or forgave.

Reports of continuing enemy progress kept arriving in Greenwood, and Loring passed them along. Pemberton's superior, Joseph E. Johnston, got wind of the Yazoo Pass expedition and wired Pemberton for confirmation. Pemberton, who, as usual, saw no need in keeping Johnston informed, confirmed the Federal campaign, but he assured Johnston that the Green-wood position was solid and would hold. He did not think, he wrote, that the enemy could "effect anything very serious." Inexplicably, Pemberton also neglected to inform the War Department in Richmond of the Union invasion. Loring thought the situation very serious and hurried his soldier and slave laborers in the construction of defenses. He wired Pemberton on March 6 to rush more guns; reports indicated that the Federals had trav-eled fifteen miles down the Coldwater.

Brown led a reconnaissance upriver with two boats and had to abandon and burn one when it ran aground. He and his men gathered cotton for the cotton-clad project and left the burning boat and headed downstream just as the Union advance came into view some seventy miles north of Fort Pemberton. Pemberton meanwhile sent a drily worded telegram to Richmond, informing the War Department that Federals had entered the Tallahatchie.

The fort meanwhile had been completed and was ready. Defenses of dirt and cotton protected the garrison, and the flanks rested on the Tallahatchie and the Yazoo. Loring had seven mounted guns and infantry that included Waul's Legion, the Second Texas, and the Twentieth Mississippi. A partly completed raft and the now sunken *Star of the West* obstructed the Talla-hatchie channel.

The Confederates spotted the Union ironclad *Chillicothe* on March 11, several hundred yards upriver. The fort's big guns spoke, and two shots hit the enemy vessel, which backed up to the cover of a bend in the Tal-lahatchie and began returning fire. This first exchange inaugurated Federal efforts that would last until April 5. In the afternoon of the 11th another exchange resulted in considerable damage to the ironclad and resulted in four Union sailors killed and nine wounded. Union commanders ordered batteries set up along the banks of the river to try and neutralize the Rebel big guns. On the 13th more fire was exchanged between the fort and the *Chillicothe*, joined by the *Baron de Kalb*. Both sides had successes, but the fighting was generally a draw. The Confederates could afford a stalemate, but the Union vessels could not stay indefinitely due mainly to potential supply shortages.[22]

A diversion arose south of Greenwood when a Union fleet commanded by David Dixon Porter entered the Yazoo from the Mississippi and turned north into Steele's Bayou. Porter hoped to use a waterway network to by-pass Confederate big guns on the Yazoo bluffs by getting to Black Bayou, then to Deer Creek, north to the Rolling Fork, across to the Big Sunflower, and down that stream to the Yazoo. If Porter could get to the Yazoo, he

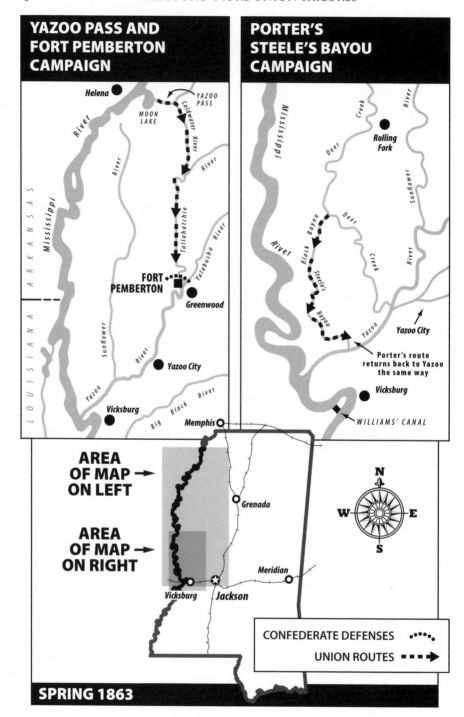

YAZOO PASS AND FORT PEMBERTON CAMPAIGN

Helena

MOON LAKE

YAZOO PASS

Coldwater River

River

River

Tallahatchie

Yalobusha River

FORT PEMBERTON

Greenwood

Sunflower River

Yazoo City

Yazoo

Vicksburg

Big Black River

Mississippi River

ARKANSAS

LOUISIANA

PORTER'S STEELE'S BAYOU CAMPAIGN

Mississippi

Creek

River

Rolling Fork

Deer

Sunflower

Deer

Black Bayou

River

Creek

River

Steele's

Bayou

Yazoo

Yazoo City

Porter's route returns back to Yazoo the same way

Vicksburg

WILLIAMS' CANAL

Memphis

AREA OF MAP → ON LEFT

AREA OF MAP → ON RIGHT

Grenada

Meridian

Vicksburg   Jackson

N
W   E
S

CONFEDERATE DEFENSES •••••

UNION ROUTES ■ ■ ■ ➤

SPRING 1863

would be between Rebel batteries and Fort Pemberton and have the option of attacking either or both.

The expedition began on March 13. Porter encountered major difficulties, from narrow streams that restricted maneuverability, to low hanging branches, to Confederates trying to fell trees both to Porter's front and in his rear, to enemy infantry and artillery setting up blockades. Finally he had to give up and have William T. Sherman's infantry help beat off the Confederates while the flotilla escaped back to the Mississippi. The campaign lasted eleven days, and the slow-reacting Confederates blew a golden opportunity to capture Union boats and use them against the Federals.[23]

In Fort Pemberton, Confederate morale soared on March 15 with the arrival of a big eight-inch naval gun. The stalemate continued, with both sides standing firm, though the *Chillicothe* suffered additional damage. Loring called up more troops when he heard that Union forces under General Isaac Quinby were headed downriver. Loring ordered defenses built up behind Fort Pemberton, a site called Fort Loring, along the Yazoo in case the enemy got past Pemberton. Loring sent word upriver to guerrilla bands to take whatever steps possible to slow Quinby.

Federal thinking, meanwhile, turned to additional levee cutting on the Mississippi, with the intent to raise water levels at Greenwood and force the Rebels to abandon Fort Pemberton. The ploy did not work; nothing seemed to be going right for the Union cause. Watson Smith became too ill to continue, and the rest of the officers present held a council of war and voted to give up the fight and return to Helena. An infantry officer, Leonard Ross, wanted to wait for Quinby. Scouts convinced Ross that approaches to the fort would be impossible. Adding to Ross's fears was news that the Confederates might be preparing a blockade of the Coldwater, which would sever the Union supply line. Ross changed his mind about withdrawing, and Confederate defenders awoke on March 22 to discover that the enemy had fled. The fight, however, was not over just yet.

Isaac Quinby encountered all sorts of delays in his efforts to reach Fort Pemberton. McPherson notified Grant and forecast another two weeks before the entire Seventeenth Corps could support the Yazoo Pass campaign. Grant responded that he wanted Quinby to get going, even if that meant leaving part of his division behind. Grant seemed to sense that the promise of the pass operation was fading fast. Grant also canceled support for Quinby when he ordered John Logan's brigade to Steele's Bayou south of Greenville, Mississippi. Grant hoped an amphibious operation up the bayou might cut Rebel supply lines from Greenwood to Vicksburg and force the abandonment of Fort Pemberton. Complicating Grant's efforts were reminders from Washington that William Rosecrans's army in Tennessee also needed transports.

Quinby did not know that his support had been canceled. With one brigade he entered the Coldwater on March 18 and ordered the transports to head toward Pemberton. Quinby met Ross and James Foster and agreed with Foster that the Union force should return to Greenwood. The Federal fleet arrived on March 23, and sporadic firing broke out.

The Confederates had been working hard since the enemy's departure. Fortifications had been strengthened, and reinforcements, both of men and weaponry, were en route. General Pemberton had toyed with weakening the fort to shore up defenses at Yazoo City and along the Yazoo north of Vicksburg. The news of Quinby's approach caused the uncertain Confederate general to change his mind. When he learned that Porter's Steele Bayou gambit had failed, Pemberton sent more men to reinforce Loring. Soon Loring had some 7,000 men on hand, many more than Quinby.

Numbers eventually became a moot point. Porter's failed campaign convinced Grant to concentrate his entire army at Milliken's Bend. Quinby received word to break off operations at Fort Pemberton and return to the Mississippi. Before he got the news, Quinby decided to try a two-pronged approach to the fort; he would send troops across the Tallahatchie and hit Loring from the rear while another column went south and tried to sever the fort's supply line. But Federal naval officers threatened to take their boats back to the Mississippi to avoid being trapped, and Confederate works blocked the planned attack on Loring's rear. Quinby finally received Grant's orders, and his soldiers boarded transports on the night and early morning of April 4–5. The Confederates had persevered, and they showed little enthusiasm for pursuit. Loring had not been aggressive, for he left the Union's long, dangling supply line stretching back to the Mississippi unbroken. As in the case of Porter's Steele's Bayou venture, the Confederates had blown an opportunity to cut off and capture Union gunboats. Confederate commanders' mind-set, from Pemberton on down, was focused on defense, not countermeasures.[24]

Undeterred, Grant pushed on with the plan he had been thinking about. He prepared to march his army down the Louisiana side of the Mississippi, transport it across to Mississippi below Vicksburg, and go from there. He experienced yet another failure in the process. To facilitate a staging area near New Carthage, Louisiana, Grant ordered a canal dug to connect the Mississippi with Walnut Bayou. A sudden drop in the Mississippi's water level killed the project, called the Duckport Canal, but Grant's ultimate goal would soon be realized. Eventually his army would cross the river, though much fighting awaited before he reached Vicksburg.[25]

6

VICKSBURG

Final Battles and Siege

The Union shift downstream from Milliken's Bend had to be accomplished in stages. The Louisiana lowlands, flood prone under normal circumstances and even more so thanks to the many breaks in levees by Grant's failed canal projects, held too much water for the Federals to move en masse. Grant ordered John McClernand, whose corps was in the forward position, to lead the way with his Thirteenth Corps. Grant still had little personal regard for McClernand, but in choosing the political general to blaze a trail for the rest of the army to follow, Grant demonstrated that he had more respect for McClernand the soldier than might have been expected, and certainly more than he ever admitted. It can be argued that Grant simply wanted McClernand out front so he could keep an eye on him. Yet this phase of the campaign could make or break Grant's career. Would he therefore put a general in the lead whom he did not trust or respect? Whatever the answer, it is an issue historians will continue to debate.

McClernand moved his men slowly down the Louisiana side of the Mississippi to Richmond and then to New Carthage, where he established a staging area. Making a route required patience in bridging bayous and challenged the army's engineers, but things went smoothly. Grant also worked with David Porter to plan the passage of the Vicksburg batteries in order to get transports south of the city to ferry the army across into Mississippi. Porter warned that once the gunboats were below Vicksburg, they would have to stay for a while, because they did not have enough power to come back upriver against the current should Grant decide to attack Snyder's Bluff instead.

Grant checked out the Snyder's Bluff area personally, and after viewing Confederate defenses shelved any notion of attacking there. He assured Porter that the plan to turn Pemberton's flank south of Vicksburg would go forward. The tasks now were clear; McClernand must lead the way and, combined with Porter's fleet, take Grand Gulf and use the town as a base for an inland campaign against Vicksburg from the south, or possibly the southeast or east. McClernand was one of the few to endorse the plan; Sherman did not like it, and Assistant Secretary of War Charles Dana informed his boss, Edwin Stanton, that it seemed risky. Stanton told Dana to keep quiet, Grant ignored the naysayers, and the plan went forward. Grant hoped that this time there would be no turning back.[1]

John Pemberton received numerous reports from John Bowen, Pemberton's best field general now stationed at Grand Gulf, that something was amiss on the Louisiana side of the river. Louisiana cavalry contesting McClernand's move south sent word that the Federals seemed to be moving in force. Bowen finally sent Francis Cockrell's Missouri brigade across to evaluate the situation. Cockrell's attempts to slow McClernand's advance elements failed, and soon the Missouri troops, heavily outnumbered, were recalled to Grand Gulf. Bowen correctly guessed what Grant had in mind, though he thought the Yankees might cross farther downriver at Rodney. Yet Bowen's urgent messages to Pemberton went unheeded. Convinced that Grant was conducting a feint and nothing more, Pemberton refused to believe Bowen. Grant's plans further confused Pemberton, for a series of diversions went into motion totally mesmerizing the Confederate commander to the point that he seemed incapable of doing anything to meet the enemy challenge.[2]

The Federal march down the Louisiana shoreline was a foretaste of what Mississippians could expect if Grant got across the river. Plantations left by escaping owners were sacked and burned; other homes received the same treatment. Some soldiers were struck by the desolation wrought by comrades; others were impressed by the beautiful landscape surrounded by debris. Many white-occupied dwellings had been burned, many by owners to deny Yankee access to valuables the owners could not carry with them when they fled. In fact, many slaves were left behind, especially the old and sickly.[3]

The first major event of this new campaign began on April 5, 1863, when Frederick Steele landed his division at the port of Greenville well to the north of Vicksburg. Sherman and Grant had decided that sending Steele north would surely get Pemberton's attention and perhaps cause him to ignore McClernand's march. Steele had orders to take his men down Deer

Creek, establish a base, and send out patrols with the goal of capturing Wirt Adams's cavalry. Other instructions included burning Confederate supplies, rounding up guerrillas, and in general clearing the area of any armed resistance.

Steele's operations got the attention of West Pointer Samuel Ferguson, who brought his troops up to confront Steele north of Rolling Fork. Stephen Lee hurried from Vicksburg with his brigade, and Tennessee West Pointer John Moore received orders to move his command from Fort Pemberton south to help. Steele's men accomplished as much destruction as possible, but in light of the Confederate concentration, he pulled his troops back to Greenville, ending the expedition on the 10th. Certainly he had gotten Pemberton's attention, but Pemberton assumed that all the noise along Deer Creek meant that Grant was merely covering a retreat upriver. For nearly a week, Pemberton and his commander in Vicksburg, West Pointer and Mexican War veteran Carter Stevenson, looked in the wrong direction.[4]

While Confederate eyes focused on Steele's diversion, David Porter readied his fleet to pass the Vicksburg batteries. Porter had his crews outfit transports with bales of cotton and hay and strapped the empty vessels to barges for protection from Confederate artillery. Some barges carrying repair equipment and other necessities were strapped to ironclads. Bad weather delayed the operation for a few days, and the flotilla did not get under way until April 16. Porter ordered the diversion of steam exhaust into the paddlewheel housing in order to muffle the sounds of engines. He did not know that in Vicksburg, music from a ball would help drown out sounds on the river; military and civilian dignitaries were gathering at a farewell gala for General Dabney Maury, who was being transferred to east Tennessee.

Porter issued orders that the boats should hug the Louisiana shoreline as they rounded DeSoto Point above Vicksburg. The trees along the banks would help cover shadows; however, if the alarm was sounded, all vessels should cross to the Mississippi shoreline where Confederate cannons, thirty-seven in all, would have difficulty effectively depressing their guns from positions along the banks. At 9:15 that evening the boats began chugging downstream.

Porter's hopes for making the passage undetected quickly dissipated. Confederate pickets on the Louisiana side saw the Union fleet, but they were too far from the batteries to sound much of an alarm. So they set fire to buildings, including a railroad depot, to warn Vicksburg gunners of what was happening. The fires also illuminated the river to give Rebel artillerymen better vision of targets. Fires did the trick, and soon additional blazes lit the Mississippi shore as soldiers ran along the bank lighting houses and other structures.

Vicksburg cannons began to roar, eventually making enough noise to break up the ball as Sherman's arrival had broken up partying back in December. Confederate gun crews hurried to their posts, and the din grew louder, compounded by the return fire of Porter's war vessels. Following orders, boat captains steered their vessels across the river to the Mississippi shoreline; the tactic worked well, as many Rebel shells overshot their target. One boat, the *Henry Clay*, turned back upstream, perhaps due to the panic of captain and crew, and a well-aimed Confederate round slammed into the boat, setting it afire, and it had to be abandoned. Pemberton's artillerymen saw the crippled ship burning and concentrated a heavy fire to make sure it did not escape. While the gunners concentrated on the *Clay*, more vessels got by and escaped. Other boats in the flotilla got hit and scarred, but all made it beyond the range of the Vicksburg batteries. The event had been one to remember, with the nighttime display of fireworks, the fires along both banks, and the eerie shadows cast across the river. Beyond the show, Porter's success assured that Grant's plan was on track, and seemed to dispel the myth that the Confederate batteries were too dangerous to pass.

Downriver, McClernand's Thirteenth Corps heard the noise and waited anxiously for Porter's boats. When the remains of the *Clay* came into view, a feeling of gloom fell over the soldiers, but soon cheering broke out as the rest of the flotilla steamed into view intact. Confederates soothed their obvious failure to stop Porter with exaggerated stories of how much damage they had inflicted on the enemy navy. Grant decided that since Porter had had a relatively easy time of it, more transports could be sent south. The two quickly organized a second fleet of eighteen barges and steamers.

The new attempt required imaginative tactics, since most of Porter's warships were now downriver. To help cover the passage of this rather defenseless second wave, Grant ordered all remaining buildings on the DeSoto peninsula fired in order to cover the river with smoke. However, Confederates on the Louisiana side of the river prevented this gambit, using the structures for cover and driving off the would-be arsonists. Grant solved another problem by getting experienced boatmen from the ranks of his army to take the boats downstream; experienced river pilots not in military service refused to be a part of what they deemed a suicide run past the Confederate batteries.

Confederate gunners were ready this time, and they did inflict more damage than before, but most of the vessels in this second passage made it by either unscathed or with only minor damage. The trust that the Confederate military had in its Vicksburg batteries to be a significant barrier to Union river traffic proved illusory, as in the summer of 1862. Several problems plagued the artillerists. Their rate of fire was slow, due to the dangers of exposure when the Yankees were shooting back. Also there were simply not enough big guns to cover the entire stretch of river in front of Vicksburg, which forced commanders to string out their guns rather than arranging them for concentrated fire. Finally, due to the thick parapets built to protect the cannons, barrels could not be depressed enough to hit enemy boats close to the Mississippi shoreline.[5]

Sadly for the Confederacy, John Pemberton still did not grasp the significance of Grant's operations. Pemberton believed that Grant merely wanted to get boats downriver to transport his troops for future operations in the Louisiana delta area. Despite Bowen's warnings, and despite the obvious fact that transports could be used to carry Grant's men across into Mississippi, Pemberton still had no inkling of what was coming. Finally he became concerned enough to send word to Johnston that Grant did not appear to be leaving and that troops being sent to other points should be sent back to Vicksburg. At this point, yet another Grant diversion got his opponent's attention.

The Union operation that mesmerized Pemberton came out of discussions between Stephen Hurlbut, a South Carolinian by birth but for several years a Republican politician in Illinois and commanding in Memphis, and William Rosecrans, now commanding Federal forces in middle Tennessee. Hurlbut wanted to send raiders to cut the Southern Railroad, which brought troops and supplies to Vicksburg from the east across central Mississippi. Rosecrans envisioned a raid against the Western and Atlantic Railroad in northwest Georgia. Both raids would disrupt enemy supply lines and force the Confederates to disperse their limited cavalry resources.

Abel Streight led the operation across northern Alabama, intended to cut the railroad in Georgia. The raid was unusual because Streight chose to mount his men upon mules, which were better suited for the rugged hill country that awaited his cavalry. Confederate cavalryman Nathan Bedford Forrest led his troopers in pursuit and captured Streight and his entire force in northeast Alabama. While Forrest had completed his assignment, his absence during the forthcoming final campaign against Vicksburg was a big plus for Grant.

The other raid, led by Benjamin Grierson, had a more immediate and direct impact on Grant's operations, for Grierson's raid gained and kept John Pemberton's attention at a crucial time. Grierson led his 1,700 riders out of

LaGrange, Tennessee, on April 17, and the horsemen soon hit the Mobile & Ohio Railroad in northeast Mississippi, tearing up track and burning Confederate supplies as they rode south. Grierson adopted the tactic of sending out small raiding parties, which caused confusing reports to be sent to Pemberton. The Yankee cavalry seemed to be in several places at once, thoroughly frustrating Pemberton's efforts to stop the raid.

Grierson followed the railroad for a time, and then led the main body of his troops on a southwesterly course through the towns of Starkville and Louisville, arriving at Newton Station on the 24th. Newton Station (present-day Newton) was located on the Southern Railroad about halfway between Meridian and Jackson. Grierson's raiders tore up much track and destroyed many supplies intended for Vicksburg, though the Confederates would have the damage repaired within a few days. Pemberton, confounded by his inability to stop Grierson, sent infantry eastward from Jackson, but of course they arrived too late. While crossing the Pearl River south of Jackson, a detachment that had broken off near Starkville to threaten Meridian rejoined the main column. Grierson continued to angle toward Baton Rouge, pausing for a moment east of Port Gibson to consider riding to the river and joining Grant's operations. Harassment by Wirt Adams's Confederate riders convinced Grierson that it would be safer to go to Louisiana, and the tired horsemen entered Baton Rouge on May 2.

The ride had been eminently successful, for Grierson's raid had produced thousands of captured munitions and guns and had resulted in thousands of dollars of property destruction that the Confederacy could ill afford. Grierson had lost only three killed and seven wounded in the process, but, most important, he had kept the enemy busy watching him instead of Grant. Other Union cavalry operations followed in north Mississippi, further tying down Rebel horsemen desperately needed in the Vicksburg area.[6]

While Grant continued to count on distracting Pemberton and on Pemberton's obvious nonaggressive generalship, he talked with his friend Sherman about yet another diversion. If Sherman took his corps and demonstrated against Snyder's Bluff north of Vicksburg on the Yazoo, perhaps Rebel commanders would shift forces in that direction, making it more difficult to send men south to the Grand Gulf area. The idea came at a bad time for Pemberton's forces, for an obstruction raft at Snyder's fell apart about this time, and the swift current made repair impossible.

Sherman's demonstration began on the last day of April, but it never amounted to much, and General Carter Stevenson, commanding locally in Vicksburg, was not fooled by the lackluster offensive moves by Sherman's

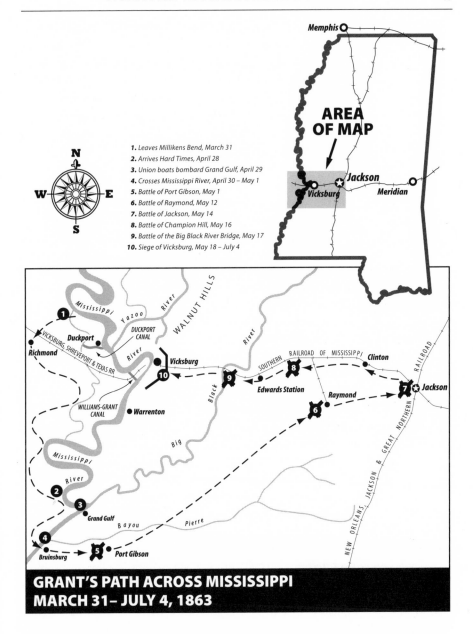

1. *Leaves Millikens Bend, March 31*
2. *Arrives Hard Times, April 28*
3. *Union boats bombard Grand Gulf, April 29*
4. *Crosses Mississippi River, April 30 – May 1*
5. *Battle of Port Gibson, May 1*
6. *Battle of Raymond, May 12*
7. *Battle of Jackson, May 14*
8. *Battle of Champion Hill, May 16*
9. *Battle of the Big Black River Bridge, May 17*
10. *Siege of Vicksburg, May 18 – July 4*

AREA
OF MAP

**GRANT'S PATH ACROSS MISSISSIPPI
MARCH 31– JULY 4, 1863**

men. At the same time, word came from Grant that Sherman should begin getting his division downstream.[7]

Downriver, John Bowen continued to plead his case, and at last Pemberton listened. Stevenson got word to have 5,000 men ready to rush to Bowen's aid if needed. Stevenson obeyed, though he argued that the Grand Gulf force should be sufficient as it was. Stevenson clung to the belief that, given the difficulties of moving a large army down the Louisiana side of the river, Union activities over there must be a feint.[8]

While all the diversions went on, McPherson and McClernand continued concentrating their divisions in the New Carthage area. McClernand sent scouts to check Grand Gulf, Grant's preferred landing spot. Reports indicated that Confederate defenses there were impressive. Two forts anchored the line of works. Fort Cobun, located some ten to fifteen yards above the river on a spot called Point of Rocks, anchored the northern approaches, and Fort Wade, slightly over six yards above water and a quarter mile from the water's edge, the southern flank. Cobun and Wade each contained four heavy guns. Behind the forts, a bluff slanted upward and was lined with rifle pits and was speckled with smaller pieces of artillery.

On April 27 Porter took his warships downriver to test Bowen's defenses. His four ironclads, plus three additional gunboats, steamed downstream and then back up, firing as they went. Confederate gunners replied in kind. The fighting went on for some time, until the gunners at Fort Wade reduced fire, largely due to the death of their commander. Porter signaled his boats to concentrate on Cobun, but to no avail. Porter's flagship, the *Benton*, took a round in the pilothouse and spun out of control, but ran aground in a spot safe from Bowen's guns.

From shortly after 8 a.m. until around 1 p.m. the shelling continued, and Cobun gunners finally had to slow their rate of fire to wait for more ammunition. Confederate resistance convinced Porter and Grant, however, that it would be costly indeed to attempt a landing at Grand Gulf, so the fighting ended. Porter had lost eighteen killed and fifty-seven wounded, while Bowen counted three dead and nineteen wounded. Grant sent word to McClernand to head his troops farther downriver to Disharoon's plantation. Porter's fleet continued to shell Grand Gulf to screen the passage of transports.

Grant found another spot to land, this one at a place called Bruinsburg, several miles south of Grand Gulf and slightly southwest of Port Gibson. On April 30 McClernand's corps began crossing the Mississippi River into Mississippi. By the time the transfer of troops ended, this would be the largest amphibious operation up to that point in American history.[9]

Once the lead elements crossed, the Thirteenth Corps began moving inland, guided by a local black man. At the head of the column, West Pointer Eugene Carr marched his division from the flatlands to high bluffs beyond. Union soldiers soon found themselves on the grounds of Windsor plantation, where a huge mansion adorned with gigantic Corinthian columns stood. Iowa troops in the lead turned briefly south, and then at Bethel Church turned east on the Rodney–Port Gibson road. The trail soon led into a landscape marked by deep ravines with much undergrowth and steep ridges, the tops of which provided farmland for locals. Night came, and still the column crept forward. By evening Illinoisan John Logan's division of James McPherson's Seventeenth Corps had landed on the Mississippi side, and these troops hurried inland to support McClernand.

On the Confederate side, John Bowen worked feverishly to meet this threat. He knew that he was in trouble once the transports passed Grand Gulf. He suspected that Grant would land at Rodney, but wherever the Yankees landed, Bowen knew that he did not have enough men on hand to drive them into the river. Help was supposedly on the way from Vicksburg, but would it arrive in time? Bowen chose not to wait; he sent a force commanded by Martin Green to Port Gibson. Green sent out patrols to scout roads leading from Port Gibson to Natchez and Rodney.

As reinforcements began arriving, Bowen's force increased, not enough, but perhaps he could slow the enemy invasion until more Confederate troops arrived. Scouting and citizen reports indicated that Grant's army was marching along two roads, the one to Rodney and the one to Bruinsburg. Bowen agreed with Green that the latter's force should take position at Magnolia Church on the Rodney road. Green worried about his right flank, which would be vulnerable if Union troops were indeed coming down the Bruinsburg road. None of McClernand's men were on that road, but Green could take no chances. He sent Edward Tracy's Alabama brigade over to the Bruinsburg road and added the recently arrived troops of William Baldwin to the position at Magnolia Church.

Tangled ravines and a creek bottom choked with undergrowth separated Bowen's two wings. Cooperation would be difficult, for troops would have to take a roundabout route to the junction of the two roads just west of Port Gibson in order to aid each other. Tracy's men, pushed to the limit by the quick march from Vicksburg, were exhausted when they finally deployed on the Bruinsburg road and would not be well rested when they went into battle. Bowen continued to shift troops from Grand Gulf to the area west of Port Gibson. He knew that he was weakening his positions at Grand Gulf and along the Big Black River, but if he could not stop the main Union

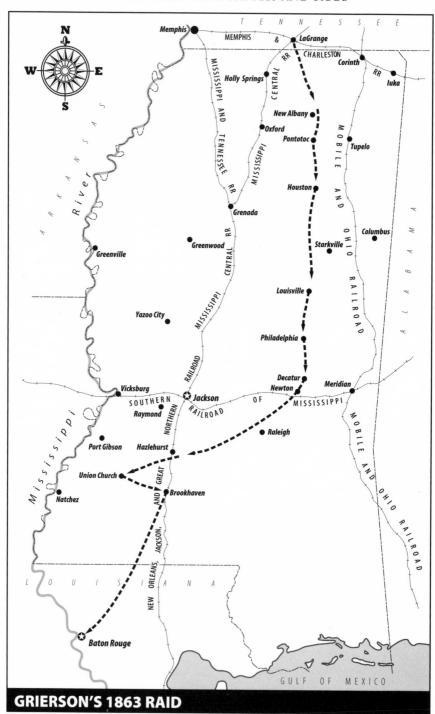

GRIERSON'S 1863 RAID

advance, he would be flanked and forced to retreat anyway. The decisive battle would be in the rugged country between Port Gibson and the Mississippi, and Bowen had to play all his cards there.

In the darkness of the night and early morning of April 30–May 1, residents of the A. K. Shaifer home west of Magnolia Church hurriedly packed wagons for a quick trip through Confederate lines and out of harm's way. General Green reassured them that they had plenty of time, but as he spoke, fire from advancing Union patrols peppered the side of the house and the wagon. The civilians hurried away in a panic, causing Green to smile. He calmly ordered his picket line to come up and hold the enemy advance as long as possible.[10]

The lead elements of the Union column pushed ahead to within fifty yards of Magnolia Church, and soon an artillery duel ensued, creating quite a specter in the black night. The flashes of cannon muzzles and fuses flying through the air lit the night, and deadly missiles of all sizes rained down into woods where soldiers on both sides huddled. Soon cries from wounded men and animals began echoing among the hills and hollows. Survivors long remembered this night.

Firing slacked, as if by mutual consent, before dawn, and as the early streaks of light split the sky of May 1, Federal officers looked incredulously at the terrain that faced them. The battlefield was even more uneven than they could have imagined, and it remained to be seen if an organized battle could be fought in such surroundings. Deep ravines contained ridges and spurs that jutted in a variety of directions. Men could very easily wind up shooting into their own ranks once the smoke of battle covered the area.

McClernand learned from a local slave that a road ran from near the Shaifer home across the hollow to the northeast where it intersected the Bruinsburg road. Supposedly the Confederates had troops there. McClernand knew he must send a force down that road or risk the enemy hitting his left flank and perhaps getting into his rear. On the Bruinsburg road, Edward Tracy's position had been weakened when he was ordered to send reinforcements to the Magnolia Church sector. McClernand sent a few companies of infantry down the connecting road to check for enemy presence, and when he received reports of Tracy's position, he sent the division of German-born Peter Osterhaus to take care of Tracy, thereby freeing Carr to concentrate on the Confederates at Magnolia Church.

Osterhaus had more men than Tracy, but the rugged terrain helped the Alabamians maintain their position for a time. The firing grew heavy as more of Osterhaus's troops came up. Soon Tracy fell dead, and Ishom Garrott, a colonel in the Twentieth Alabama, took command. Garrott, unaware

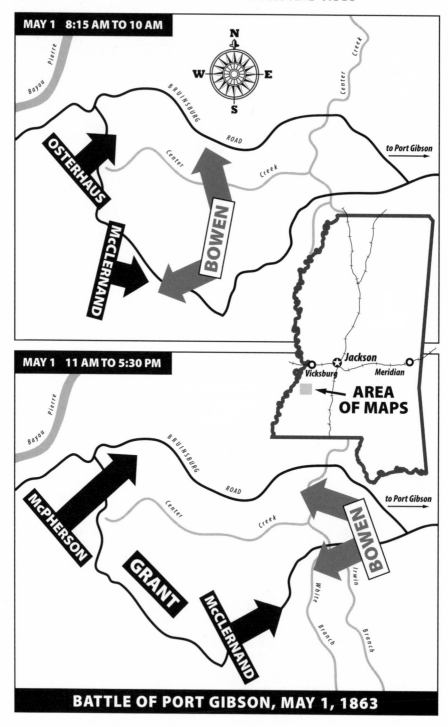

BATTLE OF PORT GIBSON, MAY 1, 1863

of any battle plans, sent word to Green about Tracy's death and asked for instructions. Green responded that the Alabamians must hold as long as possible. Beyond that general and obvious order, Garrott was on his own.

Faced with ever-increasing pressure and an ammunition shortage, Garrott had to maneuver his men to take further advantage of terrain. Osterhaus suddenly became tentative and sent word that he could not be sure of a successful attack without reinforcements. He got them when John Logan's advance arrived. Garrott got help, too, for when more reinforcements arrived from Grand Gulf to help out on the Rodney road, Bowen sent Green's tired troops to bolster Garrott's position. When Green arrived, he did not check with anyone before deploying, and Garrott soon realized that Green had put his troops in the wrong position, on the left instead of the right, to help throw back the coming Union assault. Garrott tried to remedy the situation by transferring some of his own troops to the threatened center and right of the Confederate line.

About this time Osterhaus's attack hit the Confederate right, and the line began to crumple. Green hurriedly shifted his troops to the right, and Osterhaus continued to send in more men. The fighting became confused, but clearly the Federals had the upper hand with overwhelming numbers. Around 5 p.m. Bowen sent word to Green to hold until sunset, but Green chose not to wait. An entire Missouri regiment had almost been lost in the fighting, and Green chose not to continue a conflict that was obviously lost.[11]

On the Union right, Carr had also had a tough time at the Magnolia Church front. The terrain had caused some gaps in the battle line. Carr attacked Green's left there, surprising Green, who expected the assault to come on his right across more level ground. Realizing that his flank was threatened, Green had sent word to Tracy for reinforcements. Confederate countercharges produced no results, and Green gave ground, though urged by Bowen to hold on until William Baldwin's troops arrived. McClernand planned now to hit the Rebel left a hard blow, but soon realized that he had the numbers to simply overwhelm the enemy center. When the attack came, Green's line gave way, and Confederate artillery fell into Union hands. As Green pulled back toward Port Gibson, Bowen arrived with Baldwin's brigade. Bowen instructed Green to go to the Bruinsburg road, and Baldwin, soon to be reinforced by Francis Cockrell's Missourians, took up the fight on the Rodney road.

Bowen decided to set up another line of defense in the Willow Creek bottom east of the Rodney road, where the creek forked into the White and Erwin branches. This should give his men more cover, for the bottom contained thick growths of cane. Baldwin would anchor his right across the Rodney road, and the line would form an arch from the north to the southeast. Cockrell covered the Confederate left flank. At Magnolia Church, Union soldiers cheered the speeches of the governor of Illinois and McClernand, but Grant reminded the speakers and the men that there was fighting left to be done.

Indeed there was, for Bowen's men fought tenaciously along the creek bottom, with Cockrell's men inflicting heavy casualties as they worked to keep the Yankees from turning Bowen's left flank, an event that would have likely cost Bowen his entire command. Though Cockrell hit a telling blow on the brigade of James Slack, this fight again proved that solid soldiers plus good terrain could not stop an overwhelming disparity in troop strength. Outnumbered three to one, Bowen was helpless to stop yet another McClernand tactic of bludgeoning the Confederate center.

Finally, to save his army to fight another day, Bowen issued orders for retreat and, despite some close calls, managed to get his men safely through Port Gibson and across Bayou Pierre. Bowen's rear guard fired the bridges to slow down Grant's pursuit. Grant now had a solid foothold on Mississippi soil, and he would solidify that grasp in the days to come. The cost had been 787 Union casualties, while Bowen had lost 875.[12]

Pressured by Washington, Grant considered turning south to cooperate with Nathaniel Banks to take Port Hudson above Baton Rouge, but doing so would give Pemberton valuable time to consolidate forces. Grant had the momentum, and he decided to keep going. Bowen pulled back to the relative safety of the other side of the Big Black and waited. Pemberton decided to abandon Port Hudson and transfer troops there to the Vicksburg front, but Jefferson Davis intervened and insisted that both places must be held. John Gregg's brigade had already left Port Hudson and was en route to Jackson, but Franklin Gardner, commanding the Louisiana stronghold, received word from Pemberton to keep the rest of his small army within the fortifications. The Confederates would fight on two fronts in spite of the numerical superiority of Federal forces.[13]

The Union army at Port Gibson repaired burned bridges and began moving inland north and northeast. Grant thought about hitting the Southern Railroad between Jackson and Vicksburg to cut Pemberton's supply line. Yet he wanted to keep Rebel commanders guessing about his target. McClernand's Thirteenth Corps, followed by McPherson's Seventeenth, made a broad front between the Big Black and a road that led from Port Gibson in the direction of Raymond, a small town southwest of Jackson. Troops left behind established a supply depot at Grand Gulf, which Bowen had been

forced to abandon. Heavily laden wagon trains followed Grant's army inland, but the troops would also live off the land as circumstances dictated.
Contrary to Grant's postwar claim, he did not cut himself off from his supply base, at least not right away. His army did some living off the land, but
not as much as he implied. His friend Sherman liked the idea, and he would
practice the philosophy much more than Grant ever did.[14]

John Pemberton chose, not surprisingly, to adopt a passive strategy.
Rather than send troops in an offensive thrust against Grant, Pemberton
began assembling men west of the Big Black. Joseph Johnston had advised
Pemberton to consolidate his army and attack the Federals, even if that
meant risking the loss of Vicksburg. With orders to the contrary from
President Davis, Pemberton was not about to do such a thing. It was not in
his nature, or in Johnston's for that matter, to take the offensive, especially
a risky offensive. Pemberton thought defensively, then and for the rest of
the campaign. He feared that Union forces might strike from the south
against the Warrenton area, but Grant's well-orchestrated feints along the
Big Black made predictions a dangerous game. So Pemberton decided he
would scatter his army all along the Big Black, especially watching the various fords. Pemberton figured that if Grant did hit the railroad and turn
west, the Confederates would dig in along the bluffs bordering the west
side of the Big Black and dare the Federals to attack. Clearly Pemberton
preferred a strategy of reaction to action.

His subordinates followed suit, both by choice and in obedience to orders. William Loring arrived at Bowen's front shortly after the battle at Port
Gibson had been lost, and instantly ordered a retreat to Hankinson's Ferry
on the Big Black. In the process, he let pass a wonderful opportunity to
strike McPherson's corps, which had been temporarily isolated as Grant's
troops spread out to move north. Meanwhile John Gregg received orders
to move toward Raymond when he reached Jackson from Port Hudson. In
keeping with the defensive mind-set, Pemberton ordered Gregg to observe
only and report any Federal inclination to move toward Jackson. Under
no circumstances was Gregg to get involved in a fight in which he was
outnumbered.[15]

John Gregg did not intentionally disobey, but he did make a miscalcula-
tion that changed the course of the inland campaign. At dawn on May 12,
couriers brought word to Gregg's headquarters that a Yankee force was
coming toward Raymond along the Utica road to the southwest. Gregg mis-
understood the implications of this intelligence. He decided that the enemy
on the road must be screening the Union army's right as it turned north
to hit the railroad. So he chose to attack with the notion that a threat to

the Federal right flank would disrupt Grant's march. After all, Pemberton had said it was permissible to attack the enemy flank and rear, and Gregg believed that he had an opportunity to do just that.

Actually, the troops coming up the road were advance elements of McPherson's entire corps, and when Gregg attacked with his lone brigade, he set himself up for disaster. As the battle developed initially, however, Gregg did not realize for some time just how badly outnumbered he was. The battle began along Fourteenmile Creek just southwest of Raymond, and in the early stages neither side performed in a coordinated manner. McPherson sent troops in piecemeal, beginning with regiments from Logan's division, and while Gregg's sparse troops, consisting of Tennesseans and Texans, fought well, many regiments operated without any knowledge of what was going on other parts of the battlefield.

After about two hours of bitter fighting, numbers began to tell, and McPherson's men began pushing in Gregg's right flank. Savage hand-to-hand fighting took place between the Seventh Texas and the Twentieth Ohio along the road north of the creek. McPherson soon had troops drifting far enough to the right to threaten Gregg's left. The dust and smoke of battle, plus McPherson's lack of control over the fighting, had made it possible for Gregg's men to hold the Seventeenth Corps in place for nearly three hours. In the most uncoordinated battle of the Vicksburg campaign, the Confederates lost 515 men, while McPherson counted 446 casualties. When it became obvious that the battle had not gone his way, Gregg led his men toward Jackson, the safest retreat route available. Gregg's decision to fight had not only cost him a large number of casualties, it also had assured that he would not be able to join Pemberton's army for the defense of Vicksburg. Grant's tactics of separating his corps in order to feel out the location of the enemy to his front reaped great benefits at Raymond.[16]

Citizens of Raymond were shocked by the aftermath of the battle. Wounded carried into the town soon filled the county courthouse, other public buildings, and many private homes. Local women helped nurse the slightly and severely wounded and watched helplessly as many died. Townspeople made no effort to hide their contempt for the Yankees, but John Logan and other officers warned soldiers not to pillage and raid homes, an order many soldiers ignored. Looting happened all over town, and the Federal soldiers stole from whites and slaves. McPherson's men helped themselves to stolen food, tore down fences to make fires, and generally made themselves at home. Many citizens protested that they were loyal to the Union and always had been. For some, this may have been so, but for most

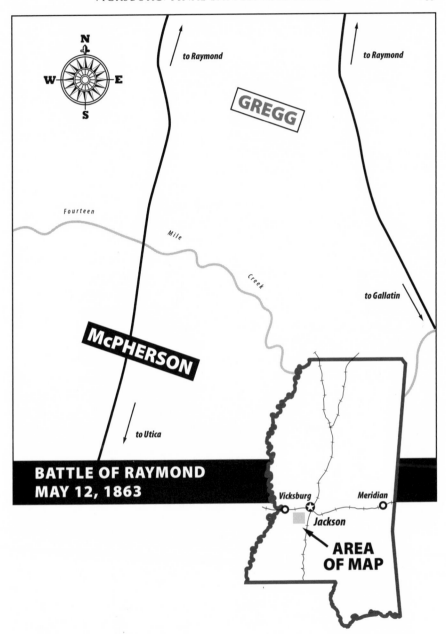

to Raymond

to Raymond

GREGG

Fourteen

Mile

Creek

to Gallatin

McPHERSON

to Utica

**BATTLE OF RAYMOND
MAY 12, 1863**

Vicksburg

Meridian

Jackson

**AREA
OF MAP**

it was an attempt to save their property. Few Union soldiers were convinced of their sincerity.[17]

While chaos and dying men overwhelmed Raymond, the fight there convinced Grant to change his strategy. Gregg had caused McPherson enough trouble to convince Grant that it might be dangerous to turn his back on Jackson. Scouts reported that Joseph Johnston had arrived in the Mississippi capital and was assembling a force there. Not wanting to risk being caught between two enemy forces, Grant decided that he must send troops to get rid of Johnston. Then he could turn and go after Pemberton and Vicksburg.

Sherman's Fifteenth Corps had finally crossed the Mississippi and had caught up with the rest of the army. Grant sent Sherman northeast from Raymond to attack Jackson from the south, while McPherson marched north to Clinton, a town fifteen or so miles west of Jackson on the Jackson-Vicksburg road. McPherson was to turn east and assault the capital city from the west. McClernand would hold the Thirteenth Corps in place between Raymond and Edwards Depot; he would provide support if needed and keep Pemberton from moving east against the flank and rear of the other two corps. Grant need not have worried.[18]

When Johnston, sent by a worried Jefferson Davis to salvage the deteriorating situation in Mississippi, arrived in Jackson, he immediately sent a telegram to Richmond with a simple message, "I am too late." Johnston had no interest in saving Vicksburg, and once he realized Grant was moving inland, Johnston decided to let the Federals have the hill city. Further evidence of his defeatist attitude was his immediate decision to give up Jackson, while at the same time ordering Pemberton to move toward the city. Johnston could have fought and held out for a time. By doing so, he would have given reinforcements on the way to Jackson by train from various points east time to arrive and detrain, and he could have then considered his options. Johnston's quick retreat fit perfectly into Grant's plans, for now there would be no one in Jackson to attack Grant's rear.

John Gregg received the assignment to put up a token resistance in Jackson, while supplies moved by wagon to Canton to the northeast. Heavy rains began to fall, slowing both the Federal advance and the Confederate withdrawal. When Sherman's troops finally crossed a flooded creek south of town, they brushed aside light resistance and soon learned that the Rebels, except for a few home guards, had disappeared. On the west side of town, McPherson, moving down the Clinton-Jackson road and on either side of the Southern Railroad where it ran west toward Vicksburg, encountered heavier resistance. Gregg's men held on to give the wagon train time

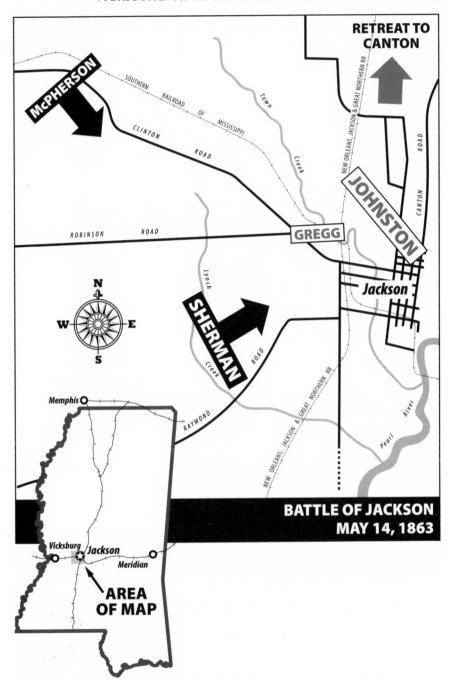

RETREAT TO
CANTON

McPHERSON

SOUTHERN RAILROAD OF MISSISSIPPI

CLINTON ROAD

Town Creek

NEW ORLEANS, JACKSON & GREAT NORTHERN RR

JOHNSTON

CANTON ROAD

ROBINSON ROAD

GREGG

Jackson

Lynch

N
W   E
S

SHERMAN

Creek ROAD

NEW ORLEANS, JACKSON & GREAT NORTHERN RR

Pearl River

Memphis

RAYMOND

BATTLE OF JACKSON
MAY 14, 1863

Vicksburg Jackson
          Meridian

AREA
OF MAP

to reach a safe distance to the north. Total casualties included some 300 for Grant and 900 for Johnston, most of the latter being prisoners sacrificed to assure the army's escape.[19]

Grant now turned his attention to Pemberton's army. A Grant informant, impersonating a Confederate scout, brought to McPherson a copy of a Johnston message to Pemberton that ordered Pemberton to march to Clinton for a junction with Johnston's Jackson force. Pemberton received the message on May 13, while Grant read a copy on the 14th. Knowing full well that Johnston was moving away from Clinton, Grant saw an opportunity to beat Pemberton in the field without having to worry about Johnston's force interfering. Orders from Grant sent John McClernand and James McPherson marching for Bolton, a town on the railroad between Clinton and Edwards Station. Should Johnston decide to turn west and effect a junction with Pemberton, the likely target would be Bolton. Meanwhile Grant left the destruction of railroads and Confederate supplies in and around Jackson to Sherman's corps. The destructive fires got out of control and spread to consume private and nonmilitary structures as well. The hard hand of war, combined with more destruction in Jackson after the fall of Vicksburg, would give the capital city the nickname "Chimneyville." The extent of damage may or may not be exaggerated, but the moniker is so ingrained in Civil War mythology it likely will never go away.

A British traveler, Arthur Fremantle, who found the war fascinating enough to travel through the South for three months, entered Jackson after Sherman's men had left. The destruction impressed him. He wrote, "All the numerous factories have been burnt down by the enemy," and he believed the Federals had a right to do so. What he did not like was the pillaging of private dwellings, which was very evident. Businesses had been gutted, and the Catholic church and other public service buildings not related to the Rebel war effort had been left in ruins. The local citizens' hatred of the Yankees impressed Fremantle, who observed that Grant's visit had surely turned them into "good and earnest rebels."[20]

Meanwhile John Pemberton had not seen Jackson, but he was wondering exactly what Joseph Johnston had done. He read with alarm the Johnston message ordering a junction at Clinton. Such a move would leave Vicksburg uncovered, though two divisions, John Forney's and Martin Luther Smith's, had been left in the city's defensive works. Pemberton also had news that a large enemy force, McClernand's, was lurking along the Raymond-Edwards road, and if Pemberton marched for Clinton, the Yankees would be in position to assault the Confederate right flank. Pemberton called his generals together for a council of war on May 14, and after much discussion

Pemberton chose to move southeast from Edwards toward Grant's supply line. Given President Davis's charge to defend Vicksburg at all costs, Pemberton decided that such a move would leave his army in position to rush back to the Big Black if necessary to block Grant's approach. At this point, Pemberton did not know that Johnston had already abandoned Jackson and was moving away from Clinton.[21]

The decision having been made, Pemberton ordered his army forward on May 15, and the advance quickly became victimized by a comedy of errors. Supplies that should have been shipped by train from Vicksburg arrived late, and then the army had to stop because Bakers Creek, which meandered along a northeast-to-southwest course east of Edwards, was flooded, and Pemberton had failed to send scouts to reconnoiter the area. More time was lost in redirecting the army's line of march to a suitable crossing. By evening the army's advance division, William Loring's, had reached the area of Jackson Creek on the Raymond-Edwards road. Behind Loring, strung out from southeast to northwest, were Bowen's and Stevenson's divisions, respectively. Supply wagons brought up the rear.[22]

As the sun rose on May 16, Pemberton received Johnston's latest message, with news of the evacuation of Jackson and another order to move toward Clinton. Why Johnston would order such a move when he was in Canton with his army is mystifying and perhaps can only be explained by Johnston's state of mind. He did not want to fight Grant, nor did he care if Grant took Vicksburg. Johnston was a disciple of the theory that armies mattered more than places, and he never abandoned that belief. His only goal seemed to be to get Pemberton's army out of Grant's way so that the two divided Confederate forces could unite. What would happen then can never be known, but it is unlikely that the combined army under Johnston would have taken the offensive, certainly not to attack Vicksburg.

Perhaps shaken by the fall of Jackson, Pemberton decided this time to obey Johnston's instructions, and he issued an order to reverse the column north to Mechanicsburg, from which point the army would march for Clinton. Before the army could reverse its march, however, the supply train had to be taken north to get it out of the way. Teamsters turned the wagons and moved out, but the army could not follow, because it suddenly came under attack from Grant's two corps closing in from the east.[23]

The battle of Champion Hill got its name from prominent heights owned by the local Champion family. The highest point, the hill, stood between the Confederate left (Stevenson) and the Union right (McPherson). If Grant won here, he would be in position to move quickly against Vicksburg. Contrarily, a Union loss could leave Grant in a precarious position.

As the battle evolved, Pemberton's army was aligned with Stevenson's troops on the left, Bowen's in the center, and Loring's on the right, with the troops extended from Loring's position on the Raymond-Edwards road on a northwesterly course to Stevenson's men strung out from the Jackson road to the railroad. To Stevenson's right, Bowen deployed from the Jackson road down Middle Road, which ran south to Loring's left. Loring's troops took their position astride the Raymond-Edwards road.

Pemberton, ignoring the ominously large number of campfires to the west on the night and early morning of May 15–16, had not organized his troops to receive any kind of attack, though his subordinates had taken some precautions. The Confederates would be outnumbered in the coming fight by 9,000 troops (23,000 to Grant's 32,000), a disparity that Pemberton could have avoided had he not left the two full divisions in Vicksburg.[24]

The fighting began badly for the Confederates and, with one brief exception, continued to deteriorate. Along the Jackson road, McPherson sent John Logan's division on the Union right and Alvin P. Hovey's division on Logan's left. Stephen D. Lee, commanding a brigade in Stevenson's division, fought effectively on the Rebel left, but reinforcements were much too long in coming. Some of Stevenson's troops did not perform well, especially in Seth Barton's brigade. Hovey's division drove a wedge into the Confederate line just north of the Jackson road. Farther north, Stephen Lee could not do much to meet Hovey's charge, for Logan's men were pressuring and in the process of turning Lee's left. By 1 p.m. Stevenson's division was in shambles, and Pemberton faced the possibility of total disaster with his left flank falling apart.[25]

At this point John Bowen, fearful of pressure on his own front, finally obeyed Pemberton's pleas for him to rush to Stevenson's assistance. Bowen's division possessed the best soldiers in the army. Led by Francis Cockrell's hard-fighting Missourians, Bowen's brigades smashed through Hovey's division and reached the crest of Champion Hill. For a time, Grant's right found itself in a shaky situation, but soon Federal reinforcements rushed in, while Pemberton had no men to send to Bowen's aid. William Loring, though lightly pressured by McClernand in his front, simply refused to send any help to the left until it was much too late. Bowen's magnificent charge came to nothing as his men grudgingly gave way and pulled back down Champion Hill. By the time Loring sent men to provide support, Stevenson and Bowen were in full retreat, forced to pull back to a lower crossing of Bakers Creek, since Stevenson's division had been flanked to the north.[26]

Loring provided cover for the other two retreating divisions, while fending off McClernand, who finally had taken the offensive. In the process,

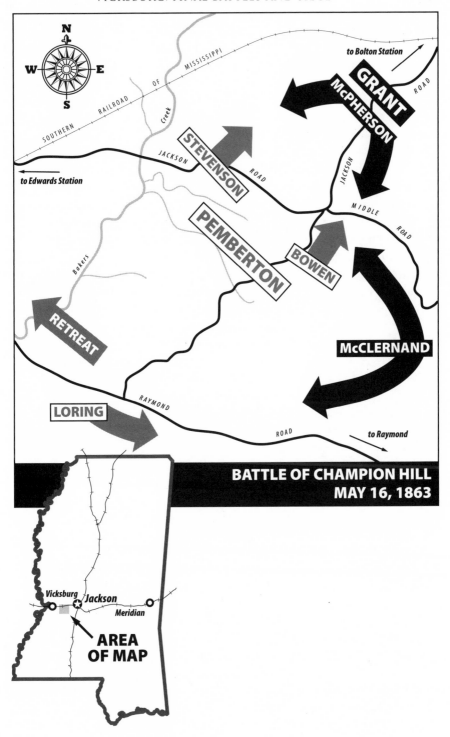

BATTLE OF CHAMPION HILL
MAY 16, 1863

AREA
OF MAP

Lloyd Tilghman, a brigade commander in Loring's division, fell dead from a cannon shot, and Loring decided that he could not get his men across Bakers Creek, because if he turned to follow, the enemy would be dangerously close on his rear. So Loring sent his men south, where they looped around McClernand and made it back to Jackson and Canton to join Johnston.

The battle of Champion Hill cost Pemberton 3,800 in killed, wounded, and missing men (the missing totaled 2,441), plus Loring's division. Grant had suffered 2,400 casualties, and he had won with only two of his three corps present. Further, whatever chance Pemberton had of joining Johnston disappeared, for the Confederate army was in disarray as it fell back to defensive works east of the Big Black along either side of the railroad crossing.[27]

Grant, elated at his army's success, now thought that total victory was within his grasp, and on the morning of May 17 he ordered his men to push on. McClernand followed the trail of Pemberton's army, while McPherson and Sherman, the latter having arrived from Jackson, moved north of the railroad to cut off any attempt by Pemberton to escape in that direction.

Pemberton, placing Bowen's three battered brigades in position in defensive works with the Big Black to their backs, decided to hold on until Loring arrived. Confederate morale was at rock bottom, and Bowen's veterans knew that they were in a vulnerable position. McClernand's men, relatively fresh, showed no mercy, as Mike Lawler's brigade broke through Tennessean John C. Vaughn's position, held by east Tennessee troops whose loyalty to the Confederate cause was minimal at best. The breaking of Bowen's line caused a general retreat, and his extreme left and his right suddenly received heavy flanking fire. The Confederates ran pell-mell toward the Big Black, some crossing the railroad bridge, some crossing the boat bridge that had been created by turning a vessel sideways, and some jumping into the water and swimming across. Bowen lost small arms, cannons, and men captured as he tried to get his troops to safety. Portions of Stevenson's division provided some cover fire from the west bank of the Big Black, and the Union assault slowed. Pemberton's engineers made sure that the bridges were aflame before following the rest of the army toward Vicksburg.

Loring, of course, never arrived, and Pemberton would not learn until much later that he had risked Bowen's division for nothing. Confederate casualties at the Big Black are uncertain, though Union reports indicated that 1,751 Rebels had been taken prisoner. McClernand's corps had light casualties of 39 killed, 237 wounded, and 3 missing. After the Confederate hasty retreat, Grant set his men to work building bridges. He wanted to push on as soon as possible, and by the next day McClernand's men were

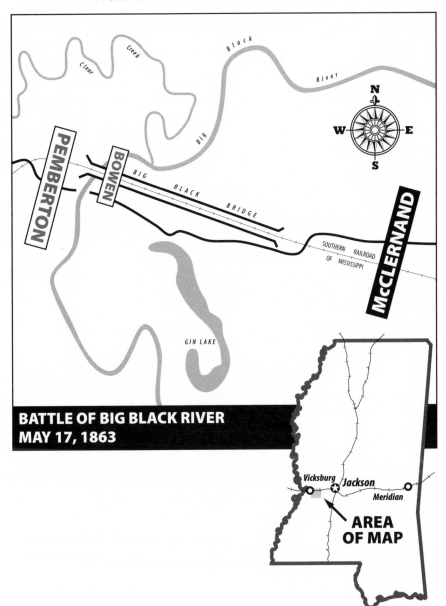

BATTLE OF BIG BLACK RIVER
MAY 17, 1863

crossing the Big Black. Upstream, McPherson and Sherman found fords
and ferries and sent their men across. The entire three corps closed in on
Vicksburg.[28]

Pemberton, meanwhile, gave no thought to trying to escape. Davis had
said hold Vicksburg, and Pemberton intended to obey, no matter the odds.
He felt sure that once Johnston learned of the events of May 16–17, help
would be on the way. He had no way of knowing that Johnston would do
nothing for the next several weeks. Upon arriving in Vicksburg, Pemberton
received word from Johnston to evacuate the city and get the army out the
best way he could. Pemberton refused, in part because even as he read the
message, sounds of Grant's artillery shelling Confederate defenses could be
heard. Pemberton had no intention of pulling out anyway, and it is certain
that even had he tried, his army would have had great difficulty. Forney's
and Smith's divisions were fresh, but Stevenson's and Bowen's would need
time to regroup before any forced march could be made. A determined
commander could possibly have led his army south out of town and gotten away, but Pemberton was only determined to make an attempt to save
Vicksburg.[29]

Though depressed by the failures of the last two days, Pemberton and
his staff went to work. He deployed Smith on the left and Forney in the
center of the works that formed a semicircle from north of town, in an
arch to the northeast, east, and southeast, and culminating to the south.
Pemberton placed Stevenson's depleted division on the right, with the ex-
pectation that any immediate assault by Grant would hit the Confederate
left and center. Bowen's division would be held in reserve. Anchoring the
long Confederate defensive line was Fort Hill on the far left, which covered both land and water (the Mississippi River) approaches; the Stockade
Redan complex a few hundred yards east of Fort Hill on Graveyard road;
the Third Louisiana Redan on the Baldwin's Ferry road; the Great Redoubt
on the Jackson road; and the Second Texas Lunette and the Railroad Redoubt, north and south, respectively, of the railroad. On the Confederate
right, Square Fort (later called Fort Garrott) protected approaches from the
Hall's Ferry road, which entered the city from the southeast. Other works
farther to the right included the Salient Work along Hall's Ferry road and,
overlooking the river and approaches from the Warrenton area, South Fort.
These latter two works played a less significant role than the others during
the two May assaults and siege operations.

Grant's approach came as Pemberton expected. Sherman occupied
the right of Grant's line, deploying on either side of the Graveyard road
that came into Vicksburg from the north. To Sherman's right, McPherson

brought his men up the Baldwin's Ferry road that entered town from the northeast and intersected the Jackson road as it curved north and entered Vicksburg from the northeast. McClernand's men deployed south of the railroad that entered town from the east. Stevenson's division would indeed be safe from combat for a time.[30]

On May 19 Grant, refusing to give Pemberton any more time to organize Confederate defenses, ordered an assault. The main effort came from Sherman's corps. Sherman's men had not seen any kind of action since the May 14 attack at Jackson, and very little at that time. Frank Blair's division led the attack down Graveyard road against the Stockade Redan, a strong work anchored on each side by two smaller fortifications. Martin Smith's division, aided by Cockrell's ever-ready Missourians, threw back the Yankees. The First Battalion of the Thirteenth U.S. Army infantry managed to get to the ditch in front of the redan and planted their colors there, giving them the right to the title "First at Vicksburg."[31]

After the first wave of the assault ground to a halt, those Federals who had made it close to the Confederate works had to endure shells rolling down the bank and exploding among them. They could not escape until nightfall because retreat in the daylight would have been suicidal. Elsewhere, McPherson's and McClernand's corps made some progress in advancing closer to Confederate defenses, but Grant had to admit failure. He had lost around 1,000 men, while Pemberton had light casualties of 200.[32]

On May 22 Grant ordered another, more general attack. A signal shot rang across the hills and ravines, and the three corps moved forward. On Sherman's front the result was about the same, though some troops did manage to gain a little ground on the corps' left. McPherson's attack also made little progress, the fire from the Great Redoubt and the lines of rifle pits anchoring it forcing the attackers to find cover quickly.

On the left, McClernand was the only commander to throw his whole corps into the fray, and his men met with enough success that the Confederates had to momentarily evacuate Railroad Redoubt, which threatened the safety of the Second Texas Lunette and the Salient Work and Square Fort positions on the far right. If the breakthrough had been permanent, Pemberton's right would have been forced well into the city, and McClernand may have produced a Confederate surrender. Reinforcements soon arrived, however, and the Rebels managed to drive the Federals back. McClernand's pleas for help were initially ignored, and by the time help came it was too late.

Grant's distrust of McClernand no doubt caused the delay; Grant simply believed, with some justification, that McClernand's claims of success were

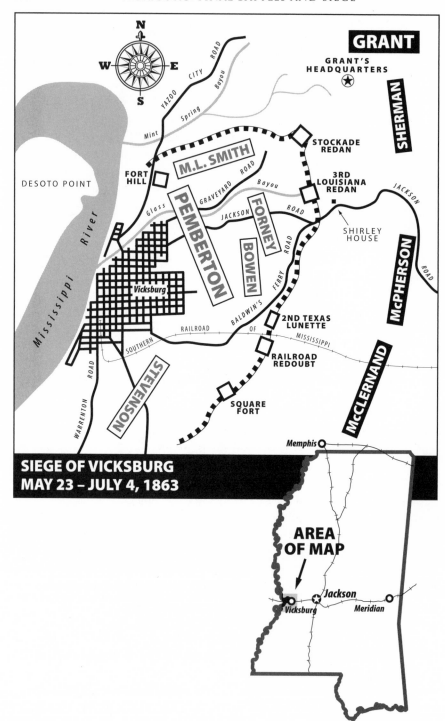

SIEGE OF VICKSBURG
MAY 23 – JULY 4, 1863

exaggerated. The events of that day set in motion a chain of circumstances, highlighted by McClernand's release of a congratulatory order that emphasized the role of his men in the May 22 assault at the expense of the other two corps. This faux pas ultimately led to Grant's dismissal of McClernand before the siege ended.[33]

Grant now decided on siege operations, and from May 23 until Pemberton surrendered Vicksburg on July 4, Union forces dug trenches and tunnels, getting ever closer to Confederate works. Using sap rollers (cylindrical, hollow contraptions stuffed with cotton or cane to ward off Rebel bullets), Federal soldiers pushed ahead, rolling the saps in front. Sometimes the Confederates successfully used lit fuses to ignite the saps, forcing a quick Yankee retreat. Mining operations met with some success, especially on June 25 and July 1 when Federal engineers exploded powder under the Third Louisiana Redan. Other mining projects might have worked, but the surrender came before explosives were detonated.

Several organized approaches were designed to threaten the Confederate strongpoints. From the Union right to left, the major approaches were John Thayer's, Thomas Ewing's, Giles Smith's, Thomas Ransom's, John Logan's, A. J. Smith's, Eugene Asa Carr's, Alvin P. Hovey's, Jacob Lauman's, and Francis Herron's. One of the most effective was Logan's approach, which was at the point of breaching the Stockade Redan defenses when the surrender came. Hovey's approach against Fort Garrott also came close to success by the time of surrender. Other approaches also almost succeeded before the surrender. The successes of the approaches demonstrated that Pemberton's decision to give up the fight was based on more than logistics.

Elsewhere in the region, feeble efforts were made to give relief to Pemberton's trapped army. Across the Mississippi, a Texas division commanded by Major John Walker attacked Union supply and staging areas at Milliken's Bend and Young's Point on June 7. At Milliken's Bend, U.S. Colored Troops, composed of former slaves from Mississippi and Louisiana, bravely fought off Walker's men, and the follow-up assault at Young's Point was equally dismal for Walker and his men.[34]

Joseph E. Johnston had his men operating in the so-called Mechanicsburg Corridor, that area between the Big Black and Yazoo rivers northeast of Vicksburg. But Grant sent patrols into the area, and other than occasional skirmishing, the Confederates did little to aggravate ongoing Federal siege operations. Grant, constantly reinforced by troops coming down the Mississippi from the north, put Sherman in charge of rotating men in and out of the Big Black bridge area east of Vicksburg to make sure that Johnston would not try an attack. There was no reason for concern, for Johnston spent most of the siege arguing with Richmond authorities that he did not have enough men to help Pemberton. His arguments lingered on so long that by the time he did make a feeble effort to move toward the Big Black in early July, Grant had enough men to negate any Johnston operation.

Arthur Fremantle found Johnston "below the middle height, spare, soldierlike, and well set up; his features are good, and he had lately taken to wear a grayish beard." Fremantle enjoyed his company. "He talks in a calm, deliberate, and confident manner; to me he was extremely affable, but he certainly possesses the power of keeping people at a distance when he chooses, and his officers evidently stand in great awe of him." Johnston told Fremantle what he had been telling Richmond: if the War Department sent him more men, he would try to relieve Pemberton. Fremantle left Johnston's camp to travel on to Alabama, and he was convinced that Johnston would be "heard of before long." Fremantle would be at Gettysburg on July 3, 1863, the day after that battle ended when Johnston was still miles away from helping Pemberton, who would give up Vicksburg the next day. When he heard Vicksburg had fallen, he did not comment further on Johnston.[35]

The forty-three-day siege tested soldiers and civilians in ways they never imagined, especially Pemberton's Confederates and Vicksburg's citizens. A big problem for the Confederate defenders was their lack of numbers. They did not have enough men to rotate soldiers in and out of earthworks, but they stayed on the move to the point of having little free time. Men in the entrenchments stood up at their own risk. Sharpshooters on both sides killed many men who forgot or got careless and stuck their heads above earthwork rims.

Pemberton had much food stored in Vicksburg, but since he did not know how long his men would be there, he immediately ordered rationing. Little by little the food supplies shrunk down to just enough food per man to keep them alive. Pemberton kept hoping Joseph Johnston would come to his aid, but after a while it became obvious that would not happen. Stories persisted that the men ate rats when all other meat, including that of mules, was consumed, and there is little doubt some ate both, though perhaps not to the extent reported. Lack of good water also became a problem as time passed. The incessant heat and humidity, interrupted from time to time by thunderstorms that turned the earthen works into mud, combined with lack of food, water, and exercise, truly made life miserable for the defenders. Many died at their posts of various illnesses, and by the end of the siege some were too weak to stand and had to be lifted out of the entrenchments by Union soldiers who were astonished that their opponents had held out so long under such circumstances.

Civilians, many of whom lived in caves decorated with items from their homes, also suffered from hunger, thirst, and heat. Inflated prices, driven up by ever-increasing shortages, sent costs out of reach for all but the very wealthy. Flour at one time reached $600 a barrel and biscuits $8 a dozen. Some people, including Confederate soldiers, took what they needed and did not worry about paying for it. Merchants were hardly in a position to protest, surrounded by armed soldiers and desperate civilians. Many homes became hospitals, which in most cases were more lethal than bullets and shells. Union artillery made life dangerous and interesting; women performed many heroic acts in hospitals, and youngsters trying to help in various ways performed their duties amid shot and shell falling to the earth in whole or in fragments. People turned to religion, which provided some hope and comfort, two rare conditions in besieged Vicksburg.

Union soldiers, aided by Grant receiving so many reinforcements, had the luxury of rotating in and out of the front lines. They spent leisure time playing cards and reading newspapers and letters from home, and they had more regular chances to take baths and boil lice out of their clothes than since the overland campaign began. Yet even these men endured misery. The heat, the likes of which many of these midwesterners were not used to, made shade a much-sought-after luxury. Poisonous snakes, mosquitoes, and other insects and vermin kept the men alert.

Some Federals regretted being involved in the siege because they knew noncombatants could be killed by the shelling and shooting. They thought of their own families and the misery they would feel if circumstances were switched. Yet they had a job to do, and they knew taking Vicksburg might bring the war to a quicker end and stop all the killing. Most simply wanted the Union restored; they cared little, with some exceptions, about the slaves they encountered, except for the labor they provided, which kept the soldiers from having to work so hard at keeping entrenchments in shape. These soldiers wanted the siege to end so they could go home, and the majority did not care how the impact of the fall of Vicksburg might affect slavery.[36]

Finally, Pemberton, tired of watching his men suffering and dying and convinced that Johnston would never do anything to help, decided that he must yield to the inevitable, and on July 3 he opened surrender negotiations with Grant. After some posturing led to a stalemate, Grant suggested that he and Pemberton allow their staffs to work out details. Finally terms were reached that allowed Confederate soldiers, minus their rifles and pistols, to be paroled rather than sent to Northern prisons. Confederate officers could retain their sidearms, clothing, and one horse each. On July 4, while angry and sad Confederates stacked their guns, Grant's army marched into Vicksburg. Not only had the Confederacy lost an army that would never fight again as a unit, it had lost thousands of weapons, including some 50,000 small arms and 172 cannons, plus a multitude of ammunition rounds. The fall of Vicksburg forced Franklin Gardner to surrender Port Hudson on July 9. That part of the Confederacy west of the Mississippi was now in effect severed from the rest, for Union forces had achieved a long-sought goal, the clearing and opening of the Mississippi River.[37]

To solidify the victory, Grant determined that he must deal with Johnston's presence east of the Big Black. Grant put together an expeditionary force of men from several corps, all under the command of William T. Sherman. Many of the troops protecting the Big Black flank were from Sherman's corps. Some of Sherman's soldiers enjoyed wrecking and stealing property on the Joseph Davis plantation, north of the Jackson-Vicksburg road near Bolton. Confederate skirmishers kept things lively. Sherman's troops would have another chance to tear apart the Davis place during Sherman's future Meridian campaign.

Johnston retreated to defensive works at Jackson, works that had been somewhat repaired and strengthened since the "battle" there back in May. However, Johnston had not seen to the stockpiling of supplies or the repair of the railroad bridge east of the city. The Confederates would not be able to fight for long and would risk being trapped in the event of a rushed retreat. Sherman's march toward Jackson began on July 9 and was hampered by heat and a lack of water. Good water became hard to find as Union troops found that Johnston's army had filled ponds and cisterns with dead cattle and horses.[38]

Arriving at the outskirts of the city on July 10, Sherman decided that Johnston's deployment of troops necessitated siege tactics. On the Federal right, Alvin P. Hovey and Jacob Lauman led their divisions into place along the Terry road, which entered Jackson from the southwest, and Bailey Hill, which overlooked Lynch Creek east of the New Orleans, Jackson, and Great Northern Railroad south of the city. Three divisions of E. O. C. Ord's Thirteenth Corps (Ord was given command after McClernand's departure) deployed to Hovey's left, south of the Robinson road, which entered Jackson from the west. Frederick Steele's division took position north of Robinson road, covering the Southern Railroad of Mississippi, which ran west to Vicksburg. North of the city John Parke's Ninth Corps came down the Livingston and Canton roads.

To defend the city, Johnston had Loring's division on the right, fronting Parke's advance, with W. H. T. Walker's division on Loring's left. Samuel

French's division faced Ord's corps, with John C. Breckinridge's troops in place to block Hovey and Lauman. Johnston had very little notion of fighting it out, for he knew he would eventually be overwhelmed. Perhaps his main reason for taking a stand at Jackson was to save face for his inaction during the Vicksburg siege. He had to know already that Jefferson Davis would harangue him for not making an effort to help Pemberton.

The major action during the siege of Jackson occurred on the Confederate left, where on July 12 Hovey and Lauman attacked. Breckinridge's men held firm, and Confederate artillery decimated the onrushing blue wave. The forty-minute attack fizzled, and the Confederates took over 200 prisoners and the colors of three Illinois regiments. Casualty figures told the story of the ill-advised assault. The total Federal list included 68 killed and 302 wounded, while the Confederates suffered only seven total casualties.

The siege dragged on until Johnston received word that an attempt to cut off a wagon train bringing ammunition to the Federals from Vicksburg had failed. A side note was that some Federal soldiers stole some of Jefferson Davis's letters from properties owned by Davis and his brother Joseph near Bolton. Many had been left with a friend, Owen Cox. Surprisingly, many of them survived the war.

On July 16 Johnston ordered his army to evacuate the city and move to the east, and for a second time he abandoned Mississippi's capital to the enemy. He had lost 71 killed, 504 wounded, and 25 missing during the brief siege. Sherman lost 129 killed, 762 wounded, and 231 missing. Sherman made half-hearted attempts to pursue, aggravated by a lack of cavalry to harass Johnston's retreat. Most of Johnston's army would wind up in the Army of Tennessee. Johnston's retreat signaled the last action of any significant Confederate military force in Mississippi. Sherman crowned his achievement by having a meal in the governor's mansion; he called it "a beautiful supper" and enjoyed a very celebratory time with his officers.[39]

MERIDIAN CAMPAIGN

An Evolution and a Portent

*A*fter Joseph Johnston evacuated Jackson for the second time, William T. Sherman decided against pursuit, mainly due to oppressive heat and the worn condition of his soldiers. But Sherman did not give up on the possibility of conducting a campaign across the middle of Mississippi, where the Southern Railroad still hauled Rebel supplies. When Johnston's army went away, most of his men transferred elsewhere, and Sherman knew that the possibility of encountering a sizable Confederate army in Mississippi was not likely. By marching a relatively small army from Jackson to Meridian, he could destroy supplies and railroads and drive off whatever Confederate troops might dare try to stop him. A successful campaign would provide more protection for the free flow of Union traffic on the Mississippi, a goal accomplished by victories at Vicksburg and Port Hudson, but not guaranteed as long as Confederate soldiers remained within striking distance of Vicksburg. There was no chance the Confederates could retake the city, but they could wreak havoc shooting at Union boats, as they had in the past.

In any event, the situation at Chattanooga, where William Rosecrans's army retreated after being beaten at Chickamauga, forced Sherman to shelve his idea. Grant wanted Sherman and other troops at Vicksburg to come to Chattanooga. Washington ordered Grant to replace Rosecrans and to chase away Braxton Bragg's army, which, after its Chickamauga victory, had occupied the heights around Chattanooga. Grant arrived and with his forces managed to force Bragg's army back into north Georgia, where eventually Joseph Johnston replaced Bragg as head of the Confederate Army of Tennessee. With Chattanooga securely in Federal hands, along with

Knoxville, where James Longstreet had given up taking that town and gone back to Virginia, time was taken for Union soldiers to work on the restoration of railroads north and east of Chattanooga. No ascent into Georgia could be made without a secure supply line that would be connected by rail to Nashville and beyond.[1]

Since the end of the Vicksburg campaign, Sherman had endured a painful personal experience and mediocre to moderate battlefield successes. In late September he and his corps prepared to travel from Memphis to help Grant. Then Sherman's son Willie became ill with what an Illinois doctor diagnosed as typhoid fever. Willie became sick while Sherman and his family were en route to Memphis from Vicksburg. By the time Sherman's boat, the *Atlantic*, reached Memphis, Willie's condition had deteriorated, and he was rushed to the Gayoso Hotel, where a more experienced doctor took over, but there was nothing that could be done. The boy died on October 3.

Sherman knew that Willie was the only one of his two sons who had expressed any interest in the military. In his memoirs, Sherman wrote he "had hardly time to pause and think of my personal loss." But he paused and thought about it quite a bit. That very evening he wrote an officer, "The child that bore my name, and in whose future I reposed with more confidence than I did in my own plan of life, now floats a mere corpse, seeking a grave in a distant land." Willie's casket was sent to Sherman's hometown, Lancaster, Ohio, but would later be disinterred and reburied in St. Louis with the rest of the family.

Sherman's heavy heart went with him to Chattanooga, and he and his corps did not perform well there, where Confederate troops led by Pat Cleburne outfought Sherman's soldiers. Cleburne eventually had to retreat when George Thomas's troops broke the center of Braxton Bragg's army on Seminary Ridge. Sherman's corps participated in clean-up operations. He also led his men toward Knoxville to pressure James Longstreet back into Virginia, thereby relieving the besieged Ambrose Burnside. Dissatisfied with the prospect of hanging around to watch railroad repairs, Sherman in early 1864 regained his enthusiasm to take to the field.[2]

Sherman talked with Grant about going back to Mississippi and doing what he had wanted to do before being interrupted by Chattanooga. A march through Mississippi, coupled with Nathaniel Banks's proposed advance up the Red River in Louisiana, would lead to destruction of Rebel supplies and free up Union troops to fight elsewhere. Sherman proposed "to break up the useless line of railroad from Memphis to Corinth, to attempt the destruction of Meridian without calling for a single man from the army in the field." He was referring to his army at Chattanooga, which would be left behind to continue railroad reconstruction. Grant agreed, and Sherman left Chattanooga and arrived in Memphis on January 10, 1864. He told Stephen Hurlbut, commanding in Memphis, to cease the occupation of Corinth, which would make the Memphis & Charleston Railroad superfluous, and to prepare two divisions, a total of 10,000 men, to leave Memphis on January 24 downriver to Vicksburg.

Sherman also talked with Sooy Smith, chief of Grant's cavalry in Memphis. Smith had returned after failing to catch Confederate cavalryman Nathan Bedford Forrest in Tennessee. Forrest led his men back into north Mississippi south of the Tallahatchie River. Sherman told Smith to concentrate his cavalry and get them ready to ride. Smith would have a projected force of 10,000 horsemen. Smith would spend his time organizing his cavalry and would be told by Sherman what to do at a later time. Sherman then went to Vicksburg, occupied by James McPherson's corps, and told McPherson to prepare two divisions for service in the field. Sherman then went back to Memphis, where he stayed until January 27, giving his commanders time to prepare.

Hurlbut chose troops from his First, Third, and Fourth divisions, a total of 12,187 men, more than Sherman asked for, but rather than split divisions to reach his 10,000 goal, Hurlbut chose all three. McPherson designated his Third and Fourth divisions, plus a brigade from the First Division and his corps cavalry, some 15,717 men. Smith's cavalry added 7,607 men, giving Sherman an army of 34,454, more than he had envisioned, but the more he had, the less likely any chances of reverses, barring an unimaginable disaster, from Vicksburg to Meridian and back. He would give special attention to Smith, whose cavalry would be a diversion. Also this many men would be able to wreck long stretches of the Mobile & Ohio Railroad north of Meridian.

Sherman wanted Sooy Smith to take 7,607 horsemen (the rest of Smith's men being left behind to guard Memphis) and to ride quickly to be in Meridian by February 10, or "as near the date I have mentioned as possible." He told Smith that such speed would "call for great energy of action on your part, but I believe you are equal to it, and you have the best and most experienced troops in the service, and they will do anything that is possible." Sherman reminded Smith that he had Benjamin Grierson along, who was very familiar with most of the area; that a diversion of boats and men was being sent up the Yazoo; and that the main movement of Sherman's force across the state would force the Confederates to divide their forces. Though Smith would be a diversion, too, he was not to be drawn into minor skirmishes that would slow his pace. Smith could attack any Confederate force encountered and drive them south. The cavalry's greatest object, wrote Sherman, was wrecking Rebel communications all the way from Okolona to Meridian along the Mobile & Ohio. Smith should take all the supplies he needed, "respect dwellings and families as something too sacred to be disturbed by soldiers, but mills, barns, sheds, stables, and such like things use for the benefit and convenience of your command." Clearly Sherman had no ideas of revenge for his son's death as was later charged by some Southerners.

If Smith had the opportunity, he should send a detachment to Columbus to destroy Rebel machinery and the bridge across the Tombigbee, but this was not essential, especially if it slowed him. Smith should try to keep in touch with Sherman from Pontotoc south to Meridian. Smith must avoid infantry; Sherman's main force would take care of any such eventuality. Sherman reminded Smith that they had already talked about this operation extensively and that the written orders "cover all points." Indeed, the written orders were clear and explicit. But Sherman did not take into account Forrest or Smith's timid leadership.

Union intelligence reports informed Sherman that Leonidas Polk, commanding in the Meridian area, had scattered his troops to collect taxes and conscript more men. The Confederates had two infantry divisions that could cause problems for Sherman. William Loring's division was at Canton, northwest of Jackson, and Samuel French had concentrated his division at Brandon, east of Jackson, where he had received reinforcements from Mobile. Sherman thought that the two divisions together totaled 12,000 men. He guessed that Forrest had about 4,000 cavalry in north Mississippi. Stephen D. Lee, commanding the southern area of Mississippi, had William Jackson's brigade, and Samuel Ferguson was moving his brigade to the state capital, where Lee was headquartered. Sherman did not know the total of Lee's force, but reports estimated his cavalry at Jackson at around 4,000 men.[3]

Sherman's information was not totally correct. Polk, who had named his command the Department of the Southwest, was told by Richmond that as of January 28, it would be changed to the Department of Alabama, Mississippi, and East Louisiana. Polk was headquartered in Meridian. Lee commanded the department's cavalry, not southern Mississippi, and he had established headquarters in Jackson. As for troops that would be directly involved in the Meridian campaign, Loring had 6,103 effectives, French had only 2,120, and Lee had 7,611 scattered cavalry. Altogether Polk would have in the field just under 16,000 men. Forrest had some 3,000 cavalry in north Mississippi, and his numbers may well have been included in Lee's total.

Interestingly, if the Confederates had all the troops on their present and absent lists, that number would have more than doubled to about 34,000. Obviously sickness, and to a greater degree desertion, had taken a significant toll since the surrender of Vicksburg.

Other troops available to Polk in his expansive department increased his possible effectives to 21,963. But he would not be able to concentrate them to meet Sherman, for to do so would have meant stripping Mobile, Alabama, and other areas that needed men to counter Yankee threats. In fact, as Sherman's march progressed, Polk became convinced that the Yankees intended to attack Mobile, perhaps in conjunction with the Union navy. So Polk did all he could to get men and supplies to Mobile; he would try to slow Sherman but not attack him. Sherman, who had no intention of going to Mobile, would be glad to find that Polk's misreading of the situation played right into Union hands.

Sherman hoped to make the march to and from Meridian a swift one, so he could return to Vicksburg in time to provide aid to Nathaniel Banks's Red River campaign. Sherman believed eliminating manpower and supplies east of Vicksburg and up the Red would go a long way toward cementing complete control of the Mississippi. As Sherman phrased it, the two campaigns would "result in widening our domain along the Mississippi River, and thereby set the troops hitherto necessary to guard the river free for other military purposes." The Mississippi had cost the Union heavily in men and casualties, and it was time to move on.

Sherman moved his army east on February 3, Hurlbut's column taking a trail north of the Big Black River bridge and the Southern Railroad of Mississippi, which connected Jackson to Meridian. McPherson followed a route south of the railroad, crossing at the Big Black bridge; Union cavalry rode south of McPherson toward Raymond before veering back toward McPherson's right. By spreading his troops out, Sherman made it much more difficult for the outnumbered Confederates to stop the Union advance. If the outnumbered Rebels concentrated an attack on either column, they would be hammered by the other. The march went quietly until Hurlbut reached the Joseph Davis plantation (brother of Jefferson Davis), and McPherson marched to Champion Hill, site of the fierce May 16, 1863, struggle between Grant and John Pemberton. Some of Stephen D. Lee's cavalry skirmished with Sherman's advance. Lawrence Ross's brigade of William Jackson's division first made contact. Ross did not remain long, for he had to rush to the Yazoo River to combat Sherman's diversion there. Wirt Adams's cavalry kept up the aggravation in Sherman's front; there was nothing cavalry could do against thousands of Union infantry but be a pest.[4]

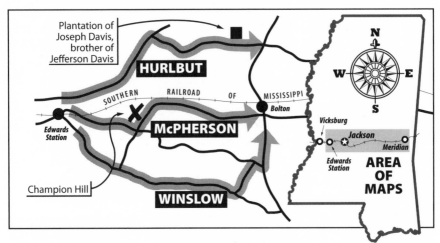

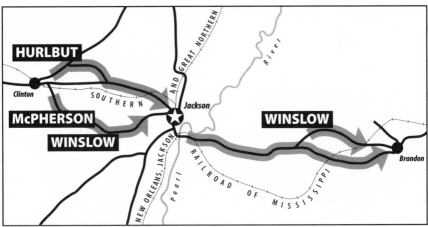

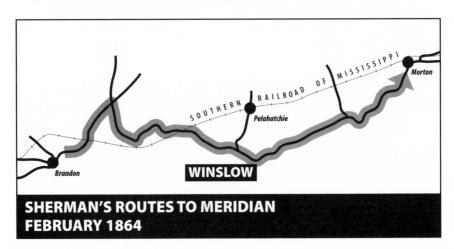

SHERMAN'S ROUTES TO MERIDIAN
FEBRUARY 1864

Sherman wrote that beginning on the 5th, the Rebels continually skirmished with his advance for eighteen miles, but by that evening Sherman's columns marched into Jackson. While Sherman moved on, Polk had gone to Mobile on an inspection trip, leaving William Loring in command. Polk's actions only make sense if he had decided he would do nothing to stop Sherman in Mississippi; he would make a stand at Mobile. Loring was at Canton. He had no chance of moving fast enough to try to block Sherman's arrival in Jackson, and he did not have enough men to do so anyway. Loring sent word to Samuel French to assume command in the Jackson area, but French's tiny division could not slow Sherman. Lee sent messages to Loring, Polk, French, and even Forrest in north Mississippi that reported the enemy's inexorable march. Wirt Adams's men, as usual, peppered away at the enemy, far more effectively than their numbers would indicate. Loring also heard about the Yazoo expedition, which added to his concerns.

The Yazoo operation started before Sherman's columns reached Jackson. The expedition was led by Colonel James Coates, Eleventh Illinois infantry, who reported on February 3 that his vessel, the *Des Moines*, had met some Confederate resistance along the Yazoo. Confederate generals Robert Richardson and Lawrence Ross had been detached to contest Coates's river maneuver. High ground on the east side of the Yazoo made life uncomfortable for Union troops, which included two regiments of U.S. Colored Troops, the Eighth Louisiana infantry and the First Mississippi cavalry.

The Confederates managed to take Yazoo City, but Union reinforcements forced Ross and Richardson to withdraw. They attacked again two days later and found that Union forces had no desire to be pinned down holding a meaningless position. The Confederates retreated back to their camps at a leisurely pace, and the little campaign ended with a whimper. Soon Confederate troops went east to resist Sherman and to aid Forrest. Coates and his men retook Yazoo City without any resistance. Out of 183 casualties, Coates lost thirty-one killed. Ross and Richardson did not detail their losses but estimated their killed and wounded to be eighty-seven. Confederate losses were likely higher and similar to Federal figures.

The Yazoo campaign had practically no impact on Sherman's overall operation. He had worried some Confederate commanders, but they knew where the real danger was. Under the circumstances, especially after the loss of Vicksburg, the Rebels had no need to hold Yazoo City, nor did Federal forces expect to protect the northern flank of Vicksburg, and no protection was needed. The Confederates did not have enough men to endanger the Yazoo. For Sherman, the Yazoo plan was militarily sound, but a waste of time.

Meanwhile William Loring, still trying to grasp what to do after Polk threw command upon his shoulders, had little idea of Sherman's location. Loring planned to take his men by February 6 toward Jackson from Canton, yet he continually received reports from Stephen Lee and French about Sherman's fast pace. Polk, reading messages from Mississippi, wired Loring that 6,000 men would be sent from Mobile to help. These men would go to Brandon, while Loring kept Sherman out of Jackson as long as possible. Loring was in no position to do so, and French and Lee together did not have enough troops to carry out Polk's orders, dated February 5, when Sherman's right column was chasing Confederates into and beyond Jackson.

Sherman noted in his report that the Confederates were trying to concentrate to block him from Jackson, but he knew they would be too late. He wrote simply, "We got into Jackson first." His men did not capture the pontoon bridge across the Pearl River before it was burned, but they quickly built one of their own 100 yards south of the other. The trip east continued, Brandon being the next major town. Certainly Polk could not get 6,000 troops to Brandon in two days to take on Sherman's men; no train of that era could cover that distance in time. The two Union corps merged at Jackson on the 5th anyway, and the Confederates, even if concentrated and adding an extra 6,000 troops, could not have been in position to stop the Federals.

Behind them, Sherman's troops had carried out the destruction he intended. The area between Jackson and Vicksburg had already been stripped and considerably damaged by war, and this was just the latest wave. McPherson's corps burned gins, barns, fences, and some houses, especially the vacant ones. Burning vacant houses had been a staple of Union activity in Mississippi since 1862. Houses burned that were not vacant usually were torched to get back at citizens who yelled obscenities at the Yankees. However, a widow had been accidentally killed where the railroad passed Bolton, a town between Jackson and Vicksburg, and Sherman did what he could to assure the care of her three children. As he had told Sooy Smith, he wanted civilians left alone and to concentrate on "railroads, warehouses, supplies, and foodstuffs in the state."

Whether Sherman understood how many Mississippians were already being victimized by Confederate deserters is not clear, but he would likely have thought such activities as justice for those who had supported the breakup of the Union. Some of the people who had food and other items stolen, however, could have been pro-Union. These people, and there were probably more than most Mississippians would have guessed, found themselves in a no-win situation, for if they made their feelings known, Rebel deserters would treat them worse, and if they told Sherman's men they were pro-Union, they likely would have been called liars. Many citizens indeed had been on the side of whichever army was closest, and Federal soldiers had become very skeptical.[5]

Large numbers of people had left the Vicksburg-Jackson countryside to get out of harm's way, and theirs were some of the empty homes that no doubt went up in flames. But many women and children, left to fend for themselves by soldiers in the Rebel armies, by husbands who had deserted, or by husbands and brothers killed in battle, barely survived. Some of Sherman's men shared their rations with such people. However, when the occupied home of a wealthy woman was found, they usually invaded the place, for they suspected that food hoarded for Confederate soldiers might well be hidden somewhere, and often they were right. They might not take all the food, but since many Yankees considered the upper class the root cause of the war, they often took whatever items caught their eyes.

Slave women had the worst of it, whether perpetrators were Union or Confederate. It will never be known how many were raped, but a few attacks are documented. However, those who committed such crimes, Rebels or Yankees, would do all they could to keep their assaults quiet. Union soldiers took advantage of slave women who trailed along with the army by forcing them to work for no compensation. Yet the women remained, for they believed freedom depended on the presence of Union soldiers.

The entrance of Sherman's army into Jackson had not gone completely uncontested. Lee's cavalry fought with much spirit until sheer numbers forced them east of the Pearl. Loring, of course, had to swing his troops to the east to avoid running into Hurlbut's corps as they marched through Jackson on McPherson's left. The divided wings now united could not be stopped by meager numbers of Confederate troops. Sherman had inflicted much damage on Jackson in two prior visits, and he loosed his men to yet another round of destruction. Much of what had been wrecked had been rebuilt, and agricultural produce had begun pouring into town once more for trips by rail to the north, east, and south. Only the line to Vicksburg was off limits due to Union occupation.

Union troops began burning supplies and accumulations of cotton and corn, and rail lines around Jackson were torn up. In Jackson, homes that had been left untouched during earlier Federal visits, including many mansions, were torched after they had been stripped of furniture, clothing, and other items. Some families already had many of their belongings stolen by the Confederates who retreated east. Sherman did not allow the burning and pillaging of private homes, but he could not watch everyone, and some of his lower-ranking officers ignored what was going on. The state capitol building was not touched, but most other public buildings that had previously escaped the torch were burned. Many citizens had already deserted Jackson, and more refugees filled roads out of town when they learned that the Yankees were coming again. The destruction was not complete; there are still antebellum homes in Jackson. (It is interesting to note that Sherman, McPherson, and Hurlbut do not mention the Jackson destruction in their official reports.)

The next day, February 6, a cold winter day by Mississippi standards, Union forces crossed the Pearl on the new bridge and marched toward Brandon, a town undefended except for about forty Rebel cavalrymen. Loring had decided to concentrate his and French's forces at Morton, east of Brandon. The Brandon townspeople had already seen their village heavily damaged by Union troops on July 19, 1863, as a result of Sherman's campaign against Joseph Johnston. The commander of Federal forces at that time was Frederick Steele. Steele's men destroyed railroad and supply depots that day, which Sherman had expected them to do, but they had done much more. Fires had already gutted the town, and stores were pillaged. Local sources indicated that the firing of some buildings spread. Now thousands of enemy troops were coming again.

On February 7 Sherman's army marched into Brandon and did not see much damage left to do. Some remaining buildings were burned, "except a block of brick buildings." The Southern Railroad was ripped up and a turntable destroyed, plus a bridge and several feet of trestle. An Illinois soldier summed up the passage through Brandon by writing simply that the army fired most of the town. Another wrote that not one commercial building was left standing. The army bivouacked for the night, and Sherman and McPherson found nice, unburned homes for temporary headquarters.[6]

Early on the 6th Loring had not yet reached Morton, but he assured French he would be there early on the 7th, though his division would not arrive for a few hours afterward. Scouting reports indicated a detachment from Sherman's forces headed north to Canton, a slight diversion ordered by Sherman, and Loring sent detachments of Lee's cavalry to the area. Lee said he would do all he could to protect Canton, though the town was in no danger at present. The next day, the 7th, Loring sent Lee a message from Morton: "My front between here and Jackson is entirely exposed, with the exception of a squadron of cavalry, and may be subject at any time to small raids of the enemy. Troops are concentrating here from Meridian." Loring added, ironically, that he had heard from Brandon late the previous day, and no Federal troops were there.

The next day Loring started toward Brandon, but he soon realized he was marching right into the teeth of Sherman's army. He advised Polk, who had returned to Meridian and was on his way to Morton, to stop in Newton. Loring realized he had to about-face to the east, despite the fact of Mobile reinforcements. He advised Polk, "The force being so much larger than ours I determined to fall back in the direction of Newton," following a trail north of the railroad to the town of Hillsborough. "The enemy is all this side of Jackson."

Sherman's columns left Brandon on the 8th and entered Morton the next day, finding the town unoccupied by Confederates. At this point, Sherman switched the marching order of his two corps, putting Hurlbut in the lead and McPherson in the rear. On the march, Confederate cavalry continued skirmishing with the vanguard of Sherman's army, and another mother was killed by Union skirmishers when she came to the door to see what was going on. The Confederates had not bothered to check the house, occupied by the woman and her five young children. As had happened east of Vicksburg, a squad of Union soldiers guarded the house and sent word to neighbors to come help with the children. When Sherman and McPherson found out about the incident, they directed men to contribute to a fund for the family and have the money turned over to a neighbor.[7]

Morton escaped the widespread destruction of Brandon. The railroad east and west of the town was destroyed, several families lost food, and some public buildings were burned. One Union soldier was not impressed with the town, and thought that once the enemy commissary building had been stripped of food and burned, the rest of the village was so dilapidated already that no more damage needed to be inflicted. Hurlbut's corps moved on toward Hillsborough and Decatur. By going north of the railroad, Sherman kept the Confederates guessing as to his whereabouts and his plans. He also made it harder for the Rebels to concentrate their forces by not marching straight alongside the railroad.

Because they were shot at from several homes, advance Union units burned much of Hillsborough. The canvas on Union wagons occasionally caught fire from embers flying through the air from the house fires. Confederate cavalry burned a creek bridge that had to be repaired before the Union wagon train could continue. In fact, fires got out of hand several times on march routes, slowing the columns, as did swampy areas and cold weather. Along the way, Sherman's soldiers found plenty of food and took most of it with them. So far, Sherman's desire to reduce greatly Confederate food supplies in this part of Mississippi was working well. Some foraging parties that strayed too far from Union columns were captured by

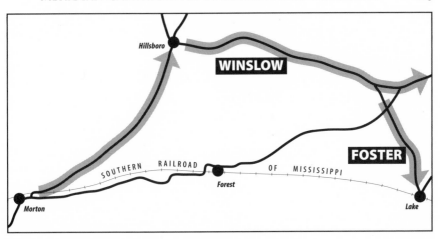

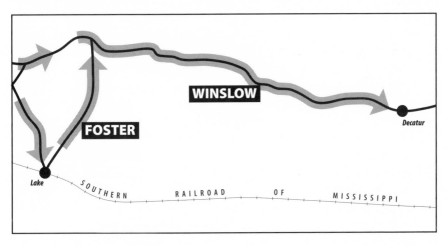

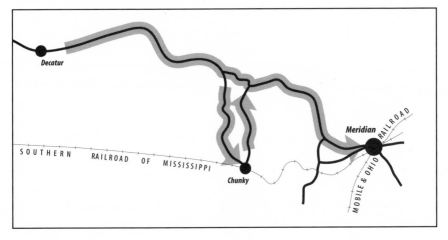

Confederate cavalry, which hovered all around Sherman's army. They were too weak to stop the Yankee march, but they did have plenty of opportunities to harass Hurlbut's and McPherson's corps.

William Loring remained unsure if Sherman intended to turn south toward Mobile rather than continuing to Meridian. Polk focused on Mobile, requesting reinforcements for the city from as far away as South Carolina. From Newton Station, where he had stopped, Polk wired Dabney Maury in Mobile that Sherman had moved on February 9 toward Newton. Loring continued retreating toward Meridian. He had never been an aggressive fighter, and he certainly knew better than to confront Sherman's legions. He might slow the Federals, but he could never defeat them, and to stand and fight would risk the capture of his entire force. Sherman had the numbers to easily flank and surround the Confederates. On February 12 Loring was fourteen miles from Meridian. He sent word to Polk that he was in a "strong position." Loring had made up his mind that Sherman indeed had targeted Meridian, both with his columns moving east and with more troops coming down the Mobile & Ohio. The validity of the former opinion was obvious, but not the latter. Loring was guessing about that. Sooy Smith had not yet left Memphis, and the Confederates knew nothing of Smith's assignment. Smith also seemed to have lost sight of his mission.[8]

Sherman's two corps continued their inexorable march, but did have memorable moments in the town of Decatur. Sherman, spending the night in a Decatur dwelling, with the woman of the house's permission, was almost captured by Confederate cavalry. Sherman had posted men to watch the house, but they had marched on past. They would return to drive off the Confederates, while Sherman and some of his aides headed to a corncrib to fight off the Rebels if they had to. If Sherman had been captured, the course of the war could have been changed, but since his army was so massive, it is difficult to conceive that the Confederates could have kept him very long. Of course, if he had been shot dead, the Union cause would have suffered a great loss.

Decatur met the fate of other towns, not necessarily because of Sherman's experience, for many fires were already burning before his near capture. The theme of the march continued with the burning of cotton gins, supplies captured and/or burned, fences taken for firewood, and foragers ranging the countryside to take food and whatever else they wanted from country homes. Most were willing to risk capture by enemy cavalry. Some of Lee's cavalry attacked a Hurlbut wagon train near Decatur and managed to kill several mules before having to retreat. Confederate cavalry continued their harassment all the way to the outskirts of Meridian. Sometimes they made strong stands against Sherman's horsemen, and they felled trees down onto roads and burned several bridges. These tactics obviously slowed Sherman's pace.

A Federal raiding party went south to Chunky Station, located on the railroad. General Manning Force, leading his brigade, pushed his men hard when he heard Confederate cavalry were nearby. His men ran off the few enemy horsemen they saw, burned seven loaded wagons and a long railroad bridge, destroyed rails, and burned a cotton warehouse that contained about 100 bales. Force's movement also broke up the concentrated enemy cavalry that had pestered the rear of Union columns.[9]

The Union corps entered Meridian on the afternoon of February 14. They had found a few empty Confederate works west of the town. The only military action the men faced was the exchange of a few rounds with Stephen Lee's cavalry, assigned to cover the retreat east of Loring's and French's divisions. Sherman learned that Polk, with Stephen Lee's cavalry covering the retreat, had left for Demopolis, Alabama, the morning of the 14th, and the Confederates had set fire to a locomotive and a train before leaving for Alabama. Sherman also learned that most rail cars had been sent south into Alabama. He decided not to pursue the Confederates, since they would probably be across the Tombigbee River onto Alabama soil before he could catch them. The Confederates had given him Meridian, the capture of which was his goal, and he saw no need of risking the lives of his men in an unnecessary chase.[10]

On February 13 Polk had told Loring that if Sherman could be held back until the evening of the 14th, there would be time to get train cars loaded with supplies past Meridian on the Mobile & Ohio to Mobile. At that time Loring was about five miles west of Meridian. Time was short, and Confederate troops had to pull into and out of Meridian at a fast pace. Loring's and French's men crossed the Tombigbee River, which meandered along the boundary between Mississippi and Alabama and was reasonably close to Meridian. They left Meridian just a few hours ahead of Sherman's advance. They had not accomplished much during Sherman's campaign to Meridian, but they, along with Lee's cavalry, had managed to hold out long enough for an estimated $12 million worth of military supplies, plus hundreds of thousands of pounds of bacon, flour, and wheat, and many train cars to escape south to Mobile. Trains picked up about 2,000 bales of cotton at Enterprise, several miles south of Meridian.[11]

The escape of the Confederate trains disappointed Sherman, but he set his men to work in and around Meridian to reduce the value of the railroad intersection to the Confederates. Sherman noted that "depots, warehouses, and length of sidetrack" were ample evidence of how significant Meridian had been. The junction made it easy for Confederate troops to be transferred, and, even more important, large amounts of supplies could be sent along the Mobile & Ohio and the Central Railroad of Mississippi. So Sherman had 10,000 of his men wreak destruction "with axes, crowbars, sledges, clawbars, and with fire, and I have no hesitation in pronouncing the work was well done. Meridian, with its depots, store-houses, arsenal, hospitals, offices, hotels and cantonments no longer exists."

Meridian was a small village at the time; the 1860 census indicated fewer than 400 residents. The railroad intersection had indeed made it valuable to the Confederates. Federal soldiers considered it a Rebel town, for most of the buildings, including homes, contained supplies or were used in other ways to support the Confederate war effort. The hospital had not been completed, and other buildings, plus several houses, were still under construction. So the soldiers in blue had few qualms about burning the entire place down. But though empty homes were burned as usual, as well as some in which people lived, not all occupied dwellings were torched. Some of these, however, were invaded by soldiers and ransacked. Other homes might have survived had not women who lived in them gone out of their way to agitate Federal soldiers. They, like other noncombatants, learned that keeping one's mouth shut when necessary was a valuable attribute. Even citizens who cooperated suffered thefts. Very few permanent residents completely escaped being terrorized by the visiting Yankees. Yet when Sherman said Meridian no longer existed, he was referring to its war-making facilities and other buildings of use to Confederate forces.[12]

Meridian was not the only place hit hard by destruction. Sherman ordered Hurlbut to send his men north and east to wreck the railroad and take supplies wherever they could find them. McPherson went south and west. Hurlbut reported to Sherman "the destruction of 60 miles of road, with ties burned and iron bent, one locomotive destroyed, and 8 bridges burned." The heating and twisting of rails gave birth to the phrase "Sherman's neckties," though Federal soldiers had used the method of destroying railroads for much of the war. McPherson's troops destroyed fifty-five miles of railroad, burned fifty-three bridges, and tore apart 6,075 feet of trestles south of Enterprise. Other destruction included "19 locomotives, 28 cars, and 3 steam sawmills destroyed and burned." Sherman rejoiced that the railroad had been made totally useless from Meridian to Jackson and from Meridian south to below Quitman and to the north to Lauderdale Springs. Unintentionally anticipating his next campaign, Sherman wrote, "The enemy cannot use these roads to our prejudice." Yet the railroads would be repaired rather quickly once the Yankees left; repairing railroads by 1864 had become a specialty by soldiers in both armies.

Stephen Lee later recalled that Sherman's men had "engaged in destroying the railroads north, south, east and west; for this purpose placing two divisions of infantry on each road. The roads were destroyed for twelve miles in every direction from Meridian. Attempts to stop the work were made by the cavalry, but the enemy's force was too large to hinder him."

Not all communities suffered the sweeping destruction of Meridian. McPherson ordered his troops moving south to be careful at Enterprise. The town, he wrote to General Marcellus Crocker, "not being a place as purely military as this, you will keep your command under control and not permit any destruction of private property." The community of Lauderdale Springs north of Meridian escaped destruction due to Union wariness about Confederate cavalry lurking about the area and reports from locals that Sooy Smith had been defeated to the north.[13]

Sherman had no idea what had happened to Smith, but he was furious that the cavalry had not showed up at Meridian. His patience vanished as days went by with no word at all from Smith. On February 20 Sherman, delighted with the destruction his men had accomplished, decided to start his columns back to Vicksburg. He had reports that all Confederate infantry had crossed the Tombigbee, so he knew that only enemy cavalry stood between him and Vicksburg. He had no concerns about Rebel horsemen; they had done little during the march to Meridian, and he expected no more than that on the return trip.

Sherman had never intended to go to Mobile anyway, but Smith's absence had wrecked his plans to have the Mobile & Ohio destroyed all the way from Meridian to Okolona, and the Southern Railroad of Mississippi destroyed from Meridian east to Selma, Alabama. His directive to Smith had included instructions to "respect dwellings and families," but his own men had certainly not always done so. During the march to Meridian, certainly he and his officers had not effectively enforced his directive to Smith. Yet there is no indication that Sherman intentionally made war on civilians. Unfortunately, he could not be everywhere at once to make sure his soldiers behaved as instructed. And too many of his officers allowed the men to do what they wanted. Also, fires started by retreating Confederates contributed to destruction, and attitudes of some citizens toward Union soldiers had proved to be very counterproductive.

As Sherman's soldiers left Meridian, there was still the burning question: what had happened to Sooy Smith? Smith did not leave Collierville, Tennessee, until February 11, the day after Sherman had told him he should be in the Meridian area. Smith chose to wait on a cavalry brigade commanded by Colonel George Waring. Waring's command had been held up during its trip from Union City, Tennessee, to Collierville. Bad roads, a ferry that could not be used, an icy stream, and muddy swamps and the like kept Waring at such a slow pace that his command did not reach Smith until February 8. Smith allowed Waring's troops to rest for a couple of days so they would be in better condition to begin the ride to Meridian. Smith's decision to wait on Waring rather than beginning his trip as Sherman had ordered doomed the operation.

Smith insisted later that Sherman had told him it was fine to wait for Waring, that to do so would certainly make the column more formidable. Sherman claimed he had said no such thing. Smith's own words seem to favor Sherman's version. On February 2 Smith wrote a message to Sherman from Memphis. In it he talks about Waring's problems causing him to be late. He noted that without Waring he would have 5,000 men instead of the 7,000 he and Sherman had discussed. Then he went on to say, "I feel in doubt as to what you would direct me to do if you were here." If Smith was sure about what he claimed Sherman had told him, he would have had no doubts. He went on to say, "My great anxiety is as to results and not as to my own connection with them." In effect, Smith was torn about whether to go or to wait. Again, if he had been certain that Sherman had told him to wait, he would have had no problem. But he had to know that by waiting, he could not carry out the role Sherman had expected of him.[14]

When Sherman received the message, he responded on February 6 from Jackson. He sent word to Memphis that he was sorry Smith had been delayed, "but trust he started then [the 2nd] and has made up his loss of time in speed." He said nothing about having Smith wait until Waring arrived. And he would have been furious, as he ultimately was, to know how much longer Smith would wait before moving.

Once Smith finally got under way, his cavalry descended in Mississippi, and he led them through the towns of Wyatt and New Albany, crossed the Tallahatchie River and Tippah Creek, and led them southeast through Pontotoc and Houston. Smith met practically no resistance, except for a few Rebel scouts and some state troops, who scattered before firing a shot. Smith then veered east to Okolona. From that point he sent a detachment farther east to Aberdeen to see if any ferry boats across the Tombigbee could be found. Smith sent reinforcements to his troopers in Aberdeen so the combined forces could attack the town of Columbus, which sat on the bluffs of the Tombigbee. There the Mississippi-Alabama state line was only about five miles to the east. With the rest of his force, Smith followed the Mobile & Ohio Railroad south toward West Point.

Nathan Bedford Forrest had received news on February 14 that Smith's column was moving toward Pontotoc. Forrest surmised that Smith would come toward the black prairie region through which the railroad passed. The area was very fertile and produced much food for Confederate forces. Forrest also knew where Sherman was and assumed that Smith intended to join him in Meridian. Forrest preferred letting the enemy come to him, which gave him time to call in his widely dispatched forces. He concentrated his men from points near the Tallahatchie and Yazoo rivers, ordering all his troops to rendezvous in Starkville, a community some twenty miles west of Columbus. Forrest reached Starkville on February 18.

The next day he received reports that Smith had reached Okolona, but that it was unclear which way the Yankees would go from there. Forrest knew Smith might attempt to cross the Tombigbee, so he sent a detachment to Columbus and additional troops, one a brigade led by his brother Jeffrey, to Aberdeen. He sent the rest of his riders to West Point, leaving dismounted men in Starkville to protect his wagon train. On the 20th Jeffrey Forrest encountered part of Smith's force, and the Confederates fell back toward West Point rather than fight a pitched battle. Forrest led the rest of his force to West Point, and he received word that Stephen D. Lee had sent reinforcements. Forrest stopped west of Sakatonchee Creek near Ellis' Bridge to wait for additional men rather than confront Smith immediately. Forrest led a foray that captured some Union soldiers who were burning a mill and capturing horses north of Ellis' Bridge. He ordered a bridge north of Ellis' to be destroyed. If Smith attacked, Forrest intended to hold the bridge he had and use it to cross and pursue the enemy. The night of the 20th passed quietly.[15]

Meanwhile Smith had concentrated his forces at Prairie Station on the Mobile & Ohio, and Federal horsemen advanced toward West Point. There was a brief skirmish north of that town with some of Forrest's scouts, and Smith's column stopped near West Point at 3 p.m. on the 20th. Reports convinced Smith that Forrest had strong forces to the Union right, center, and left, reports that greatly exaggerated Forrest's strength. Smith thought about his situation, including the 3,000 slaves who had joined the column, all mounted but not armed. There were also 700 pack mules to be concerned about. Smith concluded that he had only 5,000 effectives to take into battle. He decided, too, that the terrain was such that his men would have to dismount to fight. He believed Forrest's cavalry had better weapons, and he believed that, of his own force, only one brigade had shown proper military discipline during the trip from Memphis. Smith had also heard that reinforcements for Forrest from Stephen Lee might be on the way.

After the war, a story made the rounds that Smith became desperately ill, but remained well enough to question some Confederate prisoners. Smith, with "his mind at times bordering on delirium," told Benjamin Grierson that he should take command. Smith then asked Grierson what his plans would be. Grierson said he would continue on to Meridian, at which point Smith made a quick recovery and said Stephen Lee's cavalry was to the south somewhere, and it would be too dangerous to proceed. Smith reassumed command and decided to begin retreating back to Memphis. Lee told this story in an attempt to show that his cavalry and General Polk had done as much to restrict Sherman's success as Forrest. The incident was partially true, but certain aspects should be handled with care.

Grierson had earlier received permission from Smith to go to Aberdeen with one brigade, cross the Tombigbee if possible, and find Sherman. Grierson found a crossing and arranged to build a pontoon bridge, but he soon received a message from Smith to cancel the crossing and ride hard to West Point. So Grierson was definitely at West Point when the retreat decision was made. Smith, however, made no mention of offering the command to Grierson, nor does Grierson. Grierson does write in his memoir, however, that the pressures of command had a negative impact on Smith. Grierson wrote, "his nervous system [had deteriorated] to such an extent as to render him absolutely sick and unable to properly command in such an emergency." Grierson did talk to Smith about continuing south, and he assumed Smith agreed, but around midnight of February 20 Smith called for Grierson and said he had decided to retreat. Grierson argued strongly that with one brigade he could find Sherman, but Smith refused to consider such a movement.

Smith concluded, according to his postcampaign report: "Any reverse to my command, situated as it was, would have been fatal." Smith also guessed that Sherman might already be back in Vicksburg. So Smith talked himself into advancing no farther; he had thought of a long list of rationalizations. He wrote that his men had burned two million bushes of corn and 2,000 bales of cotton and had wrecked thirty miles of railroad. Two hundred prisoners and some 3,000 horses and mules had been taken, and the many male slaves who had flocked to the column were "well fitted for our service." In effect, Smith figured he had done enough, and it was time to go back toward Memphis. First, he would pull back north from West Point and try to draw Forrest to him.[16]

Smith's account of what he did seems a bit muddled. On Sunday morning, February 21, Nathan Bedford Forrest received reports that Smith was advancing from West Point toward Ellis' Bridge. Forrest placed his brother Jeffrey's brigade on the east side of the creek, fronting the bridge, and another brigade west of the bridge as a backup. Nathan Bedford Forrest also sent word for troops at the Starkville camp to come up just in case. He sent small detachments to guard other approaches. Smith attacked Jeffrey Forrest's brigade at 8 a.m., and after a battle of two hours, Smith's troops fell back. Jeffrey's men had thrown up hasty breastworks of logs and fence rails, and as a result had only seven casualties, all wounded. Nathan Bedford Forrest followed the Yankees with his escort, two regiments, and one section of a battery. Some of his troops were mounted and others dismounted. The Confederates moved cautiously until the battery fired a few rounds and got no response. Forrest knew then that Smith must be retreating north. Forrest and his small force, less those on foot, immediately rode on in pursuit, and he sent word for 2,000 additional riders to follow, plus a battery. For the rest of the day, Forrest fought Smith's rear guard, which made enough occasional stands to slow down the Rebel pursuit.

Strangely, Smith does not mention the clash at Ellis' Bridge, but rather focuses on his tactical successes in holding back Forrest's pursuit. He wrote that he placed his forces behind every hill, every grove of timber, anything that provided cover, and his men shot down many Confederates at "short range." Smith reckoned his own casualties were "uniformly light." Smith offers no timeline in his report. Forrest wrote that his force charged and drove the Federals repeatedly; he estimated fifteen to twenty Union casualties and several captured. As night fell, Forrest noticed that the two lines were so close that some of his men fired on their own comrades, so he decided to stop and set up camp and continue pursuit at dawn. Smith does not mention stopping to camp, and why he did not keep his men moving with just a token force left behind to slow Forrest is mystifying.

The next morning the opposing forces fought fiercely around Okolona. Smith's rear guard made a stand in Okolona and about five miles northwest of the town on the Pontotoc road. At the latter point, Forrest's brother Jeffrey was killed. Forrest's forces kept driving the Yankees toward Pontotoc. About ten miles from that town, the Federals made their final stand, deployed in three lines a few yards apart. Though some of Forrest's men on foot were lagging behind due to the hilly terrain, he decided to attack with the few he had on hand. His men had used up most of their ammunition, so he chose intimidation as his last real chance to break down enemy resistance.

Then Smith's cavalry suddenly rode at Forrest's line. Forrest called it "the grandest cavalry charge I ever witnessed," but his men stood and repulsed the first, second, and third lines of attackers. Forrest wrote proudly that Smith's cavalry "fled the field in dismay and confusion, and losing another piece of artillery, and leaving it strewn with dead and wounded men and horses." Forrest decided he had gotten all he could out of his men and conducted no further pursuit. A small command of state troops came up that evening, and Forrest ordered them to push the enemy on across the Tallahatchie if possible. Out of Forrest's 2,500 men, he lost twenty-seven killed, ninety-seven wounded, and twenty missing.

Smith claimed much of the fighting was forward and back, in effect that his troops charged and were pushed back, and Forrest's men did the same. Yet he does admit that his men rode rapidly to get away from Forrest. "Our march was so rapid that the enemy could not outstrip and intercept us, which he constantly endeavored to do." Smith does not mention his cavalry's charge at Pontotoc, and he indicates there was no more skirmishing after his forces passed through the town. If true, the state troops sent on by Forrest obviously did not accomplish much.

Smith, no doubt anticipating Sherman's anger, claimed that Sherman had told him he could get along without him "if I found it impossible to get through." He went on to say that his return to Memphis "drew the enemy after me and inflicted heavy losses upon him, and saved my command," and allowed his troops to bring back all the animals captured, several Rebel prisoners, and several slaves who had joined the column, and he described his losses as "trifling." He commented further, "Attempting to cut through to Sherman, I would have lost my entire command, and of course could have rendered him no assistance." His losses: 54 killed, 179 wounded, and 155 missing. Compared to the nearly 7,000 men he had with him, the casualty list is indeed trifling and indicated very little direct fighting with Forrest's forces. Sherman was not impressed by Smith's report, and Smith would soon depart the war.

At Meridian, Sherman decided he had waited long enough for Smith, and on February 20 he led his troops back toward Vicksburg. McPherson took the main east-to-west road, and Hurlbut took a more northerly route, along with Sherman's cavalry, so that attempts could be made to try to contact Smith or at least to find out what had happened to the absent officer and his cavalry. Union cavalry went as far north as Louisville, located about thirty miles southwest of Starkville, in search of news about Smith. The main columns moved on west, crossed the Pearl on February 25–26, and camped in the Canton area. There had still been no news from or about Smith.

Since the march west had been absent of enemy harassment, Sherman "left the army at Canton, rode into Vicksburg on the 28th, received my dispatches from General [Nathaniel] Banks." Sherman had agreed to assist Banks in planning the Red River campaign, which would prove to be disastrous. After meeting with Banks and Admiral David Porter in New Orleans to talk about that campaign, Sherman returned to Vicksburg, where he finally heard about Smith's misadventures.

Sherman thought his campaign, aside from Smith's performance, had been a great success. He had lost but twenty-one killed, sixty-eight wounded, and eighty-one missing. Aside from Forrest's total, the only Confederate report regarding casualties during Sherman's campaign came from Stephen D. Lee's cavalry, which had twenty-one killed, eighty wounded, and forty-eight missing. Perhaps the lack of reports from division commanders indicates that Lee's men were the only ones who exchanged fire with Sherman's men.

Sherman's troops captured 400 Confederates and brought back with them 5,000 slaves who could no longer serve as forced labor for Rebels, some 1,000 white Southerners who preferred going back into the protection of the Union rather than being vulnerable in central Mississippi, 3,000 animals, and a large number of wagons and other wheeled vehicles. Destruction of gins and cotton had been widespread and massive. Sherman was also delighted that a diversion by Admiral David Farragut at Mobile had created havoc there with the moving of Confederate supplies and civilians away from the city in panic. He wrote prophetically, "Their time is not yet, but will come in the due order of events."[17]

As for Sherman, he would soon be named to command Union troops concentrating at Chattanooga, from where he would begin his successful campaign to capture Atlanta, followed by his march to the sea. Sherman is credited for raising the level of hard war, beginning with the Meridian campaign. He chose to bring the war home to noncombatants, to make them feel the pain and price of war, not by personal attacks but by destruction of food, railroads, and anything else that might provide support to Confederates. He thought such destruction would break the will of Southerners and Confederate soldiers to carry on the war. Certainly some of his soldiers ignored his personal views on the sanctity of homes and families. Perhaps he should have written his views as an order and made sure every officer from regimental commanders on up received a copy and that each understood he would be responsible for enforcing Sherman's expectations.

Earlier in the war, such lack of discipline infuriated him, but he had decided that breaking the will of Southerners to fight would be more effective more quickly than winning battles. He wanted to terrorize Southern whites to the point of making them want the war to end. Yet the indiscriminate burning and wrecking of homes was often unjustified, and in such cases went beyond his stated position. There was no way to police thousands of men, and there was no doubt that his army, as well as other Union and Confederate armies, contained soldiers who had felonious, brutal, and mean-spirited attitudes and personalities that could and frequently did get out of hand. Often such men were punished, but most were not, simply because keeping civil law during a war that had spread over a very large territory was a challenge that could not be met.

Also, Sherman's style exhibited during the journey to and from Meridian had already been practiced by Union forces, and Confederate guerrillas, during the Vicksburg campaign. He did not suddenly dream up his philosophy of hard war just in time for the Meridian campaign. He built on what had been evolving in the western theater since early 1862. His earlier disgust with attacks on civilian property softened as time passed, and he, and other Union officers, including Grant, began to see that pacification would not work.

Sherman came to believe that the practice of hard war would work, and the 1,000 white Mississippians who went with his army back to Vicksburg proved to him the validity of his views. Take away the will to resist, to support a government that could not provide protection, and to make clear to Confederate soldiers that they were putting their families in harm's way and filling graveyards for no good reason, and the war would end. While the Meridian march demonstrated the evolution of his views, it also portended Sherman's march to the sea in Georgia, where he would continue his hard war philosophy on a much wider scale.[18]

Battery Robinett on Corinth Battlefield. Photograph by Michael B. Ballard.

Schaifer House on Port Gibson Battlefield. Where first shots of the battle were fired. Photograph by Michael B. Ballard

Hinds County Courthouse, Raymond, Mississippi. Used as a hospital during the Vicksburg Campaign. Photograph by Michael B. Ballard

Nathan Bedford Forrest. Confederate cavalryman who won his greatest victory at Brice's Cross Roads. Courtesy Ezra J. Warner, *Generals in Gray*, Baton Rouge: Louisiana State University Press.

Samuel Sturgis. Defeated by Nathan Bedford Forrest at Brice's Cross Roads. Courtesy Ezra J. Warner, *Generals in Blue*, Baton Rouge: Louisiana State University Press.

Andrew Jackson Smith. Victorious Union
commander at the Battle of Tupelo. Courtesy
Ezra J. Warner, *Generals in Blue*, Baton Rouge:
Louisiana State University Press.

U. S. Grant. Collection of the author.

David Farragut. Library of Congress.

David Dixon Porter. Private Collection of
Robert Younger.

Maj. Gen. Henry W. Halleck. Officer of the
Federal Army. Library of Congress.

William Tecumseh Sherman.
Library of Congress.

James B. McPerson. National Archives.

John A. McClernand. National Archives.

E. O. C. Ord. Courtesy Ezra J. Warner, *Generals in Blue*, Baton Rouge, Louisiana State University Press.

William S. Rosencrans. Library of Congress.

Maj. Gen. Benjamin H. Grierson. Library of
Congress.

John C. Pemberton.
Library of Congress.

Gen. Martin L. Smith, C.S.A. Library of Congress.

Earl Van Dorn. Henry W. Elson, *Elson's New History: The Civil War through the Camera*, 1912.

Joseph E. Johnston. Courtesy Vicksburg National Military Park Archives.

Sterling Price, C.S.A. Library of Congress.

Stephen D. Lee. Mississippi State University
Libraries, Special Collections Department,
University Archives.

Ulysses S. Grant.
Collection of the author.

Fort Hill. Only part of Confederate siege line never attacked by Union forces. Courtesy Vicksburg National Military Park Archives.

John M. Thayer's approach to Confederate lines during the Vicksburg siege. Photograph by Michael B. Ballard.

Sap Roller and Gabions. Used to protect Union soldiers digging approaches to Confederate lines during siege, exhibits at Vicksburg National Military Park. Photograph by Michael B. Ballard.

The Coker House, built in 1852, is the lone surviving wartime dwelling of the Champion Hill battlefield. Restoration of the house began in 2008 and was completed in 2010. The house is open for public tours. Photograph courtesy of the Mississippi Historical Society.

8

BRICE'S CROSSROADS

Confederates Win and Lose

After the Meridian campaign, William T. Sherman returned to Chattanooga. Significant changes were about to be made in the Union command hierarchy. In March Ulysses S. Grant was named commander of all the armies, replacing Henry Halleck, who became chief of staff, reporting to Grant. No one could have appreciated the irony more than Grant. After Shiloh, Halleck had taken away his command, and Grant reported directly to him. Now Halleck had voluntarily given up his post, and he would report to Grant. Grant appointed Sherman to command the military division of the Mississippi, an expansive area that included most of the western theater. Grant told Sherman that he should go after Joseph E. Johnston's Confederate Army of Tennessee and capture Atlanta. After that, the plans were a bit vague, but Sherman would clarify his plans after Atlanta fell.

Sherman assumed his new command on March 18, 1864, and on May 5 his force of three armies, a total of just under 100,000 men, began their march from Chattanooga toward Atlanta. As the armies moved, battling and pushing Johnston's army toward Atlanta, Sherman worried about his ever-lengthening supply line, which extended all the way north to Nashville. He believed Nathan Bedford Forrest would soon gather a large cavalry force and strike the railroad between Nashville and Chattanooga. Sherman knew he must do something to deter Forrest, and he decided his best strategy would be sending a force from Memphis into northeast Mississippi to attack Forrest and his small force and hopefully kill the Confederate general in the process. Even if Forrest were not defeated, at least he would be tied down in Mississippi.

General James McPherson, with Sherman in Georgia but still in command of the Department of the Tennessee, issued instructions to General Cadwallader Washburn, commanding in Memphis and west Tennessee, detailing Sherman's wishes. On May 20 McPherson sent word from Georgia, "Keep the enemy occupied in your district and press him at all points as far as your force will allow." A few days earlier McPherson sent word to Washburn that an effort should be made to occupy a position at Eastport, on the Tennessee River north of Iuka, to give logistical support to raids south to Columbus, Mississippi, and west to Grenada. These activities should keep Confederate troops in Mississippi occupied. On June 1, after he learned that Forrest was moving into north Alabama, McPherson told Washburn "to move into North Mississippi" and "smash things." Washburn understood that Sherman expected him to keep Forrest and other Confederate forces away from the Union supply line, even if news indicated Forrest had left or had plans to travel to Sherman's supply line. If enough noise could be made in Mississippi, Forrest might be called back.

Sherman had reason to be concerned. Stephen D. Lee, commanding cavalry in Mississippi, had ordered Forrest to go into middle Tennessee with 3,000 men, plus two artillery batteries, to destroy as much of the railroad descending from Nashville as possible, "breaking up lines of communications connecting that point with Sherman's army in Northern Georgia." Forrest left Tupelo on June 1 to carry out the operation. Two days later he received word from Lee that "the enemy were moving in force from Memphis in the direction of Tupelo, and ordering my immediate return." Lee also began concentrating other troops to join Forrest in the Tupelo-Baldwyn-Booneville area.[1]

The reason for Lee's change in plans was Washburn's hard work in putting together a large force to invade north Mississippi from the Memphis area. He thought that "prompt action was important, and that a longer delay would probably allow General Forrest to carry out his plans, which were supposed to be to operate on General Sherman's communications." By the morning of June 1, the day Forrest left Tupelo for Tennessee, Washburn had assembled 3,300 cavalry, 5,000 infantry, and 16 artillery pieces. The infantry went by train "to a point between Collierville and La Fayette, where a bridge was destroyed." The rest of his forces departed the same day. Washburn later bragged in his report, "The force sent out was in complete order, and consisted of some of our best troops." Washburn insisted that the column should travel as lightly as possible to speed up their operation. Wagons hauled ammunition and supplies to sustain a twenty-day operation. Sherman had asked for a force of 6,000, but Washburn added 2,000 more.

Sherman's choice of a commander for the expedition had unusual roots. After the Sooy Smith disaster, he promised Colonel Benjamin Grierson, the Vicksburg campaign raider, command of cavalry, which implied command of field operations in the Memphis area. Grierson wrote his wife the good news on March 13. Sherman, however, did not keep his promise. Shortly after his conversation with Grierson, Sherman gave the command to General Samuel Sturgis, also a cavalry commander, who had been serving in the Army of the Ohio and had tried and failed to catch Forrest and his cavalry as the Confederates returned to Mississippi from a raiding expedition in Kentucky and west Tennessee. During the raid, the infamous massacre of U.S. Colored Troops at Fort Pillow on the Mississippi took place. Forrest's men had shot down many black soldiers who tried to surrender.

Sturgis, a graduate of the U.S. Military Academy, had fought in Mexico and in Indian skirmishes, but his only notable battle experience since Wilson's Creek had involved Forrest. Sturgis had no luck operating against Forrest. In fact, he had broken off the chase due to worries over supplies and the condition of some of his troops, and it is doubtful Forrest ever knew that Sturgis was on his trail.

When Sturgis first arrived in Memphis, Grierson found him neither credible nor reassuring, though it must be remembered that, thanks to Sherman, Grierson had reason to resent Sturgis. Grierson feared Sturgis's presence would discourage the men. "He was a stranger to them," Grierson wrote, "entirely unknown to the troops assigned to his command, and had no knowledge whatever of the country through which he was to operate." Not only that, Sturgis's personal habits left much to be desired. Grierson wrote that Sturgis took a room at the Gayoso House, a Memphis hotel, "where, being dissipated in habits, he had a protracted drunken spree for nearly two weeks, during which he smashed looking glasses, crockery, and furniture to his heart's content, kicking up 'high jinks' generally, until his condition became notorious."[2]

Sturgis had shown timidity in the field, and he had, as Grierson noted, displayed a propensity for alcohol, and yet he seemed to impress Sherman, again for obscure reasons. Sturgis had left Memphis for a time, returning to his command to the north, but Sherman soon recalled him. Normally Sherman would not have given an officer like Sturgis a second thought, but perhaps because he had been misinformed by others, he had confidence in the nonaggressive drunkard. Another factor, which likely played a larger role in Sherman's preference, was that Sturgis had graduated from West Point, and Grierson had not. In both Northern and Southern armies, West Pointers took care of each other.

A bitter Grierson noted in his memoirs that Sherman had compounded the error he made in choosing Sooy Smith to lead the cavalry in the ill-fated Meridian operation. Sturgis, Grierson believed, would be as bad, if not worse, than Smith. Grierson asked to be relieved from his current command so he could return to Illinois and Iowa and organize a new cavalry force. His request was denied.

Washburn knew that Sturgis's return to Memphis, which made Sturgis the ranking general on hand, sent a clear signal that Sherman wanted Sturgis to lead the expedition into Mississippi. Washburn, also not enthralled with Sturgis, said, "I had no alternative" but to give the command to Sturgis. After his post-trip rest and recreational binge, Sturgis officially reported for duty three days before the expedition had been scheduled to move out. He and his staff joined his new army on June 2, and thereafter his column began moving toward Ripley in northwest Mississippi. Sturgis had orders "to proceed to Corinth, Miss., by way of Salem and Ruckersville, capture any force that might be there, then proceed south, destroying the Mobile & Ohio Railroad to Tupelo and Okolona, and as far as possible toward Macon and Columbus, with a portion of my force, thence to Grenada and back to Memphis." Sturgis had leeway to fill in the blanks for the expedition. That is, he could make his trip according to whatever guidelines had not been spelled out in his orders.[3]

Forrest had established headquarters at Jackson, Tennessee, on April 14, just two days after his men had shot down the black troops at Fort Pillow. Abraham Buford's division dispersed around west Tennessee looking for deserters and trying to recruit new men. At the time, Forrest had in mind using Tupelo as his new base, as well as making necessary repairs to the Mobile & Ohio Railroad north of Tupelo for use as a supply line. Forrest received word that his troops would soon be inspected at Tupelo by representatives of the adjutant general's office in Richmond. Forrest welcomed the inspection, and he hoped his immediate commander, Leonidas Polk, would be there. Forrest promised Polk that he would be in Tupelo by May 4, and his corps assembled there by the 6th.

Forrest's intelligence network, very effective, got word to him by April 29 of Federal plans to come after him. Before that time Forrest had scattered his troops about southwest Tennessee and northwest Mississippi to watch and raid, but Polk informed him that his cavalry would be expected to concentrate and operate against Sherman in Georgia and north Alabama as soon as Sherman's intentions became clear. Polk also sent a part of Forrest's force south toward the Yazoo River in response to news of Yankee activity below Greenwood, but the foray proved to be a waste of time. Forrest continued the task of trying to get in touch with his forces from his headquarters in Jackson, Tennessee, ordering them to concentrate at Tupelo.

Forrest, along with his escort and staff, left Jackson for Tupelo on May 2, riding along a road that led through Bolivar across the state line into Mississippi through Ripley and to Tupelo. Near Bolivar, Forrest got word of fighting going on west of the town, so he sent unarmed men into Bolivar to continue south with his wagon train. He and the 100 mounted men of his escort rode to reinforce the Confederate troops being attacked. The Union troops had repeating rifles, so at dark Forrest ordered a withdrawal. He and his men crossed the Hatchie River, burned the bridge behind them, and caught up with the wagon train at Ripley. They reached Tupelo on May 5.

Forrest spent most of the rest of May in and around Tupelo. He reorganized his force while his men gathered forage and secured additional horses and mules, and officers and staff equipped and trained a sizable body of new recruits and conscripts. He added a four-battery artillery battalion commanded by twenty-one-year-old John Morton; Morton would learn quickly that when it came to artillery tactics, Forrest had his own ideas, often unusual but frequently effective. Forrest also added a pioneer corps to repair bridges and roads. Many of his men had fine horses, but several had been stolen from farms in the area. With the great need for food for the armies, horse stealing did not create goodwill with farmers. Forrest and his officers cracked down on men who thought they were entitled to any mount they liked, no matter their rationale.

Inspectors found that Forrest's cavalry was loosely organized, to say the least, but by this time in the war, commanders could not be too picky. He recruited men where he could find them, but he would not take just anyone. At one point he sent men from his command back to their original units. Despite the confusion of disorganization and scattering of troops in the north Mississippi area to meet threats, real and imagined, by the end of May Forrest's cavalry numbered some 9,000 men on paper.[4]

But he could not concentrate them, for factors beyond Forrest's control caused the disbursement of troops across north Mississippi and north Alabama. Sherman continued to order sorties from Vicksburg to threaten the lower reaches of the Mississippi Central Railroad, and gunboats up the Yazoo continued harassing farmland production. In Georgia, as Joseph Johnston retreated before the pressure of Sherman's men, various locations from Georgia into Alabama became vulnerable to Federal cavalry raids, and Stephen D. Lee, now Forrest's immediate commander, wanted Forrest to send men to protect threatened supplies. James Chalmers left for Alabama with his three brigades, dramatically reducing the number of men Forrest had on hand. Lee had replaced Leonidas Polk as commander of the Department of Alabama, Mississippi, and East Louisiana, and Lee, aside from logistical concerns, had to protect ordnance factories at Selma in south Alabama as well as several areas in Mississippi. Forrest had to cancel a projected Tennessee raid, for he lost men to Lee, which implied he could not count on Lee for any appreciable help in Mississippi.

Despite the problems of trying to protect a wide span of geography, Lee wanted to send Forrest to attack Sherman's supply and communication lines; many in the Confederacy wondered why Forrest had not done so already. But that would not happen, not then or in the future, because Sherman's determination to keep Forrest in Mississippi worked beautifully. Even as Forrest and a portion of his command rode toward Alabama to make the strike Lee and others had envisioned, they never left Mississippi after news of Sturgis's column reached Lee.

Forrest had a force of some 2,600 men with him when he received an urgent message from Lee to return and stop the small Federal army advancing from Memphis. While the Yankees seemed to be on a course toward Corinth, there was little doubt, based on scouting reports, they intended to penetrate Mississippi and strike the food-producing area south of Tupelo. Forrest immediately issued orders to reverse his course, and he now had the challenge of assembling enough men to throw back the Union invaders. Forrest led troops down the Fulton road east of Tupelo and sent word for a brigade to come to Rienzi, where a small Union detachment of cavalry had attacked the railroad and burned the depot. John Buford sent Tyree Bell along with two batteries. Forrest and his men rode on to Tupelo, arriving June 5. There Forrest received a message that the Federal column was at Salem, about fifty miles west of Tupelo.

Two days later Forrest's scouts sent word that Yankees were now traveling in the direction of Ruckersville. Forrest left Tupelo with Buford's division and went to Baldwyn and the next day on to Booneville. Edmund Rucker and his brigade rode into Booneville on the evening of June 9. Phillip Roddey left a small portion of his command at Decatur and led the rest north to join Forrest. W. A. Johnson was on the way to Tupelo, but when Johnson reached Baldwyn, a message awaited ordering him to Booneville. Also present were Hylan Lyon's brigade, John Jackson's escort unit, a company of Georgia troops led by Henry Gartrell, and John Morton's artillery. The evening of June 9 messages reached Forrest at Booneville that the Federal column had camped several miles east of Ripley on the Guntown road.

Also on the 9th deserters were executed in Booneville. It is a measure of Forrest's disciplinary attitude that such an event took place on the eve of a battle. Three men were condemned, but one was so young he escaped the death penalty. The other two were shot and buried. Normally something of this nature would negatively affect morale, but there is no indication that it did. Forrest's men knew their commander, and they had no more patience with deserters than the general they followed.[5]

Forrest did not let the incident take his mind off his task at hand. After receiving news that Sturgis seemed to be headed toward Guntown via Brice's Crossroads rather than hitting the Mobile & Ohio Railroad somewhere south of Corinth and north of Booneville, he called several of his commanders together in Booneville. The council of war included artillerist John Morton, John Buford, Hylan Lyon, and Edmund Rucker. Forrest told them Sturgis's location and informed them that Stephen Lee thought the coming fight should be farther south in more open, maneuverable terrain. Forrest said if they waited, the Yankees might get too far ahead, making a fight more difficult. He likely also had in mind that if he was outnumbered, fighting on open ground could give Sturgis an advantage. Forrest liked to choose battle sites himself, and he believed that striking the enemy at Brice's Crosswords gave him a better opportunity to beat Sturgis. Lee had given Forrest much discretion about where to fight Sturgis, so Forrest had no concern about disobeying orders. Yet he knew he was gambling. He could not attack Sturgis with his entire force, for it would be hours before all his men reached the crossroads. In his mind, however, there were several factors that made his plan possibly workable. Shortly after the meeting, he issued orders to all his officers to be ready to move out the next morning at four o'clock.[6]

Mississippi weather had already become a Forrest ally. Had Sturgis taken Grierson's advice about returning wagons to Memphis, Union forces would have been in a much better position to cope with the weather. Pack mules could have negotiated muddy roads much better than heavily weighted wagons. June weather in Mississippi is typically hot and humid, and the intense heat often causes rainstorms, usually, but not necessarily, in the afternoon. So no matter how much the sun dried the dirt, the next thunderstorm could turn roadbeds into quagmires. Even under normal circumstances, Mississippi roads were not very good, with both wet and dry deep ruts common. The weather thus could quickly disrupt timetables and give the enemy extra time to concentrate its forces. Sturgis grew concerned, and Forrest anticipated correctly that weather could slow the enemy, giving Forrest time to assemble his far-flung troops.

Sturgis's men found clear, sunny days a rarity. The usually quick summer showers became prolonged as a wide stormy front made its way through north Mississippi. Sturgis did his best to keep his infantry off muddy roads. Grierson led his cavalry on ahead. The rain continued through June 3 and 4, and roads became practically impassable, testing the strength and patience of U.S. Colored Troops assigned to escort Sturgis's supply train. With Grierson riding ahead, the infantry forced to walk on the shoulders of roads, which also became muddy with so many feet hitting the soil, and the wagons lagging behind because they had to stay on the road to avoid trees and more mud, Sturgis's column became strung out in a manner that made it vulnerable if Forrest attacked. Sturgis sent word to Grierson to halt his advance and wait for the rest of the column.

Sturgis had instructions to destroy as much of the Mobile & Ohio Railroad as possible and as many Confederate supplies as could be found along and near the railroad. During the course of his march, his men burned the depot at Rienzi, but Sturgis found that the lack of supplies his men found limited his ability to destroy. The countryside, victimized by both sides carrying out cavalry raids during the war, had been "stripped of supplies and almost deserted by its inhabitants." Only a few remained, so Sturgis formed a provost guard unit to stop the pillaging of farms already severely depleted. The guard did not always make a difference; in one case a farmer's cow was shot. Foragers received orders not to take all the food any family had, and, in a case of an olive branch, unusual at this time in the war, racist Federal officers denied black troops the right to enter citizens' yards to get water from wells and cisterns. Foragers were not intimidated by officers' orders, and finally Sturgis put a stop to the practice altogether. Local residents accused black soldiers of all sorts of depredations, from robbing houses, to killing stock, stealing tools, and taking corn and meat. Such depredations doubtless happened, but it is doubtful all the perpetrators had dark skin. Southerners, like the Union soldiers and officers, found it easy to blame blacks for all their troubles.

Meanwhile the rain let up on Sturgis's weary army, and on the afternoon of June 5 the column picked up its pace, except when it had to go through muddy bottomland, for in the hot June it took longer for the many puddles in low areas to dry. That same day the infantry and wagons caught up with Grierson's cavalry, and the troops rested and men and horses ate. After a time, Sturgis told Grierson to send a cavalry detachment on a scouting expedition toward Corinth. The Union riders captured a few surprised Confederate soldiers and tore up Mobile & Ohio track for several miles and cut telegraph wires. The riders turned north and took a few more prisoners at the Tuscumbia bridge. Federal messengers brought word of the successes to Grierson, who replied with orders that they should turn south away from

Corinth and head toward Ellistown, northwest of Tupelo, to unite with the rest of the cavalry. Grierson apparently had decided that since his men had not encountered a major enemy force, neither Forrest nor any major portion of his command was at Corinth.

Sturgis's problems mounted. His supplies were already getting low. Grierson advised Sturgis to move on a more southerly course, as there seemed to be more food and grain available in that region. Confederate guerrillas harassed the Yankees as the Union column descended deeper into Mississippi. Confederate pickets also made life interesting for Grierson's riders. Several skirmishes broke out, with the outnumbered Confederates always disappearing into the woods. On June 7–8 the main Sturgis column entered Ripley, where locals had seen plenty of the enemy during the war and were not surprised by the looting that went on in spite of efforts by Sturgis and his officers to control their men. A local woman told Union officers that Forrest had 28,000 men and was en route to reinforce Joe Johnston. No doubt she hoped the false information would rid the town of the invaders, but the Federals were not quite that gullible.

Heavy rains continually slowed Sturgis's movements, especially the 250 wagons carrying supplies, which included a "ten-gallon keg of whiskey." With so many wagons, the small army could not travel lightly as Washburn had hoped. While in Ripley, Sturgis had second thoughts about going on. Rain continued turning roads and trails into muddy bogs, compounded by wagon and artillery wheels. He set up a meeting of his commanders and discussed the impact of the elements, including "the exhausted condition of our animals," and how the delays had obviously given the enemy time to concentrate a large force, probably at Tupelo. If the column met defeat, the loss of wagons and artillery would be great. Several agreed with his assessment, he wrote, and a few said the best thing was to turn around and cancel the campaign.[7]

Grierson was one of the several. At the meeting he said he did not know the details of Sturgis's orders, "yet under all the circumstances bearing upon the case—considering the unfavorable weather, the bad roads, the destitution of the country," problems finding enough feed for animals, "the proximity of the enemy and his knowledge of our condition—to make a further advance would be hazardous." If Sturgis wanted to continue, the column should return to Memphis with the wagons and wait for better weather. To continue the march could prove disastrous. Sturgis agreed with Grierson, but their position was not unanimous.

Other officers appealed to Sturgis's ego. He had, after all, given up his chase of Forrest earlier due to the "destitution" of the countryside. To give up the campaign now "would be ruinous on all sides to return again without first meeting the enemy." Further, Washburn's reports suggested that no major Confederate force was likely to be encountered. Washburn's scouts obviously were not very reliable, but Sturgis had no way of knowing whether they were telling the truth. Yet he did understand that to return to Memphis without "any facts to justify my course" would put him in a bad position. So, he wrote, "with a sad foreboding of the consequences," he decided to continue. His words, written after the campaign, sounded like he was groping for excuses. If he truly felt "a sad foreboding" early in the operation, he should have at least relinquished command. Any general who goes into a campaign convinced that it will turn out badly should not be leading troops. The fact that a commander not familiar with his troops, not familiar with the countryside ahead of him, and obviously not positive about his chances of success meant he led men on a mission he already thought was doomed.

Sherman ordered diversions to assist Sturgis, including frequent raiding in the Vicksburg area and to the south and east, where Union riders hoped to find that the Meridian campaign had taken the fighting spirit out of Confederates in the region. Wirt Adams still prowled the mid-Mississippi area, and he never lost his fighting spirit. He was more pest than threat, however. His men at one point burned a Union vessel, but the incident was too far from Sherman's supply line to matter.

The council of war decided to take the road to Fulton rather than Ellistown, since scouting reports indicated the road in that direction was better. So the Federals went through all the problems of changing course, moving east of Ripley. The rains came again the night of June 8 and the next day, and Sturgis had no choice but to send sick and worn-out mules and horses to pull forty-one wagons back to Memphis. Forage for animals continued to be scarce, and the men fared little better as the Federals kept moving. Torn between logistical realities and fear of reprisals from superior officers, Sturgis kept his army moving.

The evening of June 9 the column stopped at Stubbs's plantation, some fourteen miles or so southeast of Ripley, where they found a piddling amount of corn. Guerrillas fired on a foraging party during the day, but the column found some high, defensible ground to camp. As the Federals settled in for the night, they were exhausted, emaciated from the heat, and hungry, hardly in top battle-ready condition.

Grierson later recalled a comical episode at the Stubbs home. He and a few of his men went to the main house that night and found an old piano, "dilapidated violins with three strings, and a bow without about as many

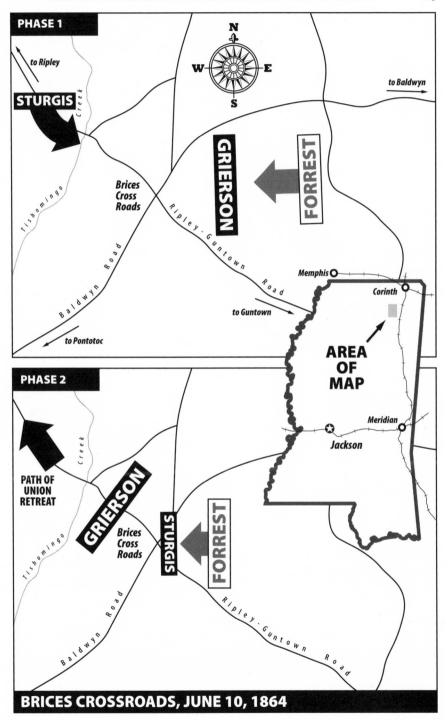

BRICES CROSSROADS, JUNE 10, 1864

hairs." They asked a young woman in the household to play the piano and sing for them. Grierson said the young woman had a "voice as tuneless and twanging as the instrument," but she sang with much power, "weeping sad and lonely" in a most emotional style, "spitting between the lines, and looking languishingly over her shoulder for our approval and admiration." His fellow soldiers talked Grierson, a talented musician, into playing an "old cracked fiddle," while everyone danced. With the benefit of hindsight, he noted, "It is well to make the most of life as it comes to us, and to be merry even under the most unfavorable circumstances. There was serious work ahead for us, and the comedy of that evening was followed by a tragedy the next day."

The force Sturgis rested that night would not rest again for a long while. His army, concentrated at Stubbs's, consisted of Grierson's cavalry, divided into two brigades, led by Edward Winslow and George Waring, and William McMillen's infantry, led by brigade commanders Alexander Wilkin and George Hoge, plus a brigade of black soldiers under the leadership of Edward Bouton. Grierson, as usual, would lead the column on the 10th toward a place known locally as Brice's Crossroads, where two roads crossed on a ridge above Tishomingo Creek. Of this group, McMillen had a well-deserved reputation, like Sturgis, as a habitual consumer of whiskey.

Early on June 10 Forrest rode with part of his army down the Wire road, so-named because of telegraph wire strung along the side of the roadbed. As he rode along with Rucker, he discussed the coming fight. He said he knew he was outnumbered, but he also realized that the Federals were on a "narrow and muddy" road, which would slow their progress. He also knew the terrain between the town and Baldwyn and the crossroads was covered with much thick timber and all sorts of bushes, so that the Confederates would be hard to see, their actual numbers disguised until the remainder of Forrest's men arrived. He knew that Grierson's cavalry would take the lead, and he figured Union horsemen would move at a pace placing them hours ahead of the rest of the column. Sturgis's army had been strung out before due to the muddy roads. Forrest firmly believed that would give his men enough time to whip Grierson. While Forrest fought Sturgis's cavalry, Grierson would send word back to Sturgis, who would hurry his infantry and artillery to get to the crossroads. Forrest well understood Mississippi weather. He told Rucker, "It is going to be as hot as hell, and coming on a run for five or six miles over such roads, their infantry will be so tired out we will ride right over them. I want everything to move up as fast as possible."

The conversation with Rucker provides an insight into Forrest's commonsense thinking. He understood the necessity of using to his advantage what was available, like the terrain, knowledge of road conditions and
how they would affect the enemy's movements, and the weather. There was
nothing complicated about his plan. The big questions that he had to ad-
dress were timelines. Could he defeat Grierson before the rest of Sturgis's
forces arrived at the crossroads? Would all his men who were rushing toward the battle site get there in time? Any number of things could go wrong
and upset Forrest's plans. But, unlike Sturgis, he went into the fight with
confidence. Sturgis had dug himself a deep hole by refusing to listen to Grierson's advice on going back to Memphis because the wagons were costing
too much time. Washburn had said reports indicated no large enemy force
in the region, so why not continue so he could at least say he had looked
several miles deep into Mississippi but could find no enemy? Railroad and
supply destruction had been accomplished. Sturgis simply had lost whatever decisiveness he possessed. He feared being accused of not doing enough,
and he had endangered his army by trying to do too much.

On the morning of June 10 Grierson recalled that Sturgis "seemed
gloomy and irritable," and in no uncertain terms told Grierson to take
his cavalry and ride out ahead, "out of the way of the infantry and train,"
and go to Baldwyn. Did Sturgis really believe that his infantry would have
to slow down due to his cavalry? He told Grierson to fight any enemy he
found, wherever he found them, and that the rest of the column would follow along "promptly." Grierson wrote, "His orders to me were imperative,
and gave me no discretion whatever but to go on and attack the enemy on
sight." What enemy Sturgis expected Grierson to find is unclear, but it is
likely he expected no trouble. After all, Washburn's scouts had said there
was no major enemy force anywhere around.[8]

The Wire road led southwest from Booneville and a few miles west of
Baldwyn. From there, "it crossed at right angles the Ripley-Fulton road" before leading southwest to Pontotoc. Brice's Crossroads was some fifty yards
above Tishomingo Creek, which flowed east to west. At the crossroads, the
man who gave the place its name, William Brice, had a home northwest and
a store northeast of the crossing. A church and small cemetery were several
yards east of the store. Though some scattered fields provided clearings, the
rest of the terrain from the crossroads east toward Baldwyn was undulating, heavily timbered, and thick with other vegetation. Forrest, of course,
counted on these factors to shield his men from the enemy and to hide the
small numbers he had until the rest of his force arrived.

As Forrest and his escort came in sight of Old Carrollville, where the Wire road from Booneville met the road coming west out of Baldwyn, he ran into several civilians who told him that Union cavalry had ridden to within about four miles of the crossroads. Forrest sent forward a detachment to find the enemy cavalry and slow their pace with a few shots into their midst. Forrest sent Hylan Lyon's troops on ahead and sent a rider to Baldwyn to telegraph Stephen Lee about the developing situation. Then he ordered Edmund Rucker's and William Johnson's troops to follow Lyon.

Early on June 10 Benjamin Grierson led his cavalry, numbering some 2,400 men, forward. Sturgis decided he needed an escort, and he took one regiment of riders from Grierson. Counting the number of sick men and worn-out horses, the loss of manpower left Grierson with around 900 men less than he had started with from Memphis. That morning he led his troopers "in a cautious manner" about three or four miles; unlike Sturgis, Grierson apparently believed reports from his own scouts that indicated somewhere ahead the Confederates did have a large force. Grierson halted his men for an hour to wait for the rest of the column to make up some of the distance, but Sturgis had not started his infantry and wagons as early as intended. When they did move, the wagon train once more slowed their progress.

Around 9 a.m. Grierson's men encountered the detachment Forrest had sent to slow them. They stopped to fix a bridge the Confederates had been in the process of tearing apart. Grierson's column reached Brice's Crossroads an hour later. Learning from scouting reports that the Rebels were indeed concentrating in the direction of Baldwyn, Grierson sent a message back to Sturgis, and he ordered out patrols on all the roads leading in the direction of the Mobile & Ohio Railroad. George Waring's brigade came up, dismounted, and deployed at the crossroads "to await further developments." The patrol that had been sent east on the Baldwyn road soon ran into Forrest's advance. Grierson left behind a few pickets and went with Waring's men toward the shooting. Grierson and his staff looked at the terrain and could see that the troops had started falling back toward the crossroads. Waring pulled back and deployed on both sides of the road, with open fields in front that might provide a good field of fire when the Confederates came after them. Grierson meanwhile went back to the crossroads to get Edward Winslow's brigade and to send another message to Sturgis. Winslow's men had stopped to shore up the bridge across Tishomingo Creek, and rode into the crossroads area at 11 a.m. Grierson, believing he did not have enough men to force his way to Baldwyn, deployed

Winslow's brigade on the Guntown road to the right of Waring. A reserve force was deployed to provide reinforcements for Winslow and to "support his artillery."

Grierson sent a third message to Sturgis, who responded that Grierson "must be mistaken" regarding the strength of the enemy, which Grierson was convinced must be 6,000–7,000 troops. Forrest's intent to keep the Yankees guessing as to his numbers could not have worked any better. Sturgis did not believe his cavalry faced more than a brigade, and he ordered Grierson to move forward to Baldwyn. Grierson insisted he faced overwhelming numbers of the enemy, and that his men could do no more than try to hold on until the infantry arrived, and then he could withdraw back to the infantry line of battle, wherever Sturgis formed to fight. Sturgis continued to dismiss Grierson's description of the situation, and he sent an aide to investigate. By then it was noon. Sturgis's officer quickly saw that Grierson was indeed in trouble and rode back to Sturgis with the news.[9]

Forrest's men had played an impressive game of bluff. Lyon's soldiers in the advance built "fortifications of rails, logs, and such other facilities as presented themselves." Forrest then sent Rucker and his brigade forward, and they dismounted and deployed on Lyon's left. Rucker sent one of his regiments, still mounted, farther left to prevent an enemy flank attack. William Johnson now moved his brigade up on Lyon's right and deployed, bending his right flank toward the enemy left to avoid a flank attack from that direction. The heavy skirmishing with Grierson's men continued until 1 p.m., and at that point Abraham Buford, division commander, and Tyree Bell's brigade arrived, along with John Morton's artillery. Forrest at once ordered the artillery to deploy and fire at the Yankees in order to get a better idea where their batteries were. When only two pieces of artillery responded, Forrest told his gunners to cease fire.

Now that all his troops were in place, Forrest ordered an assault at 1 p.m. Forrest, with his escort and Tyree Bell's brigade, moved to the left to the Guntown-Ripley road, where they advanced and dismounted. Bell sent two regiments to the right to connect with Rucker's left. Bell's other regiment was placed on the left of the road, and Forrest's escort took position on the extreme left. Forrest left orders with Buford to move forward to the center and right once the attack began on the left. The thickly wooded terrain was not as good for offense as defense, and as Bell moved forward to the attack, his men got within only thirty yards of the enemy before they could pick up enough speed to assault the Federals. Forrest noted, "In a few seconds, the engagement became general, and on the left raged with great fury." As pressure increased on the Confederate left, Forrest sent word to Buford to send Lyon and Johnson forward to press Union forces on the Confederate right.

Bell's regiment in position across the Guntown-Ripley road began to give way, and Forrest's escort charged forward and pushed Union forces back to their second line of defense. This gave Bell's regiment breathing room, and the men re-formed and moved to a less exposed position.

The battle lines evolved as the fighting spread. Eventually the Union line formed an arc, with the center bulged toward Forrest's center. Such a battle line presented problems for Union troops. Both flanks were exposed to enemy attacks, and if parts of the line had to retreat and all of the line did not follow suit, gaps would open, giving Forrest's men a chance to shoot into the flanks of segments of the line. Grierson did not intend to fight an offensive battle, not until the infantry arrived, so he and his men had to react to Forrest's varying emphases on offensives all along the Confederate line, which included feints and attacks. In effect, Grierson gave Forrest control of the battlefield. Also, Forrest's men were much more comfortable fighting dismounted as they had done many times before. Grierson's cavalry did not have much experience fighting as infantry, and their inability to see the enemy made them more tentative. Forrest also used his escort to ride to and fro behind the Confederate main line to fire into gaps that appeared in Grierson's line, a tactic that further unnerved Union soldiers.

Forrest, not sure that his message to Buford had made it through the confusion of battle, demonstrated the advantage of riding behind his battle line, "encouraging my men, until I reached General Buford." Forrest noticed only two artillery pieces firing, so he sent an aide to bring the rest of the guns up and told Buford to make sure they all got into action. "The battle was fierce and the enemy obstinate," Forrest wrote afterward, "but after two hours' hard fighting the enemy gave way, being forced back on his third and last line."[10]

Sturgis and his staff reached the crossroads at 1 p.m., accompanied by the regiment of cavalry taken from Grierson. Grierson told Sturgis that his troops needed support and urged Sturgis to send the cavalry regiment to the right of Waring's brigade. Sturgis agreed. Grierson asked that a brigade of infantry, when it arrived, also be sent to back up Waring. Sturgis still clung to the idea that his men were not fighting a big force, and he commented that "if the damned cavalry could only be gotten out of the way," the infantry would soon take care of business and whip the Rebels. The comment infuriated Grierson, who knew that getting Sturgis to listen to reason was impossible. Waring waited in vain for infantry support and, running low on ammunition, fell back about sixty yards and re-formed. Of course, Winslow had to do likewise to keep the lines connected.

The infantry finally reached the crossroads about 2 p.m. and, Grierson noted disgustedly, took another half an hour to advance and deploy on ground the cavalry had been holding. Forrest's prediction that Sturgis's infantry would be much fatigued proved to be true. Sturgis, according to Grierson, "was excited and irritable in his manner," and he seemed to blame Grierson for getting pinned down rather than riding on into Baldwyn. Sturgis remained delusional about the situation. Infantry came to relieve Waring, but Grierson refused to allow it, for the Rebels had made a heavy attack on Waring's front and to have pulled him out of line while the infantry deployed would have been disastrous. Grierson also told Sturgis that Winslow should stay in place until a sufficient force of infantry came to his relief. Sturgis soon ordered Winslow to get out of the way and take his horses with him. The infantry could not maneuver with horses standing in their way.

Grierson recalled, "It was a great mistake to withdraw the cavalry. It should have been continued in action and more infantry brought to its support, and particularly Winslow's brigade, which had so long successfully fought the enemy." Grierson thought that if Winslow had stayed in place while the rest of the infantry came up, Union victory would have been possible, or, at least the army could have held the crossroads until night. Sturgis, however, still had no grasp of what was going on, and he countermanded a move by Grierson to take cavalry artillery out of harm's way. In fact, Sturgis seemed to go out of his way to ignore Grierson's advice.[11]

Over the years historians have accepted the idea that Forrest did as he planned, that is, he whipped the Union cavalry before Sturgis's infantry got into the fight. Grierson's men, though outmaneuvered tactically, fought well and were driven back, but they did not begin withdrawing from the field until the infantry came up. Perhaps analysis boils down to what "whipped" means. There is no doubt that once the infantry arrived, Sturgis's army began a downward slide that could not be stopped. The rather cavalier statement that Forrest did indeed whip Grierson's cavalry is an overstatement.

While Union infantry struggled in vain to hold the line, mainly due to their disorganized deployment and Forrest's continual pressure, Clark Barteau, commanding one of Bell's regiments, got behind the left flank and rear of Sturgis's forces. His attack pulled Grierson's men away from the Union front to meet him, which "created confusion and dismay to the enemy's wagon train and the guard attending to it," Forrest wrote. This development seemed to spread panic and confusion among Sturgis's infantry, and his entire line began collapsing and pulling back to the crossroads and down the hill toward Tishomingo Creek. Forrest's men continued advancing and pressuring the Federals, and John Morton's artillery was sent to the front by Forrest, tactically not a normal position for artillery. Forrest, without the benefit of a West Point education, did not know or care where the artillery ought to be. Morton's guns savaged the increasingly disorganized Union infantry, and, as Forrest phrased it, "the retreat or rout began." Forrest later told John Morton that he thought Morton's artillery had led to the victory. Morton thanked him, but added, "You scared me pretty badly when you pushed me up so close to their infantry and left me without protection. I was afraid they might take my guns." Forrest smiled and retorted, "Well, artillery is made to be captured, and I wanted to see them take yours."[12]

Grierson and Sturgis agreed that among the causes that led to the collapse of the Federal line, in addition to Barteau's attack, was the wrecking of the right flank of Sturgis's line. Cavalry on that flank were pulling back to re-form, and the infantry in the same sector were trying to get set when a Confederate attack caught the whole Union flank unprepared. Forrest's men rolled up the Union right and sent the men in blue into a state of confusion and panic. Grierson also noticed a brigade of infantry still on the north side of Tishomingo Creek, and behind that unit Edward Bouton's U.S. Colored Troops were trapped in place guarding the wagon train. Infantry that could have helped stem the Confederate tide were in no position to do anything. Sturgis reported that while looking for Bouton's brigade, "the main line began to give way at various points. Order soon gave way to confusion and confusion to panic." Grierson noted, "Every effort of the infantry to form new lines" on the other side of the creek, "to oppose the advance of the foe, proved ineffectual, and the retreat became an utter rout." Grierson asked Waring to stem the stampede if possible, and Waring tried, but the panic was too great.[13]

Union forces left behind one piece of artillery, a number of caissons, and much ammunition. With the help of Grierson's cavalry, parts of Sturgis's column stopped and made several stands to hold back the pursuing Rebels. Union soldiers had become all the more panicky when they found the Tishomingo Creek bridge cluttered with their own abandoned wagons; one had overturned and effectively blocked passage across the bridge. Men took to the water to make good their escape, and, fortunately for them, the water was low, not unusual for a stream in a Mississippi summer. Much rain did not keep things wet long or make creeks rise very high due to the severe heat, which caused baked ground to soak up water as rapidly as it fell.

Bouton's U.S. Colored Troops, left to guard the wagon train, saw clearly to their front the pell-mell retreat of Sturgis's troops. Bouton decided to deploy his men to provide cover fire for the stampeding soldiers. He put two companies out front, and they held on "until they were much reduced by loss and virtually crushed back by overwhelming numbers." Bouton then rushed forward seven more companies, which made a path for retreating infantry. Soon his men "closed up and opened a well-directed fire on the enemy, which for a time seemed to hold in check his right and center." Bouton saw Sturgis and begged for help. Sturgis replied simply, "For God's sake, if Mr. Forrest will let me alone I will let him alone. You have done all you could and more than was expected of you, and now all you can do is to save yourselves." In those comments, Sturgis proved he was unfit for command and also a racial bigot.

Though his losses mounted, Bouton refused to order a total retreat. His men kept fighting and with the help of two pieces of artillery, the black troops took a position on a ridge, allowing them to pour crossfire into pursuing Rebels. Soon, however, the Confederates threatened to flank his position, so Bouton pulled his line back 200 yards. Continuing the fight, his troops slowly retreated another 800 yards. Part of Bouton's line then charged, engaging in hand-to-hand combat with Confederates. Bouton soon realized that his line was being flanked, and he must get his men farther down the road away from the onrushing Rebels. Bouton now saw that several hundred of the enemy had surrounded part of his line, and his men, "gathering around me, fought with terrible desperation." Some, who had broken their rifles in the close fighting, died defenseless. Bouton managed to get away with the survivors that evening around 9 p.m. "and by making a large circuit through the woods joined the retreating column on the Ripley road" about two hours later.[14]

Seeing black troops seemed to energize tired Confederates. Some later claimed the black soldiers just threw down their weapons and ran as fast as they could, like many of the white Union troops. Doubtless some did, but most stood and fought. They were also accused of throwing away some badges attached to their uniforms that said "Remember Fort Pillow." That was true, for Confederates found some of these badges. Some black troops likely thought that if they were captured with the badges still on their uniforms, they might be shot down, too. Forrest and his men had heard that Bouton's black soldiers had taken a vow of "no quarter" toward white troops after what happened at Fort Pillow. After the campaign, Washburn protested to Stephen Lee that the black troops seemed to have suffered a larger number of casualties than should have been the case. Washburn linked the losses to Fort Pillow. Forrest and Lee replied, with Forrest assuring Blackburn that he viewed "captured negroes" as any other property captured in battle and not as soldiers. He argued it was not the South's policy to eliminate blacks, but "to preserve and protect" them. He went on to say that all black troops "who have surrendered to us have received kind and humane treatment." Lee supported Forrest's comments, and there the matter seemed to rest.

Forrest and all his men who had not been worn down by the day's fighting pursued the fleeing Yankees well into the evening. Grierson noticed that Sturgis rode well ahead and disappeared rather than staying and trying to rally his men. Sturgis's actions were not surprising; he had given up on the battle before it was ever fought, because he had assured himself that nothing good would come of the campaign. Grierson wrote, "I presumed when I last saw General Sturgis, near Tishomingo Creek, from what he then gave me to understand, that he would remain with such infantry organizations as could be gotten together, and that with them and the cavalry, they were to vigorously dispute the advance of the foe. But I never saw the general again until he got ten miles northeast of Ripley in his hasty and disastrous retreat." Grierson finally did get a message to Sturgis, asking for the return of part of Waring's brigade, which Sturgis approved. Sturgis reached the Stubbs's farm at 10 p.m., where he found Winslow and his brigade. He ordered Winslow to take over rearguard duties. He made clear to Winslow that the saving of the troops came first, so wagons and spiked and wrecked artillery must be left behind. Horses and mules would be taken back to Memphis.[15]

Grierson continually had trouble trying to keep up with Sturgis. A few miles from Ripley, Grierson and the forces with him, the true rear guard, were attacked by Forrest, his escort, and a Tennessee regiment. Forrest had no intention of letting the Yankees go entirely in peace. As artilleryman John Morton said, the general liked to keep the "skeer" in his opponents. Forrest kept up the pressure until he and his men neared his boyhood home near Salem. There, totally exhausted, he passed out in the saddle, "and remained unconscious for nearly an hour." He soon recovered.[16]

Grierson, convinced by the fierceness of Forrest's attack, believed that a large number of Rebels still pursued Sturgis's army. Forrest, however, eventually withdrew his small force, and Grierson rode on to Ripley with an Iowa cavalry regiment. There he learned that Sturgis, with his escort and Waring's brigade, plus a number of infantrymen, "had hurriedly left the town and gone onward in their flight towards Memphis." Grierson was disgusted, for he knew Sturgis must have heard sounds of fighting but had not seen fit to send any help. Grierson found unarmed infantry wandering around Ripley, and he ordered them to go on to Memphis. The fighting in the rear continued for some time, but Union forces had little morale left and kept up the retreat rather than stand and fight. At Collierville, 2,000 men with supplies, sent by Washburn, awaited the beleaguered Federal forces. By the time Grierson reached Memphis on June 15, he heard that Sturgis had been relieved of command. He had left Memphis due to feared threats of bodily injury by furious survivors of the Brice's Crossroads fiasco.

Later, Sturgis returned to Memphis, where his loss of command became official. He wrote Grierson, asking for comments in writing, hoping Grierson would help absolve him of the claims of incompetence being heaped upon him. Grierson responded that he thought the campaign failed for reasons he had given at the conference at Ripley: the heavy wagons traveling in deep mud, the roads in horrible condition, and the movement being so slow that Forrest had plenty of time to prepare to meet the column. Grierson did say that he had heard many rumors of Sturgis being drunk on the battlefield, but that he had not observed any such condition any time during the campaign. He had heard no additional disparaging rumors.

Grierson admitted afterward that he probably should have been more "severe" in his letter. He decided to reject making comments on "hearsay evidence," and he knew that it would not be possible for Sturgis to again "be placed in command." An all-out attack on the general by Grierson or anyone else would have served no purpose. Grierson added in his memoir, however, that stories abounded about Sturgis leaving Memphis aboard a steamer and taking a train on north. "Persons who were by accident on the same steamer and train," Grierson wrote, "could have been witnesses to the fact that beastly drunkenness in man and shamelessness in women were lessened by two when he disappeared from sight." Stories of Sturgis's drinking during the battle persisted and were very likely true. Grierson simply had not seen him or been close to him at the right time. In any event, for Sturgis, the war was over. He traveled to his home in Covington, Kentucky, and remained there until the war ended. In August 1865 he took command of the Sixth U.S. Cavalry to fight Indians in the West.

One of the most astute historians of the battle at Brice's Crossroads, Parker Hills, has thoroughly analyzed the military science tenets of Forrest's victory. Forrest defined his objective, the destruction of the Union army, and demonstrated that he had considered geography, weather, conditions of enemy soldiers, and time factors. Yet it must be remembered that Forrest led a small force, not a large army, and though his commonsense strategy and tactics worked well at Brice's Crossroads, he also faced a to-tally inept opponent. In effect, his plans, while showing great energy and perception, were on a much smaller scale than if he had been leading a very large army.

Forrest went into the fight with the idea of staying on the offensive, mak-ing clear that he was not trying to defend anything. Once the fight began, he feinted attacks and made attacks, never letting his men think they were to hold a position, but rather to drive the enemy away. The long, successful pursuit of Sturgis's column further demonstrated Forrest's determination.

Forrest understood that he had to use his numbers well since he was outnumbered. He made special use of his 100-man escort to strengthen whatever parts of his line needed help; he used Morton's guns to increase firepower when his battle line needed shoring up. He also used his favorite tactic of flank and rear attacks by massing his forces to hit enemy flanks and by Barteau's rear assault. This gave the Federals less room to maneuver, reducing their numerical advantage.

Forrest masked his forces with undulating land covered with brush and undergrowth, and used his feints to keep the Federals off balance. Finally, he made sure his artillery got into the fight to wreak havoc both on the front battle line and at Tishomingo Creek, where the guns increased the panic of the enemy. He also proved especially adept at maneuvering, which made certain both Grierson and Sturgis thought they faced superior numbers.

No Civil War commander understood the principle of unity of com-mand better than Forrest. That is why he ultimately did his best work while having independent command. He trusted his own leadership abilities more than generals who outranked him, which caused him many problems when serving under such generals as Braxton Bragg, Stephen Lee, John Bell Hood, and others. As good as Forrest was in small battles, most his-torians agree that he would not have been successful as a leader of larger forces, such as divisions or corps. On the battlefield, Forrest tried to watch everything, so he could ride to trouble spots and use his mere presence to encourage his men and to make decisions. He had a "hands on" approach that worked only with his relatively small force. He also made sure his of-ficers knew what he expected of them. By riding up and down the battle line, Forrest could see for himself weaknesses in his and Sturgis's lines.

Certainly Forrest proved the value of surprise. Sturgis's ignorance of Forrest's whereabouts set the stage for trouble. Sturgis expected no attack at the crossroads, or he would have had his army closer together and ready to deploy at a moment's notice. With his cavalry well out front and his infantry in a position where they had to run to get to the fighting, clearly

Sturgis was caught off guard. Forrest's tactics with artillery, such as with Morton's battery, also confused Union commanders.[17]

Forrest's approach to the fight at Brice's Crossroads truly exemplified the last of Hill's principles, simplicity. His orders were plainly stated, and he knew down to the most basic detail what he wanted to do. Forrest understood the basics of fighting as well as, if not better than, most generals of the Civil War. Nothing his army did at Brice's Crossroads was complicated or confusing, except to the enemy. His men understood clearly what they had to do, and they worked together to get the job done.

Victory at Brice's Crossroads secured Forrest's fame in the annals of the Civil War. Military specialists still walk the battlefield to study what happened there. Yet it should be remembered that Forrest only faced one competent general, Benjamin Grierson, whose cavalry had not experienced the Forrest style of fighting. Samuel Sturgis provided no challenge at all, so Forrest's fame at Brice's Crossroads had come at least in part from inept leadership of the enemy. This truth does not detract from the innate understanding of military science Forrest possessed, but the weak competition he faced must be taken into account.

Postbattle statistics regarding casualties are always suspect, but sometimes they provide insights into why a conflict turned out the way it did. Confederate reports indicated 96 killed and 396 wounded, for a total of 492. Forrest's staff also compiled a tally of captured armaments from Sturgis's army: 16 cannons, 330,000 small arms bullets, 350 six-pounder cannon balls, and 1,500 rifles to name but a few from the list. Sturgis's report included 223 killed, 434 wounded, and 1,623 missing, though many of the missing may have eventually straggled back to Memphis. As Washburn pointed out, it took Sturgis's army ten days to get to Brice's Crossroads, and a day and two nights to get back to Memphis. Sturgis's men became so scattered, however, that the number of days it took for them to return varied greatly.[18]

Forrest's solid victory, which earned him well-deserved fame at the time, pales when placed into the larger developments of the western theater. Ironically, his defeat of Sturgis proved to be a loss to the Confederacy and a victory for the Union. While Forrest fought a relatively meaningless battle in Mississippi, William T. Sherman's supply line remained safe and secure. The Confederacy totally wasted Forrest's talents during Sherman's Atlanta campaign. Sherman's purpose in sending Sturgis into Mississippi was to keep Forrest busy, and though Sturgis totally bungled the campaign, he did keep Forrest from attacking Sherman's lifeline. Certainly Sherman was furious about what Forrest did to Sturgis, and he immediately ordered another foray into Mississippi to protect his supply line. Sherman wanted Forrest dead, but, failing that, he could at least keep the Confederate cavalryman tied down, which was, despite the outcomes of campaigns in Mississippi, a victory for the Union cause.

Sherman did not take reports coming from Memphis at face value. Washburn wrote the commanding general on June 14 that Sturgis had not lost as many men as first reported. The correct total seemed to be 1,500 or 2,000, plus the loss of 14 pieces of artillery and 130 wagons destroyed. The Rebel army had been estimated at 15,000 men. A day later Sherman wired Secretary of War Stanton, "Forrest is the very devil, and I think he has got some our troops under cower." Sherman made clear that he intended to keep sending forces after Forrest "if it cost 10,000 lives and breaks the Treasury. There never will be peace in Tennessee until Forrest is dead." Sherman now planned to send A. J. Smith and Samuel Mower after Forrest, and he wanted an investigation into stories of intoxication linked to Sturgis. He promised Mower a promotion to major general if he whipped Forrest. Sherman also berated Washburn for the stories about the Brice's Crossroads fight. He said he had learned that Forrest had a smaller number of men there than reported, certainly nowhere near 15,000 to as many as 20,000 as had been initially claimed. Sturgis "was whipped by a force inferior to his own. Let the matter be critically investigated."[19]

A board of investigation did look into the causes of the Union disaster at Brice's Crossroads and did ask questions about officers drinking. The commander of the Ninety-third Indiana, D. C. Thomas, testified that he had seen Sturgis and William McMillen drinking before the army reached the battlefield, and he saw both take a drink at breakfast but not thereafter during the battle. Thomas went on to say that he had seen McMillen drunk during the early part of the march. When asked how drunk McMillen was, Thomas said, "He was so much so that to prevent exposure I got his aides-de-camp to get him to a house and place him in bed that night, and I took command of the brigade until the next morning." When asked if others had observed McMillen in such a state, Thomas said yes, in one of the train cars after leaving Memphis. "In attempting to get from the cars he fell to the ground and had to be assisted to rise." Charles Eaton, of the Seventy-second Indiana, supported Thomas's story, but said he did not think Sturgis got drunk during the campaign. Others supported the stories about McMillen, but downplayed Sturgis's involvement. Incredibly, the board did not question McMillen about the drinking charges. Such boards usually did their best to cover up misbehavior by officers, and few officers were ever censored about anything. In fact, this board made no recommendations.

The testimony proved clearly that not only was Sturgis uneasy about the campaign, but in fact his leadership was poor, and the drinking was probably an attempt to escape in his mind from the disaster he expected to happen. Grierson testified, but he only repeated what he had already said and written earlier.[20]

Sherman did not dwell on Sturgis. There might not be peace in Tennessee until Forrest was dead, but Sherman remained determined to make sure Forrest had no peace in Mississippi until he no longer believed him to be a threat to the Georgia campaign. Sturgis had lost, but that same day Sherman led his armies toward Joseph Johnston's position in the mountainous country northwest of Marietta. Sherman did so without having to worry about what was happening to his supply line toward Chattanooga. Nathan Bedford Forrest was not there.[21]

9

TUPELO (HARRISBURG)

Forrest versus Lee

*W*illiam Sherman chose Andrew Jackson Smith to lead the second drive into Mississippi to get Nathan Bedford Forrest. Actually it was the third drive, but the second instigated since Sherman began his Georgia campaign. The additional one had been the disastrous Sooy Smith expedition in February 1864 when he had failed to join Sherman at Meridian. Except for the last name, A. J. Smith differed greatly from Sooy Smith. A Pennsylvania native who had been in Sherman's Meridian campaign, he had more recently been involved in Nathaniel Banks's ill-fated Red River campaign. Smith was passing through Memphis on his way to participate in operations against Mobile when he received orders to remain in Memphis and prepare a force to go after Forrest.

Sherman issued crisp, clear instructions. Smith and his army, elements of the Sixteenth and Seventeenth corps, must "pursue Forrest on foot, devastating the land over which he has passed or may pass, and make him and the people of Tennessee and Mississippi realize that, although a bold, daring and successful leader, he will bring ruin and misery on any country where he may pause or tarry. If we do not punish Forrest and the people now, the whole effect of our past conquests will be lost." Smith had instructions from Washington to "bring Forrest to bay and whip him if possible, and at all events to hold him where he [is] and prevent him from moving upon the communications of Major-General Sherman."[1]

While Union forces in Memphis prepared once again to occupy Forrest's attention, a debate raged in the Confederacy about whether Forrest should remain in Mississippi when he could be of greater value elsewhere. Joseph

E. Johnston urged Confederate leaders in Richmond to give Forrest, "the most competent officer in America," command of all cavalry in Mississippi and east Louisiana and unleash him on the railroad in Sherman's rear. Johnston argued cogently that Forrest and his cavalry would have greater impact "insuring the defeat of a great invasion than . . . repelling a mere raid."

Others supported Johnston. Joseph E. Brown, governor of Georgia, said his state might be spared the pain of Sherman's invasion if Forrest destroyed the Union supply line. General Howell Cobb, a prominent Georgia politician, echoed Brown's sentiments, as did Confederate cavalryman Joseph Wheeler, but logical arguments were ignored in Richmond. To understand why, one must take into account not only the relationship of some of these petitioners to the Confederate president, Jefferson Davis, but also the political realities Davis faced.[2]

Johnston and Davis had been on bad terms for most of the war. Wounded in 1862 in the battle of Seven Pines during the peninsula campaign near Richmond, Johnston had lost command of the Virginia army to Robert E. Lee. During the decisive stages of the Vicksburg campaign, Johnston argued for abandonment of the Mississippi River fortress and then did nothing to relieve John C. Pemberton's besieged army. Months later Davis reluctantly gave Johnston command of the Army of Tennessee, and Johnston's constant retreating toward Atlanta infuriated Davis. In short, Davis cared little for Johnston's advice. Joseph Brown likewise had a testy relationship with Davis. Brown considered Georgia's state's rights much more important than Confederate victory, and Davis, of course, refused to accept Brown's position. So, when it came to Forrest, Davis told Brown to mind his own business.

The Tombigbee River valley along the Alabama-Mississippi border still produced many supplies important to Confederate armies, including Johnston's. Somebody had to protect the area. If Forrest left Mississippi, Union troops there might be sent to Sherman, who already had numerical superiority over Johnston. Perhaps, too, as one of Forrest's biographers has suggested, Davis simply underestimated Forrest's ability. Davis admitted as much after the war, and the whole debate seemed to underscore Davis's misplaced priorities in the western theater. Was losing a major campaign more or less important than saving supplies?

Braxton Bragg, replaced by Johnston, was a good friend of Davis's and had gone to Richmond to advise the president. Forrest and Bragg continued to detest each other, so Bragg probably did not lobby heavily regarding Forrest's role one way or the other. Though Forrest had been very confrontational with Bragg at one point, Davis now appreciated Forrest, and Bragg had enough political sense not to try to sway his friend, the president. The bottom line was that as long as Forrest stayed in Mississippi, Sherman had no worries about keeping his supply line open.[3]

The bickering resulted in Forrest remaining where he was to satisfy a nervous Davis instead of performing more valuable service. Davis not only had logistical concerns, but some governors in states farther west than Georgia did not want Forrest being sent away. They felt vulnerable enough without having their top gun taken away. The controversy pleased Sherman greatly and doubtless tempered his anger about Sturgis's failure. As long as the Confederates were willing to cooperate, he intended to keep sending men into Mississippi.

In Memphis, A. J. Smith's men drew their pay and boarded trains headed east. After a few miles the troops detrained and marched eventually to La Grange, Tennessee, the assembly point for this latest "get Forrest" expedition.

Smith led his army out of La Grange on July 5, 1864. In all he had about 14,000 men, almost twice the number Sturgis had commanded. Benjamin Grierson, who had suffered under Sturgis, led Smith's cavalry. Black troops of the First Brigade, U.S. Colored Troops, marched with the army. These troops, still angry at the massacre of black troops by Forrest and his men in April at Fort Pillow and also upset about reported mistreatment of fellow blacks by Confederates during the Brice's Crossroads campaign—all of which Forrest had denied—continued to vow no-quarter for Rebels they encountered. Forrest's men heard of the continuing boasts, and part of the postmortem of the upcoming campaign would be even more controversy over their treatment of black soldiers. The Union infantry, artillery, and wagon supply train took the Davis' Mills road toward Ripley, Mississippi; Grierson and his cavalry rode via Grand Junction and Saulsbury and on to Ripley. Grierson's job was to scout, but not to stray too far.

Smith, traveling with the infantry, did not want to be drawn into a fight on Forrest's terms, as Sturgis had been at Brice's Crossroads. The night of July 5, the main column camped at Davis' Mills. On July 6 and 7 Smith kept his men moving, but slowly. The march was steady and controlled. To prevent straggling and desertion, Smith ordered roll calls several times daily. He wanted his men to feel secure as they descended into Forrest territory. Surviving the intense Mississippi heat challenged the resolve of the blue column as much as their dread of what might be ahead. Men fell from sunstroke every day, and the pace of the march slowed accordingly.

Skirmishing broke out a few miles north of Ripley. The noise proved to be just a few Confederate scouts trying to ascertain Smith's strength. The shooting died down quickly, and the column moved on. The march continued slowly on July 8–10, with Smith stopping in Ripley to allow his troops to carry out much destruction. Smith took to heart Sherman's idea of making not only Forrest and his men pay a high price but also the people in the area who might be supporting Forrest. But what about the people who might not be? Smith did not care. His attitude, combined with those of other Union officers, did much to create the lingering hatred of Yankees that permeated the South during postwar years.

Smith's men torched the Tippah County courthouse, Methodist and Presbyterian churches, the Masonic and Odd Fellows halls, several stores, and three homes. The army left Ripley in flames and cut a "swath of desolation ten miles across" as they moved on to New Albany. On the 10th they camped about five miles from Pontotoc. Why New Albany escaped mass destruction is unclear, unless Smith feared that carrying out such actions everywhere would slow him too much and give Forrest tactical advantages.

Word had rapidly spread to Confederate units that Smith was "slowly and cautiously advancing." Forrest initially concentrated a force at Ellistown, located between Tupelo and Ripley. Reports indicated the Yankees were coming from that direction, but he had guessed these troops were probably detachments from Grierson's cavalry or perhaps infantry conducting a feint to confuse Rebel scouts. Forrest erred. From Ripley, Smith's main column could have gone toward Ellistown, but instead took a parallel road leading toward Pontotoc. Smith had outmaneuvered, or perhaps outguessed, Forrest for the first, but not the last, time.[4]

Forrest had hoped to block Smith's route, start a fight, and draw the enemy to him. That strategy usually worked well. Now he had no choice but to pursue Smith, to harass the Federal flanks. Forrest ordered his men to fire and fall back toward Okolona; hopefully, he could lure Smith into a trap there. Forrest's men impressed area slaves to build earthworks near Okolona where "necessary arrangements were being vigorously made" to give the enemy a warm welcome. In an attempt to gain time, Forrest sent detachments on July 10 to points east of Pontotoc to spy on the slow-moving bluecoats. The Confederates had orders to fire just enough to hold up the Yankees until an adequate force could be gathered at Okolona. Opposing forces spent the day of July 11 punching and counterpunching, each side trying to determine the intent of the other. Smith sent cavalry and infantry to drive the Confederates south from Pontotoc down the Okolona road. So far, Forrest's strategy seemed to be working. Smith was at Pontotoc and apparently willing to fight. Confederates south of the town pulled back toward Okolona trying to entice him to follow.[5]

Smith thought seriously about advancing. On July 12 his main column stayed put while two regiments, one each of cavalry and infantry, ventured toward Okolona to feel out the Confederate position. Several miles south of Pontotoc, across from swampy terrain fed by two creeks, the Confederates had set up a roadblock on high ground known locally as Pinson's Hill. Aside from boggy footing, any Federal approach would be complicated by thick timber and trees felled by the Rebels. A frontal attack would have been suicidal, so Smith's scouts skirmished the rest of the day. Other Union detachments went down roads leading to Tupelo and Houston but fell back when confronted by Forrest's patrols.

Meanwhile slaves and Confederate soldiers feverishly finished the works at Okolona, and Forrest sent word to his troops around Pontotoc to soften their resistance. If the Yankees wanted to come to Okolona, Forrest would welcome them. Smith's delay at Pontotoc worried Forrest. Perhaps the Pinson's Hill blockade had been too strong. The Federals might retreat back to Memphis. Forrest's veterans likely would not have minded a Federal withdrawal, for it had not been long since they fought a major battle in the hot sun. But Forrest did not want Smith to escape unscathed, and if Smith turned back, the Confederate force at Okolona would have a hard time catching up and pressing the Yankee retreat. So Forrest discussed the situation with his commanders, and no doubt with Stephen D. Lee, who had arrived and as departmental commander was technically in charge. Lee and Forrest decided to fight Smith if the Federals kept coming or deployed to fight and to attack at the first sign of retreat.

What they could not afford to do was wait too long at Okolona, and they decided they had waited long enough. Forrest sent orders to his troops near Pontotoc to hold their positions "at all hazards" until reinforcements from Okolona reached them. One Confederate noted, "This sudden change of orders, being made at night, produced some confusion." At 9 p.m. the evening of July 11, Forrest arrived at the front. At the time, he did not realize his decision to concentrate south of Pontotoc was a serious, if understandable, mistake. Confederate cavalry on the road from Pontotoc to Tupelo had been withdrawn, leaving the road open. If Smith chose to go to Tupelo, there would be no Confederates to confront him. Forrest had gambled and lost.

So far the campaign had been classic wait-and-watch, each side looking for the other to make a decisive move or a mistake. Smith had been cautious; he had refused to be enticed by Forrest. He would not be another Sturgis and make a blind commitment. He did not intend allowing Forrest to call the tune in this campaign. Smith worried about the impact of the heat as well; if he became the aggressor, his men would suffer even more. His layover in Pontotoc may have been calculated as much to rest his soldiers as to confuse Forrest.

Smith, a veteran officer, may have sensed Forrest's trap at Okolona. The roadblock at Pinson Hill had been a bit too obvious, and Forrest had recognized that mistake too late. Smith therefore issued orders the evening of July 12 for the army to move east the next morning toward Tupelo. Grierson told Smith that Harrisburg, a small community just west of Tupelo, and Tupelo, a growing community on the Mobile & Ohio, presented the army with its best option. Smith could entrench on high ground around Harrisburg, and certainly the combative Forrest would follow. Grierson said his cavalry could ride ahead and occupy the area while the slower infantry marched. At the moment, the way was clear. The Mobile & Ohio Railroad presented destructive opportunities. Grierson's riders could destroy track and supplies stored at the Tupelo depot. Smith hesitated to embrace the plan, but he talked to other officers, and they agreed with Grierson that the high battleground at Harrisburg and Tupelo would be a good place to dig in and wait for Forrest. The march to Tupelo could be dangerous since Confederates to the south could ride up and hit the Union right flank, not to mention the threat to the Union rear from Rebel troops around Pontotoc. Yet if the army moved quickly, they could make it and dig in before the Confederates could concentrate and attack. Smith decided Harrisburg and Tupelo were his best option.

As for Forrest, he unknowingly surrendered the initiative when he decided to make a stand at Okolona. During the Federal approach to Pontotoc, Forrest had done the usual. He ordered harassment of Federal flanks and rear to try to slow Smith. In all this he had had some success, but when Smith paused at Pontotoc and decided to go no farther, Forrest realized the Okolona ruse had been a mistake. He then had to decide what to do about it.

He and Lee had no choice but to allow Smith to make the next move. No matter what Smith decided to do, they had put themselves in a position of being reactive rather than proactive. They had based their strategy on what they expected the enemy to do, and now they must find a way to salvage the campaign. Forrest knew that he was outnumbered, but he had never been intimidated by that factor. As the campaign continued unfolding, it became more apparent that Forrest would have to do what Smith forced him to do, or back off. And retreating from a fight was something Forrest could not bring himself to do. Given the situation, however, it would have been best to leave Smith alone until Confederate circumstances improved. Forrest was not the same man who had recently won his greatest victory, for he had been outmaneuvered and put in an awkward position. There were possible explanations.

He suffered terribly from boils, which made riding a horse an excruciating experience. The presence of Lee may have also affected his behavior. One could not blame Forrest for being upset with Lee's promotion to lieutenant general ahead of him, especially since the promotion came a few days after Brice's Crossroads. To Forrest, this was another indication that clannish West Pointers stuck together, and that an excellent war record, and his was more spectacular than Lee's, did not matter. Circumstances of the Tupelo campaign tend to indicate that Forrest figured Lee, as departmental commander, took credit, or at least was given credit in Richmond, for Brice's Crossroads. After that battle Lee had been promoted to lieutenant general, and Forrest had not. Forrest mentioned Lee's rank during the discussion over who should lead Confederate forces during the Tupelo campaign.

By insisting that Lee take command, Forrest seemed to want to get Lee's and Richmond's attention. Yet the campaign thus far had been primarily his, if officially Lee's. Forrest's attitude proved divisive, for it became obvious that Lee's presence at the front, at Forrest's insistence, antagonized Forrest and produced a muddled situation. Forrest and Lee had a better relationship than Forrest usually had with superior officers, but the aftermath of Brice's Crossroads created the promotion controversy. While it is easy to make light of Forrest's boils, the pain could have played a bigger role in his behavior during the campaign than has been appreciated. John Morton, Forrest's artillery commander, wrote that the day before the battle, "Forrest, from his knowledge of the enemy's position, deemed an attack unwise and declined the command." Whatever the whole truth may have been, Forrest and Lee had to set aside animosities when they awoke the morning of July 13 and learned that the enemy was moving rapidly toward Tupelo.[6]

Grierson's cavalry led the way as the men in blue hurried down the Pontotoc-Tupelo road. Despite skirmishing with small Rebel patrols most of the way, the cavalry reached Harrisburg and Tupelo relatively unscathed. The main column of infantry and artillery, especially the rear guard, had more trouble.

When word of the enemy's movement east reached Confederate headquarters, Lee ordered Forrest to take two brigades plus Forrest's escort and press the Federal rear, while Lee took the rest of the army to attack Smith's right flank. Forrest drove Smith's rear guard through Pontotoc to the Tupelo road. Pursuit was something Forrest did well, and the heat of battle temporarily overcame the pain of bouncing in the saddle. He later wrote, "I made a vigorous assault upon the enemy's rear for ten miles."

Smith had left the Seventh Kansas Cavalry and the U.S. Colored Troops infantry in the rear to keep the Rebels at bay. Colonel Edward Bouton's black soldiers, along with the cavalry, held up Forrest's pursuit before retreating toward Tupelo at the rear of Smith's main column. Rear guards often had dirty work, and there was still much prejudice in the Union army against black soldiers. Also, many in the Union army had never liked the mean, bullying behavior and attitudes of the Kansans and did not care how many of them were shot. Smith nevertheless showed confidence in his black regiments by putting them between the army and Forrest. These same men who had survived Brice's Crossroads had done well during Sturgis's retreat. The Confederates pressed hard, and Union cavalry in the extreme rear, behind Bouton's men, sent urgent calls for help.

Bouton looked for good ground to make a stand and allow the Rebels to come to him. The men of the Sixty-first Colored Regiment made good use of terrain along the road, and when Confederates rode close enough, the black Federals rose up and opened fire, emptying many enemy saddles. While the Confederates recoiled and re-formed, Bouton's men moved on toward Harrisburg for about a mile before re-forming to use the same tactic. This time the pursuing horsemen were more wary and Bouton less successful.

Forrest noted that the bluecoats took advantage of every good defensive position. In fact, the Union resistance became fiercer and more determined as fighting in the Federal rear drew close to the main column. Confederate light artillery kept the Federals alert, and cavalry detachments fanned out on Union flanks to keep Bouton from setting up other ambushes. Forrest, however, not anxious to get drawn into a stand-up fight in which he had not had time to plan strategy, decided to slow up until he heard indications of Lee's attack on the Federal right. At Brice's Crossroads, Forrest knew he could count on Barteau's flank and rear attack; he had not been in battle with Lee, and he could not be sure this time.

Bouton moved from ridge to ridge, daring the Rebels to make a frontal assault. The Confederates got more and more cautious to avoid more blasts from Bouton's infantry. Bouton's men and other rearguard cavalry had to hold off Forrest and protect the slow-moving, weighted-down wagon train, Sturgis's Achilles' heel. Bouton sent most of his force forward to protect the train while leaving part of a regiment to check the Confederates. Bouton's black troops shot down several Rebels who rode through a cornfield to within fifteen yards of the skirmish line. The exchange forced the Rebels back, and the black troops rejoined their comrades. Forrest's advance pushed ahead, harassing Bouton's flanks. Stephen Lee finally showed up on Smith's flank.

Detachments from other Union infantry regiments backtracked to assist Bouton, and more would be needed to thwart Lee. Two infantry regiments came to help; they had been protecting the wagon train when sounds of Lee's attack drifted over the hills. With Smith's column stretched out, Lee had a golden opportunity to inflict significant damage.[7]

General James Chalmers, one of Forrest's best, tried to hit Smith's flank. He heard the Yankees were moving, and he immediately put his men in motion to protect the Confederate right. Then orders from Lee instructed Chalmers to hit the enemy's right. (Smith's army's right flank, south of the road, would deploy north of the road when he got to Harrisburg area and turned west to fight.) Lee rode with Chalmers but chose not to lead in person. No matter what Forrest wanted, Lee understood that Forrest's men would fight better under Forrest. So Chalmers, one of Forrest's most trusted lieutenants, led the way and found Federals at Bartram's Shop (also known as Burrow's Shop) some eight miles west of Tupelo, where a trail intersected the main road. Chalmers immediately ordered an assault, and the surprise attack worked at first, when Rebels gunned down several mules, forcing the Yankees to abandon wagons, a caisson, and ambulances.

Chalmers's attack had a magnetic effect, drawing Union infantry and artillery to the area from both western and eastern segments of Smith's column. Chalmers saw the danger of entrapment as Federal reinforcements rushed toward his men. The scene grew chaotic, and some Confederates in the melee had to hold their fire for a time, for in the smoke of battle they could not tell friend from foe.[8]

Federal commanders had been aware that their ranks were stretched too thin in places. The slow wagon train continued to hamper Smith's deployment. One of Smith officers saw that almost a quarter of the wagons were vulnerable to flank attacks. Two Wisconsin regiments protected a portion of the wagon train at the road junction and flanked Chalmers's left.

Despite tactical challenges, Smith's men fought a textbook fight, taking advantage of terrain and reinforcing each other when needed. The coordinated defense was readily apparent, even to the Confederates, when they made a second assault on Smith's flank at Connewah Crossroads. Confederate general Abraham Buford, commanding the Second Division of Forrest's cavalry, noted his admiration for the enemy during the race for Tupelo: "About 5 o'clock Wednesday evening (13th), under order of Lieutenant-General Lee, with [Tyree] Bell's brigade and a section of artillery from

[John] Morton's battery, I attacked the enemy on his right flank during the march. At no time had I found the enemy unprepared. He marched with his column well closed up, his wagon train well protected, and his flanks covered in an admirable manner, evincing at all times a readiness to meet any attack, and showing careful generalship. After fighting him about an hour, suffering considerable loss, the enemy was heavily re-enforced and I was compelled to withdraw the brigade from action."

Edward Crossland rushed to assist Buford. When Crossland and his men arrived, they found a Buford brigade "falling back in some confusion." The brigade was Tyree Bell's, who recalled, "No blame can certainly be attached to the men for falling back, as they were completely overpowered and forced to retire." The men, mostly new troops, obviously did not have the discipline of veterans. Bell attacked with the understanding that another brigade would assist, but, unlike coordinated Union efforts, Bell got no help and had to endure frontal and flanking fire. Having severely chastised the Rebels, Federal troops continued toward Tupelo.

Thus ended the so-called battle of Connewah Crossroads. Though it was not extensive enough to measure up to most battles, it was typical of that part of the Tupelo campaign on the Pontotoc-Tupelo road. The Confederates' attempts to stall Smith's march failed at every encounter.[9]

Smith later reported his "object was to secure Tupelo, thus gaining possession of the railroad and giving me the opportunity to choose my own ground for battle." He won the race for Tupelo, and he established a battle line that took advantage of terrain. He also received welcome news that Grierson occupied Tupelo, which was on the Mobile & Ohio Railroad east of Smith's battle line. Grierson had thus secured the Union rear while the army about-faced and prepared for a Confederate attack. Smith placed his Third Division on the left of the Pontotoc-Tupelo road and the First Division on the right. The black regiments, which had been fighting most of the day, took positions in the rear behind the left flank. The First Division formed at an angle so that its infantry brigades, along with Grierson's cavalry, could keep an eye on the wagon train parked in the rear. During the coming fight, Grierson's men guarded both flanks; they were relatively fresh and could repulse any flank and rear attacks. In this position, in the area of Harrisburg, a community that had mostly died out when the railroad was built to the east through Tupelo, the Federal army camped the night of July 13.

The historian Edwin C. Bearss has written of the situation that evening: "If General Smith and his officers congratulated themselves . . . they could be excused. The day had gone extremely well. They had stolen a march on the dreaded Forrest and had occupied a strong position of their own choosing. If the Confederates assaulted them, they were confident of victory."[10]

While the Federals rested, Lee and Forrest organized their troops. Buford, with two brigades, reported to Forrest near Connewah Crossroads. Chalmers rode into camp two miles west of Harrisburg. Lee and the rest of the Confederate force drifted in during the evening. By morning there would be some 7,500 Confederate troops on hand.

Forrest and Lee privately discussed the situation, and they could not have been pleased. Smith had gotten away, but, more grating, the Federal general controlled the campaign. If left alone, Smith's men could wreck the railroad in Tupelo and destroy supplies. If the Confederates attacked, they would go against superior numbers who had terrain advantages.

Forrest was edgy. His artillery chief, John Morton, recalled many years later, with a touch of hero worship, "General Forrest, returning to headquarters about dark, dismounted from his horse, and, removing his coat, spread it upon the ground." The general seemed lost in his thoughts and very tired from the fighting and heat of the day. His staff, knowing his unpredictable temperament, stood some distance away, leaving him alone. "Suddenly springing up, he put on his coat, mounted his horse, and called to Lieut. Samuel Donelson to accompany him. They made a wide detour through the woods." With battle tactics swirling in his head, Forrest forgot his boils. He told Donelson that scouts indicated the Yankees were about a mile ahead. "He also stated that he had neglected to put on his holster, and was therefore without his pistols. Lieutenant Donelson offered him one, but it was declined, General Forrest saying that he did not think they would be needed." After an hour or so, the two rode up in the Union rear, near enemy wagons. The darkness concealed their identity, and, keeping away from campfires, they rode casually among Smith's camp. Having ascertained the information they sought, namely Smith's strength, the two rode back toward the Confederate camp. About 200 yards ahead, Federal pickets challenged them, and "General Forrest, affecting intense anger, said, 'How dare you halt your commanding officer?' and without further remark put spurs to his horse, an example followed by Lieutenant Donelson." The Yankees did not sense they had almost captured a couple of Rebels until the two riders disappeared into the darkness. The two bent over low in the saddle, and though the pickets fired a few shots, they were not hit and made it back safely. Forrest enjoyed talking about the adventure, noting he might not have minded getting shot in one of his boils if it provided some relief. There were easier ways to get them lanced. "His discovery of the enemy's strong position," Morton recalled, "occasioned General Forrest some

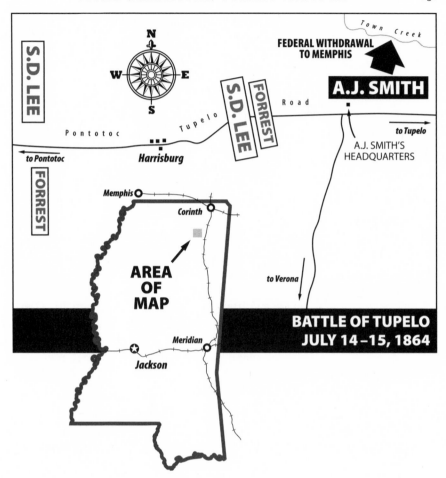

uneasiness, and his last order [to Morton] was to make his men comfortable for the night, for they had hot work before them on the morrow."[11]

Forrest's adventure might have been the only thing about the campaign he cared to remember. One can only speculate what might have happened had he been in command. Given what he had seen that night, he probably would have withdrawn or tried to maneuver Smith out of the enemy's enviable position. Lee may have sought Forrest's advice, but it is unlikely that Forrest recommended the frontal assault Lee settled on for the next day. Lee insisted many years later that he acted in accord "with the understanding to accept battle wherever the enemy offered it, and when it was found he would not advance farther." Lee further argued, "Whatever others may say," he and Forrest "were in perfect accord as to delivering battle." If Lee had made his claims immediately in a postbattle report, his comments would be more believable. In fact, by the time he wrote of the campaign, he was elderly, and the dead Forrest could not argue. John Morton commented that if Lee had written a timely report, "many matters of controversy now involved would have been settled during the lifetime of numerous distinguished and gallant comrades." One can speculate that if Forrest felt strongly about not attacking, he would have spoken up loud and clear to Lee. The fact that he did not meant either his pain or Smith's strong position had sapped his usual desire to go into battle. The night ride had been a Forrest kind of adventure, but the adrenalin rush had not lasted long. Whatever Forrest's true feelings may have been, he would not lash out at Lee until the battle had been fought and lost.

Lee never faced a situation like the one confronting him the night of July 13. He had performed well during the Vicksburg campaign, but in those days he did not have to make command decisions. Forrest had such experience, but he had never been outthought and outmaneuvered to this extent. Of course, some of Smith's moves were attributable to Confederate strategy that relied on the Federals doing as predicted. Smith had done otherwise.

Both Lee and Forrest understood the "desperate venture" they were undertaking. No reinforcements were available, since Confederate armies everywhere by 1864 faced superior numbers. At the time, Southern armies had "to fight against great odds or not fight at all. On this occasion not to fight would have been to have given up the great corn region of Mississippi, the main support of other armies facing the enemy on more important fields."

Lee may have gotten cold feet as the prospect of battle loomed the next day. He tried once more to give command to Forrest. "I said to General Forrest that a large proportion of the troops now on the ground belonged to his immediate command, had served under him in his recent successful campaigns, and had just won the splendid victory at Brice's Crossroads, having beaten some of the troops that they would have to encounter to-day, and that, knowing Forrest better than myself, they would have more implicit confidence in his leadership. General Forrest, however, positively declined to take the command, saying that I was his senior, and that I should take the responsibility." Whether Forrest still nurtured anger at Lee's promotion or believed Lee's strategy would not work, or both, he mysteriously ignored Lee's pleas, and the reason for his behavior has never been ascertained.

Lee's words indicate he was uncomfortable in command, and Forrest was uncomfortable not only with Lee's presence but also with the tactical situation. They may have agreed on the decision to fight, but not on the conduct of the battle. Who would be in charge on the field once shooting started? Forrest seemed to assume Lee would, but Forrest's actions the next day indicated he really considered himself in command. The bottom line was the two created a foggy hierarchy of leadership, going against a Federal general who so far had conducted a remarkably able campaign.

One factor missing from Lee's late report, and Forrest's reminiscences, is mention of attempts to flank Smith. If Lee and Forrest had turned north to cut off Smith's best route back to Memphis, surely Smith would have been forced to give up his chosen ground west of Tupelo. Yet there is no evidence that Lee and Forrest considered such a tactic. Forrest had seen Smith's position up close, and it seemed a logical option, but Forrest apparently never mentioned it to Lee, and why Lee did not think of it remains another unanswered question.

Smith no doubt waited for dawn with more confidence than his counterparts. He still held his strong position, but perhaps thoughts of Sturgis's failure and Sherman's wrath haunted him. Should he stay put and stare down Forrest and Lee? In retrospect, the answer is yes, but in his own mind, who knew what tomorrow might bring? He had had a good day, but he may have spent a restless night. He exhibited no killer instinct.

Daylight of July 14 gave Forrest a much better look at the Union army position than he had gleaned from his nighttime escapade. He saw the Federals held a position from which they probably could not be driven, and from a distance the Confederates could see that the Yankees were strengthening their positions. Any further frontal attack might destroy Forrest's and Lee's army. The historian Edwin C. Bearss wrote: "The position selected by General Smith to receive the Confederate attack was well suited for defense. His battle line, on the crest of a low ridge overlooking Harrisburg Branch, formed a right angle several hundred yards north of the Pontotoc road. From the position . . . the Federals looked westward toward Pontotoc, the direction from which Generals Lee and Forrest would advance. To the Union front, the terrain sloped gradually down to Harrisburg Branch," where there were large trees and little vegetation offering defensive cover. Clearings from Smith's main line to the timber would be fields of Confederate death, and in some places widely spaced trees would provide little protection for the Rebels, who would be easy targets for Union riflemen.[12]

Stephen Lee decided to fight with troops dismounted, since Forrest's men understood infantry tactics. Charging the enemy here on horseback would have been even more ridiculous than an infantry assault. Of Lee's

7,500 men, only 6,600, less than half Smith's strength, could ably participate in the attack. (Other estimates of Confederate strength go as high as
9,400, but 7,500 is more believable.) Lee placed Philip Roddey's troops on
the far right of the Confederate line. Edward Crossland's brigade covered
the center, and Hinchie Mabry's men lined up on the left. Tyree Bell supported Mabry initially but during the fight also supported Crossland. Hylan
Lyon's brigade and James Chalmers's division were held in reserve. Mabry
and Bell anchored the Confederate line north of the Pontotoc-Tupelo road;
the remainder of the troops fought most of the day south of the road. Rejecting Morton's advice to mass the artillery, Lee dispersed his guns among
divisions, thereby reducing their effectiveness. This was a curious tactic for
an experienced artilleryman. Lee had his troops up about 2 a.m., and by
daybreak most had deployed and awaited orders.[13]

The first day of the battle, July 14, was mainly a two-phase fight, fought
at times simultaneously and at other times staggered among various portions of the two armies. Part one began on the Federal left and spread along
that front to the center. The troops in these two sectors were so close that
fighting seemed to be on one line; any distinctions between the Federal left
and center and the Confederate right and center became blurred. Meanwhile combat on the Union right and Rebel left was distinguishable from
the rest of the battle. The Confederates ignited the fighting with an attack
against the Federal left-center.

False information led Lee to order Roddey's troops to charge. Two
scouts, noted for their reliability, rode into the Confederate camp with information that Smith was withdrawing toward Ripley. According to Lee,
Forrest advised the attack on Smith's left, with the idea of turning the Union
flank while the rest of the army hit the Federal front. The scouting reports
are not mentioned in Forrest's campaign reports, but, assuming they existed, Forrest possibly thought he could disrupt Smith's withdrawal as he
had Sturgis's, when he sent a detachment to hit Sturgis's left as the Federals
retreated down toward Tishomingo Creek. In effect, he could bend Smith's
left and push it against the rest of Smith's line. Lee noticed that Forrest's
"blood was up; the fire of battle was in his eye. He said that if he was in
command, he would not hesitate a moment." Perhaps that was so, but it
could be that Lee, writing after the fact, was trying to enlist Forrest was an
ally in the ultimate fatal outcome for the Confederates.

Whatever the case, Forrest obeyed. He personally delivered Lee's order to Roddey, then he moved forward to select a route for the flank attack. Suddenly he found a Kentucky brigade "had been rashly precipitated
forward," falling back under "murderous" fire. Forrest grabbed their colors

and tried to form a new line. Impressed by the "terrific" fire from Federal entrenchments, Forrest canceled Roddey's attack. The Kentuckians had bungled any chance for coordination, and Forrest, "wishing to save my troops from the unprofitable slaughter I knew would follow any attempt to charge," told Roddey to forget the assault. Forrest ordered up artillery and established a battle line. This would not be Brice's Crossroads; there would be no glorious flank and rear attack here. If Forrest had the fire of battle in his eye, it cooled quickly when he saw the effectiveness of Smith's concentrated firepower.

David Moore, commanding the Union Third Division, saw his troops gain momentum on their left and center. The Rebels advanced in column formation out in the open toward the Federal line. Moore's men lay behind the brow of the high ground until the Confederates got within twenty paces. Then the blue infantry rose up as one, gave their own version of the Rebel yell, and charged, their volleys sending the Confederates running. Some were heard exclaiming, "My God! My God!" These tactics, used effectively by Bouton on the Tupelo road, continued to work. Moore's men effectively used oblique (slanting rather than horizontal or perpendicular) firing from the right and left, leaving the Confederates hastily retreating.

The right and left oblique enabled Moore's men to move more flexibly as situations dictated, to the right or to the left, to shoot into the flanks of the charging Confederates. These shifts in fields of fire confused the attackers and reduced their ability to fight back. Once the Confederate retreat began, Union soldiers left their trenches briefly to pursue the enemy to the foot of the hill in their front. Here they halted and sent volleys into the retreating masses before returning unmolested.

Other Union accounts of action on the Federal left and center tell similar stories of dominance. At 9 a.m. the Rebels attacked, driving in Union skirmishers on the left-center of the Union line. The Rebels again made the mistake of charging across an open field and were mowed down. Holding their fire until the enemy got within 100 yards, the Yankees arose and opened fire in unison, and Rebels who survived turned and ran for their lives. Many never fired a shot.

On the Federal left, just to the right of the U.S. Colored Troops, the Confederates attacked that morning, and Union officers believed that Lee and Forrest were after Federal batteries. The Federals waited patiently and, using a right oblique, delivered a murderous flanking fire. The artillery batteries sent a devastating crossfire of shells and canister; the canister, having the effect of a plethora of shotguns, knocked down Confederates over a wide range.

An officer of the Second Illinois Light Artillery ordered his guns to change their positions to fire into the Confederate flank. The guns caused "the most terrible destruction" as deadly missiles hit Rebels with a crossfire that made it difficult to find safety. Union officer John Lowell noticed the enemy quickly disappearing in rapid retreat.

Kentuckians soon found that a frontal assault against Smith's position was suicidal. Confederate officer Edward Crossland wrote sadly of the debacle that his men charged with much enthusiasm, yelling and certain they would overrun the Yankees. Firing as they went to within 200 yards of the enemy, they met heavy fire from the front and realized they had no support on their flanks. Then, added to the fierce frontal fire, an enfilading fire coming from Federals on both flanks created an inescapable lead storm and totally wrecked the Kentuckians, who had suffered much already. The failure of other Confederate troops to advance left their comrades isolated, and the entire Union line fired into the survivors. The failure of Rebels on their right flank to move forward doomed the "decimated" Kentuckians. After the few survivors retreated, they fell exhausted to the ground and did not fight again that day. Later they moved to guard a road southeast to Verona below Tupelo, void of Yankee threats.

General James Chalmers's cavalry had similar experiences. Ordered to dismount his reserve cavalry and march his men two miles, he discovered that his orders had sent him in the wrong direction. Disgusted, he received new orders that forced a countermarch, exhausting his men and horses. While moving, he then received three conflicting sets of instructions. Forrest wanted him to move to the right, while Lee told him to move left. Abraham Buford told Chalmers that Lee wanted him in the center. Since he belonged to Forrest's command, Chalmers went right. But Lee, now taking advantage of his rank after begging Forrest to command, personally intervened and had Chalmers hold one brigade in reserve, while ordering the other to the left. Such confusion was inexcusable; all leaders involved were professional soldiers, but they had turned the field of battle into an absurd mess. This kind of uncertainty, which created absurdities, typified the Confederate experience that day.

Abraham Buford argued early in the day for an attack on the Union left. The enemy wanted frontal attacks, because they would all be beaten back. Lee and Forrest had probably already made their decision. Whatever the sequence, Buford watched furiously as everything went wrong with coordination and men not doing anything. The Kentucky disaster endangered Buford's position. His severe losses amounted to a third of his troops, and the survivors had to fall back. Confederate officers proved

slow in understanding that an attack anywhere along the Union line produced disaster. Smith's well-designed position emphasized concentrated
fire.

North of the Tupelo-Pontotoc road Federal troops continued the
slaughter of charging Confederates. Though getting some reinforcements,
Hinchie Mabry's Rebel forces fell in droves before the coordinated Union
firepower aligned along a ridge crest. Confederates in that sector did have
a few trees to provide cover, but not nearly enough. They needed the trees,
for within 300 yards of the Yankee position they received a heavy dose of
small-arms fire. They charged, though suffering from the day's heat; many
fell exhausted, some saving their lives in the process. Some escaped the
killing and wounding resulting from Union firepower. A few Confederate
survivors hunkered down and melted away, finding some cover in a hollow
behind a fence, from which they quickly retreated farther back.

Tyree Bell's brigade got to within seventy-five yards of the Federal
breastworks. His troops also suffered but fought until their ammunition
ran low. A few reinforcements came to relieve Bell, but with little effect.
Bell wrote the "place was a hot one, and the enemy's position strong and
commanding, well selected, and well fortified."

Another Confederate regiment experienced the extremities of heat.
Lee sent Edmund Rucker's brigade into the maelstrom to the left, and men
charged on the run. The men went over plowed fields and through corn, in
plain sight of the Federal line, for some 2,000 yards, and they went down,
wounded and killed from artillery and rifle fire from a ridge behind Harrisburg. Heat exhaustion again compounded the toll.[14]

The well-constructed entrenchments, masterful use of interior lines that
made it possible for Smith's men to move from one area to another without
exposing themselves to Confederate fire, and high ground made Smith's
position impossible to dent. Staying in the trenches was not enough for
some commanders. Joseph Mower sent one of his brigades in pursuit of
fleeing Rebels, clearing his front except for a few of his own men who fell
from sunstroke. Sweating, triumphant Union soldiers stayed at their forward position for a while and then returned to their original lines. Though
the Federals respected the efforts of their opponents, they celebrated when
"the enemy's last line was destroyed."

By early afternoon the fighting, except for light skirmishing, ended for
the daylight hours of July 14. At 1 p.m. the Confederates admitted defeat.
Lee sent a wire to Richmond stating that the attack had been made but that
he had been unable to force the Federals from their position. He believed
that his men had a strong position and could repel a counterattack.

Forrest also liked the Confederate position that commanded approaches for several hundred yards. Following Lee's instructions, he ordered rails, logs, and cotton bales gathered to build temporary fortifications. The farm of a Mrs. Samples supplied the necessary items. Meanwhile Lee and Forrest ordered exhausted soldiers to advance short distances and then retreat, in a vain effort to lure Smith into an attack. Forrest waited with great anticipation, perhaps anxious to redeem his lackluster performance. But, as Lee noted, Smith "did not move out of his own chosen position."[15]

Caution continued to be Smith's byword, even after a smashing victory. His men, especially those who had countercharged, needed time to recuperate from the hot weather. He had no desire to risk a counterattack, and he saw that the Confederates, given the pounding they had endured, showed no inclination to continue. Around sundown, Smith ordered most of his force to pull back several hundred yards to the supply wagons "to give [them] rest and opportunity to cook their rations." His actions seemed humane, but clearly Smith lacked the fighting instincts of a great commander.

As night fell, Confederates saw Union soldiers torching houses around Harrisburg and Tupelo as they had at Ripley. One Rebel officer wrote of the sojourn of Smith's army in Mississippi that his men committed robbery and left a trail of desolation and vandalism. They mistreated local citizens and took whatever they pleased from whomever they pleased, even widows and orphans. Livestock was killed to keep it out of Confederate hands, and carcasses were left in yards and in roads to rot in the daily hot sun. One pro-Confederate writer complained of Smith that he "laid waste this beautiful country, burning towns, private residences" plus granaries, gin houses, and plantations. Hard war had come to this stage by 1864, but after the Meridian campaign, the complainers should not have been surprised.

The destruction wrought on civilians had in many areas become predictable and was not confined to one army or the other. Soldiers in blue and gray felt inclined to take what they needed or wanted. The difference was the Yankee preference for fire. In the Harrisburg community, however, and elsewhere along the march, Smith simply continued to follow Sherman's dictum to make local people regret their support of Forrest.

While fires raged, Lee and Forrest decided on a night raid, a reconnaissance in force. They suspected and no doubt hoped the fires might mean the Federals were going to withdraw, perhaps that very night. The overall results had been devastating, but their men had not given up the fight, and they were still in Smith's front. Perhaps Smith had decided to quit while he was ahead. The Federals could not stay at Tupelo indefinitely without depleting their supplies, which, like dead livestock, were vulnerable to the summer heat.

As night blanketed the battlefield, Forrest took a brigade and rode with the men to the Federal left to read the enemy's position, strength, and intentions. The night riders at one point opened fire and drove in Federal pickets. The noise alerted the Federals, and the Yankees, Forrest noted, opened "one of the heaviest fires I have heard during the war." It seemed as if the entire Federal army had been waiting, resulting in an "unceasing roar of small-arms, and his whole line was lighted up by a continuous stream of fire." Fortunately for the Rebels, most Federal bullets went high in the darkness. The Confederates hurried back to their own lines, thankful that the enemy had difficulty seeing them.[16]

Forrest had been repulsed by white brigades and Edward Bouton's black regiments. Colonel Bouton proudly reported that his black infantry made a charge with fixed bayonets up a hill to help drive Forrest away. Smith's officers understood that their left was the key to the battlefield; if it broke, the rest of Smith's army would be subject to flank and rear attacks. Forrest's presence there came as no surprise, and Union vigilance proved decisive.

Confederate artillery lobbed shells at the Federals, who could be seen by the light of the burning buildings. Strong enemy reaction further convinced Lee and Forrest that the Yankees were not retreating.[17]

As the night of July 14 passed into the early morning of July 15, Smith held the initiative, but the big question was what he would do with it. Forrest and Lee thought the Yankees might launch an early attack. Smith might try to move south and destroy more railroad and supplies, so Lee shifted Buford's men to keep watch.

Though Smith had had his way, his actions had been defensive. To get Forrest, as Sherman had ordered, he at some point had to become the aggressor. The battered Confederate force remained before him. Smith respected the Confederates' fighting ability, and he never had any intention of attacking a stationary army in his front. He had other options. He could try to maneuver the Confederates into attacking him again. He could send Grierson's cavalry to flank the Rebels out of their position and then order an infantry charge. He could use part of his troops to conduct a holding action, while the rest sacked the surrounding countryside. Whatever he may have considered, it became evident the next day that he was not going to continue the campaign.

When morning came Smith ordered a withdrawal, mainly because, as he later wrote, his army's supply of bread had gone sour. He made the rather incredible statement in his postcampaign report that the bread had been spoiled when it was drawn from commissaries prior to the march into Mississippi. Why it took so long for him to discover the problem he did not say. What he found on the morning of July 15 was that he had only one day's ration per man on hand for the army. Of course, he might have obtained sufficient supplies from the area for several more days of campaigning. All food around his army had not been destroyed. The Confederates would no doubt have contested Federal foraging, but with his superior numbers, Smith still could have ordered his army to live off the land. He also had only about 100 rounds of artillery ammunition per gun, which may or may not have proved a problem, depending upon future actions of the Rebels. In his report Smith simply said, "It, therefore, became a matter of necessity to return." He had won a major victory; now he gave up the campaign. Had Smith lost his nerve? Had he decided to declare victory and leave while victory was still his? Only he knew the answer.

Smith held his troops in position all morning and sent cavalry to destroy the railroad five miles north and south of Tupelo. He ordered Rebel wounded who had been picked up on the battlefield to be carried into Tupelo and left there. A cavalry brigade retrieved a captured, disabled Confederate piece of artillery left behind by the Rebels the previous day. Not until noon did the Union army began withdrawing.

Before the disengagement began, action erupted on the Federal left. Abraham Buford, still guarding the road to Verona, received orders to attack at dawn. Apparently Lee tired of waiting for Smith to attack. Two Rebel brigades drove Union skirmishers to Smith's main line. Buford then ordered a halt, "threw out a line of skirmishers to hold the enemy in check, and rested my division, who were exhausted from hard fighting, the excessive heat and want of water." Eighty of his men had to be carried from the field due to heat prostration. Forrest rode up and found men fainting and otherwise in bad shape from thirst. Clearly these men were being pushed beyond their limits.

Smith's black soldiers again rose to the occasion. They moved forward toward the ridge previously held by Union forces and now by Buford's men. The bluecoats "charged, firing, with fixed bayonets," and drove the Rebels back several hundred yards.

Had the Confederates pressed that morning, they might have contacted the rear of Smith's army as it marched toward the Ellistown road northwest of Tupelo. When the black regiments chased Buford away, they were doing their usual rearguard duty and protecting the wagon train carrying sick and wounded. This portion of the army, including detachments of Grierson's cavalry guarding the flanks, joined the rest of Smith's force at Old Town Creek in the late afternoon.[18]

As Union forces departed, Lee continued his efforts to lure the enemy, but Joseph Mower's men, lagging to beat back any attack, toyed with the Rebels and suddenly bounded out from behind their lines and drove them a couple of miles. There Confederate cavalry sprang into saddles and hurried off. After clearing their front, Mower's men turned and leisurely followed the army to Old Town Creek. A cavalry brigade watched the rear just in case. There was no need. At Old Town Creek, Mower marched his division on past Moore's to take the lead. Just as Mower's men completed crossing the creek, Rebel artillery shells screamed into the creek bottom.

The Confederates had finally figured out what was amiss. After wasting most of the morning trying to pick a fight, Lee ordered troops forward. The Rebels moved slowly, held up by Smith's rear guard. Finally he discovered the Yankees were taking Ellistown road. Lee ordered his whole force to pursue. Buford's division took the lead and found the enemy in the Old Town Creek bottom and ordered his big guns to open fire.

A Union brigade turned and dealt with the Confederates. Union soldiers "scaled a fence, waded a stream, nearly waist deep in water and mud, slashed through the thick brush and timber; sloshed through a second stream as deep as the first and reached the edge of a large field of growing corn, where they confronted the rebel line." Despite the sight of Confederate flags, the sun's heat, and heavy rifle fire, the Federals pushed on, overpowering the Confederates and inflicting heavy losses. More Union troops came up to reinforce the charge, and Lee's line wavered and pulled back.

Other Union regiments ran into more Confederates and drove them away, using the oblique fire tactic of shooting from angles that had worked so well the previous day. The Rebels retreated beyond a fence, and another Union charge scattered them in confusion. Mower halted the fighting when he saw the Confederates had left for good.

Confederate commanders wrote little about the Town Creek affair. Buford admitted that the Yankees simply had too many men and that reinforcements for his troops never showed up. He decided his men had suffered enough, and he ordered a withdrawal. Tyree Bell added, "The regiments acted gallantly on this occasion until they were forced to retire in consequence of the overwhelming numbers of the enemy."[19]

Other Rebel troops, sent into battle piecemeal, received flanking fire. Then word came that Forrest had been wounded, and everyone was ready to pull out. Surviving Rebels were glad to see the Yankees go.

The campaign had come to a bitter end for Forrest. He got to the fight at Town Creek after it had started, and he was shot in the right foot. The wound posed no danger, but it was most painful. Though he would have preferred a more gallant way to exit the action, he undoubtedly was happy to see this campaign end.[20]

The action at Old Town Creek finished the Tupelo campaign. Two Confederate brigades followed Smith's retreating army. They did no damage but kept the Federals alert. The Union column reached Ellistown the next day, arrived at New Albany on the 17th, and trudged into La Grange on the 21st.

Smith had abandoned the field, but he could claim success. His army suffered fewer than 700 casualties, a low number that signified how well his troops had been positioned on July 14 and how little damage the Confederates had inflicted the next day. Confederate returns are more uncertain; casualties have been calculated at around 1,300 but could have been higher.

Cadwallader Washburn celebrated the outcome, which he called "most satisfactory"—redemption for the Sturgis disaster. The ration situation "was unfortunate," but positives overshadowed that negative. A not so subtle lesson encouraged the Union command. The U.S. Colored Troops had done well; they had fought effectively and showed themselves skilled in drill and very well disciplined. "I confess," he wrote, "that their action has moved from my mind a prejudice of twenty years' standing."[21]

Sherman, pleased at first when word spread that Forrest had died from lockjaw as a result of his wound at Old Town Creek, grew angry when he learned the truth. Forrest still lived and would recover. Sherman immediately ordered another expedition by Smith into Mississippi. Sherman's force had reached the outskirts of Atlanta, and he did not want Forrest still lurking out there somewhere.

Forrest bounced back and took to the field again. As Lee received orders to join Joseph Johnston's army in Georgia, Forrest had independent command and eventually a promotion to lieutenant general. As one of his biographers has noted, however, Forrest's fighting spirit seemed to be on the wane, reflecting the fortunes of his command and the Confederacy. Lee never wrote an official report of the battle, perhaps because he saw no point in criticizing Forrest or he was simply disappointed in himself. For whatever reason, it was the only time Lee failed to submit an official campaign or battle report.

He finally wrote about the battle in 1902, when he restated comments from reports by other officers but also editorialized: "On the Confederate side blunders and mistakes complicated matters. The troops were all of Forrest's command, and he should have had supreme command, but he insisted

on Gen. Lee [Lee wrote his account in third person], the department commander, assuming the responsibility and being present. Forrest had just won
his splendid victory at Brice's Cross Roads . . . , and his troops had confidence in him." Lee then wrote about Forrest's refusal to take command. He
said Forrest did not appear to think they had enough troops to fight Smith,
and Forrest complained about his boils. Lee's comments on the battle were
much oversimplified, but he no doubt blamed the outcome, as well as some
of the battlefield errors, largely on Forrest's refusal to take command. Lee's
account is not his finest hour, for he was in command, no matter the reason.
His decision to frontally attack, regardless of Forrest's endorsement, was
disastrous. Lee had performed well in the past and would again, but his
command performance at Harrisburg and Tupelo proved his limitations as
a general.[22]

Lee's mistakes do not absolve Forrest of a poor performance. Whether
due to boils or jealousy of Lee, Forrest seemed passive during much of the
battle. When he did fight, he made some bad decisions. Forrest's attitude
surfaced at a council of war the night of July 15. He did not want to attend
due to his wound, but Lee insisted. He asked Forrest for comments, and
Forrest said bitterly, "I'll tell you one thing, General Lee. If I knew as much
about West Point tactics as you, the Yankees would whip hell out of me
every day." Lee's response is not recorded. Having been asked to command
and refusing, Forrest had no reason to be complaining.

Forrest had more campaigning ahead with Smith, and he would enjoy
some success. But Smith and his own stubbornness had taken some fire from
Forrest. John Morton, while proud of the performance of his artillerists, admitted sadly about the battle, "The Confederates suffered an unprecedented
percentage of loss." Morton concluded, "the lack of coordination precipitated a tragic and unparalleled sacrifice." Edwin C. Bearss, commenting on
the Tupelo campaign, wrote, "The combat effectiveness of Forrest's corps
was destroyed. . . . Although Forrest would rally his force . . . , never again
would his corps be able to stand and fight Union infantry as it had at Brice's
Cross Roads."[23]

In Georgia, Sherman did not immediately hear the news of Smith's decision to go back to Memphis, and when he did, he was not pleased. But during the fighting at Tupelo, Sherman's huge army crossed the Chattahoochee
River just north of Atlanta. His supply line remained unfettered, and Forrest
had been wounded. July 15 was another day of progress for Sherman, and
had he known of Forrest's wound, he would surely have celebrated. To be
sure, Sherman was in no mood to let the Confederate general recuperate.
Forrest would have to stay busy, courtesy of William T. Sherman.

10

MORE RAIDS

Smith and Grierson

*G*eneral William T. Sherman refused to let A. J. Smith's puzzling action
deter his determination to get Nathan Bedford Forrest. Sherman, from his
faraway presence in Georgia, perhaps could not grasp all the nuances of
Smith's operation, nor could he understand what went on in Smith's mind.
Sherman assumed Smith had withdrawn in order to go to Ripley to get
resupplied. All reports indicated Smith had won a great victory, so why
march back to Memphis, leaving Forrest behind to cause more trouble, as
Sherman fully expected the Confederate cavalryman to do? Sherman did
know that whatever Smith's reasons for withdrawing, he must go back and
take care of business, and he soon received orders from General Cadwallader Washburn to return to Mississippi and destroy Forrest and his small
army. Sherman, now on the outskirts of Atlanta, would not give up, and
he would not let Smith sit and do nothing. Washburn asked about sending
Smith to help with Federal operations against Mobile, but Sherman heatedly responded that Ulysses S. Grant, commanding all U.S. forces, wanted
Smith to stay after Forrest to keep the slippery Rebel out of Tennessee.
Washburn told Smith that Sherman still demanded Forrest be pursued until he was hopefully killed in battle, and Sherman made clear that only he
and Grant had the authority to send Smith anywhere else.[1]

So Smith immediately began preparing his men for another trip into
Mississippi. They refurbished their gear, repaired everything that needed
attention, and received more ammunition, food (hopefully fresh this time),
new clothing for those in need, and fresh horses to replace those worn out
by the Tupelo foray. Smith would have no excuses this time if he defeated
Forrest and then returned to Memphis.[2]

244

Smith and Washburn determined they would not allow logistics to become an issue again; neither wanted to risk any more of Sherman's wrath, or they might find themselves out of the army, as had Samuel Sturgis. Washburn also gave Smith additional cannons, while Smith worked with maps to decide on a route into Mississippi. He chose to use the Memphis and Charleston Railroad to take his force to that line's junction with the Mississippi Central at Grand Junction, Tennessee. There he would set up a supply base and move south down the Mississippi Central, repairing the railroad along the way and rebuilding bridges. This section of the Mississippi Central had been pretty much abandoned since the winter months of 1862–63, when Grant withdrew from north Mississippi and refocused his plans for taking Vicksburg. Smith also planned to set up supply depots at Holly Springs, Abbeville, and Oxford.

Once the Federals reached Oxford, they would abandon the railroad line and cross Pontotoc Ridge. This route would carry them into the Black Prairie Region, where every effort would be made to wreak such destruction that no food would be coming from there to sustain any Confederate force. Hopefully, this would force Forrest to come to the area's rescue. If Forrest showed no inclination to fight by the time Smith reached Columbus, Smith had the option of either going on into Alabama or returning to Memphis.[3]

In late July the Federal army began concentrating at Grand Junction, where construction crews immediately went to work on the railroad to the south. As repairs progressed, the train took soldiers to Davis' Mills. There they had to leave the train and march to Holly Springs, a town that figured prominently in the early phases of the Vicksburg campaign.

The first wave of Yankees entered Holly Springs at 11:00 a.m. on August 1, 1864. Some of the town still showed the beauty of the place, but the scars of war were everywhere, and the people knew by now not to insult these men from the North. They had found out from bitter experience that the reprisals of the Union army could be severe. Thus the Iowans who first entered the place received many invitations to eat, though the locals may have had ulterior motives. Among Bouton's black soldiers, they spotted former slaves and feared that these men might be in a vengeful mood. Perhaps the white Iowans would help protect property.[4]

More Yankees arrived in Holly Springs the next day, and more were on the way, arriving from furloughs at the Memphis docks and catching up with Smith's troops. By the evening of August 3 all of Joseph Mower's division was in Holly Springs. Batteries and wagons would follow, the latter escorted by Edward Bouton's black troops. This column reached Holly Springs on the 5th, after a fifty-mile march. Next came William Shaw's division; by this time they could take the train all the way to Holly Springs, due to the good work of the fatigue parties. By the evening of August 8 Smith had 10,000 infantry assembled at Holly Springs, with a solid supply line reaching back to Grand Junction. Smith, who had remained behind in Memphis to keep things moving, arrived on the 8th. He had access to Benjamin Grierson's 4,000 cavalry, who helped the infantry repair the railroad to the Tallahatchie River. Two cavalry regiments experienced guerrilla attacks during their trip to the front, but no real harm was done, and Grierson actually had all his cavalry at Holly Springs before the last of the infantry got there.[5]

While the Federals prepared for their third foray against him since June, Forrest suffered at Tupelo with his foot wound, and still took time to see to burying the dead and getting his battered army back in shape. He wrote Stephen Lee that he would like to go to Columbus, Mississippi, to complete his recovery; if that was not satisfactory, he would go south to Okolona. Meanwhile General James Chalmers would look after things until Forrest could take to the field again. If the Federals showed no sign of life, he suggested spreading his forces around the area, gathering supplies, and finding horses in good enough shape to withstand more campaigning. He also suggested that men be sent to restore Mobile & Ohio Railroad service from Verona, near Tupelo, to Corinth. Black work gangs could do that job. Forrest asked for new Enfield rifles, 1,000 to be exact. Lee, who had traveled to Meridian after the Tupelo fight, said yes to all Forrest's requests, except the one about going to Columbus.

For whatever reason, Forrest set up headquarters at Okolona. Perhaps Lee wanted Forrest closer to the front in case the Yankees showed up again, and Okolona would be preferable. Forrest then began issuing orders to station his men where he wanted them to be, but before they left, he had them scour the countryside for anything useful to them and the army in future fighting. He also increased scouting assignments and made sure that supply depots would be established along the Mobile & Ohio to help keep his army equipped. Men, probably slaves or captured black soldiers, were put to work building earthworks at strategic places.[6]

While Forrest busied himself, Lee received scouting reports at Meridian indicating Smith had returned to Memphis and that he did not seem to be planning anything. So some of the troops attached to Forrest's command temporarily could be returned to their former units. Then Lee found himself on the road, called to join John Bell Hood's (formerly Joseph Johnston's) army in Georgia and take command of a corps in the Army of Tennessee. Dabney Maury took Lee's place. Philip Roddey's command traveled

to southern Alabama to counter Federal actions against the Alabama and
Florida Railroad. Hinchie Mabry and his brigade returned to central Mississippi, and another small battalion headed to Mobile. State Mississippi
troops that had been called up to help Forrest went south to Jackson.[7]

Forrest, when he heard that Stephen Lee had left for Georgia, went to
Columbus, and there received a message from Maury asking him to take
charge of defending north Mississippi, especially the prairie country. Maury
admired Forrest and gave him free rein to make his own decisions, form his
own plans, and make moves as he deemed necessary, and Maury promised
to provide as much support as possible. Even before he heard from Maury,
Forrest was already sending out scouts to ascertain any movements on the
part of Smith. The scouts reported to Chalmers that Smith was moving
infantry to La Grange, Tennessee, and that the Yankees were working on
the Mississippi Central Railroad. Chalmers also got an accurate count of
Smith's force, 14,000 men, and had all this information in Forrest's hands
by August 1. Chalmers also heard that the enemy was planning two other
operations that might indicate an attack on Selma, Alabama, where some
important Confederate war industries were located. Chalmers thought that
the only Confederate strategy that might work, if the reports were accurate,
would be to hit the strongest column, Smith's, beat him, and then hope to
chase off the other two.[8]

One of the other two was supposedly coming out of Vicksburg, where
supplies would be a problem, since Union forces under Sherman had raked
the area clean during the Meridian campaign. Actually, the Vicksburg story
was nothing more than rumor. Another force, supposedly in Decatur, Alabama, reportedly was small enough that Confederates in that area should
be able to take care of it. Forrest had around 5,300 men to meet Smith, not
enough to be sure, but Forrest still had a reputation of doing wonders when
outnumbered. More disturbing news came that Union ships had appeared
near Mobile Bay. No one knew what this might mean. In any event, as far
as Mississippi was concerned, the only Federal movement of any substance
was Smith's, so Mabry, at the town of Goodman in central Mississippi,
was alerted to be ready if Forrest needed him. Confederate commanders
tracked rumors as if the outcome of the war was at stake. The Confederacy
had been on a long losing streak in the western theater, with the brief exception of Chickamauga, and Robert E. Lee was locked in a life-and-death
struggle with Grant in Virginia. To almost any sober observer, it was obvious the Confederacy's life was limited, and yet the Confederates in the
West reacted to every Union move with an urgency that belied the overall
situation. And young men kept dying.[9]

In Mississippi, Maury notified Governor Charles Clark of Smith's concentration and asked for help from reserves, militia, and home guards. Clark, severely wounded earlier in the war, did not respond with enthusiasm, promising only to call upon available men if Maury thought it essential.[10]

Forrest returned to an active headquarters at Okolona on August 1, and no doubt talked at length with Chalmers. Orders were issued that each man should have ten days' rations, ammunition and ordnance were distributed, and leaves were canceled. Forrest, still not fully recovered, did not play an overly active role in getting his army ready, but he stayed in touch with all developments. He officially returned to duty on October 3, and Chalmers took a detachment toward Oxford to check information that Smith was indeed coming south toward the town. Forrest, who had found out during the Tupelo campaign how wily Smith could be, sent forces to cover Chalmers's flanks. He also sent Mabry to Grenada, in case Smith got that far. Forrest then asked the governor for the militia, told him the legislature should adjourn, and said that the politicians should go home and encourage their constituents. Again, one wonders why Forrest felt the need to sound such notes of panic over Smith's operations after Confederate armies had already suffered so many losses in Mississippi.[11]

Forrest received what militia there was, and there were not many men in condition to fight, nor did they have fit weapons for battle. He also called on Chalmers to get black work gangs to build fortifications at the Tallahatchie. Forrest still suspected that Smith would go for the prairie region, but he was not willing to gamble, not with Smith. Reports indicated Smith was still moving south, but Forrest kept pickets where he could be alerted if the Yankees turned east. Forrest, from Okolona, told Governor Clark that he was concerned about news of Admiral David Farragut leading ships into Mobile Bay. Maybe Smith was going to go and cooperate with Farragut. Forrest had all rail cars moved south of Okolona, and he warned Clark that all citizens must rally or the state would be "devastated," as if it had not been already. Then he rode to Pontotoc on August 9.[12]

Union soldiers worked during early August to repair the railroad south of Holly Springs. By the morning of the 5th they had completed the track as far as Waterford. Of course, completing it did not mean that keeping it open would be easy, for Confederate raiders and partisans would surely try to undo what had been done. Union soldiers were sent from Holly Springs to quickly occupy the area on August 5, and a strong force made ready to move on down to the Tallahatchie the next day. There Federal forces would have to build yet another bridge.[13]

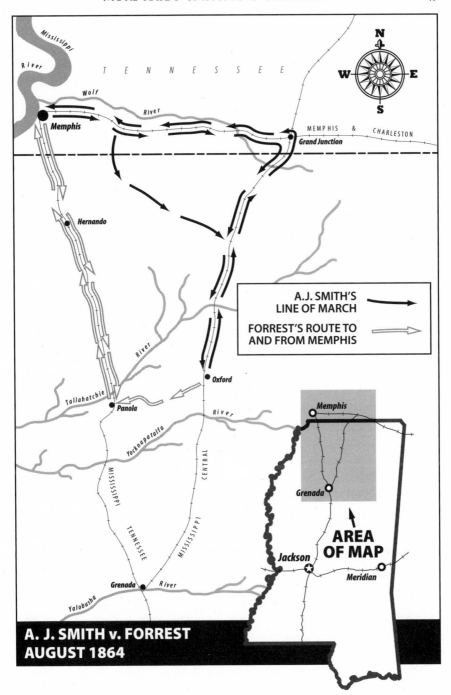

A.J. SMITH'S
LINE OF MARCH →

FORREST'S ROUTE TO
AND FROM MEMPHIS ⇒

A. J. SMITH v. FORREST
AUGUST 1864

The Confederates, meanwhile, hoped to delay the Unionists from constructing anything at the Tallahatchie. The Eighteenth Mississippi Cavalry Battalion set up a roadblock north of the river. On the southern side, at Abbeville, the First Regiment of Mississippi Partisans, reinforced with an artillery battery, was deployed. Other Rebel units encamped on Hurricane Creek, six miles north of Oxford, acting as a reserve force. Confederate hopes of stopping the Yankees' advance were not encouraging, for geographic factors, mainly open terrain on the southern side of the river, was not a good site for a defensive stand.[14]

At 2:00 p.m. on August 7 the Union "Task Force" flailed into the Rebels, and after a fierce exchange of fire the outnumbered Mississippians quickly withdrew and made the mistake of leaving a flatboat for the use of the Federal detachment. Determined to keep up the pressure, Union soldiers used the boat to begin crossing the river and before nightfall had a secure bridgehead on the south bank. Those who had not crossed camped just north of the river.[15]

Night fighting in the Civil War was relatively rare, but the Confederates, anxious to drive the Yankees back across the Tallahatchie, unleashed an artillery attack around 11 p.m. The hard-pressed Yankees, though holding their own with small-arms fire, had no artillery, and their commander sent for big guns then at Waterford. But after driving off the Rebels, the Federal commander got cold feet, and, just as dawn was breaking, he pulled back across the river, giving up his bridgehead. Soon more infantry, artillery, and Grierson's cavalry were on their way to the Tallahatchie.[16]

The Confederates built breastworks and dug in about half a mile from the river, though they were not strong enough to protect their flanks. When General Edward Hatch arrived, he must have been a bit disgusted that the task force commander, Sylvester Hill, had been so easily intimidated. Hatch placed Hill's infantry along the north bank to fire at the Rebels, while dismounted cavalry went toward the railroad bridge where the Confederates had ripped out the flooring. While Union artillery shelled the Confederates, more Union soldiers again crossed in the flatboat. William Wade, commanding the Confederates, could tell he would soon be outnumbered and probably flanked, so he ordered a withdrawal to a ridge north of Abbeville. With the Confederates gone for the moment, Union soldiers set to work building a bridge across the Tallahatchie with whatever boards and timber they could find. Soon Hatch had enough men across to safely let his troops go into bivouac.[17]

Skirmishing went on elsewhere during the day to draw attention from the Federal crossing, and when General Chalmers heard that the Confederate defense of the Tallahatchie had failed, he concentrated at Abbeville. Chalmers feared scattering his forces to counter the Union diversionary skirmishing. He also heard scouting reports that A. J. Smith had three divisions, and he advised Forrest that the ford at the Tallahatchie had been given up, and Forrest's entire army should be sent from Pontotoc to Water Valley or Coffeeville. Chalmers also fired off a message to Mabry, telling him to hurry on north. Another detachment, in the Senatobia area to the northwest, was ordered to Grenada in order to avoid being cut off from the rest of Forrest's force.[18]

Forrest agreed to send some artillery support to Chalmers, but, again, he was not ready to make a wholesale commitment until he knew for sure what Smith had planned. He told Chalmers to keep his resistance stiff and not to come all the way south to Oxford unless absolutely necessary. Meanwhile Forrest looked at maps and tried to decide how he could hit back at Smith, perhaps by a flanking movement.[19]

On the night of August 8 Chalmers withdrew most of his forces from above Abbeville south to Hurricane Creek to rest his troops. Then he went forward, north, to high ground south of the Tallahatchie, but ground lower than the opposite bank. In the early morning hours, Hatch had his troops in motion to go after Chalmers. An artillery duel erupted first, and for one of the rare times in the war the Confederates had superior guns and got the best of it, but, outnumbered and in a position that could be flanked, Chalmers, protected by a strong rear guard, ordered a withdrawal to the southern side of Hurricane Creek. Hatch's cavalry pressed hard, but had to pull up when they saw the railroad bridge across the creek in flames and Chalmers's force waiting behind the creek. However, the creek was shallow, and soon Yankees again chased Rebels south, with many of Chalmers's men in panic. Chalmers saved his artillery when a timid Union officer countermanded an order that probably would have resulted in the capture of the Rebel guns, and Chalmers pulled his entire force back to Oxford.[20]

At Oxford, along the northern limits of the town, the Confederates held their own, and Union artillery performed rather poorly, but a flank and rear move by part of Hatch's force from the west caused Chalmers, whose attention had been focused on enemy artillery in his front, to hurriedly abandon his position, losing some caissons and other supplies in the process. Confederates had already pretty much removed supplies from the town, except for a few bales of cotton. Chalmers continued south down the railroad. To the north, the remainder of Smith's men kept coming, and railroad construction crews kept rebuilding track to keep the supply line open. Forrest, hearing of Chalmers's further retreat, sent more reinforcements. Chalmers also heard that Mabry had reached Grenada.[21]

Then Chalmers's force reached the Yocona River, which was nearly at flood stage due to north Mississippi rains. He could not risk having a defeated army trying to cross the high waters. Meanwhile one of his detachments north of the river sent advanced elements of Federals scurrying to Oxford. Hatch, having accomplished his mission to drive the Rebels south of Oxford, turned on August 10 and returned to Abbeville. Compared to previous occupations, Oxford escaped a great deal of the severe destruction it had experienced in previous months, though some items were stolen from private homes. The Federals paid special attention to the home of Jacob Thompson, a Confederate diplomat and sometime spy. His wife protested about vandalism, but to no avail. Hatch, in fact, was one of the most active and successful thieves.[22]

To the south, Forrest, with Bell's brigade and John Morton's artillery, left Pontotoc for Oxford, though he left a small force behind. The Confederates reoccupied Oxford about an hour before midnight, giving the residents something to cheer about the next morning. News of Hatch's foray reached Mobile, where General Maury ordered more reinforcements from Jackson north to assist Forrest.[23]

Union general Joseph Mower, from his headquarters at Abbeville, now took over direction of operations south of the Tallahatchie, and he gave his stamp of approval to what Hatch had accomplished. Yet Mower was disappointed that persistent rains had damaged the railroad and several bridges, and so he recommended that the supply train stay at Waterford. Rebel partisans and guerrillas, some of them no doubt personally acquainted with Forrest, began pestering Union forces along the railroad between Holly Springs and Grand Junction, and they certainly would be coming south to harass Yankees there. Mower worried that his infantry, focusing on protecting the rail line, would not have time for anything else, and he asked and received more troops for the Abbeville area. Then Smith received some questionable news that Forrest and Confederate general Richard Taylor were moving north with some 20,000 men to hit La Grange and Smith's supply line. True or not, and Smith was told it was unconfirmed intelligence, he held up any further reinforcements for Mower and moved to build up defenses at La Grange. Smith also pulled some of his cavalry back north to help if needed. Union patrols found no evidence that any of the news about Forrest and Taylor was true.[24]

Forrest in fact was reorganizing his force and digging in along Hurricane Creek. There was occasional contact between the opposing forces, and then Mower decided he should not just sit and allow the Confederates to establish a solid defensive position along the creek. Thus he sent a force of cavalry, infantry, and artillery southward on August 13 from Abbeville. Hatch led the operation and intended to envelope both Confederate flanks.[25]

Forrest's advance elements slowed down the Yankees, and when his men were forced back they took a new position in well-built entrenchments. Confederate cannons and a thunderstorm also slowed the Union forces. Forrest's use of a layered defense, the placing of men at varying positions, impressed Mower, and he finally decided to give up the envelopment tactic and smash the center of the Rebel line with his power. He massed his infantry and artillery and pushed forward, crossing Hurricane Creek. On Forrest's left, Mabry's men gave way, and Forrest ordered his troops to withdraw. Hatch ordered a pursuit, but soon called it off as darkness settled over the landscape. Mower, satisfied that Forrest had been driven from the creek line, recalled his men, while Forrest had his troops deploy on the Isham plantation, some four miles north of Oxford.

All the action along the creek did not convince Smith that the Taylor-Forrest story had no merit, so he sent a detachment to watch for any signs of Confederates east of the railroad. General Buford had in mind fueling the Federal fears as he put together a force to raid Smith's supply line and hopefully hit the railroad between Holly Springs and Grand Junction as well as the Memphis and Charleston Railroad between Memphis and Grand Junction. The raid never amounted to much other than some skirmishing and narrow escapes by soldiers in blue and gray. The Confederates did tear up some track, but their hopes of doing major damage did not come to fruition.

To the south, Chalmers led a detachment across Hurricane Creek and pushed past Union sentries to near Abbeville before Federal alarms sounded. Chalmers, knowing he was heavily outnumbered, returned back across the creek, having accomplished little more than relieving the boredom along the two fronts.

Meanwhile Union crews continued repairing the railroad, making progress in spite of bad weather and guerrillas' bullets. By August 16 Smith received news that the line from Grand Junction all the way to the Tallahatchie was serviceable. Smith ordered the advance of his army to deploy at Abbeville, and he left Holly Springs to join the army at the front. By August 19 Smith had most of his entire force at Abbeville. So far, he had to feel good about his progress. But he was about to be surprised by the unpredictable Forrest.[26]

Forrest knew by August 18 that Smith had railroad trains chugging south to the Tallahatchie, and he knew, too, that the Yankees were massing at

Abbeville. Being so heavily outnumbered, Forrest realized that he could not do to Smith what he had done to Sturgis, and he certainly had no intention of repeating the mistakes of frontal attacks as at Tupelo. One thing might cause Smith to turn and get out of Mississippi, and that would be a daring and risky counterstroke, a ride around Smith's right flank toward Memphis. If the Confederates threatened Memphis, surely the Union brass would recall Smith. Of course, Smith could destroy the Confederate troops left behind as a decoy. At least Forrest believed Smith would be too shaken by the raid to keep pushing south, and it was certainly worth a try.

Forrest issued orders to his officers to pick the best units from their commands and ordered four pieces of artillery from Morton's command to be ready to accompany the raiders. Everyone was to be ready to leave Oxford at five o'clock that evening. The column consisted of 2,000 riders, the four big guns, and a few ambulances, and they pulled out in the rain on the road to Panola. The rains made roads and streams treacherous, and the column had to make a detour to get to Panola. Men had to get the artillery across flooded streams by pushing and pulling, and the ambulances required man- and horsepower to get them up muddy hills. The beleaguered riders reached Panola early on the 19th. There, due to the bad condition of some of the artillery horses, Forrest sent one section (two guns) to Grenada, and to keep the other two moving, he had ten horses harnessed to each. He also weeded out about 100 riders whose horses were obviously not in condition to stand up to the rigors of the hard ride to come. These men stayed in Panola.

The rest of the column crossed the Tallahatchie on a pontoon bridge, and rode through much mud on to Senatobia, where Forrest called a halt for the night, mostly to rest the horses. The next morning his men had to scavenge the area for planks from gin houses and telegraph poles on either side of a flatboat, used as a centerpiece, plus some strong grapevines, to construct a pontoon bridge of sorts across the flooded Hickahala Creek.[27]

The Coldwater River was even more of a challenge. The Coldwater's floodplain was wide, and Forrest realized that the one ferryboat available could carry only four horses at a time, which would require too much time to hope for a surprise attack on Memphis. So his men set to work once more building a much longer bridge, with the ferryboat serving as the middle section. Some three hours later, it was done, and the Confederates crossed, reaching Hernando, about twenty-four miles from Memphis, just before dark. Here they stopped for a lengthy visit, for this was one of Forrest's old hometowns, and he had many friends who provided him with valuable intelligence about the disposition of Union forces in the city. So far, they said, there seemed to be no indication that the Federals had detected the presence of the Rebels in the vicinity.[28]

With this information, Forrest led his men on, crossing Nonconnah Creek, four miles south of the city, where Confederate scouts gave him detailed information about Yankee posts around the city. What Forrest learned pleased him. Memphis had not been heavily fortified; there was a picket line around the town no more than ten miles long being occupied by some 5,000 men, mostly black soldiers and other men who had enlisted only for 100 days' duty. The long picket line made it difficult for Union defenders to concentrate effectively against a sudden cavalry charge on a limited front. This latter group of Yankees would not be tough, battle-hardened veterans. If Forrest could make a concentrated strike, he should be able to break through the Union line.[29]

When Forrest called his commanders together, he learned that some 500 horses were not fit to participate in a charge; the trip to Memphis had worn them out. So the horses and their riders rode back to Oxford, leaving Forrest with 1,400 men to make his attack. Undeterred, Forrest laid out his plans. His brother William would lead a small advance of scouts and take the Hernando road outpost. Then they would ride hard to the Gayoso Hotel and block all exits to attempt to capture the strongly disliked Yankee general Stephen Hurlbut and any other officers there. Another brother, Jesse Forrest, would take a patrol to Union Street and General Cadwallader Washburn's house. Washburn was commander of the Union district and would be a prize catch. Another detachment of Tennesseans would follow William Forrest and his men to the Gayoso Hotel and block Main, Beale, and Shelby streets and capture any steamboats anchored where Union Street met the Mississippi. Another detachment of Missourians, Tennesseans, and Mississippians would hit the position held by the 100-day enlistees near Hernando Road. Bell and his Tennesseans, with the two pieces of artillery, would be held in reserve, ready to ride wherever needed. Forrest warned the officers to keep their men quiet, for if an alarm was sounded too soon, the Yankees could concentrate and cause the raiders much trouble. The Memphis invasion began shortly after 3 a.m. on Sunday morning, August 21.[30]

The attack on the city went amazingly well for the Confederates. Memphis had been under Union control for more than two years, after being surrendered to a Federal flotilla on June 6, 1862. It had been in Union hands so long, in fact, that Federal military officials did not expect any Confederate presence there that amounted to anything. A reporter traveling with Smith's army had been sending back glowing reports of success on the invasion of Mississippi, especially noting how Smith had sent 10,000 Rebels flying south to Oxford. This news was published locally in the *Memphis Review* on Saturday, the day before Forrest's attack.[31]

Forrest's assault on Memphis went well at times for the Confederates and not so well at other times, especially when the Federal troops in the city began to organize and offer stiff resistance. Forrest rode his horse into the lobby of the Gayoso Hotel, hoping to capture the hated General Hurlburt. But the Rebels captured no officers and had to do some fighting, more and more the longer they stayed, and finally Forrest decided it was time to leave town. He had accomplished his mission, for he had thrown a scare into the Union occupation forces, and once the news reached A. J. Smith, he would very likely leave Mississippi and return to Memphis.

The Confederate raiders went back into Mississippi by the Hernando road, which was foggy and caused them to have to fight their way through a roadblock they had been unable to see. Ultimately Forrest managed to get his troops concentrated, and he told them to retreat slowly, so the Union soldiers in Memphis might conclude he was still a threat. If they believed that, the Memphis commanders would be even more insistent that Smith return to ensure the safety of the city.[32]

The tactic worked to a degree, for as the fog dissipated Union officers heard that some of Forrest's men still held what had been Union camps. Therefore they concluded that Forrest might have pulled back only to prepare for another attack. This kind of thinking cut down on Federal pursuit attempts and gave Forrest time to hold off Union efforts to retake their camps. With little pressure on his troops, Forrest allowed them to change horses if they could find better ones, and he looked at the some 400 prisoners, consisting of Union soldiers, some recovering from wounds and sickness, and private citizens. Many were in bedclothes due to the early attack. The Confederate column reached Crane Creek near noon. Forrest decided to try and exchange his prisoners for Confederate prisoners, so that retreat would not be encumbered.

Back in Memphis, the raid caused wild rumors, and a pursuit force had been thrown together, but it stopped when it saw Forrest's truce party approaching. Washburn sent word to Forrest that he did not have the authority to authorize any exchange, but that he would send shoes and clothing to ease the condition of the prisoners. Forrest then weeded the captured, forcing the healthy to come along with his men and sending the others back to Memphis after getting them to promise not to take up arms until exchanged.

Then the situation turned somewhat comedic. Union forces pursuing Forrest had to stand aside while supply wagons passed through to carry rations to Forrest's prisoners. The Union commander had his men take the supplies forward, but by this time delays had allowed Forrest and his raiders to ride too far ahead to be caught. Forrest sent word to Chalmers to keep pressing the Yankees on the latter's front to keep them away from interfering with Forrest's ride back from Memphis. Forrest continued to go slowly to keep the Federals guessing, but the Union pursuit finally was given up on August 23, and soon Forrest and his men had crossed the Tallahatchie on their return to Oxford. Statistics show that his foray had cost the Union 15 killed, 65 wounded, and 112 missing, compared to Confederate losses of 9 killed and 24 wounded. Both sides claimed additional casualties for the other, as usually happened, and a truly accurate count will probably never be known. While Forrest had accomplished his main goal, the only lasting effect was that Forrest was even more deified by Southern admirers for his daring and his ability to befuddle Yankees. Meanwhile General Sherman kept right on operating in Georgia without any worry of what Forrest might be doing in his rear.[33]

Back on the Mississippi Central front, A. J. Smith ordered his column to continue its march south from Abbeville on August 18, as Forrest left Oxford for his Memphis raid. Smith sent an advance detachment under Hatch to bridge Hurricane Creek. Before leaving Oxford, Forrest told Chalmers to stay active, so Smith would not realize he faced a weaker force while the Memphis raid was under way. Chalmers sent a brigade in the terribly wet weather to Hurricane Creek to keep an eye out for the enemy, and they tried to ambush Union soldiers crossing the creek, but all the wet weather had ruined their powder, so they had to withdraw.

The Federals did nothing to follow up the retreat; for all they knew, Forrest was still up ahead, and they did not want to tangle with him until Union infantry in force had crossed the creek and could provide support. Abraham Buford's force arrived to strengthen Confederate forces to contest the Union advance. Smith helped by slowing down, due to the weather, but still Chalmers worried that Smith's masses outnumbered him so heavily with Forrest gone. Situated between two flooded streams, Hurricane Creek and the Yocona River, with geography that offered little defensive possibilities, Chalmers knew he could be outflanked at any time. In preparation for a withdrawal, Chalmers sent his supply wagons on south of the Yocona. Finally, on the evening of the 20th Chalmers decided to pull his whole force south of the river. He simply could not risk staying put.[34]

Yet Maury from Mobile told Chalmers not to panic, for when Smith found out where Forrest was, the Yankees would stop their southern trek anyway. So Chalmers stayed north of the Yocona and was pleased to learn of reinforcements and ordnance at Grenada in his rear should he have to withdraw. But the Yankees kept snaking southward, and then Chalmers received a false report that caused him to panic. He heard that enemy cavalry were pushing for College Hill near Oxford, and they could cut him off from Oxford. He immediately wired Maury, who told him to pull back across the Yocona. Smith had not ordered his men to be aggressive, so the Confederates had an easy time getting south of the river, and Chalmers set up his headquarters at Springdale. He deployed his men to cover Yocona crossings. Yet the Confederates were noticeably quiet as the Federals, helped by a break in the weather, pushed on for Oxford. As their advance entered the town, they learned that the Confederates had pulled back south the day earlier. Smith ordered Hatch to take his cavalry and strike for Panola to tear up the tracks of the Mississippi and Tennessee Railroad that connected Memphis and Grenada.[35]

At this time Smith got his first news of Forrest's raid. The message from Washburn told Smith that Smith should attempt to cut off the raiders by sending detachments to Panola and Abbeville. More news from Washburn gave Smith the impression that Forrest would retreat by way of Holly Springs. So Smith forgot about Panola and began concentrating a force at Abbeville. Now Smith had to reassess his situation. His cavalry was off trying to cut off Forrest, and his forage was getting low. The roads, despite the letup of the rain, were still in awful condition, and the bridge across the Tallahatchie had broken up. Smith decided he must withdraw to Abbeville.

Once again Oxford felt the sting of war. The square downtown was "surrounded by a canopy of flame." The courthouse was burned; private and public dwellings were torched, leaving "blackened skeletons"—one of the houses was the Thompson home; stores, carpenter and blacksmith shops, two brick hotels, and the Masonic Hall went up in flames; and many residences not burned were thoroughly looted. A few occupied homes escaped total damage when residents managed to extinguish fires before they totally destroyed their houses. Some lower-ranking officers were disgusted by the soldiers' behavior, but Smith and the higher-ranking officers seemed not only to demand it but to enjoy it. Perhaps Smith's hatred of Forrest overtook his better judgment; whatever the case, there was no excuse for the gutting of the town, the blame for which fell at his feet. Smith seemed to carry to the extreme Sherman's wish to make people who supported Forrest

feel the sting of war. The blanket assumption that everyone supported Forrest left a long-lasting legacy of bitterness.[36]

Cavalry sent to find Forrest left town at 11:30 the morning of August 22,
and they immediately had to stop and fix the still unrepaired bridge over
the Tallahatchie. They crossed the next day, while other portions of the
army left Hurricane Creek toward the river. The creek bridge likewise came
apart, further slowing the move north.

When Forrest reached Panola on the evening of August 22, he heard that
Smith had pulled out of Oxford, and he sent word to Chalmers to pursue.
He especially wanted forces sent out to interrupt foraging by Smith's men.
Chalmers lost time in Oxford because he had to bring up rations to feed
the people who had been left destitute by Smith's rampage. Wade's advance
units skirmished with an Illinois detachment as they neared Abbeville, in
what became an intense skirmish. Union reinforcements eventually forced
Wade back, and the Confederates barely avoided being flanked. Confederates reported seven killed, fifteen wounded, and twelve missing, while the
Yankees lost twenty men, though the nature of the losses was not given.[37]

On August 23 a message from Sherman in Georgia ordered the division
formerly led by Smith (now by William Shaw) sent to Georgia. Washburn
could keep his cavalry and Mower's infantry. Smith got the news, and he
knew it meant he could not carry out his original plan to push across the
prairie to Columbus or Decatur or even operate south of Holly Springs.
Meanwhile Rebel raiders were busy burning bridges in the Holly Springs
area and cutting telegraph wire. Grierson also complained that his men
needed time to rest, as did their horses. Smith decided that as soon as he
could get the bridge repaired across the Tallahatchie, he would return to
Holly Springs. Shaw's soldiers were delighted to be getting out of hot Mississippi, where no matter how well they did their jobs, they ultimately had
little to show for it. Sherman, on the other hand, was in the national spotlight with his Georgia campaigning, and his casualty lists were generally
low.[38]

Forrest, too, seemed to think it was time for a rest. He allowed Chalmers
to pull back behind the Yocona River and Bell to go from Panola to Springdale. Forrest, of course, was pleased when he got the news that the Yankees
had retreated across the Tallahatchie, and he would have been all the more
so pleased to learn that Shaw's division was leaving for Georgia and that
Mower would likely be called to help out at Mobile if he went anywhere.
Memphis continued to be a place where Forrest was expected to show up,
but with Smith's entire force, less Shaw, eventually returning there, such

would not be the case. In the end, however, Forrest lived and would still be around at the end of the war after participating in John Bell Hood's disastrous Tennessee campaign in late 1864. All of Sherman's efforts to "get" Forrest had failed, but they had kept him busy enough to stay away from Sherman's supply line. On September 1 Confederates gave up Atlanta, and Sherman no longer worried about Forrest. The seemingly indestructible cavalryman did not figure in Sherman's future plans. Ironically, there would be one more major raid in Mississippi, this time by Union cavalry destroying supplies much needed by Hood's army. What Confederate authorities had kept Forrest from doing, Benjamin Grierson would do for the·Union cause.

By December 1864 the war was all but over, yet generals kept campaigning and filling graveyards, all, on both sides, for "the cause," which, especially on the Confederate side, had come to mean nothing. Rebel generals were especially vulnerable to this criticism, for if anyone understood that victory lay beyond the grasp of the Confederacy, they did, and yet not one of them had the courage to sit down with Jefferson Davis and tell him to put a stop to the killing. Therefore continual Confederate resistance left the North with no choice but to carry on the fighting.

With Robert E. Lee bogged down in a siege at Petersburg by Grant and the Union Army of the Potomac, everyone, including Lee, knew it was just a matter of time before his Army of Northern Virginia must surrender. So Washington authorities looked west to where General George Thomas at Nashville was not doing much to finish off the remnants of the Confederate Army of Tennessee, now led by John Bell Hood. Hood had decimated his army with a very foolish charge at Franklin, Tennessee, back in November, and, rather than retreat, he took the survivors on to the outskirts of Nashville, for reasons that no one but Hood understood.

Hood depended upon the Mobile & Ohio Railroad, which ran north and south and penetrated the northeast Mississippi region of the produce-producing prairie region that had been A. J. Smith's target back in August. Union army chief of staff Henry Halleck could see that fact clearly enough on a map of the region, and he decided that a devastating cavalry raid on the railroad would force Hood into an embarrassing situation. So on December 8 he wired Napoleon J. T. Dana, commanding the Department of Mississippi, to cut the railroad, so that it would be of no use to Hood.

Dana was not sure he could do it, for he only had 1,000 cavalry in Memphis who were in shape enough to carry out such a raid. However, he did have a brigade at Vicksburg, commanded by Embury Osband, and, at the time, Edward Winslow's brigade was in Memphis preparing to join

Thomas's force in Tennessee. Dana asked Halleck if he could keep Winslow to help with the raid. He was turned down, but then got Winslow anyway when news came that Thomas had finally attacked Hood and sent the battered Confederates retreating south. This made the raid all the more important, since Hood would need supplies desperately for the succor of his survivors. Joseph Kargé and his brigade were also available, so Dana's cavalry chief, Benjamin Grierson, would have three brigades of cavalry to carry out the mission of decimating the Mobile & Ohio. On December 19 at Ripley, Mississippi, the entire force came together, and Grierson planned to lead them out the next day, strike the railroad at Tupelo, and tear it up all the way to Meridian if possible.

Grierson was told that he could return to Memphis after completing the raid or, if necessary, go to Vicksburg, Natchez, or Pensacola, Florida. The men would carry tools and explosives with them on pack mules; no wagons that might slow the column would be allowed on this trip. Grierson reviewed reports, doubtless exaggerated, that there were some 5,000–6,000 Confederates at Corinth, 2,000 at Holly Springs, and 3,000 at Oxford, and supposedly the Rebels had armed detachments along the railroad to keep it safe and open.

Vain attempts by Kargé to get his brigade across the flooded Wolf River on December 19 resulted in damaged ammunition and a change in plans by Dana. The raid finally began on December 21. Grierson led the three brigades, numbering some 3,500 men, out at the same time, and followed a route between the Wolf and the Tallahatchie rivers. Infantry, led by Michael Lawler and numbering some 5,000 men, marched east, repairing the Memphis and Charleston rail line and trying to make the Rebels believe Lawler was going to strike Corinth. Hopefully this would take attention off Grierson.

The entire force, with Grierson's cavalry leading the way, was soon well ahead of Lawler's infantry, walking through the mud caused by several days of rain. Cold weather formed an icy crust over the mud, but the depth of the ice could not support horses or mules weighted down with supplies. The next day was generally uneventful, though Grierson sent a detachment to burn the railroad stations and cut telegraph wires at La Grange and Grand Junction, Tennessee. Grierson also duplicated his diversionary tactics that had made his 1863 raid during the Vicksburg campaign so successful. He sent a detachment from Ripley to destroy the railroad and supplies around Booneville to the south and another to hit the Baldwyn and Guntown areas south of Booneville. Grierson had Levi Naron, the well-known "Chickasaw," and three other scouts to help as guides. Naron, especially, knew the countryside well. In Jackson, the state capital, Franklin Gardner, who had commanded Confederate forces at Port Hudson on the Mississippi and now commanded the Department of Mississippi and East Louisiana, heard news of the Yankee movements, but he decided to do nothing until he was more certain of what the Yankees were up to.[39]

Meanwhile the mission by Federal soldiers to La Grange and Grand Junction was successfully carried out, and on the 23rd Grierson's column stopped for the night at Salem. Grierson did not know at the time that the feint toward Corinth had worked, for Gardner in Jackson had concluded that was the Federal target. Confederates in north Mississippi reacted accordingly, and Gardner sent word to Governor Charles Clark and General Richard Taylor. Clark seemed uninterested in Taylor's suggestion to call out more state troops. Perhaps Clark was just being realistic. State troops would be of little use against over 8,000 Union veterans.

On December 24, Christmas Eve, while his diversions were being carried out, Grierson led the main column on toward Ellistown and Tupelo, camping on the south bank of the Tallahatchie. On Christmas Day Grierson looked for a way to give his men some cheer from their weary days in the saddle plodding through mud. He found it while the column stopped to rest the horses and give stragglers a chance to tighten up the column. Scouts keeping an eye on his flanks reported to Grierson that at several homes they saw local citizens preparing for Christmas dinners. Though foragers had already taken some food, Grierson sent out larger detachments to take more cooked pig meat, forest turkeys, chickens, hams, and other delicacies. Grierson ordered another halt to give the men time to eat. He noted, "If the surrounding families mourned over their interrupted festivities, possibly they were better prepared to ponder on the things that would lead to peace." In effect, he justified the theft of the food due to local support of the Confederacy throughout the war. His men, their stomachs full and their demeanor cheerful, remounted after eating and rode on.

By now the Confederates understood what was happening, for scouting reports indicated Lawler's infantry had stopped its trek in the direction of Corinth, and Grierson's riders had veered south. Gardner at once began trying to concentrate a resistance force in the Tupelo area. The call for men went as far south as Morton, where Wirt Adams's cavalry received orders to ride north. Thinking it would take time for Adams to get there, Taylor told him to try to cut off Grierson's retrograde movement back to Memphis.[40]

Grierson beat the Rebels to Tupelo, and around 11 p.m. Christmas night he sent Kargé's troops to demolish a Rebel training facility and a

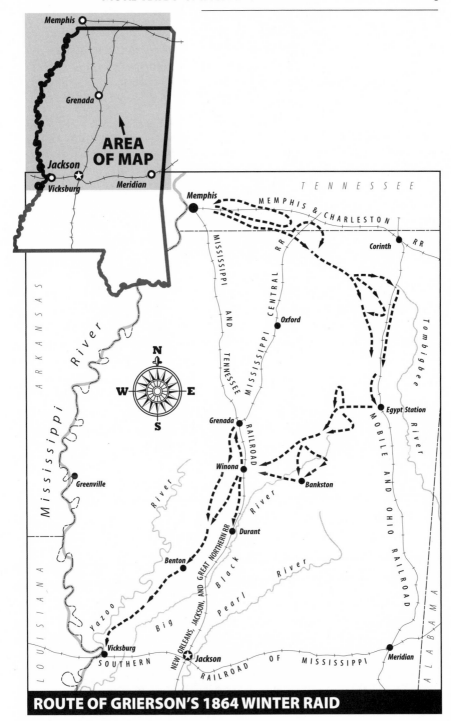

ROUTE OF GRIERSON'S 1864 WINTER RAID

quartermaster depot at Verona. Rain fell and lightning danced in the sky to help guide the Union riders. The Federals charged and quickly captured Verona, and had no problem with the Confederate trainees, but many Rebels escaped in the dark and rain of the evening. Otherwise, the Yankees destroyed thirty-two train cars and eight warehouses, all loaded with either food or ordnance. They also found 300 army wagons that had once belonged to the Union army before Forrest and his men captured them at Brice's Crossroads. These, too, went up in fire and smoke. Other of Grierson's soldiers tore up track and cut telegraph wires. By 5 a.m. the detachment left Verona, their job accomplished, and rode to Harrisburg to wait for Grierson and the main column. Meanwhile a detachment of Illinoisans sent to demolish the 900-foot rail bridge across Town Creek and to rip up rails had done both successfully before joining the main column that evening between the creek and Tupelo.

The next day, December 26, Kargé's troops rejoined the column, and Grierson sent Osband and his brigade to destroy the railroad between Tupelo and Shannon. Grierson planned to camp at Shannon, and, having arrived there before dark, sent a regiment to help Osband's brigade. Osband thus reported the destruction of 2,500 feet of rail, bridges, and trestles. Some Illinoisans also found depot and repair shops and flat cars carrying wagons that had not been destroyed by Kargé's troops, and they burned these items immediately. The Federals met some resistance but not enough to stop the destruction. With Forrest and his cavalry called to join John Bell Hood's Army of Tennessee, the cavalry left behind was weak in numbers and experience.[41]

The cut telegraph wires kept Confederates to the south in the dark regarding news from the front. Taylor, still looking for reinforcements, recalled men who had been sent toward Mobile to protect the railroad in that direction. These men received orders to go to Corinth at once. The Confederates did not have enough rail cars to send them in one trip, so they had to be transported in groups. Taylor joined the soldiers at Meridian in order to get more information from the front, and soon he learned from his staff that the railroad had been broken at Verona. Taylor ordered his commanders to concentrate at Okolona, wait for Gardner, and stop the Yankees there. The Confederate trek north ran into one unanticipated problem: there were no water tanks between West Point and Okolona, so men had to bail water from creeks to keep the train engine going. When they reached Egypt Station, they learned there was not enough water there. A railroad agent suggested the soldiers get off, then let the train engine go on without cars to Okolona for water and return to pick up the men.

At Okolona, the post commander reported that Grierson's column, estimated at 2,000 to 2,500 men, was at Shannon and that they were being shadowed by Samuel Gholson and his 250 casuals (men attached to a unit while waiting for a permanent assignment). The Confederate commanders notified Gholson that Okolona would be evacuated, and the train engineer hooked on to fourteen cars to go back to Egypt Station. A message to Taylor for reinforcements was sent, and a small Rebel detachment of 270 men deployed across Mattubby Creek, about two miles south of Okolona. Meanwhile General Gardner went to Meridian to take charge of stopping Grierson, while to the north General William Martin, who could not find enough men to pursue the Yankees, simply gave up his efforts and returned to Panola.[42]

On December 26 the beleaguered John Bell Hood first got word that Grierson had disrupted his supply line. He directed one of his colonels to try to repair the rail line; this colonel in turn contacted another colonel at Corinth, who gave the repair assignment to reserve forces commanded by yet another colonel, supervised by a major from the Confederate Railroad Bureau. Word of Grierson's activities also upset P. G. T. Beauregard and his staff, who talked about sending a wagon supply train to Hood. The problem was the distance was too great, thus the wagons could not get there in time.[43]

Unaware of all the consternation he had caused, though he would have been delighted to know, Grierson led his column out of Shannon on December 27. After a brief, meaningless skirmish with some of Gholson's men, the Union cavalry rode into Okolona around noon. Grierson, informed of the Rebel defensive line ahead south of Mattubby Creek, had his men dismount and his telegraphers tap into the line. He learned that Taylor was bringing up reinforcements from as far as Mobile. Grierson decided that he could not afford to tarry; he must attack the Confederates at the creek quickly before they received help. So he planned an assault the next day, the 28th.[44]

During the night several Rebel deserters came into the Union camp. They said they were Federal soldiers and had joined the Confederates in order to get out of the notorious Andersonville prison in Georgia. Grierson's soldiers called them "Galvanized Confederates." The former prisoners said the Confederates had offered inducements to all those of foreign birth who would join them, promising that they would be required to do only garrison duty. They further told Grierson that some 200 of their number were in the Egypt Station fortifications and would be forced to fight the next day. Grierson later claimed that slightly over 100 of these men were captured, and he recommended leniency for them to the government. However, they were placed in a prison camp at Alton, Illinois, by order of a judge advocate general. The war soon ended, and they were allowed to enlist with former Confederate soldiers in the Fifth U.S. Volunteers for service against Indians out west. They finally left the service in October 1866. By then perhaps some of them might have wished they had stayed in Andersonville, but given the death rate there, they likely appreciated their treatment.

In any event, Grierson paid them little mind at the time. They were fighting with the enemy, and a battle Grierson did not want to fight seemed imminent. His goal was to chase off the obstinate Rebels and keep moving. Meanwhile Gholson took his troops to join the Rebels south of the creek, but his men only brought the total to about 500. Thus the Confederates withdrew to Egypt Station. When Grierson heard the enemy had pulled back, he moved his column south, camping four miles south of Okolona, leaving public property there in shambles. Grierson could not afford to stop too long to burn property, but when opportunities arose, his men took advantage.

Farther south, reinforcements arrived in Meridian on the evening of the 27th, and Gardner joined them. It took fifteen hours to reach West Point, and there they learned Grierson had been through Okolona, so the train could go no farther. By telegraph to Egypt Station, Gardner promised to send 500 more men, and he learned that those men needed to be at Egypt Station early on the 28th, at least by 5:30 a.m. Due to the time factor, Gardner ordered the men back on the train and told the engineer to take it as far as he could north. Gardner stayed behind at West Point to direct the movement of more reinforcements hopefully on the way.

At Egypt Station, the Confederates nervously waited, knowing reinforcements were coming, but not knowing when they would get there. At Prairie, time was lost when troops had to retrieve water from a cistern. The train did not get under way again until after 7 a.m., and by then Grierson's cavalry was already attacking and driving back the Rebel pickets near Egypt Station. Grierson found the Rebels dug in, and flat cars held a Missouri battery that was shielded by cotton bales. Grierson had no artillery, so his commanders knew they had to charge quickly to gain the initiative. Soon they had some of the outnumbered Confederates running away. But Rebels in a stockade took a toll on some of the Yankees, and then four Confederate cannons pitched in. So Kargé put together a patrol to try to take the train. Then Grierson rode up. Confederates on the train tried to get it going, but it did not have enough steam. Finally, the engineer ordered some of the cars unhooked, and the train, with the cannons, managed to escape capture by the Yankees.

Now Osband brought his brigade up to help Kargé. This tactic allowed Federals to spread their flanks, and soon they had the stockade surrounded. New Jersey troops led a charge that broke down the gates, and, after some vicious hand-to-hand fighting, forced the Rebels to surrender. The stockade battle cost Grierson 22 killed, 101 wounded, and 1 missing. Also, Grierson lost around 100 horses, either killed or wounded, but his men captured enough Confederate mounts to replace them. Confederate losses were not recorded, but were light. Five hundred or so were captured by Grierson's men. Gholson fell wounded and later had an arm amputated.

South of Egypt Station, the train carrying reinforcements met the train that had escaped Grierson's attack. The reinforcements jumped off the cars and started for the front on the run. Grierson's men, hard at work tearing up track, saw the Rebels coming and pulled back toward Egypt Station. Then the sound of fighting around Egypt Station ceased, and the Confederate reinforcements stopped, deployed, and sent a message back to Gardner, stating that Egypt Station had probably been taken and that Grierson might keep on coming. However, Grierson had decided the increasing numbers of Confederates on his front meant that he must forget Alabama and head for Vicksburg.

Grierson told his officers of his decision, mopping up operations began, prisoner escorts were assigned, a surgeon and a hospital aide would be left behind to care for the wounded, and the rest of the column would move out, which they did by the middle of the afternoon on the 28th. That night the column camped on the west bank of Houlka Creek, near Houston. Grierson entertained a local family named Norton with his piano playing. One of the women there was inspired to sing "Hiawatha," which she apparently did very well.[45]

More Rebel reinforcements arrived, and they decided to rest before chasing the Yankees the next day. Gardner sent word to Wirt Adams in Canton and General Martin in Panola to prepare what troops they had to intercept Grierson if they had the chance. Gardner, of course, had no idea what route Grierson would take.

Grierson's column rode into Houston early on December 29, and he stopped while quickly organizing two patrols, one to demonstrate toward Pontotoc and the other toward West Point. Grierson guessed that these diversions might allow the main column to keep moving, and they headed south toward the village of Bellefontaine. An Iowa detachment rode to the small town of Bankston and burned several clothing and leather factories. The main column rode on to Winona, where the Mississippi Central Railroad ran through the town north and south. Many food supplies were destroyed there, as well as two locomotives and several train cars. The cavalry camped the night of December 31 at an unidentified point between Winona and Middleton (a community a short distance west of Winona).

That night two Iowa regiments, commanded by Colonel John Noble, were ordered to go the next morning north, riding along the Mississippi Central, to Grenada to "destroy all public property to be found" between Winona and Grenada, and then to ride south and rejoin the main column. When the Iowans reached Grenada, Noble heard about a newspaper in the town, the *Grenada Picket*, which was edited by a very strong pro-Confederate. He went to the newspaper office and asked for a copy of the latest edition. One article with the headline "GLORIOUS NEWS!!!" immediately caught Noble's attention. Underneath the headline, the editor had written, "The Yankee raid played out! Grierson and his vandals repulsed! Fleeing in great haste through Pontotoc toward Memphis!" Noble, with a wide grin on his face, informed the editor that the story was false and would be misleading to his regular readers. The newspaperman man reacted rather pompously and started pacing; Noble wondered if he was about to be asked to leave. Then the editor "suddenly grew pale with terror when he heard the order given for the destruction of the rebel press, type, and other materials pertaining thereto, together with the building in which they were contained, so there would be nothing whatever left with which to print and publish lies on the morrow."

Back in the Winona area, when daylight of December 31 came, Grierson's men began tearing up more Mississippi Central track, destroying more public property, and cutting telegraph wires. Kargé's brigade camped in Middleton that night, ahead of the other two, and the last two patrols sent out rejoined the main column that evening. The Iowans who had gone to Bankston returned; they had devastated all the public property, leaving owner James Wesson in as good a mood as those in the Grenada area. The Iowans had assured Wesson they were just cold and started the fires to warm themselves.

People in the Bankston area learned firsthand what it meant to be defenseless in a time of war. A Mrs. Edwards made a claim after the conflict that Grierson's men had stolen much from her, and she hoped for compensation. The list included six mules, one saddle horse, one mare, $550 in gold, $50 in silver, pork, meal, flour, molasses, an overcoat, pants, shirts, tin pans, buckets, knives and forks, coffee pots, a watch and chain, a Bowie knife, pot ware, bed clothing, a Colt repeater pistol, two double-barrel shotguns, one single-barrel shotgun, and forty bushels of sweet potatoes. Other families suffered similar losses, and certainly these people learned quickly there was no Forrest or anyone else able to prevent these kinds of incidents. If any of them had been Confederate supporters, Grierson's winter raid probably cooled their ardor, or made them mad and more determined. Either way, it was not a good time to be in the path of Federal soldiers.[46]

At Panola, General Martin decided that Grierson must be returning to Memphis. Reports indicated Grierson had been in Pontotoc, so it did not seem likely he would go to Vicksburg. So Martin sent a brigade to Oxford. But this was a clear case of a diversion working, and Martin did not understand the truth until another day had passed, and he heard that the Mississippi Central had been wrecked at Winona. Martin tried to get a few men together to head for Winona, and at Canton, well to the south, Wirt Adams concentrated his troops in the belief that Grierson was going to Vicksburg. Adams soon had his troops watching Goodman and Vaiden and patrolling the tracks of the railroad. He posted reinforcements at Canton. Adams, too, heard about the action at Winona, but the Vaiden telegrapher had left his post, and Adams could not learn anything new.

On January 1, 1865, Grierson divided his column into three forces, with Iowans moving north along the Mississippi Central Railroad toward Grenada, Osband pushing south from Winona, and the general himself riding with the third detachment through Lexington and Benton as a ready reserve. The Iowans wrecked the railroad and public property on the way to and in Grenada, and then turned back toward Carrollton. Osband, too, accomplished much destruction before camping a few miles south of the town of West. Grierson and the third wing rode uneventfully to near Lexington.

The evening of January 1 Wirt Adams heard about the Federals in the West area, and he ordered his men to be ready to move early the next morning. Troops at Canton rushed to Goodman, where Adams himself arrived early on January 2. Later he heard that Grierson was near Lexington and heading toward Franklin.

Osband had been told by his scouts that Rebels had gathered at Goodman; he decided to avoid that place and head for Benton or Ebenezer. North of Franklin, Confederates fired at Osband's advance, but Osband, with more numbers, pushed back the resistance of Mississippi troops. Adams rode to the rescue, spotting a detachment of Federals along the way. He sent a patrol to chase them away and kept going. Adams soon ran into a fight between some of his men and U.S. Colored Troops along Big Cypress Creek. When Federal reinforcements came up, he tried to flank them, but Osband got there and spread his line to end the threat. After fierce fighting, the shooting waned, and Osband, having lost fourteen men altogether, pulled back to the Ebenezer road and camped with Grierson's troops at

Benton. The fighting went on for about two hours, and Adams had a total of some thirty casualties, plus seven captured. The Third U.S. Colored Cavalry put up a strong defensive stand against the Confederates. Grierson did not give a casualty report for his troops, but he estimated Adams's force to be from 500 to 1,500 men, giving some indication of how muddled the fighting must have been. The Yankees made no effort to pursue, but organized a defense at Way's Bluff, where the Mississippi Central crossed the Big Black River.

Except for a brief skirmish in Lexington, Grierson's men rode unimpeded on to Benton and then to Mechanicsburg. Some of his troops had a rearguard clash with Confederates at a place called the Ponds, and the column reached the outposts that signaled they were near Vicksburg. They camped at Milldale and feasted on rations sent by Cadwallader Washburn, now commanding at Vicksburg. On January 5 they rode triumphantly into Vicksburg during a rainstorm. Grierson recalled that everyone was so muddy they were practically unidentifiable. But word spread quickly, and many fellow Federals came out in the rain to cheer them.[47]

Grierson had led his men on a 450-mile foray through the middle of Mississippi, losing twenty-seven killed, ninety-three wounded, and seven missing. They had some 600 prisoners and 1,000 blacks who had used the occasion of their passing through to desert their masters. They also had 800 head of horses and mules and 700 hogs. The Mobile & Ohio was soon working again, for cavalry and infantry, despite their destructive capabilities, never seemed to put the railroads out of business completely. Yet the Confederacy could not restock the destroyed supplies or quickly replace all the wagons and machinery that Grierson's men had burned and wrecked. Hood's army, or the remnants of it, did receive some much-needed supplies, which ran out rather quickly and led Hood's replacement, P. G. T. Beauregard, to appeal to Richmond for food to keep the men from starving.

Grierson's men, destroying many foodstuffs and other matériel, had a negative effect on the Army of Tennessee's ability to survive. Grierson recalled their ride near Lodi, when they slaughtered "a large drove of fat hogs" intended for Hood's army. His men threw the carcasses into a big bonfire, cooking the meat and thoroughly enjoying the results. They also shared supplies with poor Mississippi families they encountered. Grierson stated, "while the rich feared and deplored our presence, our kind actions gladdened the hearts of the poor—although previously all may have looked upon us as foes." Grierson received thirty days leave after his raid ended. As in 1863, he had shown that, as a raider, he was one of the best the Civil War produced.[48]

EPILOGUE

$\mathscr{B}$enjamin Grierson's winter raid was the last military campaign of any consequence in Mississippi. Skirmishing continued well into the early months of 1865, but such skirmishes were relatively few in number. On January 24 Nathan Bedford Forrest took command of the Confederate district that included Mississippi. In late March Forrest led his command on their last campaign, as he failed to stop a raid by Union cavalry general James H. Wilson from the Tennessee River to Selma, Alabama. Mississippi was among the last of the Confederate states to be surrendered; on May 4 General Richard Taylor, who by then had taken command of the district, surrendered his troops. Robert E. Lee had surrendered on April 9 and Joseph E. Johnston on April 26. The rest of the Confederacy, the so-called trans-Mississippi, was, in effect, surrendered on May 26 by Simon Bolivar Buckner on behalf of Edmund Kirby Smith. On June 2 Smith officially accepted the terms negotiated by Buckner.

Although this book has focused on major campaigns and battles, those soldiers who participated in countless skirmishes and fights should not be overlooked. The men fighting those fights, in life-and-death situations, were soldiers, no matter the scope of their conflicts. To many of them and their families, their efforts and sacrifices were important. Fighting and killing define war, no matter the size of the battlefield.

In the subconscious minds of many those who fought for and/or supported the Confederacy, the war did not end in 1865. The emotional, physical, and psychological trauma of defeat, the impact of the war dead on families, the lingering effects of severe wounds, and the losses of homes and property left scars that filtered down through many generations. Women especially were determined that no one should forget the conflict that wrecked their worlds. Racial issues produced threads of discontent, and violence that led to the freedom of slaves continued into a Reconstruction period when most of that freedom was taken away. From the late nineteenth century through the mid-twentieth century, struggles for black freedom and resistance to change continued. The significant battles and campaigns in Mississippi indeed produced long-lasting echoes.

THE FORGOTTEN

*E*thnic and racial groups in Civil War Mississippi have been largely ignored by historians. Their stories could have been integrated into the preceding chapters, but I prefer shining a spotlight on them. To have immersed them in chapters would have diminished their stories, and that is not my purpose for including them. They need to be recognized to flesh out the history of Mississippi's Civil War era. Hopefully, they will receive more attention in the future.

Mississippi Choctaw Indians did not play a major role in the Civil War, but many participated on the Confederate side, and sometimes they saw action, albeit unorthodox in nature. For example, in the summer of 1863, during the Vicksburg campaign, reinforcements came by rail from the east to help John Pemberton's besieged army. In June a trainload of these soldiers were en route to Jackson, where they would join Joseph Johnston's force, but heavy rains in the Meridian area had submerged the railroad bridge across the Chunky River. The train stayed on the water-covered track until the last car came loose and tumbled into the "raging waters with nearly one hundred soldiers" on board.

Choctaw soldiers happened to be nearby, perhaps acting as scouts, and unhesitatingly jumped into the rapidly flowing stream and pulled most of the soldiers out of the water, though many were already dead. Some "twenty-two were resuscitated and returned to their commands." The rest were buried near the railroad, though families later came and disinterred some bodies to take them home. For the Choctaws, this incident of bravery was the highlight of their service in Mississippi, yet they never received recognition.

An outfit called the First Mississippi Choctaw Battalion participated in the Confederate army and trained at Camp Moore in Louisiana, but many became prisoners when a Union detachment captured the camp. Most white officers escaped, and what happened to the captives is uncertain; it has been presumed they were sent to Oklahoma Territory, where other Choctaws had been deported prior to the war. Whatever the case, the role of the Mississippi Choctaws in their state's Civil War needs further exploration.

Another Confederate Choctaw unit, the First Choctaw Battalion Cavalry, was organized in the state capital of Jackson in the summer of 1862. Most of the members were Choctaws from southern Mississippi, and the battalion served in the Department of Mississippi and East Louisiana, in the Fourth Military District commanded by General John Adams. As far as can be determined, the battalion stayed within the boundaries of Mississippi and did not see any major action. During the siege of Vicksburg, the battalion disbanded on June 9, 1863, and apparently was reorganized as the Third Regiment, Choctaw Cavalry. These troops may have left Mississippi to campaign in Indian Territory, but whatever military action they participated in after leaving the state is unclear. Even if they saw no major action, they, too, should be remembered. The numbers of Mississippi Indians who participated in the war is not known and may be impossible to calculate.[1]

Soldiers who have not been ignored, but on the other hand have not received a proper amount of attention, are Mississippi African American soldiers who served in the Union army. There is a seemingly never-ending debate, started by lost causers who defend or dismiss slavery as the cause of the war, over whether and/or how many blacks fought for the Confederacy. Yet until near the end of the war, the Confederate government forbade the use of slaves as soldiers. There has long been a story that black soldiers fought for the Confederacy at the battle of Chickasaw Bayou, north of Vicksburg, in December 1862, because some Union soldiers insisted they saw them. None of the Confederate accounts, whether official or in letters and diaries, reveals anything of the kind. Most historians have concluded that the Federal soldiers saw Louisiana soldiers, some of whom had dark complexions due to their French-Cajun heritage, their faces made even darker by powder and smoke from the firing of guns. Many reject that argument, but until evidence is found to prove that black Confederate soldiers participated in that fight, the complexion explanation is the only one that makes sense.

Did some slaves pick up guns and fire at Union troops during the war? There is some indication in scattered sources that at times they did, but if so, they certainly did not fight in numbers large enough to change the out-come of any battle, or the war. There are those who insist some regimental records indicate black soldiers served in Confederate units, but they could not have done so in any official capacity that would have been recognized by the Confederate government. Even if they received pensions after the war, and some did, they were not, due to government policy, official sol-diers in the Confederate army. Only in the last few weeks of the war did the Jefferson Davis government and the Confederate Congress give in and per-mit slaves to be organized as military units. Some few marched around the streets of Richmond, but most who saw them dismissed the whole project as ludicrous. It is certain that the change in policy came much too late to benefit the Confederate military in any way.

In the following discussion, black participation is limited to those who fought in U.S. Colored Troop units. A student of this topic estimates that former slaves in Mississippi who fought for the Union numbered between 16,000 and 18,000. Coming up with an exact count is impossible, but the totals are based on the best research materials available. If black Confeder-ate units existed, there is no known documentation to support their exis-tence. Such outfits would have drawn the ire of Jefferson Davis, the Confed-erate Congress, Confederate state governments, and most of the Southern white population in general.[2]

A cavalry unit, originally designated the First Mississippi Cavalry (Af-rican Descent) was authorized at Vicksburg by Brigadier General Lorenzo Thomas, following a "suggestion" by General Ulysses S. Grant. Formally organized and accepted in U.S. service in October 1863, the unit eventually became known as the Third U.S. Colored Cavalry. One of their initial du-ties, which they must have thoroughly enjoyed, was escorting Confederate prisoners captured north of Vicksburg into the town in December 1863. The outfit operated in various capacities in the Vicksburg region, especially in Louisiana and Arkansas, before occupying Yazoo City in 1864, and was commanded by white officer Embury D. Osband, who loved paperwork, and made possible the Third being the only black cavalry unit to have a regimental history. Written by Edwin M. Main, who doubtless drew heav-ily from Osband's records, it is entitled *The Story of Marches, Battles, and Incidents of the Third United States Colored Cavalry: A Fighting Regiment in the War of the Rebellion, 1861–5.*[3]

The First Mississippi Volunteers of African Descent, organized at Mil-liken's Bend, Louisiana, and Vicksburg in May 1863, played a dramatic role in the battle of Milliken's Bend, June 7, 1863, on the west side of the Mis-sissippi River northwest of Vicksburg. They received Belgian rifles, which were not considered very good weapons, the day before the battle. They obviously did not have time for proper training, yet they fought well beside black Louisiana troops and "held off a larger force of Confederates in heated hand-to-hand combat." Yet the Union troops were driven back to the edge of the Mississippi where a Union gunboat, the *Choctaw*, provided cover fire, and the attacking Confederate Texas troops had to retreat. The black troops proved they were not afraid to fight, for "the vicious hand-to-hand struggle on the levee near Milliken's Bend created new respect for African American fighting men." The unit remained in Vicksburg until 1864 and was eventually designated the Fifty- first U.S. Colored Troops.

Other Mississippi African American units included the Second Mississippi Regiment of Infantry, African Descent, which also served in the Vicksburg area and was designated in 1864 as the Fifty-second U.S. Colored Troops. The Third Regiment of Black Infantry, African Descent, likewise was in the Vicksburg region and became the Fifty-third U.S. Colored Troops. The Fourth Regiment was also organized at Vicksburg and served there, becoming the Sixty-sixth U.S. Colored Troops. The Fifth Regiment never completed its organization and did not officially serve in the war. The Sixth Infantry, African Descent, served at Natchez and Vicksburg and was designated the Fifty-eighth U.S. Colored Troops. Other predominantly Mississippi troops included the Second Regiment of Heavy Artillery, before having its name changed to the Fifth and then the Sixth U.S. Colored Heavy Artillery, assigned to the Vicksburg district. The First Regiment of Heavy Artillery became the Fourth and then the Fifth U.S. Colored Heavy Artillery, likewise serving at Vicksburg. Another African American unit, the First Regiment Mounted Rifles, was mostly Mississippian, though organized at Memphis, where it served in the defense of that city and later participated in Grierson's 1864–65 raid on the Mobile & Ohio Railroad.[4]

A group that has received practically no attention is the number of Mississippians who fought in the Union army. According to records of the U.S. Adjutant's office, published by the National Archives on microfilm, slightly over 900 Mississippi men fought for the preservation of the Union. Other sources give a lower number, in the 500 range. Whatever the truth, they all fought in an outfit called the First Battalion, Mississippi Mounted Rifles. Other pro-Union Mississippians did not wear uniforms. Some, like Levi Naron, scouted for Union armies, while others quietly worked as spies for the Union cause or aided and supplied escaped Federal prisoners. Because they operated in secrecy, and few let their true feelings be known after the war, their story will probably never be told with any degree of certainty. Ironically, many of these Unionists were and are forgotten because they wanted to be.

NOTES

PROLOGUE

1. Emory M. Thomas, *The Confederate Nation, 1861–1865* (New York: 1979), 41–42; John K. Bettersworth, *Confederate Mississippi: The People and Policies of a Cotton State in Wartime* (Philadelphia, 1978), 5–8. The actual vote apparently was 84-15; one delegate was unable to attend, but apparently was counted as a yes vote, though it was unofficial, hence the 85-15 total. Glover Moore, an authority on Mississippi history, in his chapter, "A Separation from the Union, 1854–1861," in *A History of Mississippi*, 2 vols., ed. Richard Aubrey McLemore (Jackson, Miss., 1973), 1:444, goes with the 84-15 count. For additional information on voting, see http://www.csawardept.com/documents/secession/ms/index.html.

2. Bettersworth, *Confederate Mississippi*, 8, 11–12; Michael B. Ballard, *Vicksburg: The Campaign That Opened the Mississippi* (Chapel Hill, N.C., 2004), 5–6.

3. Bettersworth, *Mississippi*, 12–13; Ballard, *Vicksburg*, 9.

4. Ballard, *Vicksburg*, 11–13.

5. Ibid., 13–15.

6. Charles E. Hooker, *Mississippi*, vol. 9 of *Confederate Military History*, ed. Clement Evans (Wilmington, N.C., 1987), 30–31; Dunbar Rowland, *Military History of Mississippi, 1803–1898* (Spartanburg, S.C., 1978), 36–37.

7. Bettersworth, *Mississippi*, 213–45. See also Victoria E. Bynum, *The Free State of Jones: Mississippi's Longest Civil War* (Chapel Hill, N.C., 2001).

8. Levi H. Naron, *Chickasaw: A Mississippi Scout for the Union, The Civil War Memoir of Levi H. Naron as Recounted by R. W. Surby*, ed. Thomas D. Cockrell and Michael B. Ballard (Baton Rouge, La., 2005), 5–20; Kristy Armstrong White, "Life in Civil War Tishomingo County, Mississippi" (M.A. thesis, Mississippi State University, 1998), 7–10.

9. Rowland, *Military History*, 38–39.

10. Bettersworth, *Mississippi*, 18–21; Ballard, *Vicksburg*, 11.

11. Bettersworth, *Mississippi*, 21.

12. Ballard, *Vicksburg*, 20; Rowland, *Military History*, 39; Thomas D. Cockrell and Michael B. Ballard, eds., *A Mississippi Rebel in the Army of Northern Virginia: The Civil War Memoirs of Private David Holt* (Baton Rouge, La., 1995), 63–67.

13. Warren E. Grabau, *Ninety-eight Days: A Geographer's View of the Vicksburg Campaign* (Knoxville, Tenn., 2000), 34–36, Map 1, 535; Bettersworth, *Mississippi*, 11; Ballard, *Vicksburg*, 16.

14. Hooker, *Mississippi*, 9:14. The figures are from Pamplin Park, a museum complex in Petersburg, Virginia, devoted to the common soldier. The park has stone monuments to each state, and figures denoting participation and casualties. The figures, which resulted from exhaustive research, seem more reasonable than any I have found elsewhere.

15. Herman Hattaway and Archer Jones, *How the North Won the Civil War: A Military History of the Civil War* (Urbana, Ill., 1991), 44–49, 53, 62–63, 65–77, 157–58, 163.

16. Ibid., 163–71; F. W. Richman diary, "Rebel Strategy at Shiloh Praised by Yank," in *The Civil War and the Battles of Corinth and Shiloh, The Daily Corinthian Special Civil War Centennial Souvenir Edition, 1961–1965* (Corinth, Miss., 1965), Section 1, 7.

CHAPTER 1. CORINTH

1. John F. Marszalek, *Commander of All Lincoln's Armies: A Life of General Henry W. Halleck* (Cambridge, Mass., 2004), 123.

2. *The War of the Rebellion: A Compilation of the Official Records of Union and Confederate Armies*, 128 vols. (Washington, D.C., 1880–1901), 10-2, 99 (hereafter cited as *OR*, followed by volume number, part number when applicable, and page number[s]; all citations are from Series 1); Roy P. Basler, ed., *The Collected Works of Abraham Lincoln*, 8 vols. plus index volume (New Brunswick, N.J., 1953–55), 5:210.

3. *OR*, 10-2, 99, 105; Ulysses S. Grant, *Memoirs and Selected Letters: Personal Memoirs of U. S. Grant, Selected Letters, 1839–1865*, 2 vols. in 1 (New York, 1990), 248.

4. *OR*, 10-1, 672.

5. Mildred Throne, ed., *The Civil War Diary of Cyrus F. Boyd, Fifteenth Iowa Infantry, 1861–1863* (Baton Rouge, La., 1998), 40.

6. Committee of the Regiment, *The Story of the Fifty-fifth Regiment, Illinois Volunteer Infantry in the Civil War, 1861–1865* (Huntington, W.Va., 1993), 136.

7. Stanley F. Horn, *The Army of Tennessee* (Norman, Okla., 1952), 148; Horatio to Josie, April 12, 1862, http://misandy.home.tsixroads.com/Corinth__MLSANDY/josie .html.

8. W. H. Tunnard, *A Southern Record: The Story of the 3rd Louisiana Infantry, CSA* (Dayton, Ohio, 1970), 164–65; H. Grady Howell Jr., *Going to Meet the Yankees: A History of the "Bloody Sixth" Mississippi Infantry* (Jackson, Miss., 1981), 98, 101.

9. Joseph E. Chance, *The Second Texas Infantry: From Shiloh to Vicksburg* (Austin, Tex., 1984), 43–45; Samuel R. Watkins, *"Co. Aytch," Maury Grays, First Tennessee Regiment; or A Side Show of the Big Show* (Jackson, Tenn., 1952), 49.

10. *OR*, 10-1, 389–99.

11. Ibid., 403, 405, 440.

12. *OR*, 10-2, 414, 422, 453.

13. Ibid., 421, 457–58; Horn, *Army*, 145.

14. *OR*, 10-2, 424–25; Horn, *Army*, 146; Alfred Roman, *The Military Operations of General Beauregard in the War Between the States, 1861–1865; Including a Brief Personal Sketch of his Services in the War with Mexico*, 2 vols. (New York, 1884), 1:380–81.

15. *OR*, 10-2, 457–58; Roman, *Beauregard*, 1:382–83.

16. Roman, *Beauregard*, 1:383–84.

17. Ibid., 384; Ballard, *Vicksburg*, 22, 38–39.

18. Michael B. Ballard, *U. S. Grant: The Making of a General, 1861–1863* (Lanham, Md., 2005), 57–59.

19. Grant, *Memoirs*, 248, 250; *OR*, 10-2, 182–83; Ballard, *Grant*, 58–59.

20. Marszalek, *Halleck*, 123, 125; Basler, *Collected Works of Abraham Lincoln*, 5:210.

21. *OR*, 10-1, 673.

22. *OR*, 10-2, 171, 177; Peter Cozzens, *General John Pope: A Life for the Nation* (Champaign, Ill., 2000), 67.

23. *OR*, 10-1, 665–66.

24. Ibid., 739.

25. Ibid., 738–43.

26. Ibid., 673–76.

27. *OR*, 10-2, 160–61; *OR*, 10-1, 801–2; Roman, *Beauregard*, 1:386–87.

28. *OR*, 10-2, 160–61.

29. Ibid., 164, 167, 169.

30. Roman, *Beauregard*, 1:387–88.

31. *OR*, 10-1, 804, 807–8.

32. Cozzens, *Pope*, 69–70.

33. Grant, *Memoirs*, 252.

34. *OR*, 10-2, 506–7.

35. *OR*, 10-1, 660–61; Roman, *Beauregard*, 1:388.

36. Horn, *Army*, 150–51; Roman, *Beauregard*, 1:388.

37. *OR*, 10-2, 225–30.

38. Ibid., 252; Roman, *Beauregard*, 1:395.

39. *OR*, 10-2, 242, 249, 635–37; Stephen D. Engle, *Don Carlos Buell: Most Promising of All* (Chapel Hill, N.C., 1999), 244–45; Grant, *Memoirs*, 251–55.

40. *OR*, 10-1, 772–73.

41. Marzalek, *Halleck*; Grant, *Memoirs*, 255.

42. *OR*, 10-1, 671.

43. Grant, *Memoirs*, 262–63; Basler, *Lincoln*, 5:300, 312–13; Marszalek, *Halleck*, 126–28; Ballard, *Grant*, 65–66; *OR*, 17-1, 245–46.

44. *OR*, 10-1, 774–77, 786.

45. *OR*, 17-2, 601, 606, 614.

46. Grady McWhiney, *Braxton Bragg and Confederate Defeat* (New York, 1969), 266–70.

CHAPTER 2. VICKSBURG: FIRST ATTACK

1. Admiral [David Dixon] Porter, *Incidents and Anecdotes of the Civil War* (New York, 1885), 95–96; Thomas L. Connelly, "Vicksburg: Strategic Point or Propaganda Device?" *Military Affairs* 34 (April 1970): 49–53; on New Orleans, see Chester G. Hearn, *The Capture of New Orleans, 1862* (Baton Rouge, La., 1995); Benjamin F. Butler, *Private and Official Correspondence of Benjamin F. Butler, during the Period of the Civil War*, 5 vols. (Norwood, Mass., 1917), 1:428; *Official Records of the Union and Confederate Navies in the War of the Rebellion*, 31 vols. (Washington, D.C., 1894–1927), 18:245, 462, 465, 473–78, 489–92, 494–95, 528–32, 533, 782–83, 810 (hereafter cited as *ORN* followed by volume, part if applicable, and page numbers; all citations are to volumes in Series 1 unless otherwise indicated); William N. Still Jr., *Iron Afloat: The Story of the Confederate Armorclads* (Nashville, Tenn., 1971), 63; Edwin C. Bearss, *Rebel Victory at Vicksburg* (Vicksburg, Miss., 1963), 15, 20; *OR*, 15:423, 736; F. W. Curtenius diary, May 15, 1862, Journals/Diaries/Letters Subseries of Vicksburg Campaign Series, Vicksburg National Military Park, Vicksburg, Miss. (hereafter cited as VNMP).

2. *OR*, 15:6–7; Still, *Iron Afloat*, 64; William Y. Dixon diary, vol. 1, May 2–4, 9, 12–13, 17, 1862, entries, Dixon Papers, Louisiana State University Special Collections Library, Baton Rouge (hereafter cited as LSU); J. M. Doyle to Josiah Knighton, May 24, 1862, Josiah Knighton and Family Papers, LSU; Charles K. Marshall letter, June 30, 1862, printed in *Jackson Daily Mississippian* (Summer 1862), clipping, Marshall File, Old Courthouse Museum, Vicksburg, Miss. (hereafter cited as OCHM).

3. *OR*, 15:6–7; Marshall letter, June 30, 1862, OCHM; *ORN*, 18:493, 498–99, 507, 704–5, 725, 810.

4. *ORN*, 18:507, 519–22.

5. Ibid., 508–10, 575–76.

6. *OR*, 15:22–24; *ORN*, 18:534, 761; see Mark Grimsley, *The Hard Hand of War: Union Military Policy Toward Southern Civilians* (New York, 1995), esp. 42.

7. *OR*, 15:7–8, 22, 24; *ORN*, 18:520, 535.

8. *OR*, 52-2, 316–17; Bearss, *Rebel Victory*, 51.

9. *ORN*, 18:783; Dixon diary, vol. 1, May 30, 1862, LSU; Rowland Chambers diaries, Diary 6, May 26–27, 1862, LSU; Mahala Roach diary, May 28, 1862, Duke University Perkins Library, Durham, N.C. (hereafter cited as DU); *OR*, 15:8.

10. *ORN*, 18:520, 535, 546–47, 762, 785, 789–90, 797–98, 802, 816, 820; William Smith to brother, June 16, 1862, Smith Letters, LSU; John D. Winters, *The Civil War in Louisiana* (Baton Rouge, La., 1963), 110–11.

11. *ORN*, 18:547, 798, 802; Bearss, *Rebel Victory*, 61.

12. *ORN*, 18:552–53.

13. *OR*, 15:752–53; *OR*, 17-2, 591; William Leroy Brown to wife, June 7, 1862, Brown Papers, U.S. Army Military History Institute, Carlisle Barracks, Pa. (hereafter cited as USAMHI).

14. *OR*, 15:754, 756, 758; *OR*, 17-2, 612; Dixon diary, vol. 1, June 19, 1862, LSU.

15. *OR*, 15:742, 746, 761–63, 766, 770; *OR*, 17-2, 622; *OR*, 52-2, 324; *OR*, 15:15, 767; George Henry, *History of the 3rd, 7th, 8th, and 12th Kentucky, C.S.A.* (London, Ky., 1970), 34; William Pitt Chambers, "My Journal," in *Publications of the Mississippi Historical Society, Centenary Series* (Jackson, Miss., 1925), 5:240; "During the First Siege of Vicksburg: From the Diary of a Confederate Soldier," *Confederate Veteran* 2 (January 1894): 11.

15. *OR*, 52-2, 316–17, 324; *OR*, 15:15, 742, 746, 767; Bearss, *Rebel Victory*, 51; Henry, *History*, 34; Chambers, "My Journal," 240; "During the First Siege," 11; Spencer Bowen Talley memoir, 15, USAMHI; W. E. Holloman journal, July 4, 1862, Forty-sixth Mississippi File, VNMP; Allen C. Richard Jr. and Mary Margaret Higginbotham Richard, *The Defense of Vicksburg: A Louisiana Chronicle* (College Station, Tex., 2003), 51, 56.

16. *ORN*, 18:546–47, 554, 562–65, 580–83, 785, 789–90, 797–98, 802, 816, 820; William Smith to brother, June 16, 1862, Smith Letters, LSU.

17. *ORN*, 18:555–59, 561, 571–72, 664–66; Chester G. Hearn, *Admiral David Dixon Porter: The Civil War Years* (Annapolis, Md., 1996), 124–25.

18. *ORN*, 18:586–87, 639, 727, 750; *OR*, 15:8.

19. *ORN*, 18:584–85, 23:241; Jay Slagle, *Ironclad Captain: Seth Ledyard Phelps and the U.S. Navy, 1841–1864* (Kent, Ohio, 1996), 249–50.

20. *ORN*, 18:585–86, 619–20, 623, 640–41, 727, 751, 798.

21. *OR*, 15:9; Jefferson Davis to John J. Pettus, February 3, 1862, RG (Record Group) 27, Mississippi Department of Archives and History, Jackson (hereafter cited as MDAH); G. W. Freeman to John J. Pettus, August 9, 1862, RG 27, MDAH.

22. *ORN*, 23:242–43, 590–91; Ballard, *Vicksburg*, 50, 56.

23. *ORN*, 18:593, 599–608, 632–36, 675; *ORN*, 23:235; James P. Duffy, *Lincoln's Admiral: The Civil War Campaigns of David Farragut* (New York, 1997), 139.

24. *ORN*, 18:626–32.

25. Ibid., 647–52; *ORN*, 23:244; *ORN*, 19:40–41, 68–69, 132–33; Still, *Iron Afloat*, 64–66; I. E. Fiske to John Comstock, July 24, 1862, Comstock Papers, University of North Carolina at Chapel Hill (hereafter cited as UNCCH).

26. *ORN*, 19:4–7, 9–11, 13, 15, 40, 46, 60, 133–34.

27. Ibid., 19:18, 45–46, 50, 61; Slagle, *Ironclad Captain*, 277.

28. *ORN*, 19:17, 19, 59–60, 62.

29. Ibid., 5–7, 50–51, 52–55, 63–64; Dabney Maury Scales to father, July 31, 1862, *C.S.S. Arkansas* file, OCHM; *OR*, 15:31–32.

30. *ORN*, 19:772, *OR*, 15:16, 746, 766, 778; Sidney Champion to Matilda Champion, July 9, 1862, Champion Papers, DU; Bearss, *Rebel Victory*, 281.

31. *ORN*, 19:722; *OR*, 15:16; Sidney Champion to Matilda Champion, July 9, 1862; Bearss, *Rebel Victory*, 281.

32. *OR*, 15:15, 17, 54, 76–77, 79, 80, 82–83, 330–31, 548, 550–51, 786, 791; *ORN*, 19:130; Sidney Champion to Matilda Champion, [August 1, 1862], Champion Papers, DU; I. N. Brown, "Confederate Gun-Boat 'Arkansas,'" in *Battles and Leaders of the Civil War*, 4 vols., ed. Robert Underwood Johnson and Clarence Clough Buell (New York, 1956) 3:579 (hereafter cited as *B&L*); C. W. Read, "Reminiscences of the Confederate States Navy," in *Southern Historical Society Papers*, 52 vols. (Millwood, N.Y., 1977), 1:350 (hereafter cited *SHSP*); George W. Gift, "The Story of the Arkansas," in *SHSP*, 12:205–12; William C. Davis, *Breckinridge: Statesman, Soldier, Symbol* (Baton Rouge, La., 1974), 319–20.

33. See Ballard, *Vicksburg*, 73–76.

CHAPTER 3. IUKA

1. McWhiney, *Bragg*, 266–70.

2. Albert Castel, *General Sterling Price and the Civil War in the West* (Baton Rouge, La., 1968), 88–89.

3. Hattaway and Jones, *How the North Won*, 205–8, 212–19.

4. *OR*, 17-2, 705–7.

5. *OR*, 17-1, 73; Grant, *Memoirs*, 272; Peter Cozzens, *The Darkest Days of the War: The Battles of Iuka and Corinth* (Chapel Hill, N.C., 1997), 64.

6. William M. Lamers, *The Edge of Glory: A Biography of General William S. Rosecrans, U.S.A.* (Baton Rouge, La., 1999), 104.

7. Ibid.; Grant, *Memoirs*, 272, 285.

8. Grant, *Memoirs*, 272, 275; Cozzens, *Darkest*, 64; *OR*, 17-1, 65.

9. Ballard, *Grant*, 75.

10. *OR*, 17-1, 66.

11. Ballard, *Grant*, 76.

12. *OR*, 17-1, 66–67, 118–19; *OR*, 17-2, 222, 227–28; Grant, *Memoirs*, 276.

13. Naron, *Chickasaw*, 62.

14. Ibid.; *OR*, 17-1, 69.

15. Lamers, *Edge of Glory*, 108; Cozzens, *Darkest*, 72; *OR*, 17-1, 68, 116.

16. *OR*, 17-1, 67, 69; Grant, *Memoirs*, 276.

17. Cozzens, *Darkest*, 72–73, 127–28; Lamers, *Edge of Glory*, 109–10, 117–18; *OR*, 17-1, 67.

18. Ballard, *Grant*, 171–74; *OR*, 17-1, 74.

19. *OR*, 17-1, 67, 90.

20. Cozzens, *Darkest*, 78; *OR*, 17-1, 122; John K. Mizner quoted in Phil Gottschalk, *In Deadly Earnest: The History of the First Missouri Brigade, CSA* (Columbia, Mo., 1991), 127; *Marching Through Dixie: A History of the 80th Ohio Vol. Inf.*, Chapter 1, 1862, http://freepages.genealogy.rootsweb.ancestry.com/~keller/ovi80/work/80thch1.html.

21. *OR*, 17-1, 90–92, 123–27; Cozzens, *Darkest*, 87; Tunnard, *Southern Record*, 188; Bell Irvin Wiley, ed., *"This Infernal War": The Confederate Letters of Sgt. Edwin H. Fay* (Austin, Tex., 1958), 158; Stephen E. Ambrose, ed., *The Selected Letters of James K. Newton* (Madison, Wis., 1961), 34.

22. Cozzens, *Darkest*, 133; *OR*, 17-1, 126–27; Ephraim McD. Anderson, *Memoirs Historical and Personal, Including the Campaigns of the First Missouri Confederate Brigade* (Dayton, Ohio, 1972), 224; Franklin J. Higgins to father and mother, September 22, 1862, http://www.3battery.org/61-65frank mhiggins.html; *Marching Through Dixie*.

23. *OR*, 17-1, 77–78.

24. Ibid., 99, 104, 122, 134; C. S. Hamilton, "The Battle of Iuka," in *B&L*, 2:735.

25. Castel, *Price*, 102; R. S. Bevier, *History of the First and Second Missouri Confederate Brigades, 1861–1865* (Independence, Mo., 2006), 130.

26. *OR*, 17-1, 119; Grant, *Memoirs*, 276; Lamers, *Edge of Glory*, 119; Cozzens, *Darkest*, 129–30, 125–26; Hamilton, "Battle of Iuka," 735.

27. Castel, *Price*, 102–3; *OR*, 17-1, 122.

28. *OR*, 17-1, 67–68, 70–71, 74.

29. Lamers, *Edge of Glory*, 115–30; *OR*, 17-1, 68, 167–68.

CHAPTER 4. CORINTH

1. Arthur B. Carter, *The Tarnished Cavalier: Major General Earl Van Dorn, C.S.A.* (Knoxville, Tenn., 1999), 66.

2. Castel, *Price*, 104–6. For the full text of the Price-Snead exchange, see *OR*, 52-2, 366–67.

3. *OR*, 17-2, 710–11, 713.

4. Anderson, *Memoirs*, 229; Tunnard, *Southern Record*, 190.

5. *OR*, 17-1, 374–75, 378.

6. Ibid., 376; *OR*, 17-2, 712; Cozzens, *Darkest*, 132.

7. *OR*, 17-1, 377–78.

8. Carter, *Van Dorn*, 50; Cozzens, *Darkest*, 136–39; Castel, *Price*, 106–7; *OR*, 17-1, 45, 441; *OR*, 17-2, 716–17.

9. *OR*, 17-2, 235, 237, 243, 250–54; Ballard, *Grant*, 75–76.

10. *OR*, 17-1, 167, 337, 352, 378, 422–23; Carter, *Van Dorn*, 93; Lamers, *Edge of Glory*, 135; Castel, *Price*, 112.

11. *OR*, 17-1, 168, 252–53, 404, 412, 426; Cozzens, *Darkest*, 37, 165–68, 174; Joseph E. Johnston, *Narrative of Military Operations during the Civil War* (New York, 1990), 332, 572–73; Howell, *Going to Meet the Yankees*, 131.

12. Cozzens, *Darkest*, 182–86; *OR*, 17-1, 344–45, 354, 426; Bevier, *History*, 140; Gottschalk, *In Deadly Earnest*, 149.

13. *OR*, 17-1, 179, 205, 252–54, 256, 359, 389–90; Cozzens, *Darkest*, 216–18, 205.

14. Naron, *Chickasaw*, 72; *OR*, 17-1, 167–68, 256–57.

15. *OR*, 17-1, 155, 157, 160–61, 168–69; Cozzens, *Darkest*, 238–39.

16. Cozzens, *Darkest*, 223; *OR*, 17-1, 379; Richard Lowe, ed., *A Texas Cavalry Officer's Civil War: The Diary and Letters of James C. Bates* (Baton Rouge, La., 1999), 185.

17. *OR*, 17-1, 379, 387, 390; Bevier, *History*, 149–50.

18. *OR*, 17-1, 405, 408, 411–12; Cozzens, *Darkest*, 271–72.

19. *OR*, Cozzens, *Darkest*, 237; *OR*, 17-1, 206–7, 391; Lowe, *Texas Cavalry*, 186–87.

20. *OR*, 17-1, 69, 181, 206–7, 259–60, 257, 387, 398–99, 402; *Marching Through Dixie*; Whitfield-Ross Texas Cavalry Brigade, http://www.geocities.com/sixtxcavrgtcsa/blog. html?p=31; Anderson, *Memoirs*, 237; Gottschalk, *In Deadly Earnest*, 150–51.

21. *OR*, 17-1, 381, 388, 398–99, 185–86, 181, 190–91; Cozzens, *Darkest*, 258, 262–65; William S. Rosecrans, "The Battle of Corinth," *B&L*, 2:751–52.

22. *OR*, 17-2, 720; Carter, *Van Dorn*, 104–5; Cozzens, *Darkest*, 278.

23. *OR*, 17-2, 265–66; *OR*, 17-1, 399–400.

24. *OR*, 17-1, 322-23; Cozzens, *Darkest*, 286.

25. *OR*, 17-1, 403; Wiley, "Infernal War," 165.

26. *OR*, 17-1, 323–24, 395; Lowe, *Texas Cavalry*, 190.

27. *OR*, 17-1, 306, 323; Cozzens, *Darkest*, 299–300.

28. *OR*, 17-1, 368, 413.

29. Cozzens, *Darkest*, 297–99; Tunnard, *Southern Record*, 193.

30. Ballard, *Grant*, 77–78; Lamers, *Edge of Glory*, 177, 181.

31. *OR*, 17-1, 176, 383–84; Cozzens, *Darkest*, 209, 212, 305–6; Franklin J. Higgins to father, October 7, 1862, Third Battery, First Michigan Light Artillery Web site, http://robinsonsbattery.org/4022.html.

32. Michael B. Ballard, *Pemberton: A Biography* (Jackson, Miss. 1991), 109–15; *OR*, 17-1, 414–59.

33. Two excellent studies of Perryville are Kenneth W. Noe, *Perryville, This Grand Havoc of Battle* (Lexington, Ky., 2001); and James Lee McDonough, *War in Kentucky: From Shiloh to Perryville* (Knoxville, Tenn., 1996).

CHAPTER 5. VICKSBURG: MORE UNION FAILURES

1. *OR*, 17-2, 237, 294, 296–97, 308; Grant, *Memoirs*, 281; Edwin C. Bearss, *The Vicksburg Campaign* (Dayton, Ohio, 1985–86), 1:22–23, 31; Simpson, *Grant*, 155; see also *OR*, 13:778–79.

2. Richard L. Kiper, *Major General John Alexander McClernand: Politician in Uniform* (Kent, Ohio, 1999), 129–31, 132–43; *OR*, 17-2, 274–75, 282, 312–13, 315–19.

3. Simon, *Grant Papers*, 6:243, 256, 261–63, 268, 278; *OR*, 17-2, 338–40.

4. Ballard, *Pemberton*, 1–113, contains an overview of the pre-Vicksburg life of Pemberton; *OR*, 17-2, 715–17, 724, 727–29, 733; *OR*, 52-2, 381.

5. *OR*, 52-2, 382; *OR*, 17-2, 728, 736, 738, 745–47, 776–77, 782, 797–98, 800, 802; Bearss, *Vicksburg*, 1:51; J. R. Waddy to John Gregg, November 4, 1862, RG 109, chap. 2, vol. 57, Letters and Telegrams Sent, Department of Mississippi and East Louisiana, National Archives (hereafter cited as NA).

6. *OR*, 17-2, 368–70, 374; *OR*, 17-1, 471–72, 528–30, 533–37, 539–40; W. A. Montgomery to sister, December 12, 1862, Bailey Papers, USAMHI; David G. Jones to parents, December 4, 1862, Wisconsin Historical Society Archives, Madison (hereafter cited as WHSA).

7. Thomas J. Blackwell diary, December 5–6, 1862, Thirty-first Mississippi File, VNMP.

8. *OR*, 17-1, 627–28, 635–36, 642, 648, 651, 677, 687, 696; *ORN*, 23:573–74, 581, 592; Bearss, *Vicksburg*, 1:166; Committee of the Regiment, *Story of the Fifty-fifth*, 188–89; Chambers, "My Journal," 255.

9. *OR*, 17-1, 641, 643–44, 647, 651, 687, 690–91, 695, 696; David Palmer to parents, January 3, 1863, Palmer Papers, University of Iowa Libraries, Special Collections, Iowa City (hereafter cited as UI). In the *OR*, the Twenty-ninth Louisiana is sometimes mistakenly called the Twenty-eighth, and the Seventh Kentucky is erroneously called the Third.

10. *OR*, 17-1, 649–50, 656, 658–59, 682–83; Gary Ray Goodson Sr., *The Confederate Georgia 7,000: Part II, Letters and Diaries*, 1996, excerpts from writings of Henry W. Robinson, Georgia File, OCHM; William Marsh to parents and brother, February 17, 1863, Marsh Papers, Illinois State Historical Library (hereafter cited as ISHL); S. A. Black, *A Soldier's Recollections of the Civil War* (Minco, Okla., 1911–12), 28; George W. Morgan, "The Assault on Chickasaw Bluffs," *B&L*, 3:469–70; Frank Moore, ed., *The Rebellion Record: A Diary of American Events*, 12 vols. (New York, 1977), 6:310, 314.

11. *ORN*, 23:491–92, 24:107–8; *OR*, 17-1, 701–2, 704, 707, 708–9, 716–19, 723–24, 780–81; *OR*, 17-2, 546; *OR*, 22-1, 887; Kiper, *McClernand*, 157–59, 161, 167–68, 170; William T. Sherman, *Memoirs of William T. Sherman*, 2 vols. in 1 (New York, 1984), 220–21; Porter, *Incidents*, 130–31; Simon, *Grant Papers*, 7:209–11; Bearss, *Vicksburg*, 1:418–19; R. R. Hall diary, January 9, [1863], OCHM; Steve Meyer, *Iowa Valor . . .* (Garrison, Iowa, 1994), 169–71; William Eddington memoir, 6, ISHL; David Holmes to parents, February 2, 1863, Holmes Papers, ISHL; Andrew McCormack to parents and sisters, January 18, 1863, Wiley Sword Personal Collection; Samuel Gordon to wife, January 10–12, 1863, Gordon Papers, ISHL; Joseph P. Lesslie to wife and folks at home, January 20, 1863, Fourth Indiana File, VNMP; George Marshall, "Civil War Reminiscences," 35–36, Marshall Papers, Indiana State Library (hereafter cited as ISL); Black, "Recollections," 33–34; Abernethy, "Incidents," 410; John H. Ferree to brother, May 9, 1863, Ferree Papers, Indiana Historical Society (hereafter cited as IHS); James Russell Soley, "Naval Operations in the Vicksburg Campaign," in *B&L*, 3:559. The *Cairo* was salvaged in the early 1960s and is on exhibit at the Vicksburg National Military Park.

12. *OR*, 17-1, 604–6, 629–30; *OR*, 15:953–54, 962–63, 983–84; Jacob T. Foster memoirs, 43, WHSA.

13. *OR*, 17-1, 606, 666, 656–56, 672–73; *OR*, 17-2, 803, 807; Ballard, *Pemberton*, 128; Joseph Dill Alison diary, December 26, 1862, UNCCH; Chambers, "My Journal," 253–54; Sherman, *Memoirs*, 216–18.

14. Lee, "Details of Important Work," 53–54; "What Telegraph Men Did for Vicksburg," *Confederate Veteran* 10 (February 1902), 72; "How Telegraphs Saved Vicksburg: A True Story of the Civil War," M. J. Smith Papers, MDAH; Bearss, *Vicksburg*, 1:152–54; *OR*, 17-1, 606; Lynda Lasswell Christ et al., eds., *The Papers of Jefferson Davis*, 11 vols. to date (Baton Rouge, La., 1995) 8:565–79, 582.

15. Bearss, *Vicksburg*, 1:152–54; Sherman, *Memoirs*, 216–18; *OR*, 17-1, 606, 666; *OR*, 17-2, 807.

16. *OR*, 17-1, 627, 635, 642, 648, 654, 686–87, 690, 695–96; *ORN*, 23:573–74; Bearss, *Vicksburg*, 1:166–67; Committee of the Regiment, *Story of the Fifty-fifth*, 188–89.

17. *OR*, 17-1, 606, 627–28, 635–36, 641, 643–44, 647, 649, 654–55, 666, 677, 687, 690–91, 695–96; *OR*, 17-2, 807; *ORN*, 23:581, 592; Sherman, *Memoirs*, 216–18; David Palmer to parents, January 3, 1863, Palmer Papers, UI; Bearss, *Vicksburg*, 1:183; Moore, *Rebellion Record*, 6:316; Chambers, "My Journal," 255.

18. *OR*, 17-1, 607–8, 628, 633–34, 677–79, 646, 649–50, 652, 655–56, 658–59, 682–83, 688, 692, 697; *OR*, 17-2, 608–9, 634, 661, 679; *ORN*, 23:585, 592; Sherman, *Memoirs*, 218–19; Morgan, "Assault on Chickasaw Bluffs," *B&L*, 3:464–67, 469–70; Richard M. Hunt, "Battles of Chickasaw Bayou and Arkansas Post," n.p., Hunt Papers, USAMHI; Goodson, *Confederate Georgia*, excerpts, Robinson, Georgia File, OCHM; William Marsh to parents and brother, February 17, 1863, Marsh Papers, ISHL; Black, "Soldier's Recollections," 28; Boyd diary, December 28, 1862, ISHL; Dabney H. Maury, "Winter at Vicksburg," *Philadelphia Weekly Times*, January 3, 1885; Price F. Kellogg journal, December 29, 1862, Kellogg Papers, ISHL; William Kennedy to wife, January 2, 1863, ISHL; Samuel Burdick diary, December, 28, 29, 31, 1862, WHSA; William R. Eddington memoir, n.p., Ninety-seventh Illinois File, VNMP.

19. *OR*, 17-1, 609, 662–63; *OR*, 17-2, 609–10, 625, 671; *ORN*, 23:588; Marshall, "Reminiscences," 29, Marshall Papers, ISL; John A. McGregor, "Chickasaw Bayou," *National Tribune*, July 21, 1904; Andrew McCormack to parents and sisters, January 2, 1863, Wiley Sword Personal Collection; Sanders diary, excerpt from *Louisiana Genealogical Exchange*, March 1970, OCHM; Andrew J. Sproul, Narrative, February 12, 1863, Sproul Papers, UNCCH; Maury, "Winter at Vicksburg"; Foster memoirs, 46, WHSA; Black, *Soldier's Recollections*, 29; Mahala Roach diary, December 31, 1862, UNCCH.

20. *ORN*, 23:491–92; *OR*, 17-1, 701–2, 708–9, 716–19, 781; *OR*, 17-2, 546; *OR*, 22-1, 887; Kiper, *McClernand*, 157–59, 161, 167–68; Sherman, *Memoirs*, 220–21; Porter, *Incidents*, 130–31; Samuel Gordon to wife, January 10–12, 1863, Gordon Papers, ISHL; Joseph P. Lesslie to wife and folks at home, January 20, 1863, Fourth Indiana Cavalry file, VNMP; Marshall, "Reminiscences," 35–36; Black, "Recollections," 33–34; Abernethy, "Incidents," 410; John H. Ferree to brother, May 9, 1863, Ferree Papers, IHS; Eddington memoir, 6–7; Hunt, "Chickasaw Bayou"; Henry Clemons to wife, January 15, 1863, Clemons Letters, WHSA.

21. Simon, *Grant Papers*, 7:223, 233–34; *OR*, 24-3, 44, 78–79; Bearss, *Vicksburg*, 1:470, 472; J. K. Newton to father and mother, February 28, 1863, Eleventh Wisconsin File, VNMP; C. P. Alling, "Four Years with the Western Army in the Civil War of the United States, 1861–1865," 6, Eleventh Wisconsin File, VNMP; James C. Vanderbilt to mother, February 26 and March 6, 1863, Vanderbilt Papers, ISL; Seneca Thrall to wife, February 14, 1863, Thrall Papers, UI; Lewis Trefftzs to brother, March 14, 1863, Louis Trefftzs Papers, ISHL; Charles Thompkins to wife, February 10, 1863, Thompkins Papers, DU; William C. Caldwell to mother, March 29, 1863, Caldwell Papers, University of Michigan, Bentley Library (hereafter cited as UM); William A. Lorimer memoir, n.p., Seventeenth Illinois File, VNMP; P. C. Bonney letter, March 3, 1863, excerpts from Winifred Keen Armstrong, ed., *The Civil War Letters of Pvt. P. C. Bonney*, Publication of the Lawrence County Historical Society, Lawrenceville, Ill., 1963, in Thirty-first Illinois File, VNMP; Bearss, *Vicksburg*, 1:477–78.

22. *ORN*, 23:709; *ORN*, 24:244, 246–47, 251, 255, 262–64, 266, 268, 272–76, 280–84, 294, 296–97, 299–300; *OR*, 24-1, 17, 20, 368, 378, 373–74, 380–83, 389, 390, 393–94,

396–98, 403, 405–6, 412–17; *OR*, 24-3, 36, 56–57, 86–87, 94, 98, 105, 112–14, 118, 123, 662, 626, 629–30, 638–39, 641, 643–46, 649, 652, 656–57, 622, 680, 721–22; Bearss, *Vicksburg*, 1:482–83, 510–11, 521–26; Katherine Polk Gale, "Reminiscences of Life in the Southern Confederacy, 1861–1865," 10–11A, Gale and Polk Family Papers, UNCCH; L. C. Sheppard, "A Confederate Girlhood," 25–27, Sheppard memoir, UNCCH; S. H. M. Byers, *With Fire and Sword* (New York, 1911), 50–51; "An Account of Lyman Baker in Union Army," 4, Baker Papers, ISHL; Frances Marion Baxter, "My Service in the Confederate Army from April, 1861 to May 22, 1865," Baxter Papers, MDAH; John V. Boucher to Mrs. J. V. Boucher, April 12, 1863, Boucher Papers, USAMHI; "An Account of Lyman Baker in Union Army," 4, Baker Papers, ISHL; A. T. Mahan, *Gulf and Inland Waters* (New York, 1883), 145; Karl Kreible to Wilhelmine, March 21, 1863, Kreible Letters, Journals/Diaries/Letters Subseries of Vicksburg Campaign Series, VNMP; Golden, unpublished history of Thirty-seventh Alabama, 382–83, T. Michael Parrish Personal Collection.

23. James L. Alcorn to wife, March 16, 1863, Alcorn Papers, MDAH; *OR*, 24-1, 21, 432–39, 448, 460, 455–59, 465–66, 474; *OR*, 24-3, 112–13; *OR*, 52-2, 436, 680, 682, 684; *ORN*, 24:474–77, 485, 487–88, 493–95, 668; Pemberton to commander, Yazoo City, March 19, 1863, RG 109, chap. II, vol. 60, NA; Porter, *Incidents*, 160–61; Sherman, *Memoirs*, 230–33; Sidney Champion to Matilda Champion, March 29, 1863, Champion Papers, DU; Bearss, *Vicksburg*, 1:566; Pemberton to Jefferson Davis, March 28, 1863, RG 109, vol. 60, chap. II, NA; E. D. Willett, *History of Company B (Originally Pickens Planters): 40th Alabama Regiment, Confederate States Army, 1862–1865* (Jackson, Miss., 1963), 31.

24. *OR*, 24-1, 407–9, 419–20; *OR*, 24-3, 127, 134, 669, 671, 677–80, 686–96; *ORN*, 24:287; Bearss, *Vicksburg*, 1:537; Robert Shields to sister (Nellie Constant), March 29, 1863, Shields Papers, ISL; E. P. Stanfield to father, March 30, 1863, Stanfield Papers, IHS; James K. Newton to father and mother, April 18, 1863, Fourteenth Wisconsin File, VNMP.

25. Bearss, *Vicksburg*, 2:43–51.

CHAPTER 6. VICKSBURG: FINAL BATTLES AND SIEGE

1. Grant, *Memoirs*, 295–96, 305; *OR*, 24-3, 151–52, 168, 179–80; *OR*, 24-1, 74; *ORN*, 24:520; Bearss, *Vicksburg*, 2:27.

2. *OR*, 24-3, 724, 730–31, 745, 752–53, 760, 773.

3. Crooke, *Twenty-first Iowa*, 49, 53; Daniel Buchwalter diary, April 4, 1863, 120th Ohio File, VNMP; S. H. Stephenson to brother, April 18, 1863, Forty-eighth Ohio File, VNMP; W. H. Raynor diary, April 16, 1863, Fifty-sixth Ohio File, VNMP; W. L. Rand to parents, April 20, 1863, Rand Papers, ISHL; Bernard Schermerhorn to wife, April 19, 1863, Schermerhorn Papers, IHS; Asa E. Sample diary, April 14, 1863, Sample Papers, IHS.

4. Ballard, *Vicksburg*, 208–10.

5. *OR*, 24-3, 132, 186, 188, 740, 212, 215–16; *OR*, 24-1, 70–78, 567–68; *ORN*, 24:553, 555–58, 563–64, 566, 682, 697–98, 704; Bearss, *Vicksburg*, 2:53, 58–59, 65–68, 73–74, 76–79, 80–82; Porter, *Incidents*, 175; Nathan Dye to father and family, April 16, 1863, Dye Papers, DU; F. Grant, "General Grant," *National Tribune*, January 20, 1887; Walker, *Vicksburg*, 151–52; A. B. Balch, "Memories of Soldiers by One of Them," Joseph Forrest Papers, ISHL; A. L. Dorsey to father and mother, April 21, 1863, Forty-third Georgia File, VNMP.

6. Jack Hurst, *Nathan Bedford Forrest: A Biography* (New York, 1993), 117–24. On Grierson's raid, see Dee Alexander Brown, *Grierson's Raid: A Cavalry Adventure of the Civil War* (Urbana, Ill., 1962); and Benjamin Grierson, *A Just and Righteous Cause: Benjamin Grierson's Civil War Memoir*, ed. Bruce J. Dinges and Shirley A. Leckie (Carbondale, Ill., 2008), 134–86.

7. Ballard, *Vicksburg*, 212–13.

8. Bearss, *Vicksburg*, 2:258; *OR*, 24-1, 256, 678; *OR*, 24-3, 797, 800, 804.

9. Bearss, *Vicksburg*, 2:269–70, 311, 314; F. Grant, "General Grant," *National Tribune*, January 20, 1887; William Warren Rogers Jr., ed., "'The Prospects of Our Country Are Gloomy Indeed': Stephen Crooms at Vicksburg (April 1863)," *Journal of Mississippi History* 59 (Spring 1997): 43–44; *OR*, 24-1, 663–64; *ORN*, 24:626–28, 607–8, 610–11, 613, 615–23, 625–26; Crooke, *Twenty-first Iowa*, 53–54; W. H. Raynor diary, April 29, 1863, Fifty-sixth Ohio File, VNMP; Bevier, *History*, 412; Hobbs diary, April 29(?)/30(?), 1863, Ninety-ninth Illinois File, VNMP; Grant, *Memoirs*, 317.

10. *OR*, 24-1, 48, 143, 601, 615, 621, 628, 631, 663–64, 672, 678, 658; Grant, *Memoirs*, 317–18, 321; A. B. Hubbell to William T. Rigby, April 30, 1908, Forty-second Ohio File, VNMP; F. Grant, "General Grant," *National Tribune*, January 27, 1887; Bearss, *Vicksburg*, 2:318, 346, 353; S. C. Jones, *Reminiscences of the Twenty-second Iowa* (Iowa City, Iowa, 1993), 29–30; Hobbs diary, May 1, 1863, Ninety-ninth Illinois File, VNMP; L. B. Jessup diary, May 2(?), 1863, excerpts in letter to William T. Rigby, June 10, 1902, Twenty-fourth Indiana File, VNMP.

11. *OR*, 24-1, 143, 413, 586–92, 643, 668, 670, 673, 678, 664, 679–81; Hobbs diary, May 1, 1863, Ninety-ninth Illinois File, VNMP; Minor Ellis to uncle (W. W. Thomas), June 2, 1863, Thomas Papers, IHS; Frances Obenchain to William Rigby, July 4, 1903, Virginia Botetourt Artillery File, VNMP; William Milner Kelly, "A History of the Thirtieth Alabama Volunteers (Infantry), Confederate States Army," *Alabama Historical Quarterly* 9 (Spring 1947): 135–36; "Journal of the 46th Regiment, 1861–1865," Augustus Sinks Papers, ISL.

12. *OR*, 24-1, 145, 180–81, 585, 593, 603, 627, 652, 672–73, 144–45, 599, 602, 606–7, 610–11, 662, 664, 668, 675–76; Hobbs diary, May 1, 1863, Ninety-ninth Illinois File, VNMP; Bearss, *Vicksburg*, 2:379; Chambers, "My Journal," 264; Bevier, *History*, 177–78; Joseph Bowker diary, May 1, 1863, Forty-second Ohio File, VNMP; William R. Eddington, "My Civil War Memoirs and Other Experiences," 8, Eddington Papers, ISHL; Anderson, *Memoirs*, 298–99.

13. Bearss, *Vicksburg*, 2:431–35; Ballard, *Pemberton*, 134, 144–45; *OR*, 24-3, 810–13, 828, 830, 835, 839, 841–45, 850; Charles S. Howell to father, May 5, 1863, Howell-Taylor Family Papers, USAMHI; *OR*, 24-2, 69, 336; *OR*, 24-1, 259.

14. *OR*, 24-1, 32–33; Ballard, *Vicksburg*, 257–59.

15. *OR*, 24-1, 259, 261; *OR*, 24-3, 849, 851–66; Bearss, *Vicksburg*, 2:479–81.

16. *OR*, 24-3, 853; *OR*, 24-1, 737, 646, 715–17, 718, 728, 740–46, 748, 775, 782; *OR*, 24-2, 297; Henry D. Dwight, "A Soldier's Story," USAMHI; Bearss, *Vicksburg*, 2:498, 511; Jones, *Reminiscences*, 33.

17. Bowker diary, May 15, 1863, Forty-second Ohio File, VNMP; John P. Davis diary, May 13, 1863, Davis Papers, ISHL; Lavinia to Emmie, [June(?) 1863], Crutcher-Shannon Papers, MDAH; Letitia D. Miller, "Some Recollections of Letitia D. Miller," 10–11, Miller Collection, UNCCH; Sample diary, May 16, 1863, IHS; George Hovey Cadman, quoted in Grimsley, *Hard Hand of War*, 157.

18. Bearss, *Vicksburg*, 2:512–13; Grant, *Memoirs*, 332; *OR*, 24-3, 300–301; *OR*, 24-1, 638, 729, 734; *OR*, 24-2, 198.

19. *OR*, 24-1, 51, 215, 239, 639, 751, 753–54, 759–60, 766, 770, 775, 782, 785–87; *OR*, 24-3, 310; Johnston, *Narrative*, 172, 174–75; Grant, *Memoirs*, 333, 337–38; F. Grant, "General Grant," *National Tribune*, February 3, 1887; Feis, *Grant's Secret Service*, 162.

20. *OR*, 24-1, 754; *OR*, 24-2, 251; *OR*, 24-3, 315; Grant, *Memoirs*, 338; John J. Pettus to Jefferson Davis, May 16, 1863, Pettus Papers, RG 12, MDAH; Davis diary, May 15, 1863, ISHL; Anonymous to mother, May 26, 1863, Sixth Ohio File, *Civil War Times Illustrated* Collection, USAMHI; William McGlothin diary, May 14, 1863, McGlothin Papers, USAMHI; Sherman, *Memoirs*, 242; Scott, *Story of a Cavalry Regiment*, 85; Arthur J. L. Fremantle, *Three Months in the Southern States* (Edinburgh and London, 1863, 1884), 109–10.

21. Ballard, *Pemberton*, 154–56; *OR*, 24-3, 877; *OR*, 24-2, 125; *OR*, 24-1, 261.

22. *OR*, 24-1, 262; *OR*, 24-2, 74–75, 87, 90, 93, 107, 110–14, 124; Smith, *Compelled to Appear in Print*, 96; Ballard, *Pemberton*, 158–59; William A. Drennan diary, May 30–July 4, 1863, 4, MDAH.

23. *OR*, 24-2, 75, 83, 91, 93–94; *OR*, 24-1, 263; *OR*, 24-3, 884.

24. *OR*, 24-2, 104, 108, 110, 116; Drennan diary, 4, MDAH.

25. *OR*, 24-2, 41–42, 48–49, 53, 55, 57–58, 75, 95, 99, 100–105, 110, 122; *OR*, 24-1, 52, 639, 640, 647, 709, 717–18; Samuel L. Ensminger to William T. Rigby, September 29, 1900, Eleventh Indiana File, VNMP; Jessup diary, May 16, 1863, Twenty-fourth Indiana File, VNMP; Charles Wood diary, May 16, 1863, Twenty-ninth Wisconsin File, VNMP; Lee, "Campaign of Vicksburg," 40, 42; Samuel Gordon to wife, May 25, 1863, Gordon Papers, ISHL; Ulysses S. Grant, "The Vicksburg Campaign," *B&L*, 3:511.

26. *OR*, 24-2, 110–12, 116, 120–21, 49–50, 55–56; Anderson, *Memoirs*, 311–13; Bevier, *History*, 187–88; Bearss, *Vicksburg*, 2:608; A. H. Reynolds, "Vivid Experiences at Champion Hill," excerpted from *Confederate Veteran*, Nineteenth Arkansas File, VNMP; Byers, *With Fire and Sword*, 78–79; "Experiences of Lyman Baker," 9, Baker Papers, ISHL.

27. *OR*, 24-1, 265; *OR*, 24-2, 74, 76–78, 81, 89–90, 92, 256; Smith, *Compelled to Appear in Print*, 135; George H. Forney to Ma, May 27, 1863, Forney Papers, DU; B. J. Williams to William T. Rigby, June 30, 1905, Fourth Indiana Cavalry File, VNMP; Ballard, *Vicksburg*, 308.

28. *OR*, 24-1, 266, 268–69, 617, 640–41, 648; *OR*, 24-2, 27, 33, 73, 113, 132, 139, 205, 251, 400–401, 23, 119–20, 137; Bearss, *Vicksburg*, 2:655–56; Bevier, *History*, 194–95; J. G. Fox diary, n.d., ISHL; Joseph W. Westbrook memoir, 4, Westbrook Papers, USAMHI; S. H. Lockett, "The Defense of Vicksburg," *B&L*, 3:488; Anderson, *Memoirs*, 319; Bowker diary, May 17, 1863, Forty-second Ohio File, VNMP; Sherman, *Memoirs*, 352.

29. Ballard, *Pemberton*, 3–4, 165–66; Lockett, "Defense of Vicksburg," *B&L*, 3:488.

30. *OR*, 24-2, 172, 179, 199–200; Bearss, *Vicksburg*, 3:905.

31. Bowker diary, June 23, 1863, Forty-second Ohio File, VNMP; W. H. Raynor diary, June 3, 28, 1863, Fifty-sixth Ohio File, VNMP; Charles Schenimann to mother, June 26, 2863, Twenty-ninth Missouri (Union) file, VNMP; S. H. Stephenson to parents, July 2, 1863, Forty-eighth Ohio File, VNMP; E. J. Irwin to mother, June 28, 1863, Irwin Family Papers, UM; Henry Brush to father, June 26, 1863, Brush Family Papers, ISHL; John Harris to mother, June 15, 1863, Harris Papers, ISHL; Richard Hall to mother and father, July 2, 1863, Hall Papers, LSU; Pinckney S. Cone diary, June 14, 1863, Cone Papers, ISHL;

John Travis to sister, May 25, 1863, Travis Family Letters, UM; Clark Whitten to wife, June 23, July 11, 1863, Whitten Papers, USAMHI.

32. Ballard, *Vicksburg*, 320–24; *OR*, 24-2, 13, 19, 33, 159–60, 229, 268, 237, 266–67, 402, 406–7; *OR*, 24-1, 17, 154, 230–31, 273–74; Committee of the Regiment, *Story of the Fifty-fifth*, 237–40; Bearss, *Vicksburg*, 3:766–67.

33. *OR*, 24-3, 334–35, 843–44; *OR*, 24-1, 719, 756–57, 760, 768; *OR*, 55-6, 172–73; *OR*, 24-2, 264, 269, 273, 282, 351–52, 361, 407, 257–58, 297, 300, 415; J. W. Larabee statement on May 22 attack, Fifty-fifth Illinois File, VNMP; Henry S. Nousse to William T. Rigby, November 9, 1901, Fifty-fifth Illinois File, VNMP; George Hildt to William T. Rigby, February 8, 1902, Thirtieth Ohio File, VNMP; W. B. Halsey diary, May 23, 1863, Seventy-second Ohio File, VNMP; Tunnard, *Southern Record*, 239; J. M. Pearson to Stephen D. Lee, May 17, 1902, Thirtieth Alabama File, VNMP; Bearss, *Vicksburg*, 3:840–41, 843–44; Ainsworth diary, 42–49, UM; John W. Niles diary, May 22, 1863, Ninth Iowa File, VNMP; Alonzo Abernethy diary, May 22, 1863, Ninth Iowa File, VNMP.

34. *OR*, 24-3, 368–74, 384, 386, 934, 937–40, 946–47, 951, 953, 955–56, 978, 978; *OR*, 24-2, 214, 325, 436–41, 440, 442; *OR*, 24-1, 194, 224–28, 244; *OR*, 52-1, 359; *ORN*, 25:57–58; Johnston, *Narrative*, 199; Bearss, *Vicksburg*, 3:1010.

35. Ballard, *Vicksburg*, 374–88; Fremantle, *Three Months*, 116, 120, 126.

36. *OR*, 24-2, 107, 155–57, 172–74, 176–77, 179, 181–87, 189–97, 199–203, 207–9, 285, 289–90, 294, 312–13, 317–23, 332–34, 339, 342–43, 363–65, 368, 372, 376–77, 390–91, 407–13, 416, 420–21, 438, 441; *OR*, 24-3, 356, 387, 391–92, 396, 410, 435; *OR*, 24-1, 94, 103, 107–8; Committee of the Regiment, *Story of Fifty-fifth*, 251; Tunnard, *Southern Record*, 246–48; Anderson, *Memoirs*, 345; Grant, *Memoirs*, 345; Andrew Hickenlooper, "The Vicksburg Mine," *B&L*, 3:539–40; O. J. Burnham to father and mother, June 12, 1863, Sixth Wisconsin Light Artillery File, VNMP; William Taylor to Jane, June 28, 1863, 100th Pennsylvania File, VNMP; W. H. Bently to William T. Rigby, February 18, 1903, Seventy-seventh Illinois File, VNMP; Dana, *Recollections*, 82–83; Simpson, *Grant*, 207–8. Siege caves are now closed to the public due to the dangers of cave-ins. According to former director of the MDAH, Elbert Hilliard, one of the caves was added to the National Register of Historic Places in the 1970s. The Vicksburg National Park has a few photographs of the exterior openings of the caves, and exhibits in the Visitors Center at the park demonstrate what cave life was like for civilians. Another site designated as a Mississippi Landmark, according to Hilliard, is high ground called Bailey Hill, where several Union siege guns were located. Some Union earthworks north of the park are on property owned by the University of Mississippi Medical Center, located in Jackson.

37. *OR*, 24-1, 281–86; *OR*, 24-3, 982–83; John Pemberton, "The Terms of Surrender," *B&L*, 3:544; Ballard, *Pemberton*, 180–82; Grant, *Memoirs*, 375–81; Bearss, *Vicksburg*, 3:1302, 1311; Grabau, *Ninety-eight Days*, 502; Bevier, *History*, 218; Tunnard, *Southern Record*, 271; Barney, *Recollections*, 200; William P. Henderson to friend, July 11, [1863], Seventeenth Illinois File, VNMP; O. J. Burnham diary, July 4, 1863, Sixth Wisconsin Light Artillery File, VNMP; Edwin Dean, "Edwin Dean's Civil War Days, 1861–1865," Dean Papers, USAMHI.

38. *OR*, 24-2, 245–46; *OR*, 24-3, 427–28, 430–31, 439, 449; Bearss, *Vicksburg*, 3:1086; William Taylor to Jane, July 11, 1863, 100th Pennsylvania File, VNMP; Willis Herbert Claiborne diary, July 13, 1863, Claiborne Papers, UNCCH; John K. Street to Melinda Street, July 6, 1863, Street Papers, UNCCH; David W. Reed, *Campaigns and Battles of the Twelfth Iowa Regiment, Iowa Veteran Volunteer Infantry* (Evanston, Ill., 1903),

128; MacCutcheon autobiography, "Down the Mississippi," UM; J. W. Pursley to Mary Frances Pursley, July 28, 1863, Pursley Papers, DU; Ballard, *Vicksburg*, 406; Buckley Thomas Foster, *Sherman's Mississippi Campaign* (Tuscaloosa, Ala., 2006), 49.

39. *OR*, 24-2, 541–42, 575; Edwin C. Bearss, *The Siege of Jackson, July 10–17, 1863* (Baltimore, 1981), 81–82, 84–95, 97, 100–103, 105; Johnston, *Narrative*, 211–52; Dunbar Rowland, ed., *Jefferson Davis, Constitutionalist: His Letters, Papers and Speeches*, 10 vols. (Jackson, Miss., 1922), 5:579; Lloyd Lewis, *Sherman: Fighting Prophet* (New York, 1932), 297; Lynda Lasswell Christ, "A Bibliographical Note: Jefferson Davis's Personal Library: Some Lost, Some Found," *Journal of Mississippi History* (August 1983): 186–93.

CHAPTER 7. MERIDIAN CAMPAIGN

1. *OR*, 32-1, 173–74.

2. E. B. Long, *The Civil War Day by Day, an Almanac, 1861–1865* (New York, 1971), 385, 396–98, 408–9, 413, 415, 425–30, 432–36, 443–44, 447, 449; Sherman, *Memoirs*, 260–61, 280–83.

3. *OR*, 32-1, 172, 174, 181–82; Sherman, *Memoirs*, 288.

4. Sherman, *Memoirs*, 335; *OR*, 32-2, 583, 627, 671–72, 574–76; *OR*, 32-1, 174–75, 215, 315–16, 320–26, 357, 382–91; Margie Riddle Bearss, *Sherman's Forgotten Campaign: The Meridian Expedition* (Baltimore, 1987), 35, 64–65.

5. Buckley Thomas Foster, *Sherman's Mississippi Campaign* (Tuscaloosa, Ala., 2006), 50–51; Ballard, *Vicksburg*, 84–85, 102–3, 105–6, 126–27. See also M. Shannon Mallard, "'I Had No Comfort to Give the People': Opposition to the Confederacy in Civil War Mississippi," *North & South* (May 2003): 78–85.

6. Foster, *Sherman*, 52–53, 65–66; Ballard, *Vicksburg*, 270, 285–86; Bearss, *Sherman's Forgotten Campaign*, 79, 90–93.

7. *OR*, 32-2, 684, 690, 692–93; Bearss, *Sherman's Forgotten Campaign*, 108, 100–101; *OR*, 32-1, 175.

8. *OR*, 32-1, 211; Bearss, *Sherman's Forgotten Campaign*, 110–11, 117–19; Foster, *Sherman*, 80; *OR*, 32-2, 693, 700–701, 722, 725.

9. Sherman, *Memoirs*, 293–94; Foster, *Sherman*, 87–88; *OR*, 31-1, 227; Bearss, *Sherman's Forgotten Campaign*, 137–55.

10. *OR*, 32-1, 175–76; Stephen D. Lee, "Operations of the Cavalry in Mississippi, from January to March, 1864," *SHSP*, 9:99.

11. Bearss, *Sherman's Forgotten Campaign*, 160–61; *OR*, 32-2, 733–34.

12. *OR*, 32-1, 176; Bearss, *Sherman's Forgotten Campaign*, 164–65; Foster, *Meridian*, 109–11.

13. *OR*, 32-1, 176; Bearss, *Sherman's Forgotten Campaign*, 184, 188; Stephen D. Lee, "Sherman's Meridian Expedition and Sooy Smith's Raid to West Point," *SHSP*, 8:54.

14. *OR*, 32-1, 176, 181–82; *OR*, 32-2, 316–17; George E Waring Jr., "The Sooy Smith Expedition," in *B&L*, 4:417–18n; Foster, *Meridian*, 127–28.

15. *OR*, 32-2, 346; *OR*, 32-1, 256–57, 351–52.

16. *OR*, 32-1, 257; Grierson, *Memoir*, 217–18, 220; Lee, "Sherman's Meridian Expedition," 57.

17. *OR*, 32-1, 176–78, 194, 257–58, 352–55, 369.

18. See John F. Marszalek, *Sherman: A Soldier's Passion for Order* (New York, 1993), 255–56, 294; Foster, *Sherman*, 173–75. See also Grimsley, *Hard Hand of War*, 162–70.

CHAPTER 8. BRICE'S CROSSROADS

1. Grant, *Memoirs*, 471–72, 475; Sherman, *Memoirs*, 368; *OR*, 39-2, 33, 73; *OR*, 39-1, 221–22.

2. Grierson, *Memoir*, 235. On the Fort Pillow massacre, see John Cimprinch, *Fort Pillow; A Civil War Massacre and Public Memory* (Baton Rouge, La., 2005).

3. Grierson, *Memoir*, 227, 233–34; *OR*, 39-1, 85–86, 90.

4. Edwin C. Bearss, *Forrest at Brice's Cross Roads and in North Mississippi* (Dayton, Ohio, 1979), 10–11, 12–13, 20; *OR*, 39-1, 221–22.

5. Bearss, *Forrest*, 221–22, 26–30, 30–32, 62; *OR*, 38-4, 690; *OR*, 39-1, 221–22; *OR*, 39-2, 222; John Watson Morton, *The Artillery of Nathan Bedford Forrest's Cavalry, "The Wizard of the Saddle"* (Kennesaw, Ga., 1962), 174.

6. *OR*, 39-1, 222; Bearss, *Forrest*, 62–63; Papers of the Blue and Gray Education Society; Parker Hills, *A Study in Warfighting: Nathan Bedford Forrest and the Battle of Brice's Crossroads* (Saline, Mich., 1996), 24.

7. Grierson, *Memoir*, 235, 239–40, 237–41; Bearss, *Forrest*, 11, 44–51; *OR*, 39-1, 86, 90–91.

8. *OR*, 39-1, 89–90, 172; John Allen Wyeth, *Life of Lieutenant-General Nathan Bedford Forrest* (New York, 1908), 400; Grierson, *Memoir*, 243.

9. Bearss, *Forrest*, 65–66; *OR*, 39-1, 129, 222–23; Grierson, *Memoir*, 243–45.

10. *OR*, 39-1, 223; Bearss, *Forrest*, 134; Morton, *Artillery*, 175–76.

11. *OR*, 39-1, 92–93, 104, 129; Grierson, *Memoir*, 247–48.

12. *OR*, 39-1, 223–24; John A. Wyeth, *That Devil Forrest: Life of General Nathan Bedford Forrest* (New York, 1959), 364.

13. Grierson, *Memoir*, 248–49; *OR*, 39-1, 93, 129, 133.

14. *OR*, 39-1, 125–26, 214; Morton, *Artillery*, 177.

15. Bearss, *Forrest*, 135–36; Grierson, *Memoir*, 250–51; *OR*, 39-1, 94; Morton, *Artillery*, 179–80. See Morton, *Artillery*, 184–91, on the controversy over black troops.

16. Grierson, *Memoir*, 251; Wyeth, *That Devil*, 369; Bearss, *Forrest*, 118.

17. Grierson, *Memoir*, 255–56; Bearss, *Forrest*, 138; Hills, *Study in Warfighting*, 52–58.

18. *OR*, 39-1, 227, 230–31; Wyeth, *That Devil*, 371.

19. *OR*, 39-2, 118, 121, 123–24, 130.

20. *OR*, 39-1, 172, 176, 181, 197, 198, 113.

21. Grierson, *Memoir*, 256.

CHAPTER 9. TUPELO (HARRISBURG)

1. *OR*, 39-2, 121, 121, 123; *OR*, 39-1, 249; Mark W. Boatner III, *The Civil War Dictionary* (New York, 1959), 290; Marszalek, *Sherman*, 269–70.

2. Joseph E. Johnston, "Opposing Sherman's Advance to Atlanta," *B&L*, 4:276; Wyeth, *That Devil*, 377–78.

3. Wyeth, *That Devil*, 242–43, 378; Hurst, *Forrest*, 198; Steven E. Woodworth, *Jefferson Davis and His Generals: The Failure of Confederate Command in the West* (Lawrence, Kans., 1990), 244.

4. *OR*, 39-1, 250, 259, 279, 295, 300; Thomas Jordan and J. P. Pryor, *The Campaigns of Lieut.-Gen. N. B. Forrest and of Forrest's Cavalry* (Dayton, Ohio, 1977), 519; Frank

Allen Dennis, "Tupelo: 14–15 July 1864," in *The Civil War Battlefield Guide*, ed. Francis H. Kennedy (Boston, 1990), 196; John Scott, *Story of the Thirty Second Iowa Infantry Volunteers* (Nevada, Iowa, 1896), 290–91; Reed, *Campaigns*, 151; *OR*, 39-1, 250, 320; Bearss, *Forrest*, 168.

5. *OR*, 39-1, 250, 320–21; Stephen D. Lee, "The Battle of Tupelo, or Harrisburg, July 14, 1863," in *Publications of the Mississippi Historical Society*, vol. 6, ed. Franklin L. Riley (Oxford, Miss., 1902), 42.

6. *OR*, 39-1, 250–51, 321, 325–26; Hurst, *Forrest*, 199–200; Lee, "Battle of Tupelo," 41; Grierson, *Memoir*, 262–63; Morton, *Artillery*, 206; Bearss, *Forrest*, 200.

7. *OR*, 39-1, 234, 251, 321, 301, 322, 265.

8. Ibid., 265, 326; Lee, "Battle of Tupelo," 43; Bearss, *Forrest*, 183–84.

9. *OR*, 39-1, 276–77, 330, 336, 347.

10. Ibid., 251, 304; Reed, *Campaigns*, 153–54; Bearss, *Forrest*, 189.

11. Bearss, *Forrest*, 189, 193; Dennis, "Tupelo," 197; Morton, *Artillery*, 204–5.

12. Lee, "Battle of Tupelo," 44–45; Morton, *Artillery*, 210; Lee quoted in Wyeth, *That Devil*, 386; Wyeth, *That Devil*, 400–401; Bearss, *Forrest*, 197.

13. Bearss, *Forrest*, 197–98; *OR*, 39-1, 322, 330, 347; Bearss, *Forrest*, 194; Lee, "Battle of Tupelo," 42; Dennis, "Tupelo," 197; Herman Hattaway, *General Stephen D. Lee* (Jackson, Miss., 1976), 120–21.

14. Lee, "Battle of Tupelo," 45; *OR*, 39-1, 322–23, 280, 282, 295, 299, 326, 336, 331, 349–50, 326, 347.

15. *OR*, 39-1, 252, 257–58, 267, 272, 277, 320, 322–23; Dennis, "Tupelo," 197; Lee, "Battle of Tupelo," 48.

16. *OR*, 39-1, 252, 323, 328; Lee, "Battle of Tupelo," 48; Bearss, *Forrest*, 213, 214; Wyeth, *That Devil*, 375, 396.

17. *OR*, 39-1, 252, 280–81, 295–96, 302, 327.

18. Ibid., 323, 252–53, 331–32, 303.

19. Ibid., 253, 258, 263, 327, 332, 337, 348, 281, 187; Lee, "Battle of Tupelo," 49.

20. *OR*, 39-1, 323–24, 327; Wyeth, *That Devil*, 398.

21. *OR*, 39-1, 249, 253, 256; Wyeth, *That Devil*, 398.

22. Wyeth, *That Devil*, 406–7; Hattaway, *Lee*, 124; Brian Steel Wills, *A Battle from the Start: The Life of Nathan Bedford Forrest* (New York, 1992), 231; Lee, "Battle of Tupelo," 51–52.

23. Hurst, *Forrest*, 207; Morton, *Artillery*, 210–11; Bearss, *Forrest*, 232.

CHAPTER 10. MORE RAIDS

1. *OR*, 39-2, 184, 201, 203–4.

2. Ibid., 202, 217, 219.

3. Grierson, *Memoir*, 271; *OR*, 39-2, 207, 222–33.

4. Bearss, *Forrest*, 241; *OR*, 39-1, 375.

5. *OR*, 39-1, 377; Grierson, *Memoir*, 272.

6. *OR*, 39-2, 715–17; Bearss, *Forrest*, 248–49; Jordan and Pryor, *Campaigns*, 521.

7. *OR*, 39-2, 719–20, 731.

8. Ibid., 743–44

9. Jordan and Pryor, *Campaigns*, 521–22; Wyeth, *That Devil*, 407–8; *OR*, 39-2, 731; Bearss, *Forrest*, 252.

10. *OR*, 39-2, 747. See also Bearss, *Forrest*, 253–54, 256.

11. *OR*, 39-2, 749; Bearss, *Forrest*, 252–53; Jordan and Pryor, *Campaigns*, 521, 523.

12. Bearss, *Forrest*, 253–56; Jordan and Pryor, *Campaigns*, 526–28; Wyeth, *That Devil*, 408.

13. Bearss, *Forrest*, 259–60; *OR*, 39-1, 375–76; Wyeth, *That Devil*, 409.

14. Jordan and Pryor, *Campaigns*, 529; Wyeth, *That Devil*, 409; Bearss, *Forrest*, 260.

15. *OR*, 39-1, 375–76; Bearss, *Forrest*, 261; Jordan and Pryor, *Campaigns*, 528.

16. *OR*, 39-2, 235–36, 764; *OR*, 39-1, 388; Wyeth, *That Devil*, 409; Bearss, *Forrest*, 261–62.

17. Jordan and Pryor, *Campaigns*, 528–29; Bearss, *Forrest*, 262–63; *OR*, 39-1, 372, 376, 388–89, 394.

18. Bearss, *Forrest*, 263–64; Jordan and Pryor, *Campaigns*, 532; *OR*, 39-2, 765–66.

19. *OR*, 39-2, 765; Bearss, *Forrest*, 264.

20. *OR*, 39-1, 372, 389, 395; Bearss, *Forrest*, 264–66; Jordan and Pryor, *Campaigns*, 528–29.

21. *OR*, 39-1, 389–90, 395, 400; *OR*, 39-2, 238–39, 767; Jordan and Pryor, *Campaigns*, 529–30; Bearss, *Forrest*, 266–67.

22. Bearss, *Forrest*, 268; Jordan and Pryor, *Campaigns*, 530–31; *OR*, 39-2, 389.

23. Jordan and Pryor, *Campaigns*, 530–31; Bearss, *Forrest*, 268–69; *OR*, 39-2, 769.

24. *OR*, 39-2, 242, 377–78, 382, 385, 393; Hurst, *Nathan Bedford Forrest*, 211.

25. *OR*, 39-1, 382, 389; Bearss, *Forrest*, 273–74; Jordan and Pryor, *Campaigns*, 532; Wills, *Battle*, 238.

26. *OR*, 39-1, 372, 374–75, 377–78, 382, 385, 387, 389, 390–91, 393; *OR*, 39-2, 261, 267; Bearss, *Forrest*, 275–78; Jordan and Pryor, *Campaigns*, 532–33; Hurst, *Forrest*, 212; Wills, *Battle*, 238–39.

27. Bearss, *Forrest*, 281–82; Jordan and Pryor, *Campaigns*, 533–36; Hurst, *Forrest*, 212; Wills, *Battle*, 239–40; Wyeth, *That Devil*, 411; *OR*, 39-1, 469; *OR*, 39-2, 765, 783.

28. Bearss, *Forrest*, 283–84; Jordan and Pryor, *Campaigns*, 536–37; Wyeth, *That Devil*, 412; Wills, *Battle*, 239–40.

29. *OR*, 39-1, 471; Jordan and Pryor, *Campaigns*, 537; Wyeth, *That Devil*, 412; Bearss, *Forrest*, 284.

30. Wyeth, *That Devil*, 412–13; Jordan and Pryor, *Campaigns*, 536–38; Bearss, *Forrest*, 284–85.

31. Bearss, *Forrest*, 285–86.

32. Since Forrest's raid did not happen in Mississippi, I have offered only a very brief summary of the details of the attack on Memphis. I have, however, indicated its significance and its success. For more on the raid, see Bearss, *Forrest*, 286–92, 298n16; Wyeth, *That Devil*, 413–16; Jordan and Pryor, *Campaigns*, 539–43; *OR*, 39-1, 469, 472–75, 477–79, 482–83.

33. *OR*, 39-1, 471–74, 476–77, 480–81, 484; *OR*, 39-2, 792, 795; Jordan and Pryor, *Campaigns*, 546–48; Bearss, *Forrest*, 295–97; Wills, *Battle*, 244–45; Wyeth, *That Devil*, 420–21; Jordan and Pryor, *Campaigns*, 547–48.

34. Bearss, *Forrest*, 301–3; *OR*, 39-2, 265–66, 783, 276–77; *OR*, 39-1, 377, 378, 380, 382, 383, 389, 377, 396–98.

35. *OR*, 39-1, 372–73, 376, 379, 381, 391, 393, 378, 380–82, 385, 387, 389, 391–92, 399, 400, 469–70; *OR*, 39-2, 791; Jordan and Pryor, *Campaigns*, 549, 550–52; Bearss, *Forrest*, 304–7, 309–10.

36. *OR*, 39-1, 372–74, 376, 377, 379, 381, 382, 383, 387, 388, 389, 392–93, 395, 399; Jordan and Pryor, *Campaigns*, 552; Bearss, *Forrest*, 309–10.

37. *OR*, 39-2, 270, 298, 301, 305; Bearss, *Forrest*, 312–13.

38. Bearss, *Forrest*, 313–38; *OR*, 39-1, 388–90, 392; *OR*, 39-2, 797–99, 301–2, 310.

39. Grierson, *Memoir*, 282–303. Some of Grierson's account of his raid in his memoir is taken from his report in *OR*, 45-1, 844–47. The only other published account of the raid is Edwin C. Bearss, "Grierson's Winter Raid on the Mobile and Ohio Railroad," *Military Affairs* 24 (June 1960): 20–37.

40. *OR*, 41-4, 782.

41. Ibid., 903–4.

42. Grierson, *Memoir*, 301–2; Naron, *Chickasaw*, 143.

43. Grierson, *Memoir*, 302; *OR*, 45-1, 866–67.

44. Grierson, *Memoir*, 302–4, 312–13; *OR*, 45-1, 848, 854, 862, 871.

45. Grierson, *Memoir*, 304–6; *OR*, 45-1, 861, 863–64, 870–71; Naron, *Chickasaw*, 145, 151–52.

46. Grierson, *Memoir*, 306–8, 313; *OR*, 45-1, 868–69, 872–73; J. P. Coleman, *Choctaw Chronicles: A History of Choctaw County, Mississippi, 1830–1973* (Spartanburg, S.C., 1981), 78–79; Edwards property claims, December 30, 1864, Edward D. Edwards Family Papers, Manuscripts Division, Special Collections Department, Mississippi State University Libraries.

47. Grierson, *Memoir*, 308–9, 313; *OR*, 45-1, 858, 875; Naron, *Chickasaw*, 157.

48. Grierson, *Memoir*, 309–14, 411; *OR*, 45-1, 846–47; Naron, *Chickasaw*, 147, 161.

APPENDIX

1. S. G. Spann, "Choctaw Indians as Confederate Soldiers," http://www.choctaw.org/history/confederate.htm; "The Civil War in Mississippi, http://www.researchonline.net/mscw/unit20.htm; "Confederate Troops," 2, http://rebelcherokee.labdiva.com/cwit/rebeltroops.html; Charles E. Hooker, *Confederate Military History*, vol. 9, ed. Clement A. Evans (Wilmington, N.C., 1987), 130.

2. I am indebted to James Hollandsworth of Jackson, Mississippi, for sharing information regarding the number of Mississippi black troops.

3. Noah Andre Trudeau, "Proven Themselves in Every Respect to Be Men: Black Cavalry in the Civil War," in *Black Soldiers in Blue: African American Troops in the Civil War Era*, ed. John David Smith (Chapel Hill, N.C., 2002), 279, 284, 291, 301n8; Frederick H. Dyer, *A Compendium of the War of the Rebellion*, 3 vols. (New York, 1959), 3:1343; Edwin M. Main, *The Story of Marches, Battles, and Incidents of the Third United States Colored Cavalry: A Fighting Regiment in the War of the Rebellion, 1861–5* (Lexington, Ky., 1908).

4. John David Smith, "Let Us All Be Grateful That We Have Colored Troops That Will Fight," in Smith, *Black Soldiers*, 55; Richard Lowe, "Battle on the Levee: The Fight at Milliken's Bend," in Smith, *Black Soldiers*, 110, 117–18, 126; Dyer, *Compendium*, 3:1343–44; see also David Slay, "Abraham Lincoln and the United States Colored Troops of Mississippi," *Journal of Mississippi History* (Spring 2008): 67–86.

SUGGESTED READINGS

Ballard, Michael B. *Civil War Mississippi: A Guide*. Jackson, Miss., 2000.

———. *Pemberton: A Biography*. Jackson, Miss., 1991.

———. *U. S. Grant: The Making of a General, 1861–1863*. Lanham, Md., 2005.

———. *Vicksburg: The Campaign That Opened the Mississippi*. Chapel Hill, N.C., 2004.

Bearss, Edwin C. *Forrest at Brice's Cross Roads and in North Mississippi*. Dayton, Ohio, 1979.

———. *Rebel Victory at Vicksburg*. Vicksburg, Miss., 1963.

———. *The Vicksburg Campaign*. 3 vols. Dayton, Ohio, 1985–86.

Bearss, Margie Riddle. *Sherman's Forgotten Campaign: The Meridian Expedition*. Baltimore, 1987.

Brown, Dee Alexander. *Grierson's Raid: A Cavalry Adventure of the Civil War*. Urbana, Ill., 1962.

Bynum, Victoria E. *The Free State of Jones: Mississippi's Longest Civil War*. Chapel Hill, N.C., 2001.

Carter, Arthur B. *The Tarnished Cavalier: Major Earl Van Dorn, C.S.A.* Knoxville, Tenn., 1999.

Castel, Albert. *General Sterling Price and the Civil War in the West*. Baton Rouge, La., 1968.

Cozzens, Peter. *The Darkest Days of the War: The Battles of Corinth and Iuka*. Chapel Hill, N.C., 1997.

Davis, William C. *Breckinridge: Statesman, Soldier, Symbol*. Baton Rouge, La., 1974.

Dubay, Robert W. *John Jones Pettus: Mississippi Fireater, His Life and Times*. Jackson, Miss., 1975.

Duffy, James P. *Lincoln's Admiral: The Civil War Campaigns of David Farragut*. New York, 1997.

Foster, Buckley Thomas. *Sherman's Mississippi Campaign*. Tuscaloosa, Ala., 2006.

Giambrone, Jeff T. *Beneath Torn and Tattered Flags: A History of the 38th Mississippi Infantry, C.S.A.* Bolton, Miss., 1998.

Grabau, Warren E. *Ninety-eight Days: A Geographer's View of the Vicksburg Campaign*. Knoxville, Tenn., 2000.

Grant, U. S. *Memoirs and Selected Letters: Personal Memoirs of U. S. Grant, Selected Letters, 1839–1865*, 2 vols. in 1. New York, 1990.

Grierson, Benjamin. *A Just and Righteous Cause: Benjamin Grierson's Civil War Memoir*. Ed. Bruce J. Dinges and Shirley A. Leckie. Carbondale, Ill., 2008.

Grimsley, Mark. *The Hard Hand of War: Union Military Policy toward Southern Civilians, 1861–1865*. New York, 1995.

Hattaway, Herman. *General Stephen D. Lee*. Jackson, Miss., 1976.

Hattaway, Herman, and Archer Jones. *How the North Won: A Military History of the Civil War*. Urbana, Ill., 1991.

Hearn, Chester G. *Admiral David Dixon Porter: The Civil War Years*. Annapolis, Md., 1996.

———. *Ellet's Brigade: The Strangest Outfit of Them All*. Baton Rouge, La., 2000.

Hoehling, A. A., ed. *Vicksburg: 47 Days of Siege*. Mechanicsburg, Pa., 1996.

Howell, H. Grady, Jr. *Chimneyville: Likenesses of Early Days in Jackson, Mississippi*. Jackson, Miss., 2007.

———. *Going to Meet the Yankees: A History of the "Bloody Sixth" Mississippi Infantry*. Jackson, Miss., 1981.

———. *To Live and Die in Dixie: A History of the Third Regiment Mississippi Volunteer Infantry, C.S.A.* Jackson, Miss., 1991.

Hurst, Jack. *Nathan Bedford Forrest: A Biography*. New York, 1993.

Jordan, Thomas, and J. P. Pryor. *The Campaigns of Lieut.-Gen N. B. Forrest, and of Forrest's Cavalry*. Dayton, Ohio, 1977.

Kiper, Richard L. *Major General John Alexander McClernand: Politician in Uniform*. Kent, Ohio, 1999.

Kitchens, Ben Earl. *Rosecrans Meets Price: The Battle of Iuka*. Florence, Ala., 1987.

Lamers, William M. *The Edge of Glory: A Biography of General William S. Rosecrans, U.S.A.* Baton Rouge, La., 1999.

Marszalek, John F. *Commander of All Lincoln's Armies: A Life of Henry W. Halleck*. Cambridge, Mass., 2004.

———. *Sherman: A Soldier's Passion for Order*. New York, 1993.

Miers, Earl S. *The Web of Victory: Grant at Vicksburg*. New York, 1953.

Naron, Levi H. *Chickasaw: A Mississippi Scout for the Union: The Civil War Memoir of Levi H. Naron, as Recounted by R. W. Surby*. Ed. Thomas D. Cockrell and Michael B. Ballard. Baton Rouge, La., 2005.

Sherman, William T. *Memoirs of William T. Sherman*. 2 vols. in 1. New York, 1984.

Smith, Jean Edward. *Grant*. New York, 2001.

Smith, Timothy. *Champion Hill: Decisive Battle for Vicksburg*. El Dorado Hills, Calif., 2004.

Symonds, Craig L. *Joseph E. Johnston: A Civil War Biography*. New York, 1992.

Wills, Brian Steel. *A Battle from the Start: The Life of Nathan Bedford Forrest*. New York, 1992.

Winschel, Terrence J. *Triumph and Defeat: The Vicksburg Campaign*. Mason City, Iowa, 1999.

Winschel, Terrence J., and William L. Shea. *Vicksburg Is the Key: The Struggle for the Mississippi River*. Lincoln, Neb., 2003.

Woodworth, Steven E. *Jefferson Davis and His Generals: The Failure of Confederate Command in the West*. Lawrence, Kans., 1990.

Wyeth, John A. *That Devil Forrest: Life of General Nathan Bedford Forrest*. New York, 1959.

Wynne, Ben. *Mississippi's Civil War: A Narrative History*. Macon, Ga., 2006.

INDEX

Adams, Wirt, 72, 141, 144, 176, 178, 204, 262, 267, 269–70
Arkansas, C.S.S., 41, 44–45, 48–54, 80
Autry, James, 37

Baldwin, William, 151–52
Barteau, Clark, 211–12
Barton, Seth, 123, 127
Battery Robinett, 96–98
Beauregard, P. G. T., 12–13, 16–22, 25–26, 28–29, 31–33, 43–44, 86, 265, 270
Bell, Tyree, 200, 209–11, 228–29, 234, 237, 241, 252
Big Black River, Battle of, 162–64
Blair, Frank, 122–28, 165
Bouton, Edward, and U.S. Colored troops in the Brice's Crossroads and Tupelo campaigns and battles, and in A. J. Smith's and Grierson's 1864 raids, 202, 212–13, 222, 227–28, 235, 239–40, 242, 245, 270
Bowen, John: and Battle of Corinth, 82–83, 85–88, 92–94, 101, 103; and battles of Champion Hill and Big Black, 160, 162; and campaign and Battle of Port Gibson, 140, 143, 146–47, 149, 151–52; and Siege of Vicksburg, 164
Bragg, Braxton, 16, 17, 28, 33–34, 43, 54–59, 63, 65, 75–76, 78–80, 82, 103, 107, 128, 172, 221–22
Breckinridge, John C., 17, 43–45, 52–53, 57, 65, 82, 171
Brown, Isaac, 49–50, 53, 133
Buell, Don Carlos, 11, 12, 14, 17, 22, 25–27, 30, 33–34, 54–58, 60, 76, 81, 102
Buford, Abraham, 198, 200–1, 209–10, 228–29, 236, 240, 241, 253
Burbridge, Stephen, 125, 127
Butler, Benjamin, 37, 45

Cabell, William L., 87, 92, 94–96, 99–100
Carr, Eugene, 147, 151
Chalmers, James, 199, 228, 234, 236, 246–48, 250–53, 257–59
Champion Hill, Battle of, 159–62
Chickasaw Bayou, Battle of, 118–29
Clark, Charles, 7, 248
Cockrell, Francis, 140, 151–52, 160, 164
Corinth, 15–16, 19
Crossland, Edward, 229, 234, 236

Davies, Thomas, 83, 85–86, 88–92, 94–95
Davis, Charles, 45–46, 48–52
Davis, Jefferson, 4, 5, 6, 17–18, 32–33, 36, 43, 57–58, 80, 110, 118, 152–53, 221, 260
De Courcy, John, 122–24, 126–27
Dickey, Lyle, 64–65, 114

Ellett, Alfred W., 46, 48–49, 129

Farmington, 25, 27
Farragut, David, 35, 37–42, 44–46, 48–51, 54
Forney, John, 158, 164
Forrest, Nathan Bedford, 111, 118, 143, 174, 195, 271; and the Campaign and Battle of Brice's Crossroads, 196–203, 206–19; and the Campaign and Battle of Tupelo, 220–28, 230–36, 238–43; and Meridian Campaign, 189–92; and A. J. Smith's 1864 Mississippi Raid, 244, 246–48, 251–60
French, Samuel, 171; and Meridian Campaign, 175, 178–79
Fuller, John, 96–97

Gardner, Franklin, and Grierson's Winter Raid, 262, 264–67
Garrott, Ishom, 149, 151

Gates, Elijah, 94–95
Gholson, Samuel, 265–66
Grand Gulf, 41–42, 45, 53; Battle of, 146
Grant, Julia, 81, 115
Grant, Ulysses S., 153–54, 156, 162, 173, 195, 244; and actions prior to crossing the Mississippi below Vicksburg, 139–40, 142–44, 146; and Battle of Champion Hill, 158–59; and Battle of Iuka, 56–57, 59–66, 71–75; and Battle of Port Gibson, 152; and Corinth, 11, 13, 14, 20, 22, 27, 31–32, 39, 54; and Corinth (Battle of), 80–82, 92, 98, 101–4; and efforts to bypass Vicksburg, 130–38; and North Mississippi campaign, 105–11, 113–17, 128–30; and Siege of Vicksburg, 164–65, 167–70
Green, Martin, 89–90, 93–95, 147, 149, 151
Gregg, John, 123; and Battle of Jackson, 156, 158; and Battle of Raymond, 153–54
Grierson, Benjamin, 174, 190; and Campaign and Battle of Brice's Crossroads, 197–98, 201–4, 206–12, 214–15, 217, 219; and Campaign and Battle of Tupelo, 222, 226, 229; and 1864–1865 Winter Raid, 260–62, 263–71; and 1863 raid, 143–44; and A. J. Smith's 1864 Raid, 246, 259
Griffith, John S., 108, 111

Halleck, Henry, 13, 14, 16, 18, 20–23, 26–33, 39, 41–42, 48, 54, 58, 62, 75, 79, 81, 105, 195
Hamilton, Charles, 61, 63, 66–71, 73, 75, 85–86, 90–92, 94–95, 106
Hatch, Edward, 250–53, 257–58
Hatchie River, Battle of, 98–101
Hebért, Louis, 68–70, 72, 78, 85, 92–93, 95–96, 129
Hills, Parker, analysis of Forrest victory at Brice's Crossroads, 215–17
Holly Springs, 106–7, 117; raided, 115–16
Hovey, Alvin P., 108, 160, 170–71
Hovey, Charles, 123–24, 128
Hurlbut, Stephen, 98, 100–1, 143, 255–56; and Meridian Campaign, 174, 176, 181–82, 184, 186

Jackson, Battle of, 156–58; second battle and Siege of, 170–71
Johnson, W. A., 200, 208, 210
Johnston, Joseph E., 87, 108, 117–18, 128, 134–35, 156, 158–59, 167–68, 172, 195, 199, 219, 220–21, 242; and Siege of Jackson, 170–72

Kargé, Joseph, 261–62, 264, 266–67

Lagow, Clark, 64–65
Lee, Samuel Phillips, 37–38, 40
Lee, Stephen D., 118–19, 121, 124–26, 129, 160, 246–47; and Campaign and Battle of Brice's Crossroads, 196, 199–200, 208, 214, 216; and Campaign and Battle of Tupelo, 224–28, 230–43; and Meridian Campaign, 175–76, 179–81, 185, 187, 189
Lincoln, Abraham, 5, 14, 28, 31–33, 35–36, 38, 56
Little, Henry, 67–68, 71
Logan, John, 137, 154, 160
Loring, William, 133–35, 153, 160, 162, 170; and Meridian Campaign, 175, 178–82, 184–85
Lovell, Mansfield, 43–44, 78–79, 85–87, 89–90, 92–94, 96–98, 102–3
Lyon, Hylan, 200–1, 208–10, 234

Mabry, Hinchie, 234, 237, 247, 251, 253
Martin, John, 68–69
Martin, William, 265, 267, 269
Maury, Dabney, 69, 71, 78–79, 85–86, 92–93, 95, 98, 100, 121, 128, 141, 246–48, 252, 258
McArthur, John, 85–89
McClernand, John A., 106, 109, 130, 132, 139–40, 142–43, 146, 156, 158; and Battle of Port Gibson, 149, 151–52; and battles of Champion Hill and Big Black, 160, 162; and Siege of Vicksburg, 165, 167
McKean, Thomas, 82, 85–89
McMillen, William, 206, 218
McPherson, James, 101, 106, 137, 146, 196; and Battle of Champion Hill, 158–60; and Battle of Jackson, 156; and Battle

of Port Gibson, 147, 152; and Battle of Raymond, 154; and Meridian Campaign, 174, 176, 179–82, 184, 186; and Siege of Vicksburg, 164–65

Mississippi: 1861 military situation, 9–12; minority groups in the Civil War, 273–76; secession of, 3, 4, 6–8

Moore, David, 235, 241

Moore, John, 86–89, 96, 98–99

Morgan, George, 121–27

Morton, John, 199, 201, 209, 212, 216, 226, 229–31, 243, 252, 254

Mower, Joseph, 70, 91, 237, 241, 252–53, 259

Murphy, Robert, 114–16

Naron, Levi (Chickasaw), 7, 63, 91, 261

Oliver, John, 82–83, 85–88

Ord, E. O. C., 59–69, 71–75, 81, 98–100, 170–71

Osband, Embury, 260, 267, 269

Osterhaus, Peter, 149, 151

Oxford, 109, 117

Palmer, James, 40–42

Pemberton, John C., 17, 80, 130–31, 133–35, 137, 140–41, 143–44, 146, 152–53; and Battle of Champion Hill, 158–60, 162; and Battle of Chickasaw Bayou, 117–18, 121, 128; and Grant's North Mississippi campaign, 107–11; and Siege of Vicksburg, 164–65, 167–69

Pettus, John J., 3–9, 37

Phifer, C. W., 96, 99

Polk, Leonidas, 17, 198, 200; and Meridian Campaign, 175–76, 178–79, 182, 184–85

Pope, John, 14, 22, 25–31

Port Gibson, Battle of, 147–52

Porter, David, 45–46, 109, 128–29, 131–32; and Battle of Grand Gulf, 146; and passage of Vicksburg batteries, 139–43; and Steele's Bayou campaign, 135–38

Porter, William D., 50–51

Price, Sterling, 27, 34, 106; and Battle of Corinth, 77–80, 82, 85–86, 90–96, 98–99, 102–3; and Iuka, 54–76

Quinby, Isaac, 81, 137–38

Raymond, Battle of, 154–56

Roddey, Philip, 234–35, 246

Rogers, William P., 97, 99

Rosecrans, William, 143, 172; and Battle of Corinth, 79, 82–83, 85–86, 89–93, 90–91, 95, 97–98, 101–2; and Battle of Iuka, 57, 59–76

Ross, Lawrence, 176, 178

Ross, Sul, 99–100

Rucker, Edmund, 200–1, 206–7, 209, 237

Rust, Albert, 85–86, 92–94

Shaw, William, 246, 259

Sherman, William T., 20, 23, 29, 31, 81, 137, 140, 164, 173, 195, 260; and Battle of Chickasaw Bayou, 117–30; and Battle of Jackson, 156, 158; diversion by, 144–45; and Grant's North Mississippi campaign, 106–7, 109–10; and Meridian Campaign, 173–76, 178–82, 184–90, 192–94; and Mississippi campaigns against Nathan Bedford Forrest, 196–200, 204, 217–23, 242–44; and sieges of Vicksburg and Jackson, 164–65, 167, 170–72

Smith, Andrew Jackson, 122, 125, 127; and Campaign and Battle of Tupelo, 220, 222–35, 237–43; and 1864 Mississippi Raid, 244–48, 251–54, 257–59

Smith, Giles, 127–29

Smith, Kirby, 17, 18, 34, 55–56, 76

Smith, Martin Luther, 37–38, 40, 42–45, 48, 110, 113, 118, 158, 165

Smith, Morgan, 122, 124

Smith, Sooy, and Meridian Campaign, 174–75, 179, 184, 187–93, 197–98

Stanley, David, 61–64, 66, 70, 73, 75, 85, 89–91, 95–96

Stanton, Edwin, 30, 31, 106, 140, 218

Steele, Frederick, 122–23, 129, 140–41, 170

Stevenson, Carter, 121, 128, 141, 144, 164; and Battle of Champion Hill, 159–60

Sturgis, Samuel, and Campaign and Battle of Brice's Crossroads, 197–98, 201–4, 206–19

Swayne, Wager, 97

Taylor, Richard, 262, 264–65, 271
Thayer, John, 123, 126–27
Thirteenth U.S. Infantry, 127, 165
Thomas, George, 21, 23, 29
Tilghman, Lloyd, 133–34, 162
Tracey, Edward, 128, 147, 149, 151

U.S. Colored Troops. *See* Bouton, Edward

Van Dorn, Earl, 11, 12, 17–18, 25–28, 34,
    43–44, 52–60, 65, 72, 76; and Corinth,
    77–83, 85–86, 90–94, 98–103; and
    Grant's North Mississippi campaign
    and Holly Springs raid, 107, 110–11,
    113–16, 118
Veatch, John, 99–100
Vicksburg, 4, 5, 20, 35–36, 38, 44, 46; Siege
    of, 164–70
Villepigue, John, 85–87, 93–94, 100

Wade, William, 250, 259
Waring, George, 206, 209–12, 214
Washburn, Cadwallader C., 108, 196,
    198, 204, 213–15, 217–18, 242, 244–45,
    255–56, 258–59, 270
Waul, Thomas, 133–34
Welles, Gideon, 37, 40, 42, 45, 48, 51
Williams, Thomas, 39–41, 45, 49, 51–52,
    130
Winslow, Edward, 206, 208–9, 211, 214,
    260–61
Withers, William, 121–23, 129

Yazoo Pass Campaign, 131–38
Yazoo River 1864 expedition, 178